DR BEATRICE LEUNG tea⟨...⟩ ⟨...⟩
of Political Science at the ⟨...⟩
Kong. She has been invol⟨...⟩
church for more than twe⟨...⟩ ⟨...⟩er of
the religious order of the S⟨iste⟩rs of the Precious
Blood, as editor of the *Kung Kao Po* (Hong Kong's
Catholic Chinese Weekly) (1967–70) and more
recently as editor for a series on International
Economic Regulations for the Guizhou People's
Press in China. She has also written numerous
articles on church–state relations.

How can the contemporary claims of Communism and national culture be reconciled with a universal religion? How can the government of the People's Republic of China with its claim to absolute sovereignty exist alongside the spiritual authority of the Roman Catholic church? This conflict between two centres of authority has been at the core of recent relations between the Catholic church and China. In this first book-length study of the subject, Dr Beatrice Leung analyses the interactions between China and the Holy See from 1976 to 1986.

Dr Leung examines the historic relationship between the Catholic church and China both prior to 1949 and from 1949 to 1976. She then analyses the major problems between these two institutions as they tried to establish a dialogue for future reconciliation. These include the need for the Vatican to transfer its recognition of China from Taiwan to Beijing; the role of the Pope with his spiritual leadership of Chinese Catholics; and the handling of the Chinese Catholic Patriotic Association. The book concludes with suggestions for a basis for church–state rapprochement.

Throughout her work, Dr Leung uses Chinese language sources, both on the Catholic and Communist sides. These are supplemented by a wide range of interviews which the author has conducted in the Vatican, in Hong Kong and with members of the official and unofficial Catholic churches inside China itself.

Sino-Vatican relations: problems in conflicting authority 1976–1986

LSE MONOGRAPHS IN INTERNATIONAL STUDIES

For a list of titles out of print please see back of book.

SINO-VATICAN RELATIONS

Problems in conflicting authority 1976–1986

BEATRICE LEUNG

Department of Political Science, University of Hong Kong

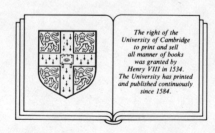

The right of the
University of Cambridge
to print and sell
all manner of books
was granted by
Henry VIII in 1534.
The University has printed
and published continuously
since 1584.

CAMBRIDGE UNIVERSITY PRESS

Cambridge
New York   Port Chester
Melbourne   Sydney

Published by the Press Syndicate of the University of Cambridge
The Pitt Building, Trumpington Street, Cambridge CB2 IRP
40 West 20th Street, New York, NY 10011-4211, USA
10 Stamford Road, Oakleigh, Victoria 3166, Australia

© Cambridge University Press 1992

First published 1992

Printed in Great Britain at the University Press, Cambridge

British Library cataloguing in publication data

Sino-Vatican relations: problems in conflicting authority
1976–1986. – (LSE monographs in international studies)
1. Vatican. Foreign relations, history. China 2. China.
Foreign relations, history. Vatican
I. Title II. Series
327.45634051

Library of Congress cataloguing in publication data

Leung, Beatrice.
Sino-Vatican relations: problems in conflicting authority,
1976–1986 / Beatrice Leung.
p. cm.
ISBN 0-521-38173-8 (hardback)
1. Catholic Church – Relations (diplomatic) – China. 2. China –
Foreign relations – Catholic Church. 3. China – Foreign
relations – 1976– 4. China – Church history – 20th century.
I. Title.
BX1665.L48 1991
322′.1′095109047 – dc20 90-39988 CIP

ISBN 0 521 38173 8 hardback

To Mr Leo F. Goodstadt, my teacher and my friend,
who has encouraged me to work for
Sino-Vatican reconciliation.

Contents

ix

Illustrations

Foreword

Michael B. Yahuda

It may be thought that the problems of the relations between China and the Vatican are of only marginal significance to both sides. After all only some 5–10 million Chinese out of a population of more than 1,100 million actually profess the Christian faith. The Vatican itself disposes of little effective power and there is some truth in Stalin's cynical dismissal of the Vatican with the question 'how many tanks does the Pope have?' And yet the interactions between China and the Vatican have been troublesome to both sides as they have brought to the fore uncomfortable questions about their respective claims to moral authority. More broadly some of these questions illustrate graphically one of the fundamental dilemmas of contemporary international society regarding the competing claims of state sovereignty and universal human rights. How can the contemporary claims be reconciled of Communism and national culture on the one side and, on the other, those of a universal religion with a centre in Rome that is at once holy and secular in the shape of the Vatican state.

The difficulty has been compounded in the Chinese case because of the recognition by the Vatican of the Republic of China (i.e., Taiwan) as the legitimate government of China. Alone of the states in Europe, the Vatican did not shift its recognition to the People's Republic of China in Beijing in the 1970s. Indeed to this day the position has not changed. But, as Dr Leung shows in her wide-ranging study, the problem here has less to do with formal diplomacy than with the special character of the spiritual authority of the Catholic church and the claims to totalist authority over its citizens by the Communist government of the People's Republic of China (PRC).

The Vatican's claim to universal religious authority is challenged by the PRC's insistence on the national autonomy of the officially

xiii

sponsored patriotic Catholic church with its Bishops appointed separately from the apostolic succession. In the event of a possible compromise on this issue the Vatican would have to accommodate the so-called 'underground church' whose members for more than thirty-five years have refused to foreswear allegiance to the Holy Father in Rome. Many of those who have survived are restricted under house arrest or, still worse, suffer in labour camps. Moreover the Catholic church would have to ensure continued pastoral access to the hundreds of thousands of its adherents on Taiwan.

For its part, the Communist party is challenged by the prospect of several million of its citizens professing spiritual loyalty to an alien authority that challenges the fundamental tenets of its ideology. In principle that conflicts with the PRC government's claim to absolute sovereignty – a claim that has been advanced with particular vehemence because of the alleged threats of bourgeois liberalism and of an international conspiracy that seeks to undermine socialism by peaceful means. Dr Leung explores these conflicting claims on the basis of deep knowledge and thought. She charts the complex historical legacies to which the two parties are heir as necessary to an understanding of the different ways in which the problems are perceived. As befits a member of the Catholic order in Hong Kong, Dr Leung, is sensitive to the constraints affecting both sides and is yet able to suggest possible ways by which the conflict may be settled.

The appeal of this book, however, transcends the subject matter with which it is directly concerned. It can be read with profit by those with an interest in interactions between cultures as by those concerned with China, the Catholic church and international relations.

Preface

Since 1949, religions have had problems of adjustment and accommodation with the ruling communist party in China. To some extent, this state of affairs has resulted from a Marxist distaste for religious belief. In part, it has reflected suspicions about the political role of religions in Chinese life, especially where such religions have links with the outside world, Buddhism, Islam and Catholicism being by definition 'world religions'. In the case of the Roman Catholics these difficulties were aggrevated by the institutional nature of the Vatican* and its conflicts with the Kremlin prior to the rupture in Sino-Soviet relations, its continued diplomatic relations with Taiwan and by the Chinese belief that the Vatican served the ends of foreign imperialism.

However, the CCP found it very difficult to tolerate the believers in religions who have their world-view, while they themselves being Marxist by nature take dialectical Materialism as their ideology which is the opposite to that of the religious believers. Therefore when dealing with morality the religious believers and party members have their own separate sources of inspiration. The Catholics go to the Catholic doctrine, which is based on the teaching of the Gospel, party members go to the party which points to Marxism–Leninism as the orthodox teaching.

In Deng's era, when relaxation of economic and social policies are

---

* For convenience sake, the expression 'the Vatican' is used in all this work. As far as international law is concerned, when referring to the supreme authority of the Catholic church, the correct expression should have been: 'The Holy See'. It is the Holy See, and not the Vatican City State, which enters into diplomatic relations with the States (even if the Vatican City State may enter certain specific international agreements, such as l'Union Postale Universelle). Even after the suppression of the Pontifical States (1870) until the creation of the Vatican City State (1929), when the Holy See did not have any territorial configuration, it maintained diplomatic relations with a great number of countries and was recognised as a juridical person in international law.

practised, it is hoped that a continuing clash between these two centres of authority, which have conflicting concepts of what constitutes the true source of authority, may change into reconciliation. In its pragmatic policies in the foreign sphere the Chinese government have a role to play in the world community as well as in seeking to attain the recovery of territory such as Taiwan. The Vatican has foreign ties with Taiwan but the Chinese government's view is that Vatican–Taiwan relations must be severed in favour of Beijing.

This study focuses primarily on the interaction between China and the Vatican as they tried to establish a dialogue as a basis for future reconciliation. The core of the conflict of authority stems from the dual character of the Vatican as both a sovereign state and the spiritual leader of a universal church. Thus at one level there is the problem of when and how the Vatican should transfer its recognition of China from Taiwan (the Republic of China) to the People's Republic. But at another level, the problem arises as to what may be meant by the exercise of the Pope's spiritual leadership of the Catholics in China and as to how to handle the independent Chinese Catholic Patriotic Association that rejects the authority of the Pope and those Chinese Catholics who since the 1950s have been persecuted and driven underground for refusing to disavow their allegiance to the Holy See. As both sides have attempted to develop a dialogue these problems have taken special forms, such as how bishops should be appointed, how independent can the Chinese Catholic church be and how Vatican–Taiwan relations should be severed in favour of the PRC. These and various developments in China's new policies towards religion are examined in detail as well as the complex process of establishing Sino-Vatican communications. However, this study concludes with a consideration of the possible basis for an accommodation.

In order to place this analysis in a proper perspective, it also surveys the historical experience of China's encounters with Christianity in general and the Catholic church in particular. Similarly, it surveys the experience of the Vatican's encounter with other communist regimes. It shows that the historical legacy is still relevant to both sides. Finally, by way of background, we also examine the development of the policies of the Communist party towards the church and other religions from the 1920s, focusing in particular on the period from the establishment of the People's Republic in 1949 to the end of the Cultural Revolution in 1976.

This study is a revised version of a doctoral dissertation presented to the London School of Economics and Political Science, the University of London in 1988. In the process of writing the thesis, my deepest gratitude goes to my supervisor, Mr Michael Yahuda, Reader in the Department of International Relations, London School of Economics and Political Science. Not only did he give guidance during the process of writing, but also made very detailed corrections and comments on each draft. Mr Leo F. Goodstadt of the Centre for Asian Studies, the University of Hong Kong, and of the Hong Kong Government's Central Policy Unit has been my staunch friend throughout and has given valuable help in many ways. As a matter of fact, he was the one who first led me to view Sino-Vatican relations from a political angle, and promised me any kind of help for this research I needed. His promise gave me much confidence in launching into this study. Dr Rosemary Quested, former Reader in History, University of Hong Kong, who was the supervisor of my MA research at the University of Hong Kong (1980–2), took great interest in this research from beginning to end. She polished the language of the final draft of this thesis and made it readable, having to work under great stress at the final stage, when we were pressed for time.

To Father Bernard Quintus O.M.I., the Second Assistant Superior General of the Missionary of the Oblates of Mary Immaculate (1984–7), I also owe my gratitude, for it was through his assistance and arrangements, that I was able to have interviews with the Vatican officials without difficulty. His help in translating some important Italian articles into English, and polishing the first draft of the thesis was very valuable indeed. Father Robert Murray, S.J. of Heythrop College, University of London offered his valuable help by reading some of the manuscripts and helped me in the search for the Latin text of the Papal Documents. I also thank Mr Peter Hebblethwaite, the author of *In The Vatican*, who led me to view the Vatican from a new angle which I never thought of.

At different periods of revision, I have had the good fortune of receiving substantial comments and warm encouragement from various sources. I would like to express my thanks to the teaching staff of the London School of Economics and Political Science, for example Mr Michael Donalan, Dr Eileen Barker, Professor Fred Halliday, Mr George Schopflin and Professor Michael Leifer. They gave their valuable advice on various points in the process of writing.

Professor Audrey Donnithorne of the Australian National University, Father L. Ladanay S.J. and Father M. Masson S.J. the former and present editors of *China News Analysis* kindly read the whole typescript and offered valuable suggestions for its publication. Father Joseph Garland S.J. and Fr William Joyce S.D.B. kindly gave their time and effort in polishing the text for publication. I am also grateful for the help offered, in a variety of ways, by my colleagues at the Department of Political Science, University of Hong Kong who provided stimulating suggestions and intellectual challenges on church and state relations.

The German Missio generously granted me a partial scholarship for three years so that I could have peace of mind to do this research on a full-time basis without worry about the financial problems. The Central Research Fund of the University of London assisted one of my trips to the Vatican for my interviews. I am thankful to the Superior General and the General Councillors (1985–9) of the Sisters of the Precious Blood, Hong Kong, for releasing me from my duties so that I could stay in London to do the research.

My thanks are also extended to Father Louis Tchang, the Director of the London Catholic Chinese Centre for helping me to translate Chinese names from Chinese to Pinyin. I would like to give a special thanks to Archbishop Dominic Deng Yiming, and Fr Louis Ha, the Editor General of Kung Kao Po, the Hong Kong Catholic Chinese Weekly, for allowing me to use their valuable collection of photos.

I would like to thank Mr Kamal Khan for helping with the technical problem of printing this thesis from the word processor, and Miss Cecilia Wai Yuan Wah, and Miss Linda Chow for their generous help in typing some of the manuscripts. Of course I myself am responsible for all the mistakes.

Hong Kong   B. Leung

Abbreviations

AFP	Agence France Presse
ANSA	Agenzia Nationale Stampa Associate [Associated National Press Agency] (Italy)
ASEAN	Association of South East Asian Nations
CPA	Catholic Patriotic Association (China)
CPPCC	Chinese People's Political Consultative Conference
IRA	Irish Republican Army
KMT	Kuomintang
NCNA	New China News Agency [Xinhua]
NPC	National People's Congress
PLO	Palestine Liberation Organization
PRC	People's Republic of China
ROC	Republic of China (in Taiwan)

CHAPTER I

Introduction

On 1 October 1949 Chairman Mao in Tiananmen Square, Beijing solemnly declared the establishment of the People's Republic of China (PRC). After he himself had hoisted the five-star national flag, he proclaimed that the Chinese people from then on would stand on their own feet. The proclamation was short but contained a wealth of historical connotations. It declared that, in the days to come, the Chinese Communist Party (CCP) led by Mao would do all they could to 'liberate' the Chinese from grinding poverty and oppression by feudalism, bureaucratism and foreign imperialism.

At the same time in Nanjing, Mgr. Antonio Riberi, the Papal Nuncio to the National government, was anxiously waiting for a reply from Mao, whom he sought permission to meet. In spite of the fact that most of the western diplomats had left China he had stayed on in the hope of formulating a relationship with the new government. After waiting for nearly two years in Nanjing, on 6 September 1951, a reply was given to Mgr. Antonio Riberi from Beijing. Instead of allowing him the chance to discuss religious matters with the CCP, he was ordered to leave China forever. After his expulsion, Mgr. Riberi moved to Taibei together with the Papal Nunciature, after a short stay in Hong Kong. From 6 September 1951 onwards, there were no diplomatic relations between China and the Vatican. The expulsion of the Papal Nuncio was the prelude to the long drama of conflicting Sino-Vatican relations, in which the principal players were the CCP and the Vatican, and in which Chinese Catholics and to some extent Catholics outside also played their parts. This state of affairs has lasted for more than thirty years and it is still unfinished.

In China, one could not expect decent treatment to be accorded to any world religion in general and to Catholicism in particular in the immediate aftermath of the establishment of the PRC. This was because the CCP, as patriotic Communists, demanded the severance of ties with western 'imperialist' cultural institutions, and because they wished to stamp out all alternative sources of political authority, and furthermore as believers in atheist Marxism they were unfavourably disposed to any religion. The anti-imperialist mood in China reached its peak in the course of China's participation in the Korean War (1950–4). The already tense Sino-Vatican relations went from bad to worse. Subsequently, foreign missionaries were expelled (including the Papal Nuncio), church property was confiscated and the Catholic church was ordered to cut off all ties with the Holy See. The government sponsored Chinese Catholic Patriotic Association (CPA) was established. The CPA is a semi-official organisation staffed by religious cadres acting as a liaison between the state and church body somewhat like the PAX association in eastern European countries. Obviously in the 1950s the CPA became the home for those Catholics who yielded to the demands of the CCP. (Later on in the 1970s the CPA had its own developments.) Those who refused to sever spiritual relations with the Pope and put themselves in a position of being 'schismatic', had no choice but to go underground. After confronting several years of resistance led by local bishops such as the Bishop of Shanghai, Ignatius Gong Pinmei, and the Bishop of Guangzhou, Dominic Deng Yiming, Beijing could not completely control Chinese Catholics, and these two prominent Catholic leaders, together with numerous Catholic laity, were thrown into jail in 1955 and 1957 respectively. The Vatican responded to the Chinese situation by issuing three Papal encyclicals to denounce China for its rough treatment of the Catholics there. These encyclicals were: 'Cupimus Imprimis' (1952), 'Ad Sinarum Gentem' (1954) and 'Ad Apostolorum Principis' (1958).

Despite many attempts over the years by the Vatican to normalise relations with China, little progress was made as these advances were coldly rebuffed by Beijing. It was not until November 1987 that the ice began to break. China consented to have the Secretary General of the Party, Zhao Ziyang, meet Cardinal Sin, who was entrusted by the Pope to contact China for a dialogue. Subsequently it was confirmed that China had agreed to hold discussions with the Vatican on Catholic related problems. Only then was a new page turned in Sino-Vatican relations.

On the surface, the dispute between China and the Catholic church rested on the struggle as to who was to exercise religious authority over Chinese Catholics. On closer examination, however, the problem goes beyond religious questions. The particular nature of the Catholic church with the Vatican, a tiny sovereign state, as its central administration causes the complexity of the problem.

Sino-Vatican relations have not received much attention in the literature on international relations. This is perhaps due to the insignificance of the issue in the context of the major problems of security and economics in world politics. Moreover the Vatican is a tiny state occupying less than half a square mile in the heart of Italy and, although it is the spiritual leader of over 700 million Catholics world-wide, the 5 million Catholics in China account for less than $\frac{1}{2}$ a per cent of China's population and they play an insignificant role in Chinese politics and society. Thus, even if it were acknowledged that Catholics and the Catholic church play significant political roles in many countries and that they exercise significant moral leadership there, China is manifestly not one of those countries. Nevertheless the topic is of considerable interest for students of international relations. When China demanded the independence of the Chinese Catholic church it was the first sovereign state in the modern age (except Albania) to create an independent church after the example of Henry VIII of England in the sixteenth century.

Although the dispute between the Vatican and China is not an 'eye-catching' issue even in 'low' politics, it is nevertheless relatively important and worthwhile studying simply because it is a complicated issue relating to the accommodations between religion and communism. This book is a study of how a universal religion of long tradition encountered newly arising nationalism and patriotism. Furthermore it also casts light on the problems encountered by a revolutionary regime, which demands complete control over every aspect of social and political life including religion, in confronting a universal religion with a spiritual leader who also acts as an absolute monarch of a sovereign state. In a very real sense this involves a clash between two centres of authority who have conflicting concepts of what constitutes the true source of authority and who differ fundamentally on the scope and limits of that authority. In carrying out this study, we have to deal with ideology and belief, authority and political legitimacy, human rights and sovereign power. All these are very pertinent to the core problems in international relations.

Sino-Vatican relations are very special for several reasons:
1 The evidence is that the CCP hostility towards the Catholic church is more sustained than against any other Christian group.
2 There is a readiness to suffer in defence of the Catholic church of such proportions that it has attracted external attention, e.g. by heads of state of foreign countries who ask for clemency and by Amnesty International.
3 World opinion on such matters is seen as important by China, as evidenced by the criticism of US Congressmen's remarks on Tibetan human rights.
4 The level of tolerance or of persecution can be linked directly to the internal ideological situation: the tighter or more leftist the control by the CCP over ideological matters and the more 'politics take command', the worse the treatment of all religions, including the Catholic church. The more open the ideological situation, the less harsh the treatment of the church. But political controls are never relaxed enough to allow what the west would regard as freedom of religious activity.
5 The Vatican would like to protect Catholics from this harsh treatment and, at the same time, to encourage them to remain faithful to their essential beliefs, which creates a conflict between condemnation of the CCP and concessions.
6 The Vatican's position is complicated by its need to have a consistent policy in dealing with foreign states, especially the Soviet bloc and by the trends in favour of dialogue, localisation and so on, which emerged earliest in the case of China (the accommodation of policy of the Jesuits and the Chinese rites dispute) but are now widespread throughout the church after the Second Vatican Council (1963–5).
7 China finds it hard to deal with the Vatican as a sovereign power because of the ideological complications of recognising a world religious leader and the political implications of its access to Chinese Catholics. Worse still, China cannot follow its usual pattern for dealing with former hostile powers (cultural exchanges with pro-China groups, trade and financial contacts, state-to-state economic contacts, political negotiations on recognition) in its dealing with the Vatican. For the Vatican is a state only in the juridical sense: it has no cultural or economic capacity of any significance for China.

8 One concession that China wants from the Vatican is closure of its office in Taibei, which it demands as a matter of principle.

As a world religion, Christianity has a two-dimensional requirement. It demands of the believer as an individual that he/she embrace the belief privately and internalise the faith so that it may be expressed in life on a personal level. Secondly, on the communal level, it requires that each individual be attached to a religious organisation whose regulations always go beyond the boundary of a state. In a Communist party state, due to ideological differences (atheism versus theism), the political leaders always have problems in dealing with a universal religion. These problems are, firstly, in the field of ideology: religious belief is seen as a product of the pre-Socialist stage of history destined to be superseded eventually when mankind reaches the stage of Socialism. Meanwhile religious bodies and religious believers are viewed as a carry over from the old society. Secondly, from the view point of politics, the degree of tolerance to be accorded to 'religious dissenters' is dependent on the stage of historical development the society is thought to have reached and the problems and policies of the Communist rulers. These problems cannot be called too difficult, so long as the state can retain its authority over the religious believers. For example, the Chinese government does not appear to have great problems of authority with Chinese Buddhists, Chinese Protestants or Chinese Muslims (except that, because of ethnic rather than for religious reasons, some of the latter seek greater autonomy from the central government). Despite the differences in belief, the Chinese government can exercise its authority over these believers apparently without irreconcilable conflict. For political and social reasons, such as for the promotion of its international reputation and for the purpose of uniting with the national minorities, the Chinese government can be even more tolerant of the Buddhists, Muslims and Protestants by granting some privileges to them, for example, by sending some of their elites abroad on cultural exchanges, provided of course that they are docile enough to accept China's authority and are willing to promote the broad interests of the state and the party. China cannot apply such privileges to Catholics simply because this particular branch of Christianity has a unique feature – it is administered by the Vatican which is recognised by international law as a sovereign state, while the Roman Catholic church has the characteristics of a transnational actor in world politics.

The gauntlet thrown down by China in splitting Chinese Catholics from Rome by demanding independence for the Chinese Catholic church is not an innovation in history. After Henry VIII, in the Reformation period, all Protestant countries did this. The French Revolution also tried to prise the French church from its loyalty to the Pope.

The Vatican, the Holy See, and the Catholic church

The city state of the Vatican is the smallest state in the world, of 108.7 acres, created in 1929 by the treaty of the Lateran Pacts. It is located at the eastern side of Rome on the left bank of the River Tiber. Through the Lateran Pacts, the new state of the Vatican was placed under the absolute sovereignty of the supreme pontiff, to the exclusion of all interference by any government. The Vatican is a state in the strict legal sense, since it possesses all the necessary attributes and functions. This is widely admitted in the community of nations. It has territory, population and sovereignty. This territory, limited as it is, suffices to guarantee the spiritual and temporal independence needed for the exercise of the Holy See's spiritual mission to Catholics over the world.[1] Sovereignty over the Vatican is exercised by the Pope in his function as supreme head of the Catholic church. In its governmental form, the Vatican is unique in being an elective absolute monarchy. The Pope alone has the fullness of legislative, executive and judicial power and represents the Vatican in international relations.[2] The Vatican and the Holy See, though distinct entities, are both recognised internationally as such and are subjects of international law, but they are united in the person of the Pope, who is the ruler of the state and head of the Catholic church, although the former is temporal in its purpose and the latter is spiritual. Therefore the Vatican is functioning for the interests of the Catholic church, while the Catholic church can free itself from any state control because of the existence of the Vatican.

A state is a territorial, political entity. Thus while non-territorial types of political entities may exist and may wield considerable power they cannot be states. It is true that the Holy See has long been considered a subject of international law with the capacity to make treaties (concordats) and to send diplomatic representatives

---

[1] *The New Catholic Encyclopaedia*, 1967 edn, s.v. 'Vatican City, State of' by L. Barbarito.
[2] Ibid.

(nuncio). It was not regarded as a state, however, until it achieved a measure of territory and became the Vatican state.[3] The Vatican city state is a useful adjunct of the Holy See, but not essential to it as an international entity any more than it is essential to it as a doctrinal entity. From 1870 to 1922, the Pope had no territorial jurisdiction, yet the Holy See remained an international entity, sending ambassadors, who held the position of doyens of the diplomatic corps, to many of the great powers of the day.

It is the Holy See and not the Vatican city state which enters into diplomatic relations with the states. Antony Judge even classified the Holy See as an international body with special status in international law. It is because the Roman Catholic church is centred on the Holy See which is recognised on a par with governments by some countries and as such has a special status in international law.[4]

The Catholic church is the basic reality underlying the position of the Pope as a subject of international law. She is a unique international phenomenon, an organism rooted in many countries but constituted as a super-national body which has its own law, its own lawcourts and its central government consisting of the Pope and the central office in Rome. It is described collectively as the Holy See[5] which is the real head of the Catholic church and which is invested with the supreme authority over the Catholic church coming down from St Peter. When a Cardinal is elected as the Pope, immediately he is invested with the authority of the Holy See. In exercising his authority to administer the universal church the Pope is assisted by the Roman Curia, which is the bureaucracy, or the administrative office of the Holy See. The authority of the church does not rest with the Roman Curia or the Vatican city state but with the Holy See.

However, in many written works of the Chinese government, and in speeches of Chinese officials, with very few exceptions, 'the Vatican' and 'Roman Curia' has been wrongly used to refer to the head of the Catholic church; and it is interesting to note that the bishops and priests in mainland China who should have enough

---

[3] H. M. Blix, 'Contemporary aspects of recognition', *Recueil des Cours* 130 (1970, II): 632.
[4] Antony Judge, 'International Institutions: Diversity, Borderline Cases, Functional Substitutes and Possible Alternatives', in Paul Taylor and A. J. R. Groom (eds.), *International Organization* (London: Francis Pinter, 1978), pp. 50–1.
[5] Sidney Z. Ehler, 'The recent concordats', *Recueil des Cours*, 104 (1961 III): 8–11.

theological training to distinguish which is which, follow the government's conceptual framework in Catholic matters all the same.[6]

There are two levels to the relationship of the Holy See to a state. Firstly the Holy See as the head of the universal church has authority over the local church of that particular state. (Although there is constant debate on the matter of the Pope's authority and the level of autonomy of the local church headed by a bishop.) The Holy See also establishes diplomatic relations with national governments, fosters religious development and the spiritual welfare of the people as well as taking care of church and state relations.

On the other hand, the Catholic church itself possesses the characteristics of a transnational actor, with the Holy See residing in the Vatican as the centre that co-ordinates and shapes the actions of the subsidiary field units by supplying them with general norms, symbolic leadership and authoritative decisions.[7] Backed up by a sovereign state, the Catholic church with its transnational character also ties itself to many organisations, such as the United Nations and the EEC, just to mention two.

Moreover, the Catholic church itself has a highly structured hierarchy and its central administration headed by the Pope exercises an authoritative leadership over the local churches by laying down ultimate guidelines mainly on three aspects of church life: ultimate sanction, orthodoxy of doctrine and appointment of the leader of the local church, the bishop. All these three areas of church authority proved to be problematic in China.

The picture is somewhat complicated by the fact that large numbers of Catholic organisations conduct activities and maintain contacts with state agencies and political institutions independent of the Vatican. Catholics, even bishops, travel on their own national passports and very rarely on Vatican ones. The extent of Vatican

[6] 'Zhonggong Zhongyang' Guangyu Woguo Shehui Zhuyi Shiqi Zhongjiac Wenti De Jiben Guandian He Jiben Zhence' (Wenjian no. 19: 1982) [Document 19 Issued by CCP Central Committee in 1982 – regarding our nation's basic view points and policies towards religion in socialist stage], *Zhonggong Yanjiu* (Taibei) 3 (15 March 1983).

   Catholic Church in China 3 (30 October 1981). (In this issue there are many articles written to protest against the appointment of the Archbishop of Guangzhou. The focus of attack was on the Roman Curia.

   The head of the Religious Affairs Bureau in one of his speeches to Catholic leaders on 20 April 1983, explicitly centred his attack on the Vatican City State, a political entity with its head the Pope invested with religious authority. See *Catholic Church in China* 7 (15 August 1983): 30–1.

[7] Ivan Vallier, 'The Roman Catholic church: a Transnational Actor', *International Organisation* 3 (1971): 479–95.

control over all Catholic activities is debated within the Catholic church itself, and actual or potential centrifugal tendencies can be seen in the Liberation Theology clergy of the third world, and recently in the Hong Kong church. This is a factor which must be considered by both the Vatican and the Chinese government.

The nature of the interactions between the People's Republic of China (PRC) and the Catholic church immediately after the 1949 Revolution belongs to the dimensions of a state-to-state relationship. The problems lying between these two states are not only religious ones with the implication of authority, but they also have implications for general relations among states in the international community. For example, Beijing could not have good relations with any state that has diplomatic relations with the Republic of China on Taiwan, because the PRC is following its own principles in having no formal relations with the Vatican which has diplomatic ties with Taiwan. From Beijing's perspective, the Papal appointment of Chinese bishops for China is not only a religious question but an issue of sovereignty. How can it be entertained that the Pope, a foreigner, should interfere in Chinese internal affairs by appointing a Chinese religious leader, accountable to Rome, to administer ideological affairs amidst Chinese Catholic believers? Since the founding of the PRC the state machinery has been holding the principle of 'under the leadership of the CCP and the guidance of Marxism–Leninism and Mao Zedong Thought', therefore the CCP has a special difficulty in competing with other systematic value systems such as organised religion (the more organised and structural, the greater the conflict perhaps), and it also has a sensitive spot in its need to win the support of minority peoples, who tend to be more ardent religious believers than the Han. Thus religious believers such as Catholics come under all the same suspicions voiced and condemnations made of intellectuals who know about Trotsky, Freud, Rousseau and all the other writers whom 'orthodox' Marxists dislike, while conversely some religious activities are tolerated by the CCP because they are regarded as folk customs or traditional practices which have no direct ideological content.

In spite of the fact that the conflict began soon after the 1949 Revolution, some of its roots went back many generations in Chinese history to the clash of authority between the Chinese emperor ('the Son of Heaven') and the Pope (the Vicar of Christ) which arose out of the struggle between orthodoxy and heterodoxy after the arrival of Matteo Ricci in the late Ming period. It was because of the endeavour of Matteo Ricci and the Jesuits' accommodation policy that Matteo Ricci began to win Chinese converts. The quarrel between the Dominicans and the Jesuits in China over the accommodation policy resulted in the Chinese rites and the ban of Catholicism by Emperor Kangxi. Then, in the late nineteenth century, the return of missionaries behind the gun-boats of imperialists after the Opium War 1840 met Chinese people who were saturated with anti-foreign and anti-imperial sentiments. The so-called 'hundred years of shame' (1840s–1940s) also explained why the CCP, moved by patriotic nationalism, projected their negative feelings towards Catholicism, a branch of a foreign religion.

Beginning in the early 1960s, the Vatican made several overtures towards China. The successor of Pope Pius XII, Pope John XXIII, made a goodwill gesture by ceasing to call the CPA a schismatic church. Pope Paul VI in 1970 made an accommodating speech to China from Hong Kong. But none of this reaped much fruit due to the intolerant ideological line of the Cultural Revolution in China during that period. The ice began to break only after Mao's death in 1976, which marked a watershed in the history of China. That is why our attention is focused on the post-Mao period of 1976 to 1986, which resulted in the November 1987 turning point in Sino-Vatican relations, as signified by the official meeting of Cardinal Sin and Zhao Ziyang. They discussed the problems relating to Catholics and subsequently agreed that their own specialists might go ahead to make further preparations for discussion of the detailed technical problems.

Moreover, since the launching of the programmes of modernisation in 1978, the question of authority in China has been allowed to lapse in many ways: a greater degree of ideological non-conformity has been tolerated than before and the United Front has been much broadened; academic and intellectual life enjoy more autonomy, and more vitality and diversity is found in many aspects of life in China. Therefore religion too has had its opportunity to revive. These developments consequently provide a considerably more positive context in which to view the whole issue of the Vatican and the Catholic church.

On the Catholic side, the Second Vatican Council (1962–5) introduced a drastic change for the Catholic church in its whole outlook towards Marxism in particular and towards pluralism in ideology in general. Also the same Council gave a great amount of autonomy to local churches to allow the greater expression of local culture and customs, both liturgically and institutionally. All these things give positive ground for reconciliation and negotiation. It also explains why our research concentrates on the ten years of 1976–86 and does not go beyond that. This does not mean that the Sino-Vatican relations did not develop further after 1986. Far from it; just because there will be a new era in Sino-Vatican relations other new approaches will be needed to study the new problems arising, which are beyond the scope of this book. In the development of Sino-Vatican relations, the ten years 1976–86 are important ones and deserve our attention because they laid the foundations for the later development of church and state relations.

Moreover, on a personal note, the Catholic church in Hong Kong began in 1978 to initiate some programmes to study Sino-Vatican relations, aiming at establishing a dialogue with China at the grassroot level. I have been observing the progress of these studies, and the development of the dialogue, and became convinced that the dispute should be studied from both the Chinese and Catholic points of view in a political context in order to understand properly this political game. The ancient Chinese strategist, Sunzi, put it graphically in a maxim that still applies: 'Know yourself, know your enemy; then if you fight a hundred battles, you will win a hundred victories.' The attempt is made in this book to interpret the dispute in the context of international politics in the hope of reaching a better understanding of China's way of dealing with Catholics.

On the scope and organisation

Over these ten years, 1976–86, the attempts by the Vatican reaped various kinds of fruits. There have been successes and failures, positive and negative results. The attempts will be discussed from various points of view. Also the treatment of Chinese Catholics by their government is described and analysed to give a clearer picture, and to see how their treatment has been reflected in the dispute between China and the Vatican.

It is intended that Sino-Vatican relations should be discussed in the context of history, therefore in chapter 2 considerable weight will be given to the historical background – the first encounter between China and Catholicism introduced by Matteo Ricci, the Chinese

rites controversy, the banning of Catholicism by the Kangxi
Emperor, the re-entry of Christianity accompanied by foreign
imperialists and the response of Chinese intellectuals to these cultural encounters. In chapter 3, we try to discuss the Ostpolitik of the
Vatican in the hope of throwing some light on how the Vatican dealt
with other Communist states, because its diplomatic experience in
eastern Europe set the tone for its accommodation of other political
regimes with conflicting ideologies. In addition to that, the PRC, as
well as the eastern European countries, was under the great
influence of the USSR model of the state machine, including its
religious policy.

Chapter 4 depicts the clash of authority between China and the
Vatican for political, cultural and ideological reasons, when both of
them were less tolerant of each other in the 1950s. We look at the
evolution of China's religious policy in chapter 5 to set a proper
perspective for the discussion of Catholic problems in the modernisation era, as well as to enable us to examine the scope of China's
tolerance of diversified ideologies. Some obvious constraints have
been inflicted on Chinese Catholics, therefore in chapter 6 the
constraints will be discussed in order to cast light on Sino-Vatican
relations in the ten years between 1976 and 1986. In chapter 7, the
interactions between China and the Vatican are surveyed from
political and diplomatic points of view. 'Bridge-churches' are also
discussed to see how they may have facilitated rapprochement. In
chapter 8, we shall discuss the possibility for negotiations with
feasible concessions and compromises.

Due to problems of access to sources, some areas cannot be dealt
with as fully as could be wished. Where sources are more abundant,
episodes can be written about with more confidence. For example,
due to my personal acquaintance with Bishop Dominic Deng
Yiming, the controversy over his appointment as Archbishop of
Guangzhou can be discussed with greater insight. After observing
the Hong Kong Catholics in their endeavours to contact China with
different motives and orientations, the 'bridge-church' can be portrayed without much difficulty. However when it comes to the
meeting of Zhao Ziyang and Cardinal Sin in November 1987, due to
the difficulty in obtaining first-hand information when I was in
London, the discussion of the negotiations has had to be undertaken
mainly on the basis of negotiations theory with some degree of

speculation.[8] I have been better supplied with inside information from the Catholic side, as might be expected.

On sources of research materials

All the relevant published documents of both the Vatican and the Beijing government have been used. I have also read some internally circulated Catholic materials, e.g. *The Correspondence* (of the Jesuits) which, due to their sensitive nature, could not be obtained when I was in Hong Kong but were consulted in London. I was also able to consult some confidential reports written mainly for the high officials of the Vatican on the situation of the underground non-CPA Catholics, as well as on their meetings with the CPA Catholics.

Many of my confidential, private sources of information about non-CPA Catholics have had to be treated with extra care, so that no real names of living persons or locations can be traced, lest the disclosure of identities expose people to unnecessary danger and trouble. In dealing with the CPA Catholics, for the sake of preserving reputations as well as conveying the truth, vague descriptive words are used over some sensitive issues, such as their marital status and their loyalty to Rome.

Interviews have also been an important source. However, most of these were held within Catholic circles. Vatican high officials like Cardinal Casaroli, the Secretary of State of the Vatican, and Mgr. C. Celli, the director of the China Desk, as well as the high officials of the Congregation for the Evangelisation of Peoples (the former Propaganda Fide) were interviewed more than once during the course of the research. My greatest regret is that I was not able to interview any high Chinese officials on Catholic matters, but I was advised by my superiors not to do so in view of the delicacy of the situation. In the course of interviewing Catholic visitors to China about the non-CPA Catholics, cross-checking was carried out by asking the same question on the same issue of at least two overseas visitors from different places, e.g. Hong Kong and Manila.

Newspapers and journals both in English and Chinese, published in China, Hong Kong, London and other places have been utilised. The newspapers only provide a general background to the current

---

8 G. Windham, 'Negotiation as a management process', in R. O. Matthews (ed.), *International Conflict and Conflict Management* (Scarborough, Ontario: Prentice-Hall of Canada Inc., 1984), pp. 465–75.

developments in Chinese politics as well as to the involvement of the Vatican in global affairs and much more can be learnt by searching the specialist religious and political journals for particular issues. The publications of the Christian centres on China studies constantly provide information on grassroot contacts. They contain important data allowing us to examine the informal interactions between the Vatican and China, especially after the dispute over the appointment of the Archbishop of Guangzhou. At that time the Vatican had no formal way to contact China and the Chinese Catholic church.

Even though interviews and reports and published materials both at first-hand level or second-hand level are not lacking in this study, in some critical areas these cannot be compared with being personally present on the spot with the persons that were involved in the events. In the case of the meeting of Cardinal Sin and Zhao Ziyang for example, through some personal contacts in Hong Kong who had met Sin after his second trip to China it was possible to obtain information on the possible way the discussions between China and the Vatican would move, but there is no way of knowing how Sin and Zhao actually conducted their discussions. For example, under what auspices were they conducted, how much did they agree and disagree with each other, what was their agenda and so forth. Such details would be of inestimable value.

The meeting of Party General Secretary Zhao Ziyang and Cardinal Sin in November 1987, signified the start of a new period in Sino-Vatican relations. This study that basically ends in 1986 covers what may be considered the preparatory stage. The issues and problems identified in this study will doubtless cast long shadows into the new era. But the preparatory stage is important in its own right, and it has demanded a particular approach, while the new era will obviously raise new questions that will require special studies in their own right. It is hoped that this book will identify the central underlying problems and explain the complicated process of accommodation between China and the Vatican that is now beginning to bear fruit.

CHAPTER 2

The cultural encounter of China and Catholicism, 1552–1949

Introduction

Historians have shown that Christianity was introduced to China on four separate occasions. The case of the Russian Orthodox church mission is not numbered among them as it did not attempt to proselytise and only played a rather insignificant role in Beijing and a few places to the north-east. The first wave of Christianity was the Nestorian, a Christian sect condemned by the Catholic church as heresy, which came from Persia via the famous silk route during the Tang Dynasty. People at a later period would not have known of its existence in China had not the famous Nestorian Tablet (A.D. 781) been unearthed in Xian in 1625 in the late Ming.[1] This sect survived for about 250 years in China, before disappearing. The second coming of Christianity arose out of the Mongol conquests that reached into the heart of Europe. Pope Innocent IV, while in exile in Avignon, France, sent his representatives headed by Joannes de Plano Carpini to the Mongol capital, Karakorum, in 1246, with the intention of saving the Catholic church in Europe from the Mongol cavalry. A friendly relationship was established between the Pope and successive Mongol Khans. The King of France, Louis IX, while on a crusade to recover the Holy Land sent Andrew of Longjumeau in 1249, and William Ruisbrock in 1253 as ambassadors to the Mongol Khans in order to win them as allies against the Muslims.[2]

Then the first mission to China was inaugurated through the efforts of Joannes de Monte Corvinto, a Franciscan, who arrived in

---

[1] *The New Catholic Encyclopaedia*, 1967 edn, s.v. 'China'. The inscription in Chinese and Syriac states that it was erected in 781 A.D. in honour of Bishop Wang She-cheng. It also gives a narration of the Creation and other Christian doctrines.
[2] *The New Catholic Encyclopaedia*, 1967 edn, s.v. 'China'.

Beijing, the capital of China, in 1292.[3] One hundred years later, with the withdrawal of the Mongols from intramural China back to the northern Steppes, all vestiges of Catholicism disappeared from the Middle Kingdom, because most of the converts were Mongols and not Han Chinese. The arrival of Matteo Ricci and his companions in the sixteenth century was the third coming of Christianity to China. Even though these Jesuits found some diaspora Jews at Kaifeng in Henan Province, they found no trace of any Chinese Catholics from the Mongol period.[4] The Jesuit policy of accommodation that Matteo Ricci and his companions had taken up from their predecessor Francis Xavier[5] in evangelising the Chinese was not without beneficial effects when applied to the high officials and literati in the Ming court. Converts from these circles co-operated closely in translating literature on Catholic doctrine and western science.[6] Within eight years of his arrival in China (1591) Ricci had converted eighty Chinese, and at the time of his death (1601) there were only 2,500 Catholics. By 1700 the infant Catholic church in China had barely 300,000 converts,[7] a tiny number compared with the vast Chinese population. Five years later, after working in China for 200 years, the Jesuit missionaries were forced to leave the country, and Catholicism was banned by the Kangxi Emperor due to the Chinese rites controversy.

3 Lo Guang (ed.), *Tianzhujiao Zai Hua Chuanjiao Shiji* [The history of Catholic missions in China] (Taibei: Zhengxiang Press, 1967), pp. 69–72 (hereafter cited as Lo Guang, *The History*). P. A. Van Den Wyngaert, *Sinica Franciscana* (8 vols., Florence: Collegium S. Bonaventurae, 1929), vol. 1, pp. 3–130 on Johnnes de Carpini; pp. 335–55 on Monte Corvinto. That Franciscans were the first Catholic missionaries to China was not accidental, because Pope Nicholas IV was a Franciscan monk and had been the Prior General of the Franciscan Order before he became the Pope in 1288.

4 Chen Sui-jeng, 'The Jewish community in Kaifeng', *Tripod* (Hong Kong) 17 (October 1983): 36. Chen stated that Matteo Ricci sent two young Jesuits to Kaifeng to meet the Jews.

5 Francis Xavier (1506–1552) born in Spain the co-founder of the Society of Jesus. He went to India to evangelise and later went to Japan. He died in Shangchuan Dao, a small island on the southern border of China. He was a renouned missionary who was convinced of the accommodation policy, to win converts a missionary has to become an integral part of a culture. However, he knew mission work was contradictory to the current practice in that it imposed Christian teaching on local culture.

6 The term 'Policy of accommodation' was used by the historian John Young in his work *Confucianism and Christianity: The First Encounter* (Hong Kong University Press, 1983), pp. 9–24 (hereafter cited as Young, *Confucianism and Christianity*).

7 Lo Guang, *The History*, pp. 23–9 and *The New Catholic Encyclopaedia*, 1967 edn, s.v. 'China'.

In the fourth phase, Christianity came to China behind the gunboats of western Imperialists of the Opium War of 1841. In 1948, there were 3.2 million Catholic and 1.4 million Protestant converts in China.[8] Of the huge population of China only 0.8 per cent were Catholics.[9] Not only did missionaries see that the results of their hard labour were minimal compared with those of their Spanish and Portuguese contemporaries who had set sail to the Philippines and South America, but also that, the longer the missionaries stayed in China, the more they became 'persona non grata', and that the more missionaries were sent to China, the more the Chinese literati (gentry and officials and later on students) expressed their resentment at the message of Christ.[10]

It is interesting to note why the Chinese were so difficult to convert. Even though the Catholic doctrine was preached by Ricci and his companions after much prior study of the Chinese classics and language, as required by the Jesuits' policy of accommodation, still the Chinese literati rejected their teachings. Then, hardly six years after the death of Ricci, the first dispute between missionaries and Chinese literati, called the Nanjing Missionary Case, occurred, in which Shen Que (d.1640), Vice President of the Nanjing Board of Rites, three times wrote to the emperor denouncing the Jesuits and suggesting that they should be expelled.[11] One of his contemporaries compiled a collection of writings refuting Christianity, called *Po Xie Ji* [An anthology of writing smashing heterodoxy]. The book was widely circulated among Chinese literati for many years. Paul Cohen called the dispute between Chinese literati and missionaries an intellectual conflict;[12] another writer, E. T. Kelly, argued that

---

[8] The detailed statistics on the Catholics and Protestants and the mission activities appeared in *Annuarie de l'Eglise Catholique en Chine 1949* (Shanghai: Bureau Sinologique de Zi-ka-wei, 1949), Table 'B', pp. 12–15 and *Bilan Du Monde* (Louven: Encyclopaedia Catholique du Monde Chretien Caterman), Tome II, 1960 edn, s.v. 'China'.

[9] *Bilan Du Monde*, Tome II, 1960 edn, s.v. 'China', p. 202.

[10] Anti-Christian sentiment was much stronger in the Qing Dynasty than in the Ming and 1860 to 1874 saw the peak of hatred of Christians by Chinese literati. See Lu Shiqiang, *Zhongguo Guanshen Fanjiao De Yuanyin 1860–1874* [Causes of anti-missionary activities of Chinese officials and gentry, 1860–1874.] Series in *Zhongguo Xueshu Zhuzuo Jiangzhu Weiyuanhui Congshu*, no. 16 (Taibei: Zhongguo Xueshu Zhuzuo Jiangzhu Weiyuanhui, 1966), Introduction, pp. 1–8 (hereafter cited as Lu, *Causes*).

[11] This incident is described in Shen Que's biography in the Ming Shi 218 Chuen, pp. 11b–12b, quoted in Young, *Confucianism and Christianity*, p. 59.

[12] Paul Cohen, *China and Christianity: The Missionary Movement and the Growth of Chinese Antiforiegnism 1860–1870* (Cambridge, Mass.: Harvard University Press, 1963), p. 21.

the literati felt that the missionaries were the agents of foreign powers and should be expelled.[13]

This chapter aims to discuss the encounter between Catholicism and Confucianism from 1552 to 1949 as a clash of moral and political authorities. The year 1552 is chosen as the starting date because in that year St Francis Xavier died on Shangchuan Dao, a small island on the southern border of China, before reaching the mainland. His death marked the beginnings of the China Mission, because his brethren in the Society of Jesus took up his mission in China and the accommodation policy. The year 1949, being the start of Communist rule in China, needs no explanation. From then on the Catholic church had to face another type of conflict and clash of authority generated from Marxism–Leninism and Mao Zedong Thought, that has constituted the orthodox teaching of China in recent times.

The Millennial Kingdom in the west and the Middle Kingdom in the east

The world views and social orders in the west, from where the missionaries were sent, and in the east, where they were received, were very different, causing different political and cultural behaviour in the Chinese than in the foreign missionaries. In Europe around the middle of the fifteenth century people experienced the Age of Discovery. One of the striking features of that time was the apocalyptical expectations of its many travellers. Great explorers like Christopher Columbus and Vasco da Gama viewed exploration and colonisation as the fulfilment of the prophecies of the apocalypse – the coming of the new heaven and earth, the way to a universal Christian empire.[14] Christopher Columbus claimed that it was not from scholarly books or learned men that he reached his decision to sail westward.[15]

During the Middle Ages, it was commonly believed that part of

[13] E. T. Kelly, 'The anti-Christian persecution of 1616–1617 in Nanjing' (Unpublished Ph.D. dissertation, Columbia University, 1971), pp. 259–75, quoted in Young, *Confucianism and Christianity*, p. 59.

[14] John Phelan, *The Millennial Kingdom of the Franciscans in the New World* (Berkeley: University of California Press, 1970) and Samuel E. Morison, *Admiral of the Ocean Sea: A Life of Christopher Columbus* (New York: Time Incorporated, 1962), pp. 3, 252, 271, 536–7, quoted in Young, *Confucianism and Christianity*, p. 11.

[15] Washington Irving, 'The life and voyage of Christopher Columbus', in *Life and Works of Washington Irving* (New York, n.p. 1883), vol. 3, p. 182, quoted in Young, *Confucianism and Christianity*, p. 11.

the duty of a king was to spread the gospel among the heathens.[16] With the discovery of new lands and sea routes in the fifteenth century, the conversion of the whole earth seemed closer than ever.[17] Thus, after the Portuguese King John III obtained Macau, a tiny spot of land at the southern tip of China, in 1540, he asked Pope John III to send missionaries there.[18] The first group of Jesuits was sent to China in the late Ming dynasty at the request of the Pope and the Portuguese emperor. After a century of Spanish–Portuguese rivalry in the east, came the British, the French, the Dutch and the American expansionists who set up the unequal treaty system in the mid nineteenth century. These nations basically believed in the nation state, the rule of law, the benefits of individual rights, Christianity and scientific technology, and the use of warfare in the service of progress.[19]

When the first group of foreign missionaries landed in China, they found themselves thrown into an entirely different world with a Sinocentric world view. The Chinese, especially the old ruling class, believed in the classical Confucian teachings and the universal supremacy of the Son of Heaven, the emperor, who maintained his rule by the edifying example of his virtuous conduct at the head of a harmonious social order or hierarchy and status. In this ancient regime, the classical learning tolerated only change-within-tradition, the extended family system dominated the individual, a doctrine of duty eclipsed any doctrine of rights. Civil administrators controlled the military and used the merchants; the principles of moral conduct took precedence over human passions, material profit, and the letter of law.[20] With the stimulisation of the coming of the foreigners and the disturbance they brought, the ancient and less rapidly changing civilisation gradually gave way before the more modern and dynamic, and there arose in the nineteenth century a pioneer generation of Chinese scholars and administrators who pursued reform. Gradually they worked out a new view of the world and China's place in it. When the central authority declined, in a

---

[16] James Bryce, *The Holy Roman Empire* (New York: Schock Books, 1961), pp. 104–6, 113, quoted in Young, *Confucianism and Christianity*, p. 11.

[17] Young, *Confucianism and Christianity*, pp. 11–12.

[18] Gu Zhangsheng, *Chuang Jiaoshi Yu Jindai Zhongguo* [Missionaries and contemporary China] (Shanghai: Renmin Press, 1981), p. 1 (hereafter cited as Gu, *Missionaries and China*).

[19] J. Fairbank (ed.), 'Late Ching [Qing], 1800–1911', Part 1 in D. Twitchett and J. K. Fairbank (eds.), *The Cambridge History of China*, vol. 10 (Cambridge University Press, 1978), p. 2.

[20] J. K. Fairbank (ed.), 'Late Ching', p. 2.

confusion of new ideas, the Chinese nationalists in an expanded international world of nationalism were prepared to embrace democracy and science to save China, and found no other ideology relevant – not even Christianity, one of the cultural heritages of the western world. Eventually in the mid twentieth century, China established a new orthodoxy through the application of atheistic Marxism–Leninism, and through the work of Mao Zedong and other Chinese Marxist thinkers. In spite of the fact that Christ was born in the east, Christianity is clothed with a Greco-Roman cultural heritage which could not easily be accepted by the Chinese, who had Confucius as their great master and teacher, and the whole orientation of Chinese culture was coloured by him. For two thousand years, Confucianism was regarded as the orthodox teaching while every other school of thought was heterodox.[21]

Orthodoxy versus heterodoxy

In the ninth century when Buddhism was accepted by some emperors of the Tang Dynasty, a very prominent prose writer, a high official, Han Yu (A.D. 768–824), holding the view that Buddhism was unorthodox, presented a letter to the emperor dissuading him from giving too much honour to the Buddha and Buddhism by receiving the Buddha's relic at a grand ceremony. The following was the argument Han Yu presented to the emperor:

Your servant begs to say that Buddhism is no more than a cult of the barbarian people which spread to China in the time of the Latter Han. It did not exist here in ancient times ... Now Buddha was a man of the barbarians who did not speak the language of China and wore clothes of a different fashion. His sayings did not concern the ways of our ancient kings nor did his manner of dress conform to their laws. He understood neither the duties that bind sovereign and subject, nor the affections of father and son. If he were still alive today and came to our country by order of his ruler, Your Majesty might receive him condescendingly, but it would be no more than one audience in the Xuan Zheng Hall, a banquet by the Office for Receiving Guests, the presentation of a suit of clothes; and he would be escorted to the borders of the nation, dismissed and not allowed to delude the masses. How then, when he has long been dead, could his rotten bones,

---

[21] Paul Cohen, *China and Christianity*, pp. 3–60 (chapter on 'The anti-Christian tradition in China') discusses the antithesis of orthodoxy and heterodoxy in Chinese tradition.

the foul and unlucky remains of his body be rightly admitted to the palace? Confucius said: 'Respect ghosts and spirits, but keep them at a distance.'[22]

Han Yu's refutation of Buddha was mainly based on cultural grounds of Confucian tradition, not on political reasons. He dwelt on the concept of orthodoxy which he often referred to, and implied that Buddhism was a heterodox cult of barbaric people. The act of receiving the relic of Buddha with grand ceremony was against the orthodox tradition of Confucianism that ghosts and spirits should be respected yet kept at arm's length.

In the mind of Han Yu, as well as other Chinese literati, anything coming from abroad was barbarian and inferior to anything Chinese in every way. China was the Middle Kingdom, denoting that China was the centre of the earth, and the neighbouring people were barbarians who paid tribute to her to learn a high standard of civilisation; while the Middle Kingdom granted protection to the barbarians. There was a one way traffic of learning in the whole cultural intercourse – for the Chinese mostly felt they had nothing to learn from barbarians.

Han Yu took up the self-imposed responsibility of a Chinese gentry-official to defend Confucianism as the orthodoxy *vis-à-vis* heterodoxy in spite of the possibility of offending the absolute monarch. His attitudes and his arguments were so well accepted, not only by his contemporaries but also by Confucian scholars from generation to generation, that this letter was regarded as an outstanding piece of literature and was included in a collection of outstanding essays by the best Chinese scholars, and widely read by nearly all literati of all ages until modern times.

The non-responsiveness exemplified by Han Yu's essay was perhaps caused by the fact that Chinese traditional society had created such an effective and balanced structure of ideas and practices, all much superior to those of its neighbouring states. Geographical isolation had prevented any challenge from other cultures of equal maturity but different in expression, form and order. Thus the Chinese were unprepared for the coming of the European culture of Greco-Roman origin.

---

[22] Han Yu, 'Jian Ying Fogu Biao' [Treaties persuading against receiving the Buddha's relics] *Guwen Pingzhu* [Classical proses with commentary and annotations] (Hong Kong: Guangzhi, n.d.), vol. 2, pp. 18–21.

The coming of the Jesuits to China

The re-introduction of Catholicism to China was through the Portuguese traders in the sixteenth century. St. Francis Xavier's death in 1552 on a small island on the southern border of China before he reached the interior was partly explained by China's general unwillingness, intensified by the disturbance of Japanese pirates along the coast, to welcome barbarians from across the oceans. But the most important reason was that Chinese officials had heard about the uncivilised conduct of the Portuguese towards the Asian peoples. They had gained control of the sea route over the Indian Ocean, effecting mass conversions on the one hand and gross exploitation and slavery on the other.[23]

Though Xavier had made large-scale conversions in India, he took on a new approach after he had visited Japan and had been challenged by Buddhist monks there.[24] Xavier and later the Jesuits in China took up the 'organic' missionary policy, which is that to win converts a missionary has to become an 'integral' part of a particular civilisation. Ricci's great effort to study Confucian literature and other aspects of Chinese culture was not accidental, nor did it grow out of any admiration for Chinese civilisation, it was done only because he aimed at communicating with the Chinese in their own language and at conducting a dialogue with them in terms relevant to their own culture.[25]

Historians of the Catholic church have written much on Matteo Ricci and his contribution to the Chinese Catholic church, regarding him as the first and greatest missionary to China. Even Pope John Paul II on the 400th anniversary of Ricci's arrival in China (1583–1983) paid him tribute by honouring him as the bridge between east and west.[26] Historians of the Ming period, for example Fang Hao, revealed that Matteo Ricci was well accepted both inside and outside Catholic circles in China.[27] Later, in the controversy of the Chinese rites, Ricci was identified with the Catholic church in

[23] H. J. Coleridge (ed.), *Life and Letters of St. Francis Xavier* (London: Burns and Oates, 1881), p. 89.

[24] Young, *Confucianism and Christianity*, p. 14.

[25] Ibid., p. 25.

[26] John Paul II, 'Fr. Matteo Ricci established a bridge between the church and Chinese culture', in E. Wurth (ed.), *Papal documents Related to the New China 1937–1984* (Maryknoll, N.Y.: Orbis Books, Probe Series, 1985), pp. 161–6.

[27] There are numerous works on Matteo Ricci in Chinese and Italian written from a Catholic point of view. See Fang Hao, *Zhongguo Tianzhujiaoshi Renwu Chuan* [Biographies of prominent persons in the Chinese Catholic church] (Hong Kong: Tianzhujiao Zhenglixuehui, 1967),

the mind of the Kangxi Emperor, who regarded the Catholic rites adapted by Ricci as acceptable.[28] Ricci and his companions obviously did not aim at mass conversion as other contemporary Catholic missionaries did in the Fujian Province. Ricci's own encounter with Chinese officials and society at large convinced him that, in order to gain converts, he had to allow them to continue to practise the Confucian rites and ancestor worship. In spite of opposition even from those within his own religious congregation, such as Nicholas Longobardi (d. 1654), Ricci strongly believed that these Confucian ceremonies were only part of the Chinese tradition; they had no religious significance, nor were they in conflict with the Christian doctrine.

In essence, Ricci tried to make his instructions closely related to Confucian teachings, hoping to make Christian teachings an integral part of the Chinese civilisation.[29] The first group of Jesuits came at a time when China was lagging behind in one of the more important aspects of modern civilisation – science. Being an agricultural state, China needed a proper calendar to forecast the approximate times for sowing and harvesting, vital data for farmers. Most of the astronomical knowledge and techniques used in the Ming Dynasty were those of Guo Shoujing (1231–1315), and they proved to be obsolete, with weather forecasts going wrong on many occasions. The late Ming rulers desperately searched for a scientifically based calendar that could be used more accurately.[30] Ming emperors tried to compile a new calendar based on accurate astronomical tables as offered by the newly arrived Jesuits. Together with his early companion, Mechele Ruggieri, Matteo Ricci displayed scientific instruments from the west, engaged in conversation and discussion with the literati and gained their respect. The contribution by the Jesuits in late Ming and early Qing to mathematics, astronomy, geography, hydraulics and the manufacturing of cannon has been positively accepted even by Chinese Marxist historians, despite their

vol. 1, pp. 72–82. This is a collection of writings of Chinese non-Catholic literati eulogising Matteo Ricci.
[28] Chen Yuan (ed.), *Kangxi yu Luoma Shijie Guanxi Wenshu Yingyinben* [Facsimiles of a collection of documents on relations between Kangxi and Rome] Zhongguo Shixue Congshu no. 23 (Beijing: Gugong Yingyinben [Museum facsimile], 1931; reprinted Taibei: Xueshen, 1956), document no. 4, pp. 13–14 (hereafter cited as *Collection of Documents*).
[29] Young, *Confucianism and Christianity*, p. 26.
[30] Ibid., p. 24.

general view of the missionaries as the forerunners of the western
imperialists who aimed at turning China into their colony.[31]

The conversion of some high Ming officials such as Xu Guangqi,
Li Zhizao and Yang Tingyun greatly contributed to the introduction of Catholicism and western science to China through their co-
operation with the Jesuits in various translations. It was the scientific
contribution of the Jesuits that enabled them to win the favour of
emperors, consequently enabling the Catholic church to survive in
China for more than two hundred years, even under the persecution
of the Qianlong Emperor that was caused by the famous Chinese
rites controversy. At the death of Matteo Ricci there were only 2,500
converts and nine out of eighteen Jesuits in China were Chinese;
whereas by the end of the Ming Dynasty there were 150,000 Chinese
Catholics (though no figures are available for Yunnan and Guizhou,
the two remotest provinces), and Catholic missionaries were found
in every province.[32] Nevertheless one could look at the mission of
Matteo Ricci from the other perspective, and argue that, although
the modern church hails him and his work and although he is an
example of tact and scholarliness, he was not as successful as Xavier.
Nor was he successful like St. Paul, who was 'all things to all men'.
The reason is that Paul preached Christ crucified, in season and out,
but Ricci preached science and astronomy. It might be argued that
he failed to tell the Chinese the true meaning of Christianity because
he fell into the error of 'reductionism' or 'indifferentism', trying to
make the differences between Catholicism and non-Catholic beliefs
as small as possible – smaller than the truth.

The controversy over Chinese rites: political and cultural conflicts at top level
The Chinese rites issue has been called by a Chinese historian a
purely European concern with complicated political overtones.[33]
The Bull 'Ex Quo Singulari' of 1715 was the official opinion of the
Catholic church on this controversy. The making of this decision had
evolved over more than a century, through seven popes and two

[31] Chen Yulu, Forward to *Missionaries and China*, by Gu Zhangsheng. Chen holds the opinion
that the western missionaries were 'hypocrites engaging in aggression in China. For a long
time the Chinese have regarded them as Imperialists in a religious cloak. The imperial
capitalists have been using these deceitful missionaries as their forerunners to turn China
into their colonies', pp. 1, 10.

[32] Chia Tianyao, 'Yesuhui Chuanjiaoshi Zai Zhongguo' [The History of Jesuit mission in
China] in Lo Guang, *The History*, pp. 17–23 and *The New Catholic Encyclopaedia*, 1967 edn,
s.v. 'China'.

[33] Young, *Confucianism and Christianity*, pp. 118–23.

apostolic delegates, two Chinese emperors, the kings of Portugal, Spain and France, the Jesuit confessor of Louis XIV, the Holy Office and the Sacred Congregation of the Propagation of the Faith, the Theology Faculty of the Sorbonne, the Jansenists, preachers like Fenelon and Bossuet, writers like Voltaire and Leibnitz, the missionaries, their religious congregations and superiors.[34] But it is a most puzzling thing that not one Chinese Catholic Confucian scholar was directly involved or consulted, although the decision by the church touched the lives of the Catholics in China, and affected in an irrevocable way the course of the church in the Middle Kingdom. Perhaps it was regarded as a matter of church discipline, and the church thought that it could handle its own questions as it saw fit. In the same way, the Chinese emperor made up his own mind on the rites without understanding the Pope's position. The controversy was aroused when the Jesuits' policy of accommodation was challenged by the Dominicans and Franciscans. The latter could never agree with the Jesuits' practice of allowing Catholics to perform rites before the tablets of ancestors and burn incense to honour Confucius. There was also a dispute as to whether the Chinese terms Shang-di and Tian-zhu were really identical to the word 'God' in the Chinese language. In 1701, Pope Clement XI sent a Papal delegate to China to settle the dispute. Charles Thomas Maillard de Tournon, the Apostolic Visitor to the East Indies and the Chinese Empire, was chosen as his representative. Kessler, a European scholar, held the opinion that the Kangxi Emperor was very displeased with this because he believed that this was a gesture challenging his absolute power in China.[35] Kessler was right because the quarrel between missionaries over the question of honouring Confucius and ancestors would not alone have been the cause of the banning of Catholicism, had Kangxi not felt that his absolute authority was being challenged by the religious authority manifested by the Pope.

Apparently when de Tournon first arrived, the first audience in 1705 was held in a cordial and friendly atmosphere with a good deal of courtesy. In one of his edicts, the emperor showed his concern over de Tournon's illness, and treated him as a state guest.[36] On the other hand Kangxi was already fully aware of the sharp divisions

[34] Minamiki, 'Introduction', *The Chinese Rites Controversy* (Chicago: Loyola University Press, 1985), pp. IX–XVI.
[35] Kessler, *Kanghsi and the Consolidation*, p. 154, quoted in Young, *Confucianism and Christianity*, p. 18.
[36] Chen Yuan (ed.), *Collection of Documents*, document no. I.

and struggles among the different European nationalities in general, and within the missionary circles in particular. He exercised his moral authority to request the foreign missionaries to stop quarrelling and observe what they had preached on universal brotherhood.[37]

In 1706, after he had listened to Tournon's 'plea' on church affairs, Kangxi issued a more substantial edict laying down regulations that those from the west who came and left within a year's time would not be allowed to live in the interior. Kangxi passed remarks on the way the missionaries quarrelled and meddled with Chinese customs on honouring Confucius and ancestors as follows: 'They (the missionaries) were like men standing outside a house criticising what the people inside were doing. How can people accept this kind of behaviour ... As for members of the various societies and nationalities, since they all worship the same Master of Heaven, they should not make distinctions among themselves. They are all under the same roof, thus they should not cause any trouble.'[38] This was the second time that the emperor exercised his moral authority by requesting the foreign missionaries to behave properly. Unfortunately the missionaries were rather insensitive to his request.

The appearance of Maigrot, Vicar Apostolic of Fukien, in Beijing to assist Tournon changed the whole matter from bad to worse. Maigrot suggested they discuss the choice of a candidate for the Pope's representative in China with the emperor. The emperor then lost his temper with the arrogant Maigrot when the latter exhibited his ignorance of Confucian tradition, whilst he did not even know the Chinese language.

In an Edict of 1707 Kangxi took a firm attitude and acknowledged Ricci's rites for honouring ancestors and Confucius. The tone of the edict itself was resonant with the authority of a head of state. Solemnly he declared:

Henceforth those who do not follow the rites of Ricci are not permitted to stay in China.[39]

The real clash of authorities became manifest when Pope Clement XI in 1715 issued the bull 'Ex Illa Die' to confirm his anti-rites stand of 1704. He demanded that the missionaries and Catholics observe it

---

[37] Young, *Confucianism and Christianity*, pp. 118–19.
[38] Chen Yuan (ed.), *Collection of Documents*, document no. 2, p. 10.
[39] Ibid., document no. 4, pp. 13–14.

under pain of ex-communication and pronounced that this was the final decision on the Chinese rites and no further dispute would be allowed.[40] At this stage Kangxi in no ambiguous terms expressed his mind on the whole conflict especially on Maigrot and Tournon, who as envoys of the Pope had failed to convey his opinion to the Pontiff. He declared:

Again I say, if you do not follow the rules of Matteo Ricci, the western teaching preached for two hundred years in China will be discontinued, all Westerners will have to leave. Many times I have pointed out to you the ruinous conduct of Tournon and Maigrot, asking you why you have not given my views to the Pope . . .[41]

After all, as the leader of China, Kangxi felt he had to exercise his authority to uphold the orthodox Confucian tradition. From his viewpoint the Chinese rites laid down by Ricci to honour Confucius and ancestors, were not only permissible but also necessary. Kangxi even asked the missionaries 'Don't you westerners also have saints and honour them because of their deeds?'[42]

To explain the controversy of the Chinese rites, according to Pope Clement XI, Chinese Catholics were not allowed to honour the ancestor tablets, Confucius and various spirits and ghosts. In the context of Confucianism, the honouring of ghosts and spirits is not considered an act of superstition, but an act of honouring the virtues of ancient sages. Confucianists long for immortality, and Confucius himself encouraged his followers to maximise their limited physical existence to build up an everlasting spiritual life by being virtuous, doing great and heroic deeds and leaving valuable academic theses to signify that in spite of their physical mortality their spiritual life would live forever from generation to generation. Therefore in Chinese society great honour has been given to those who have made great contributions through heroic deeds, and academic and professional achievements. These heroes were thanked, commemorated and honoured by successive generations. To honour these heroic figures as patron spirits for their honourable personalities and the contributions they had made was only to give them their due on the part of later generations. It was also meant to stimulate everyone in

[40] Ibid., document no. 14 in which the Papal Bull was translated into Chinese, pp. 87–96.
[41] Ibid., document no. 7, pp. 21–3.
[42] Ibid., document no. 11, pp. 33–7.

society to contribute his best for his fellow men. Usually it resulted in encouraging good conduct, by which the Chinese hoped to remain virtuous and immortal in the hearts of their descendants. Besides every good deed was to be noted down in the family record as a mark of honour to the whole family, while any fault was noted as a shame going down even to the later descendants. The Chinese Confucianists could not but conclude Catholicism to be barbaric because of the Chinese rites controversy.[43]

Yet from one's observation the Chinese practice of veneration of ancestors, involves a great deal of worship in a very religious sense. For example, the spirit of the dead person is expected to return to the family on a particular day. There are rites connected with this return. Paper houses, money, clothes and so on are burnt, and many people believe that these offerings have a relevance to the sort of world in which the spirit lives. If graves are not clean and tidy, it is believed that the body will be uncomfortable. In the villages, the bones are dug up and cleaned in order to make the dead comfortable. It must be said that a great deal of ghost worship, spiritualism, magic and other practices, which are not acceptable to Catholics, are to be found in the ordinary beliefs and practices of Chinese society. In modern cities like Hong Kong, it is possible for Catholics to be more tolerant because the strength of such superstitions has declined. So, if someone lets off fire crackers in a cemetery, one need not think it is to frighten away ghosts. But, in the past, many people believed in such things very strongly. So it is difficult to say that Rome was wrong on the ancestor worship of Confucianism, even though the educated class may have known that Confucius was not a god and that ancestors were not gods either. But what did ordinary people think?

After all Kangxi had been in contact with the Catholic missionaries for over half a century and he appreciated their scientific skill and respected their morality, dedication and loyalty. But, in the process of dealing with the rites controversy, the manoeuvring of the Papal delegates totally ignored his authority. He was disillusioned with the foreign Catholic missionaries who preached moral righteousness, but had difficulty in observing it themselves. Eventually an edict banning Catholicism and ordering the expulsion of foreign missionaries

[43] Lu, *Causes*, p. 30. His argument on the ancestor worship is very much accepted by many scholars both Chinese and non-Chinese. It forms a sharp contrast to the anti-Chinese rites attitudes held by the Vatican at that time.

was written by him in 1721 in vermilion to signify its gravity. Part of the edict runs as follows:

In reading this declaration (of the Pope), one can only ask how these mean people of the west could discuss the principles of China? They do not understand our literature and their discussions are merely ridiculous. The content of this declaration is identical with the heterodox teachings of the Buddhists and Taoists. All these wild sayings are generally the same. Hereafter, to avoid further problems, the westerners will be prohibited from practising their teachings in China.[44]

The ultimate motive for banning Catholicism rested on the fact that Kangxi could not accept that his authority over the Chinese rites should be undermined by the Catholic authorities, whose papal delegation repeatedly ignored his suggestions and refused to give him the chance to have his final word on the decision.

When Kangxi interpreted the whole issue from the framework of Confucianism he may have had little or no idea of the state–church relations prevalent at that time in Europe. The impact of the Reformation on the Catholic church had led it to defend itself by adopting a hard dogmatic line demanding assent from all its members. Furthermore the missionaries came from a Europe which had just gone through an experience of turmoil and division over religious beliefs. The gestures and the symbolic objects involved in the Chinese rites to some extent resembled, to their perceptions, the scene of the reformation in their home milieu. Though the Chinese rites issue was completely different, in fact, the missionaries were reacting to the rites situation in China as if it were a Reformation scene.[45]

Even though the prohibition by Kangxi was not enforced very meticulously, the Yong Zheng Emperor (1724–36) carried out a severe persecution, ending with the deportation of most of the missionaries to Macau. In his long reign (1736–96), the Qianlong Emperor, as part of this campaign against heterodoxy, went even further by decreeing the death penalty for preaching or embracing Christianity. Numerous Catholics suffered death in the persecution of 1784–5. After that only a handful of missionaries remained in the countryside in hiding, and worked in secret under untold hardships, while some Jesuits such as the famous court painter Giuseppe

---

[44] Chen Yuan (ed.), *Collection of Documents*, p. 96.
[45] Minamiki, *The Chinese Rites Controversy*, p. 11.

Castiglione and other missionaries in the service of the emperor at Beijing enjoyed imperial favour and tried to exert an influence against the persecutions to a limited degree.

During the controversy over Chinese rites there were 300,000 Chinese Catholics. When the prohibition on honouring Confucius was imposed by Rome on the Chinese Catholics under the pain of ex-communication, most of the literati-officials refused to be part of the Catholic church; understandably they wished to keep themselves free to perform the state ceremony of honouring Confucius. However, conversions continued among the lower strata of society.[46] With the disbanding of the Jesuit Society in 1773, no missionaries were sent to replace the aged Jesuits at the court. The outbreak of the French Revolution and the Napoleonic wars diverted the Europeans from foreign missions. Thus by the first half of the nineteenth century missions in China were in a deplorable situation. Intermittent persecutions reduced the number of European missionaries to less than forty. The number of Chinese priests never exceeded this figure. Between 1800 and 1840 the number of Catholics stood at between 200,000 and 250,000.[47]

Return of the foreign missionaries in the nineteenth century

The re-entry of the missionaries to China after the Opium War in 1840 together with western traders behind the gunboats marks the start of the fourth phase of the coming of Christianity. In fact the humiliating and unequal treaties allowed the western powers to squeeze as much profit as possible, and left China in a desolate situation.[48]

Political and cultural conflict on the middle level: missionaries versus Chinese literati-gentry

After the Sino-Papal conflict between the Kangxi Emperor and the Catholic missionaries in general and the Pope in particular, we shall look at the response to Catholicism at the mid-level of Chinese

---

[46] Lo Guang, *The History*, p. 32.
[47] *The New Catholic Encyclopaedia*, 1967 edn, s.v. 'China'.
[48] The works of Latourette and Paul Cohen did not convey the feelings and reactions of the Chinese concerning the cultural, economic and political activities of missionaries. The works of Gu Zhangsheng, Li Siyu and Lu Shiqiang conveyed a very strong reaction and resentment at these activities. See Gu, *Missionaries and China*; Lu, *Causes*; and Li Siyu, *Jindai*

society, in which the literati constituted the majority and played a prominent role, and see how the literati reacted to the coming of the so-called 'heterodox teaching of Christianity'. In the old society of China, the illiterate or semi-literate peasants formed up to $\frac{4}{5}$ of the total population, and only $\frac{1}{5}$ of the total population belonged to the literate class. Yet the roots of the literati reached into the masses from whom they originated, and by whom they were accepted and trusted. On the other hand the literati were the source of manpower for the bureaucracy, the ruling elite, appointed through the public examination system. Sandwiched between the masses and the ruling elite, the literati became the link and channel of communication between them, and they were accepted and depended upon equally by each. This same literati-gentry class had the self-imposed responsibility of upholding the orthodoxy of Confucianism since obviously most of the literati were tutors and teachers of all levels of studies. With the coming of Christianity, the literati were threatened not only in their position as teachers but most of all by an encroachment on their pristine culture by foreign barbarians.

In the Chinese political arena, a change of dynasties was for the literati only a change of political leadership, political rulers and the ruling families; but the replacement of the Song dynasty by the Mongols and of the Ming dynasty by the Manchu Qing, were for the literati signs of the crumbling of the traditional and cultural heritage handed down from the ancient sage kings. These changes were seen as a threat to the Han race causing it to degenerate into barbarism.[49] This was very true in the Yuan dynasty when the Mongols rejected the Han intellectuals. However, the situation was better in the Qing dynasty (except for secret societies), for many of the Han could get along with the Manchus well because the Manchu rulers from the beginning tried hard to embrace Confucianism and they had successfully bridged the gap between the civilised Han and the barbaric Manchus. Then the flooding in of missionaries together with western traders and gunboats after 1800 once again aroused a keen awareness of the difference between the civilised Chinese and the barbarian, and the fear of cultural encroachment. The orientation of the Tongzhi Reform as suggested by Zhang Zhidong, to have Chinese learning as the basis of society and western learning for

Zhongguo Fan Yangjiao Yundong [The late nineteenth-century anti-missionary movement in China] (Beijing: Renmin, 1958, Facsimile, 1971).
[49] Lu, *Causes*, pp. 15–16.

utility, clearly revealed what the Chinese mandarins preferred. The reform evinced a degree of willingness to change within the framework of Confucianism, by accepting the need to learn western political systems and scientific technology, but it was by no means so far-reaching a reform as to embrace Christianity. One of the reasons of the conservative officials for opposing the establishment of the Tongwen School (as part of the Tongzhi Reform in the 1860s), for the teaching of astronomy and mathematics to young degree holders, was that they did not wish the young to come in contact with foreign teachers. In effect, many officials identified foreigners as missionaries. The Chinese officials feared that once the foreigners became teachers they would be able to promote Christianity. Although the reformers strongly advocated that the Tongwen School be inaugurated, they too shared the same fear of their conservative counterparts that, in the guise of teachers, the foreigners might indoctrinate the young with their Christianity. For this reason the teachers at the Tongwen School, who were employed to teach only foreign languages and other assigned subjects, were strictly forbidden to teach the Christian religion there.[50]

Most of the officials – conservative or progressive alike – disliked Christianity, and to them foreign missionaries were no more than foreign traders, who only drained wealth from the Chinese economy, or worse, stole away the hearts of the people from the Confucian heritage, becoming agents and heralds of political encroachment. Take Wang Bingxie's argument for example. Wang himself had been serving Premier Li Hongzhang for years, and was very friendly with the progressive officials who were engaged in reform. He had the opportunity to listen to the preachings of foreign missionaries as well as of reading their religious books and the Holy Bible. Besides, he also read certain Chinese scholarly works on the events in the world like Wei Yuan's *Illustrated Treatise on Maritime States*. Wang himself had great suspicion of missionaries and regarded them as trail-blazers of the westerners. His theses were well accepted by the high officials of his time. He held the opinion that the more the Chinese were converted the greater was the danger facing the nation, and his arguments read as follows:

The foundation of a nation lies in the hearts of its people, which can never be allowed to be bound to foreigners. Now if we allow them to spread their

[50] Lu, *Causes*, pp. 14–15.

religion, the unlearned masses could easily be manipulated by them. Once the masses have embraced the foreign religion, their hearts will be turned towards the heads of their religion, and they will push aside the laws and order of our state. This will shake the nation from its foundation.[51]

Wang further buttressed his arguments by pointing to some dissolved or dissolving empires nearby, where the British and the French had made use of missionary activities for their own political purposes, such as in Java, India and the Philippines.[52]

A scholar from the Hanlin Academy, Yin Shouyun, in a letter to the emperor also revealed the same doubts regarding the missionaries. He even held the opinion that the missionaries possessed double identities: spies to gather intelligence on one hand and agents to overthrow China on the other.[53] Zhang Guanying, a famous progressive reformer of the Qing Dynasty, had once spent some years working as a middleman in foreign trade and became an authority on foreign affairs. He affirmed that these missionaries were the cause of discord because according to him they spied on Chinese affairs with the intention of drawing away the hearts of the Chinese.[54]

When Hong Xiuquen, the leader of the Taiping Rebellion, claimed that he was the second son of the Heavenly Father and Jesus Christ was his elder brother, the Qing mandarins were confirmed in their belief that Christianity was the cause of all trouble in China. Zeng Guofan succeeded in appealing to the young literati of Hunan Province to take the lead to combat the Taiping Rebellion. The following was part of his public appeal:

The bandits in Guangdong embraced the religion of God, and called themselves emperor and premier. They call everyone brethren, even the lowest class of soldiers and manual labours. Only the being in heaven do they call father, while they regard every male as brother and female as sister ... Their literati do not study the classics of Confucius but they have other literature on Jesus Christ as well as the New Testament. Have we been so blind as not to notice the complete sweeping away of the rites, classics, standards in human relations, and righteousness which have been prevailing among us for thousands of years in China? Is it not only the most drastic change during the Qing dynasty but also a tremendous cultural collapse which would cause Confucius and Mencius to weep bitterly in the

[51] Lu, *Causes*, pp. 18–20.
[52] Ibid.
[53] Ibid., p. 20.
[54] Zhang Guanying, *Shengshi Weiyan* [The alarming words in a peaceful age], vol. I. on business, quoted in Lu, *Causes*, p. 20.

underworld? How can we who can read and write, sit comfortably with folded arms, not doing anything to redeem the situation?[55]

The aggressive nature of some Christian missionary activities

Although the foreign missionaries contributed much to medical and educational work in China (in fact it was they who introduced western medicine and the western education system to China), and there were many genuine missionaries who were really zealous in preaching the gospel, dedicating their whole lives to working in China, some of them too fell into the category of imperialists. The aggressive nature of missionary work became prominent only after the signing of the series of unequal treaties starting from the Opium War in 1840. The thing which had the most far-reaching effects on the Christian mission in China was the protection given to missionaries by foreign powers. Although protection was meant to eliminate discrimination by the Chinese who were by that time saturated with anti-foreign feelings, the chasm of rejection and abhorrence into which it cast the Christian church including the Catholic church was the direct result. Furthermore the French protectorate in particular separated the Chinese Christians from the masses making them live in an 'imperio in imperium', which caused serious conflict with the sovereignty of China.

Thus not only did the cannons and the gunboats of foreigners cause a great deal of resentment in the Chinese, but the foreigners' arrogance and their interference with Chinese government in an attempt to protect the Catholics caused great resentment on the part of the literate class towards the missionaries.

Moreover interference in Chinese administration by the missionaries was not uncommon. In fact, during the making of the Sino-French Treaty of 1846, it was discovered that the Chinese translation of the text done by a French missionary was not identical with the original French text. In the Chinese translation, a clause 'the French missionaries can purchase land in all provinces and are free to construct churches' was added. Article 6 of the French text of the Sino-French Treaty (1846) reads thus in French:

Conformement à l'édit imperial rendu le 20 mars 1846, par l'auguste Empereur Tao Kouong, les établissements réligieux et de bien faisance qui

---

[55] It was said that this appeal drew much support from the literati not only from Hunan Province but also from many other provinces throughout China, cited in Lu, *Causes*, p. 23.

ont été confisqués aux Chrétiens pendant les persecutions dont ils ont été les victimes, seront rendus à leurs propriétaires par l'entremise de son Excellence le Ministre de France en Chine auquel le Gouvernement Imperial les fera délivrer avec les cimetières et les autres édifices qui en dépendaient.[56]

Its English translation should read like this:

In conformity with the Imperial Edict granted on 20 March, 1846 by the great Emperor Dao Guang, the religious and philanthropic establishments which were confiscated from the Christians during the persecutions of which they have been the victims, are to be restored to their proprietors through the intervention of his Excellency the French Minister in China, to whom the Imperial government is to have them handed over, with the cemeteries and the other buildings which were attached to them.

But the Chinese translation of that treaty which was in the hands of the Chinese read as follows:

In conformity with the Imperial Edict granted on 20 March, 1846 by the great Emperor Daoguang, the religious and philanthropic establishments which were confiscated from the Christians during the persecutions of which they have been the victims, are to be restored to their proprietors through the intervention of his Excellency the French Minister in China, to whom the Imperial government is to have them handed over, with the cemeteries and other buildings which were attached to them; and the French missionaries have the freedom to purchase land in all provinces and are free to construct churches.[57]

Given the fact that the Chinese text did not tally with the original French text of the treaty, both Chinese Catholic and non-Catholic scholars have shared the opinion that a French Catholic missionary should be held responsible for the addition of the extra clause, because in the process of formulating the Treaty of 1846, a missionary would have served as interpreter and translator on the Chinese side.[58] Some Chinese historians have even passed much stronger criticism, condemning the fact that a missionary who professed to preach the good news of God should engage in such devices in matters of such importance.[59]

---

[56] From the original French text of the Academica Sinica, Taiwan, quoted in Lu, *Causes*, p. 100.
[57] The English text is translated from the Chinese text of the treaty in Lu, *Causes*, p. 101.
[58] See K. S. Latourette, *A History of Christian Mission in China*, p. 276. Paul Cohen, *China and Christianity*, pp. 298–9, note 13, as quoted in Lu, *Causes*, p. 101.
[59] Lu, *Causes*, p. 101.

The case of returning church property is a classic example of the aggressiveness of the missionaries. It was decided in the Sino-French Treaty of 1860 that the religious and charitable institutes whose property was confiscated under Kangxi in 1721 should be restored to the Catholic church through the French Minister in China.[60] The ban on Catholicism began in 1721, and since then many confiscated church properties had either fallen into the hands of unidentified owners or the buildings themselves had been converted into various sorts of private and public edifices, and some even had been demolished or rebuilt. It was extremely difficult to trace the records and identify the real owners. Very often the missionaries sought the support of their own government, refusing to consider the difficulties faced by the Chinese side, often insisting on some unreasonable compensation and refusing to accept alternative locations when the displacement of the local people occupying some of these buildings or land proved to be most awkward. Numerous disputes in more than thirty cities and towns all over China gave rise to untold problems in this matter of restoration of church property. These disputes lasted till the end of the Qing dynasty in 1911. In the Academica Sinica in Taiwan, there are twenty-three big volumes of national archives covering 1860–1911, on religious affairs involving foreign governments and over the restoration of church property. In reading these Chinese documents, one finds it hard to understand why those missionaries on the one hand preached the love and compassion of Jesus Christ, while on the other they appeared extremely insensitive and inconsiderate in dealing with the restoration of church property. Willy-nilly they projected themselves as hypocritical, by holding double standards in what they did and what they preached.

The French apparently had a rather notorious record of stirring up storms in a tea cup over religious affairs for their political gain, because they had the so-called 'Right of Protectorate'.[61] In Sichuan Province for instance, in November 1862, the French Minister in China had openly made a suggestion to the Chinese government that, in future, all dealings on religious affairs in Sichuan, Yunnan

[60] See K. S. Latourette, *A History of Christian Mission in China*, p. 276.
[61] Lu, *Causes*, chapter 2, pp. 61–129. In this chapter Lu shows how the French government and the French missionaries behaved over the restoration of church property and the settling of disputes between the Catholic and the non-Catholic Chinese, to illustrate the aggressive nature of Catholic missionaries.

and Guizhou Provinces should be managed by Chongshi, the general of Chengdu, who constantly made concessions to the French. The same French Minister also suggested the transfer of the Governor General of Sichuan, Luo Bingzheng, the General Secretary of Sichuan Province, Liu Yun, and the Governor of Chengdu, Yang Zhongya, from Sichuan Province because these three officials had not always complied with the French.[62]

It is true that missionaries were arrogant. From missionary records one can see that too. They were astonishingly ignorant of the real outlook and practices of the Chinese. But there is something that few Chinese scholars are fully aware of. The missionaries did not go to China to help find an empire for the western world as their main motive for leaving family and friends, safety and comfort for the loneliness, danger and disease of China; most of these missionaries gained no material rewards from their China mission. They often thought that the only solution for China was foreign ways and foreign presences. That was an understandable feeling on their part, just as many Hong Kong people feel that the Philippines' economy would be much improved if it were run by Hong Kong Chinese.

However, the Chinese literati-officials and the gentry whipped up more antagonism towards the foreign religion because the French Protectorate was extended to Chinese Catholic converts and Chinese Catholics were protected from Chinese laws and orders. It was obvious that in local court cases whether civil or criminal, that the Catholics under the protection of foreign missionaries always won the cases or obtained whatever they wanted, while the Chinese court could not act against their wishes. In Guizhou Province it was recorded that people were converted because they wanted to seek protection from missionaries against local banditry; and some of the one-time bandits and pariahs joined the Catholic church just to seek its protection from the local Chinese court. Thus it appeared that the Catholic church rendered its protection to its Chinese converts whilst usurping the judicial power of the legitimate authority – the literati-officials. In moral and social practice, the Catholics went to the missionaries to learn and seek advice instead of going to the literati-gentry as traditionally used to be the case. In the struggle for authority to teach and afford protection, the Catholic church could not simply be on friendly terms with the Chinese literati-gentry.

[62] This case was one of a few cited by Lu Shiqiang to illustrate interference in Chinese internal administration by the French missionaries. See Lu, *Causes*, pp. 150–3.

Further research is needed before passing judgement as to whether the complaints about the Catholics are justified. If the Catholics were as despised as the Chinese historians suggest, why did people still join the church in a century when the Boxer Rebellion had proved how dangerous it was to be a Catholic? Why did the Chinese join during an upsurge of nationalist and anti-western feeling? In spite of the small number of converts they proved to be of very good quality. Why did the sons and grandsons of these Catholics accept persecution and martyrdom under the Communist party? Why did so many priests accept prison and death when it would have been easy to renounce Rome? A western scholar who is familiar with Catholic affairs in modern China admits that more bishops and priests – and many laity too – suffered in China under the Chinese Communist party than were willing to suffer under Henry VIII in England when the whole country was supposed to be Catholic. If the Catholic church was able to produce so many people willing to suffer first under the Boxers and then under the Chinese Communist party, can one deny that they were truly part of China and truly involved in their own society, and willing to pay the highest price to bear witness within China?

To a certain extent, the missionaries became the victims of foreign governments. For many, the missionaries epitomised the foreign threat. Foreign government personnel and foreign traders remained in the international settlements of treaty-ports and associated among themselves. Missionaries however travelled from village to village and had the chance to contact the populace through the orphanages, education, famine relief, medical service and so forth. Therefore, it was easy for the Chinese to see them as spies collecting intelligence. It was true that for westerners and the Chinese of that time there was no clear boundary between ideology and government. Many Chinese could not differentiate an evangelist from a political emissary, or between different nationalities, such as French, German, British, Russian and American. They had no idea that there was struggle, competition, between other nationalities. They had not noticed that the French and Germans were at odds with each other in Europe. The traditional rivalry between the French and British in acquiring colonies and trade routes was not known to many Chinese. The arrogance of the French missionaries in one place, was blamed on all foreign missionaries. In fact some foreign missionaries did not always receive the whole-hearted support which they sought. As quoted by Jessie G. Lutz, Sir Ernest Satow, British ambassador to China announced that the British missionaries were not accredited agents of the British government; and the British had not confered on missionaries any right of intervention on behalf of native Christians.[63]

In one of the anti-foreign movements, the Boxer Rebellion in 1900, the Catholic missions were one of the targets to be attacked. It was reported that around 30,000 Catholics mainly in north China were victimised because the rebellion was the result of an eruption of the unbearable hatred of the Chinese towards foreigners. In spite of this great resentment from the Chinese, the number of missionaries increased. Even women of missionary orders went to China to help in the many missionary schools, hospitals and orphanages that mushroomed in all areas.

In 1900 there were 886 male missionaries belonging to ten institutions, and by 1949 the number had gone up to 6,889 in forty-seven institutions. Female religious congregations grew from ten in 1900 to fifty-eight in 1949, and their membership rose from fifty-nine to 7,463 in the same period. Catholics totalled 742,000 in 1900 and 3 million in 1938. On the eve of liberation the total number of Catholics had mounted to 3,274,740 with 5,788 priests and ninety-seven bishops.[64] Among the many Catholic social institutions conducting education, social services and medical work, there were three Catholic universities. In 1946, the Chinese Catholic hierarchy was established.

Although the development of the Catholic church during this period was considerable, with missions spread over practically everywhere, the church was full of foreign elements with foreign bishops in the majority of the Catholic dioceses in China. More than half of church personnel, both priests and sisters were foreigners and foreign mission societies supported the missions financially.[65] The Vatican in 1926 had already taken the first steps in implementing the inculturalisation policy suggested by Pope Benedict XV in his encyclical 'Maximum Illud' (1919) by ordaining the first six Chinese bishops. Moreover, the First Chinese Synod was called in 1924 in

---

[63] Jessie Gregory Lutz, *Chinese Politics and Christian Missions*, (Indiana: Cross Cultural, 1933), p. 23.

[64] The figures are quoted from *Annuaire de L'Eglise Catholique en Chine 1949*, p. xiii and *The New Catholic Encyclopaedia*, 1967 edn, s.v. 'China'.

[65] J. Charbonnier, *Guide to the Catholic Church in China 1989* (Singapore: China Catholic Communication, 1989), pp. 20, 55, 78, 119 and 162.

Shanghai under the leadership of Archbishop Constantini, the first
Vatican delegate to China, to formulate more detailed plans on
Chinese missions, aiming at implementing this policy at the grassroots level. Unfortunately the implementation was carried out too
slowly and was started too late, during the KMT period. Twenty-
five years later, when the political leaders in Beijing demanded that
ties with foreign missions should be severed and foreign missionaries
expelled, the blow to the Chinese church was severe, with the
departure of foreign church personnel and the drying up of financial
support from abroad. Indirectly it spoke for itself, a truly Chinese
Catholic church, embedded in Chinese culture and fully accepted
and identified with by the Chinese people had not yet been
developed.

The search for wealth and power: Christian teaching or Marxist teaching

After the 1911 Revolution, the Chinese intellectuals searched for the
key to national salvation and they found traditional Confucian
beliefs and institutions too authoritarian and anachronistic. In their
quest for modernity and national strength, many intellectuals turned
to western science and learning.[66] In the late nineteenth century
and early twentieth many western ideas were introduced into China,
many of them rationalist ideas either of eighteenth and nineteenth-
century Europe, or later additions of Anglo-American utilitarianism
and pragmatism. In the realm of religion, anti-clericalism prevailed
in Europe at this time. Darwin's theory of evolution, in particular,
was widely studied and accepted by Chinese intellectuals. Hu Shi,
one of the leading intellectuals of the period, wrote in 1922, 'With
the appearance of Darwin, evolutionism first clashed wih the view
that the universe was created by God.'[67] Influenced by their
counterparts in Europe, the Chinese literati were converted to so-
called scientism and were confident that reason would break the
bondage imposed by religion and superstition. The spirit of that time

[66] There are many books on this period which saw the transformation of modern Chinese
thought. Among the numerous scholarly works are Benjamin Schwartz's *In Search of Wealth
and Power: Yen Fu and the West*, (Cambridge, Mass.: Harvard University Press, 1964) and
Reflections on the May Fourth Movement: A Symposium (Cambridge, Mass.: Harvard University
East Asian Research Centre, 1972), also Chow Tse-tsung, *The May Fourth Movement*
(Cambridge, Mass.: Harvard University Press, 1964).
[67] Hu Shi, 'Wushi Lianlai Shijie Zhexue' [Philosophies of the world during the last fifty years],
Hu Shi Wen Cun (Shanghai: Yadong, 1924), vol. 2, pp. 217–304.

could be seen in Chen Duxiu's declaration in *Xinqingnian*, the journal for progressive intellectuals, in January 1919. He proclaimed:

To advocate democracy, we have to oppose Confucianism, propriety, chastity, old ethics and old politics. To advocate science, we have to oppose old art and old religion. To advocate democracy and science, we have to oppose the national heritage and the old literature.[68]

When President Yuan Shikai tried to promote Confucianism as a state religion, he provoked much opposition from the progressive intellectuals who had so vehemently opposed it as being irrelevant to a modern Chinese society.[69] Thus the strong rationalist strain in traditional Chinese thought made its contribution to their stand against Christianity. In the 1920s, the Chinese intellectuals generally took Christianity to be irrational, superstitious and unworthy of the attention of serious-minded people.[70]

For the Chinese literati who embraced western science and learning they had a dilemma when faced with Christianity. They shied away from total identification with western tradition because that would have deprived them of their self-respect and a distinct cultural identity.[71] The leading literati picked up various schools of atheism and anti-clericalism from different European thinkers of their time, and so took religion to be an obstacle to human progress. They advocated that spiritual freedom would permit one to develop one's intellectual skills to the fullest. Hu Shi, a disciple of John Dewey, argued that everything was refutable unless it could be proved by scientific methods. Social immortality should take the place of religion. The immortality of human society or the Greater Self should replace the notion of immortality of the soul. For Hu Shi, to live for the sake of the species and posterity is a religion of the highest kind.[72] Another leading intellectual and educationalist Cai Yuanpei proposed that religion be considered part of aesthetic education.[73] The Marxist intellectual Chen Duxiu thought that

[68] Chen Duxiu, 'Ben Zhi Zuian Zhi Dabian Shu' [In defence of the 'Sin' of this magazine], *Xinqingnian* (15 January 1919), pp. 15–16.

[69] Yip Ka Chi holds the opinion that Chen's initiative in launching the *Xinqingnian* was to propagate opposition to the monarchical movement and oppose the promotion of Confucianism as a state religion. See Yip Ka Chi, *Religion, Nationalism and Chinese Students. The Anti-Christian Movement of 1922–27* (Washington: Western Washington University, 1980) (hereafter cited as Yip, *Chinese Students*).

[70] Paul Cohen, *China and Christianity*, pp. 3–60, 262–73.

[71] Yip, *Chinese Students*, p. 17.

[72] See Hu Shi, 'Bu Xiu' [Immortality], *Xinqingnian* 2 (15 February 1919): 113–23.

[73] Yip, *Chinese Students*, pp. 19–20.

social progress was incompatible with religion.[74] Led by Chen Duxiu, other Marxist literati in China also drew upon Lenin's theses on imperialism, and argued that western capitalists in their attempt to prevent their own collapse had turned to economic as well as cultural aggression. The purpose of introducing Christianity was to benumb the Chinese and weaken their will to resist. Since Christianity was regarded as a tool of imperialism, the Chinese had to do more than simply reject it. They had to rid China of the source of oppression – the whole structure of western Imperialism in China. In the 1920s the anti-Christian movement saw its peak.

While the Nationalists and Christians seemed to have come to terms with each other, the Communists still regarded Christianity and all other religions as the 'opiate of the people' and as the tools of Imperialism. The co-operation given by Christian churches including the Catholic church to the Nationalist government was an additional incentive to the Communists' anti-Christian campaign. Under Mao Zedong, Zhu De and He Long, the Communists continually harassed Chinese Catholics, ill-treated foreign missionaries and occupied church properties in the domain of the Jiangxi Soviet from late 1927 to early 1930. A similar policy was followed in the Yenan period. Edgar Snow in his work *The Red Star Over China* recorded that all temples, churches and church properties were confiscated, while monks, nuns, priests, catechists and foreign missionaries were deprived of the rights of citizenship.[75] The anti-Christian attitude of the Chinese Communist party was carried on to the year 1949 and after.

THE RESPONSE FROM THE CATHOLIC CHURCH

Establishing Sino-Vatican relations

The Qing Court tried to rid itself of the French protectorate over the Chinese Catholic church by attempting to establish direct diplomatic relations with the Holy See. Through the Qing Prime Minister, Li Hongzhang, and the British Ambassador, China expressed its desire to formulate a direct diplomatic relationship with the Vatican so that it could negotiate directly with the Holy See over religious

---

[74] Chen Duxiu, 'In defence of the 'Sin' of this magazine', *Xinqingnian* 1 (15 January 1919): 15–16.
[75] Edgar Snow, *Red Star Over China* (Harmondsworth: Penguin Books, 1972), p. 396.

affairs and everything related to foreign missionaries could go straight to the headquarters of the Catholic church, the Vatican, without going through the French. Opposition came from France which still possessed the 'Protectorate Right'. The French threatened to break Franco-Vatican relations and stop subsidising any church and philanthropic endeavour in France. Eventually the Vatican had to give in, and postponed negotiations with China on the question of establishing diplomatic relations.[76] In 1918, when China wanted to gain international support for the abrogation of the unequal treaties, it again proposed establishing diplomatic relations with the Vatican. The same kind of opposition came from the French. Pope Benedict XV again had to postpone establishing diplomatic relations with the Chinese nationalist government.[77]

Yet the Vatican was not willing to be under the thumb of the French. In 1919, a special papal delegate, Bishop J. B. Goesbriart, was sent to visit all the important missions in China, and gave questionnaires to Chinese Catholics and clergy asking them to express their opinion on the mission affairs of the Chinese Catholic church. Then Bishop Goesbriart tabulated a report that was presented to the Pope on his return to Rome. Goesbriart suggested that a special papal delgate should be sent to China to take care at least of the internal church affairs of China.[78] Discreetly the Pope appointed Archbishop Celeso Constantini to be the Apostolic Delegate to China without diplomatic status. Constantini's appointment was not announced until he had arrived in Hong Kong and was on his way to Nanjing, in order to avoid unnecessary opposition from the foreign missionaries in China. With instructions from the Pope, Constantini announced that he would carry out his duty according the following principles:

1 His mission was mainly for the evangelisation of the good news of God, therefore immune from political motivation.
2 He would respect every nation which came within his sphere of dealing. He would first of all respect the sovereignty of China and

---

[76] Zhang Chunshen, *Fandigang Yu Woguo De Waijiao Guanxi* [The Diplomatic Relations of the Vatican and the Republic of China] (Tainan: Wendao, 1980), pp. 23–4 (hereafter cited as Zhang, *The Diplomatic Relations*).
[77] Ibid., p. 25.
[78] Ziyou Taipingyang Yuekan She, *Lei Mingyuan Shenfu Chuan* [The biography of Father F. Lebbe] (Saigon: Yuenan Ziyou Taipingyang Xiehui, 1963), p. 542 (hereafter cited as *The Biography of Father Lebbe*).

all other legitimate governments, but give primacy to the Holy
See, and not to any other political entity.

3 He also announced that the Pope did not want to interfere with
any political issues, but, if and when political affairs came into the
realm of religion, then the Holy Office would deal with the
problem.

4 The Holy See was in no way an imperial power, and the political
interactions of the western powers over China were of no concern
to it. The Pope loved China and sincerely wished for its well-
being, and he was trying to work on the principle that China
should belong to the Chinese in every sense of the word, including
religious matters.

5 Mission work in China was the enterprise of the Catholic church
in China, therefore on the question of candidacy for local bishop-
rics the Holy See would usually select a candidate from the local
native clergy.[79]

Despite the difficulties it faced in the Chungking Period during the
Second World War, the nationalist government in 1942 sent Xie
Xiukang as the first Chinese ambassador to the Vatican, although
the Vatican had not appointed a Papal Nuncio to Chungking. The
successor of Constantini, Archbishop Zanin, was still holding the
title of Apostolic Delegate and was supposed to exercise his power in
the internal spheres of the Catholic church and not in the capacity of
an ambassador of the Pope dealing with the Chinese government.[80]
After the Second World War, Sino-Vatican relations turned a new
page when Archbishop Riberi was sent by Pius XII as the first Papal
Internuncio to the Chinese government in 1946, and the Chinese
Catholic church hierarchy was established in the same year. Then
full diplomatic relations were established between the Vatican and
China until Riberi was expelled by the PRC government in 1951.
From 1946 to 1951, Riberi was not only the Papal delegate in church
affairs but on a diplomatic level he was the ambassador of the Pope,
with residence in Nanjing.

The development of the Chinese Catholic church

Putting foreign missionaries in China under the authority of Chinese
bishops and gradually replacing foreign missionaries by Chinese

---

[79] Zhang, *The Diplomatic Relations*, pp. 26–7.
[80] Ibid.

clergy marked the indigenisation of the church, which was integrating itself with the local culture in theology, liturgy, hierarchy and structure. From a political point of view, it was a gesture from the local church in China that it was ridding itself of the domination of foreign missionaries in particular and foreign powers in general. It was an inevitable step if the Catholic church in China wished to lose the image of being a foreign institution and to prove that Christianity and Chinese culture were compatible and that salvation was universal. Some far-sighted missionaries who genuinely longed for the well-being of the church in China were eager to have the first group of six Chinese bishops consecrated in Rome by Pope Pius XI in 1926, and even worked hard to make the Catholic church in China fully sinicised in church art, music and architecture, as well as in liturgy and prayer. The life of Fr F. Lebbe, a Belgian missionary, was an excellent example of the effort to strengthen the Chinese church by promoting good religious education for native Chinese clergy with the aim of raising up qualified Chinese church leaders.[81]

The first Chinese Synod 1924

Under the leadership of Archbishop Constantini the first synod of Chinese bishops was called in Shanghai. It was important not only because it was the first meeting on Chinese church administration but it also served as a landmark in the China mission. Participants included heads of all Chinese diocese, representatives of missionary societies and Chinese clergy. The focus of discussion centred on the implementation of Pope Benedict XV's encyclical 'Maximum Illud' issued in November 1919 giving guidelines on how to build up local churches by setting up local hierarchy and training native clergy. In the meeting Archbishop Constantini requested that all the bishops in China should correctly implement the Vatican's guidelines on establishing the local church. By ridding the Chinese church of the domination of foreign powers, influenced by Constantini who had the authority to supervise the entire Chinese church, the Synod made a resolution to open all church posts to local clergy without any reservations. Foreign missionaries were asked to follow the

[81] See *The Biography of Father Lebbe*, chapter 9 'The birth of Chinese Bishops' and chapter 7, 'Struggle for the church in China'. The writer illustrates in great detail how Father Lebbe accelerated the sinicisation of the Catholic church in China even at the expense of antagonising foreign missionaries, pp. 262–319, 359–87.

directives issued by Propaganda Fide and to revoke the 'privilege of precedence' which granted the foreign missionaries with the title apostolic missionary priority status in all things over the native clergy. In the Synod it was decided that the date of ordination became the one and only criterion for seniority among priests. The same Synod also echoed the Vatican's request to missionaries that they should avoid as much as possible any contact with foreign diplomats and gave guidelines for such contacts as were deemed necessary.

Therefore, this eased the problems of the existing tension between native and foreign clergy, the promotion of Chinese priests and the consecration of Chinese bishops, the creation of new church commissions for apostolic work and the liberation of the church from the political influences of the foreign protectorates. During the meeting Rome proposed a new plan to redraw the sixty-four mission territories, making them into seventeen ecclesiastical regions.[82]

In 1939, in the same spirit of inculturation, the Propaganda Fide lifted the ban on Chinese rites making a clear stand on the age-old church–state dispute.

In theory, the Vatican wished the Chinese church would take root in the native soil. However, this church reform was not thorough enough to reap prominent fruit. It was a reform circumscribed by a western framework for the utilities of the Chinese. Take the law for example, in China as in other countries the Chinese Catholic church has to be operated according to the Canon Law issued in 1917. Governed by the church Canon, which was saturated with European culture, it was too difficult for the Chinese church to rid itself of its foreign colour even though the church was led by Chinese clergy and bishops. Also in the area of priestly formation the theology taught to the young Chinese seminarians was European in approach. So far, indiginisation of theology has not experienced much success. Also tensions arose from the transference of leadership from foreigners to local clergy.

However, the Chinese church hierarchy was established in 1946, and a Chinese bishop, Thomas Tian of the Divine Word Order, a German congregation, was conferred the red hat to be the first Chinese Cardinal. To appoint a Chinese of a German founded

---

[82] Patrick Taveirne, 'The missionary enterprise and the endeavours to establish an ecclesiastical hierarchy and diplomatic relations with China: 1307–1946', *Tripod*, 54 (December, 1989), pp. 53–66.

missionary order illustrated the fact that the Catholic church could not completely stand on its own feet, and that it had to go through a transitional period in the shadow of indirect foreign protection. The Vatican, although it saw the remote picture of an indiginised Chinese church, had to map out its strategy in this unchartered land and proceed step by step. When all this did not map out too well, in the short period of twenty-five years, the coming of Communist rule was a great blow to this rootless Chinese church.

The Catholic church also realised the importance of its work among Chinese intellectuals who had always played such an important role in Chinese society. Three Catholic universities were established as well as many secondary schools in several parts of China, with the purpose of filling the young Chinese with Christian values. Catholic daily and weekly newspapers, together with Catholic books began to be published in major cities like Beijing, Shanghai and Tianjin in the hope of transmitting the Catholic faith and values through mass media.[83] Gradually some Chinese intellectuals were attracted to the Catholic church.[84]

The young Chinese Catholic church was nipped in its bud by the overpowering hand of the Chinese Communist Party, during and after of the establishment of the PRC. When all foreign clergy were compelled to leave the Middle Kingdom, nearly 70 per cent of dioceses were left without bishops. Thus it gave the excuse to the CCP to have self-election and self-consecration of local bishops without the consent of the Holy See, which was the start of the thorny question of setting up a Chinese Catholic church under the patronage of the government completely independent of the Vatican.

[83] *The Biography of Father Lebbe*, pp. 200–2 gives details of the successful publication of Catholic newspapers in Tianjin.
[84] Ibid., p. 201.

CHAPTER 3

The Vatican's Ostpolitik

Introduction

'The Christian Faith is not a secret cult but needs publicity. Therefore the church has always done everything it can and will do everything in the future to guarantee publicity for the exercise of religious faith', said Cardinal Franz König,[1] the man who had worked for the past thirty years in the Vatican Ostpolitik – the eastern policy – with its architect Cardinal A. Casaroli, also chosen by Pope John Paul II as the President of the Vatican's 'Secretariat for Non-Believers' in 1978. He explained in an interview with a Catholic weekly the ultimate purpose of the Vatican's eastern policy, established after it was finally realised that the Concordat principle did not provide an adequate basis for the Vatican to cope with the challenges posed by Lenin and the Bolshevik government after the 1917 Revolution. In Ostpolitik the Vatican responded by re-designing its pastoral devices into pastoral diplomacy so as to serve the fundamental objectives of the Catholic church. In effect what Pope Paul VI told the graduates from the Pontifical Diplomatic Academy on 24 April 1978 was a succinct reiteration of the new policy: namely that to assure the existence of the local churches in totalitarian regimes with atheist ideologies it is necessary to seek points of contact with a sense of realism, and to motivate the atheist political leaders to take religion into account as a useful card in world politics.[2]

Papal eastern diplomacy or Ostpolitik – seen as a means to an end, a technical device, as the art of the possible – follows, as we shall see,

---

[1] Quoted in König's interviews with the Catholic weekly *Rheinischer Merkur* (Cologne), 23 June 1978.

[2] Pope Paul VI spoke to graduates of the Pontifical Diplomatic Academy, on 24 April 1978. Cited by H. Stehle, *Eastern Politics of the Vatican 1917–1979*, translated by S. Smith (Ohio University Press, 1981), p. 1 (hereafter cited as Stehle, *Eastern Politics*).

the basic pattern underlining all international intercourse: defence of one's own interests through confrontation where coexistence is impossible, through compromises where they seem to be tolerable, and through co-operation where there are partners for it. Like every policy, it oscillates between allegiance to principles and expediency, and – often with no alternative – is entangled in national and ideological contradictions.[3] It is important to review the relations between the Vatican and the Soviet Union and its east European allies as this will suggest the experience and range of expectations held by the Vatican in its dealings with Communist party states on the eve of its overtures towards China. This review will also serve to establish which aspects of the problems in Sino-Vatican relations derive from the special character of Communist party states and which may be due to the particularities of China and its relationships with the outside world. It must never be overlooked that the CCP right from its foundation was heavily under the influence of Soviet beliefs and policies regarding religion in general and the Catholic church in particular, and that this influence did not end with the Sino-Soviet split in the early 1960s, because China's claim to hold Communist leadership precluded it from showing itself soft towards religion.

Vatican–Soviet relations in 1917

Until 1917, Moscow controlled a sizeable Catholic population. In general its policies were quite repressive, particularly towards the Uniate Catholic churches in the Ukraine and Belorussia, which were forced to join the Orthodox church in 1839 and 1946 under the Tsarist and Bolshevik regimes respectively.[4] The Catholic church under the Soviet regime has continuously received the same kind of treatment and worse from the atheist Communists as it did from its Tsarist oppressors due to ideological incompatibility. If one looks into the tenets of Communism and Catholicism that requires no further explanation.

---

3 Stehle, *Eastern Politics*, pp. 5–6.
4 For an excellent study of this issue see D. Dunn, *The Catholic Church and the Soviet Government 1939–1949* (New York: Columbia University Press, 1977). B. Bociurkiw, 'The Catatomb church: Ukrainian Greek Catholics in the USSR', *Religion in Communist Lands* 1 (Spring 1977): 4–12.

Opposing ideologies: Marxism–Leninism versus Catholicism

Communism and Catholicism are not only irreconcilable but also incompatible with each other, and that is one of the main reasons why the Soviet government gives little accommodation to religions, including Catholicism, especially since the Communist party itself does not accept pluralism in ideology, nor loyal opposition in political affairs. Historically Communism, while deriving its inspiration from the theories of Marx, Engels and Lenin, firmly roots itself in historical materialism,[5] according to which a world view without a spiritual dimension is asserted. It claims that all reality is in the first instance material, and that the evolution of human society is ultimately determined by economic laws pushing mankind dialectically and inexorably forward through various economic and corresponding social stages towards Communism. Marx claimed that the basic concept of history is:

The basis of this concept of history is, therefore to disclose the real production process, with material production of immediate life as the starting point, to conceive the form of intercourse connected with and engendered by this mode of production – hence civil society in its various stages – as the foundation of history, to represent this society in its state activity and to explain by society all the various theoretical products and forms of consciousness, religion, philosophy, morals etc., and to trace their coming into being to it.[6]

This was developed further by Lenin into what might be called the Bolshevik view as follows: man has values, not as a free personality but as one element of the collectivity and man must be subordinated to the Communist party and its political struggle to fashion an economically 'classless society'. In the Communist world view, man is defined by his class position, economy controls history and determines social organisation, and political activity is very important. Society from the Communist point of view is not only changeable but perfectible.

The Catholic world view not only embraces the spiritual aspect of the world, it also acknowledges the material side of the universe, placing the spiritual order above the material and claiming that man's life on earth is a beginning of his life with God leading him

---

[5] For a comprehensive understanding on Marx's view on religion see Karl Marx and F. Engels, *On Religion* (Moscow: Foreign Language Press, 1954) (hereafter cited as Marx and Engels, *On Religion*).

[6] 'German Ideology', in Marx and Engels, *On Religion*, p. 77.

progressively to a consummation of it after death. Therefore man's activities, his ideas and behaviour should conform to that view. Endowed by God with human life man is not geared to or fashioned by the laws of dialectical materialism.[7]

For a Communist, religion is the fantasy of man alienated from himself, from others and above all from reality by the division of his labour caused by Capitalism. The Marxists believe that to terminate the division of labour one must liquidate the 'opiate of the people' – religion.[8] Religion as seen by a Marxist is an important instrument of exploitation of the proletariat by the bourgeoisie. It was declared by Engels that religion is an exclusive possession of the ruling classes who apply it as a means of government, to keep the lower classes in their power.[9] Therefore when the proletariat gains control of the means of production, religion would lose its value and vanish together with the bourgeoisie. Here Engels claims:

When society, by taking possession of all means of production and using them on a planned basis, has freed itself and all its members from the bondage in which they are now held by these means of production which they themselves have produced but which confront them as an irresistible alien force; when therefore man no longer merely proposes, but also disposes – only then will the last alien force which is still reflected in religion vanish; and with it also vanish the religious reflection itself.[10]

Therefore the task of the proletariat, according to Marx, is to 'liberate the conscience from the witchery of religion'.[11] The Catholic church will never accept that its existence depends upon such moorings. It considers itself to be a sacramental and apostolic church founded by Jesus Christ, the God incarnated man, for the purpose of helping man to obtain eternal salvation. It rejects altogether the Marxist–Leninist notion that religion is a fantasy, a creation of man to soothe his pains caused by exploitation, nor that religion is simply a mechanism manipulated by the ruling class to exploit the working class. On the contrary, it is religion that makes man's existence meaningful. Without one or the other changing

---

[7] Denis Dunn, *Detente and Papal-Communist Relations, 1962–78*, a Western Replica edn (Boulder, Colorado: Westview Press, 1979), pp. 6–8 (hereafter cited as Dunn, *Detente*).

[8] Lewis S. Fever (ed.), *Marx and Engels: Basic Writings on Politics and Philosophy*, New York, 1959, p. 263, cited in Dunn, *Detente*, p. 7.

[9] Ibid.

[10] Engels, 'Anti-Duhring', in Marx and Engels, *On Religion*, p. 149.

[11] K. Marx, 'Critique of the Gotha Programme', in Marx and Engels, *On Religion*, p. 143.

fundamentally its philosophy or world view, philosophical reconciliation is impossible since Communism and Catholicism entertain no common ground for interpretation of reality, of man and of history.

The persecuted church under the Soviet regime

After the October Revolution in 1917, when the atheist Communist party took power in Russia, on top, as it were, of the traditional hostility towards Rome, Russian (or Soviet)–Vatican relations sank to their lowest ebb. At that time there were not many Catholics in the Soviet Union. Not until the Soviet Union acquired parts of Poland, western Ukraine and the Baltic states during the Second World War did Moscow exercise control over a substantial number of Catholics. Yet, in the 1920s right after Papal relief had been given to the victims of the 1920 famine, the Soviet government launched a brutal onslaught against the Catholic church. This was due to various reasons, including the suspicion by the government that the church had supported anti-Communist elements during the civil war, and that by its nature the Catholic church, as an independent institution with its own ideology, lay beyond the party's control. As seen by the Bolsheviks this was particularly dangerous, because its supreme head resided in Rome not Moscow and above all because of the fact that the Catholic church was overwhelmingly a religion of national minorities with strong emotional attachment to the west – the Poles, Germans, Lithuanians, some Belorussians and some Latvians and Ukrainians. This meant that the beleaguered Bolsheviks faced a tightly knit organisation built on a belief that was hostile to Russia and to Communism, that looked to a spiritual head in a capitalist country and that was fused with local nationalism. They clearly regarded the potential security risks as very grave. Apart from the introduction of anti-god legislation by Lenin, in 1923 the Soviet government started a campaign of anti-religion which included the arrest of members of the Catholic hierarchy with the aim of liquidating the Catholic church, the confiscating of church property and the closing down of church institutes. By the time of Lenin's death in 1924 only one Catholic bishop and several hundred priests remained. In 1925 and 1929 respectively, the Leagues of the Godless and the Militant Godless were founded to conduct anti-religious propaganda in a more systematic manner.

The Catholic church responded to this religious persecution of a political nature by pastoral means, e.g. by sending, in September

1925, the Jesuit bishop, Michael d'Herbigny to tour Russia and consecrate some bishops secretly to save the local church from possible extinction through the loss of all its bishops. The Bolsheviks found out and d'Herbigny was expelled.[12] Consequently the vigilance of Moscow became greater than ever, and more persecutions were carried out in retaliation. In the 1930s the Pope called for a Crusade of Prayer against the ruthless persecution of the church.[13] Later Pope Pius XI instructed the universal church that a special prayer should be said at the end of each mass for the 'conversion of Russia'. The reaction from the Soviet government was total: removing the whole Catholic church hierarchy. By 1940 all the bishops and nearly all the clergy had been eliminated through exile, imprisonment or death. The issuing of the papal encyclical *Divini Redemptoris* in 1937 by Pius XI, condemning Marxism–Leninism openly at an international level, indicated that Vatican–Soviet relations were at dead-lock.[14] The total sweeping away of the Catholic hierarchy in the 1930s taught the Vatican a new lesson: namely that something more than pastoral means, or a kind of diplomacy to serve pastoral ends, should be undertaken and that clandestine and offensive gestures like d'Herbigny's mission should be halted. The new goal was to try to initiate a rapprochement in the hope that Catholic problems could be discussed and solved on the negotiating table with the Soviet officials. This was not possible in Lenin's lifetime nor in Stalin's.

The turning of the tide: peaceful co-existence

After the death of Stalin, the Soviet leaders wanted better relations with the west and more genuine support from the Communist ruled nations in east Europe, and as a result the Catholic church became an object of their interest. This was because of its significance in eastern Europe, especially in Poland, Hungary, Czechoslovakia, Yugoslavia, Ukraine, Belorussia and Lithuania. Moreover, in January 1961, John Kennedy, a Roman Catholic, was elected President of the USA; and, at the same time in Europe, the Chancellor of the

---

[12] For the detailed description of d'Herbigny's secret mission see H. Stehle, *Eastern Politics*, chapter 3, pp. 67–111.
[13] For the details of the Crusade of Prayer see H. Stehle, *Eastern Politics*, chapter 4, pp. 112–49.
[14] For *Divini Redemptoris* see Claudia Carlen (ed.), *The Papal Encyclical*, 5 vols. (US, Raleigh: MaGrath Publishing Co., 1981), vol. 3, pp. 537–54.

German Federal Republic, Konrad Adenauer, a renowned states-man, was a staunch Catholic. The presence of these two leading Catholic figures on the political stage of the west added more weight to the side of the Vatican, making the Soviet–Vatican rapproche-ment a useful instrument for promoting confidence when the Soviet Union was building up goodwill both in the west and in the countries of eastern Europe. At the request of John Kennedy, Pope John XXIII stepped into the Cuban missile issue by making a plea for peace to the US and USSR ambassadors in Italy, stating: 'We implore all rulers not to remain deaf to the cry of humanity for peace ... to resume negotiations ...'.[15] Khrushchev withdrew the rockets from Cuba and this event he felt confirmed the view that the close alliance between the Vatican and the western powers could not be ignored.

Political intercourse between a theocratic state and an atheistic nation could pose some dangers for both sides. For Khrushchev no doubt there were dangers if he were to go out of his way to pay attention to the concerns of the Catholic church; the main one being vulnerability to the charge by ideological rivals that he was emascu-lating Marxism–Leninism. The dangers were to become clearer in the case of some of the east European allies, but not in the Soviet Union itself. This was largely because the Catholics there were so few in number and because they were subdued by the revival, on a large scale, of the anti-God campaign of 1959. Khrushchev realised that the Soviet–Vatican rapprochement brought him much more benefit than unwanted side effects. He found that he could make friends with the Vatican for his own purposes and at the same time keep tight ideological control in his domains, taking the line that religious freedom was an internal affair with which no outsider should meddle.

The association with the Papacy helped the Soviet Union to create a more positive image among religiously conscious people and help gather world opinion behind Soviet foreign policy goals. Moscow embraced two objects in its foreign policy which at least which could be accepted by the Vatican. These were to avoid nuclear war and to keep stability in eastern Europe. The Soviet–Vatican rapprochement no doubt also helped the infiltration of Marxism among the leftist Catholics in the west and in the third

[15] Reported by Luitpold A. Dorn, 'Zweten Deutschen Fer nsehen', 29 April 1973, quoted in Stehle, *Eastern Politics*, p. 305.

world, which the Soviet Union was not unhappy about. After the Second Vatican council, the Catholic church seemed to give the impression that it concentrated more on social problems than on spiritual and supernatural ones and that it was trying to reach a modus vivendi with the Communist states. Some sceptical scholars even suspected that Moscow's overtures to the Vatican were a smoke screen to obscure the major anti-religious campaign which began in the USSR in 1959, and lasted until Khrushchev's downfall. The rapprochement was also part of the flurry of activity in 1961–2 which saw the Russian Orthodox church and the All-Union Congress of Evangelical Christian-Baptists join the World Council of Churches.[16]

Vatican's motivations in the rapprochement

After the failure of d'Herbigny's mission, the Vatican could not think of any practical way to help the Catholic church in the Soviet Union or in the Soviet-controlled territories resist the persecutions of the anti-religious campaign. On the other hand, the Vatican was aware that Stalin's systematic and violent anti-god campaign was only part of a great domestic political adventure through which he was trying finally to consolidate the Soviet state. Stalin thought that the Soviet Union could only live and become a great power in the long run by industrialisation and the extension of Soviet controls to the countryside through the collectivisation of its 137 million peasants and the destruction of the traditional rural structures to which church and clergy belonged.[17] After the Second World War, Stalin's anti-religious programme included a violent determination to end the independence of the Catholic church in eastern Europe, to subordinate the church to the government, and finally to sever all ties between the Papacy and Catholics in Soviet-controlled territories with the exception of East Germany where the church's social base had been undermined. Undoubtedly the Catholic church in the Soviet controlled areas was seriously hampered by those assaults, especially in the Ukraine where 1.5 million Uniate Catholics were forced to amalgamate with the Orthodox church. The church life in

---

[16] Dunn, *Detente*, pp. 45–6.
[17] The long-time correspondent of the Berlin *Tageblatt*, Paul Scheffer, was one of the few contemporary observers to see through this; as quoted in Stehle's *Eastern Politics*, chapter 1, pp. 11–33.

this part of the world was very much eroded by these anti-religious campaigns. The Vatican at that stage began to give some thoughts to a rapprochement with the Communists whom it had strongly condemned, for the sake of arresting the decline of church life behind the Iron Curtain. Since there were far more Catholics in the eastern European countries than in the USSR itself, the Vatican–Soviet rapprochement was aimed at Communist states in general and eastern Europe in particular. There is 10 per cent of the total world Catholic population in eastern Europe, estimated at 60 million.[18] Yet contact between the Vatican and individual eastern European states would not be possible without the consent of the Soviet government, the 'big brother'. The Communist take-over in 1949 of the whole continent of China, and the wiping out of the Chinese Catholic hierarchy built up by Pius XI and the declaration by the Communist leaders of China of independence from Rome for the Chinese Catholic church caused great alarm to the Vatican and to the universal church.[19] The events in China re-confirmed to the Vatican that something had to be done to arrest the rapid erosion of the Catholic church at the hands of these Communist governments.

Some political observers remarked that detente between the Holy See, the Soviet Union and the eastern European countries was part of the Vatican's programme of expanding its influence in world politics as a mediator between east and west. Success in such a programme would greatly enhance the Vatican's reputation and the personal popularity of the Pope. Pope Paul VI's intensive travels to Jerusalem, India, Constantinople, the United Nations and Geneva seemed to re-affirm that his quest was for peace on earth.[20] The endeavour to bring peace between the Communist bloc and the free world was part of this ambitious programme. Anyone who could succeed in this would certainly go down in history.

Pope Pius XII, who responded positively to the Soviet's overture, had thirty years earlier, when he was Archbishop Pacelli and the Papal Nuncio of Pope Pius XI in Berlin, once witnessed Hitler's national socialism that sent millions of Jews to the gas chambers as a lesser evil than Bolshevik Communism.[21] The Soviet–Vatican rapprochement was carried out in spite of the fact that the Vatican after

[18] *Annuario Pontificio*, the city state of the Vatican, 1961.
[19] For the treatment of the Catholic church in China, see chapter 4 and chapter 6 of this book.
[20] Claudia Carlen (ed.), *Papal Encyclicals*, vol. 4, pp. 107–29.
[21] Stehle, *Eastern Politics*, p. 154.

World War II regarded the USA as fulfilling the old imperial role of temporal arm against the enemies of the church, with the Vatican acting as the spiritual vicar to the western alliance.

The Vatican's role in east–west co-existence

In 1955, the first east–west summit conference took place in Geneva, an initial indication of rapprochement between the Capitalist and Communist governments. A further step towards detente was taken when the new leadership in the Kremlin invited Adenauer, the Catholic German Chancellor (regarded as their most dangerous opponent in Europe), to visit Moscow. After obtaining endorsement from the USA, Adenaeur accepted the invitation. While Adenauer was still considering the pros and cons of his Moscow trip, and a few days before he announced his acceptance of the Soviet invitation, Pope Pius XII changed his tune even more when compared with his Christmas speech in 1954, expressing his acceptance of peaceful co-existence as a prospect that could lead to world peace.[22]

In November 1954 a declaration was made by of the Central Committee of the Soviet Communist party, emphasising that the feelings of the faithful and the clergy must not be injured in the struggle between scientific-materialist and anti-scientific religious ideologies. The declaration also warned that oppressive measures which damaged the goals of the Communist party and ultimately resulted in entrenched prejudices, were to be avoided.[23] The Vatican took this as a positive message which reflected a swing of the Soviet political pendulum from Stalin's cold war to a cold peace period of detente. Moreover, when Cardinal Roncalli was elected as the successor of St. Peter, it became apparent that a more moderate wind would blow through the Roman Catholic church. In convoking the Second Vatican council, Pope John XXIII ushered in the most epoch-making reform of the Catholic church in modern times.

The Second Vatican Council (1963–5) called by Pope John XXIII was meant to bring renewal to the church through 'aggiornamento'. That meant that the church did not intend blindly to follow the trends of the modern world, but that it would rather listen carefully and respond to what it perceived to be its real needs. Accordingly the militant and triumphant self-image that had dis-

[22] *Observatore Romano*, 3 January 1955, quoted in Stehle, *Eastern Politics*, p. 287.
[23] Stehle, *Eastern Politics*, p. 286.

figured the church had to give way to a caring and serving attitude. Instead of denouncing Communism as they had before, the Council Fathers humbly invited the whole church to engage itself in self-criticism and self-examination before condemning others. In the Council document 'The Pastoral Constitution of the Church in the Modern World', they wrote:

Yet believers themselves frequently bear some responsibility for this situation. For taken as a whole, atheism is not a spontaneous development but stems from a variety of causes, including a critical reaction against religious beliefs and in some places against the Christian religion in particular. Hence, believers can have more than a little to do with the birth of atheism. To the extent that they neglect their own training of faith, or teach erroneous doctrines, or are deficient in their religious, moral or social life, they must be said to conceal rather than reveal the authentic face of God and religion.[24]

Thus the council sought to affirm the universality of the Catholic church on a new and broader base by establishing dialogue with non-Christians and non-believers. Therefore it might be fairer to say that the reign of John XXIII, the son of the Bergamo peasant, was a red-letter page in the history of the church, with great repercussions for the long-meditated eastern policy, and which would not have occurred by any stretch of the imagination had the previous climate in the church prevailed.

The Vatican–Soviet relations

For outsiders, the most prominent sign of a Soviet–Vatican rapprochement was the invitation to send representatives to the Second Vatican Council sent by the Vatican in 1962 to the Russian Orthodox church through Cardinal Willebrands. The rapprochement could not have got into full swing if Khrushchev had not affirmed and agreed in a five-point summary to his willingness to establish an informal line of communications with the Vatican. The five points were as follows:

1 The USSR values the mediation of the Pope, and Khrushchev agrees that it is not only a question of offering useful mediation during the final moments of a crisis, but it is also one of a continual and lasting effort by the Pope on behalf of peace.

---

[24] Abbot (ed.), *The Document of Vatican II*, translated by J. Gallagher (London: Geoffrey Chapman, 1966), p. 217.

2 Khrushchev confirms that he desires to establish a communication line with the Holy See through private contacts.

3 Khrushchev recognises that the church respects the principle of the separation of church and state in various countries.

4 Khrushchev recognises that the church wants to serve all humanity from the perspective of the higher values of life and is not only concerned for Catholics.

5 Khrushchev recognises that the Pope has exhibited courage in acting as he did, since he knows that the Pope has encountered problems and opposition within the church which have not been altogether dissimilar from those that he, Khrushchev has experienced within the Soviet Union.[25]

So representatives, presented as government delegates, were sent from the Orthodox church even though traditionally it had not enjoyed harmonious relations with Catholics in the USSR. The Vatican at that stage acted very discreetly in the Council. Prior to the coming of the Soviet delegates, 450 bishops – one quarter of the whole world's episcopal hierarchy – appealed to the Council to condemn Communism, but the petition was tactfully put aside to smooth the way for the participation of the Russian Orthodox observers.[26] Then began a concerted dialogue and programme of exchanges between these two churches, including a five-day conference of Catholic and Orthodox theologians in Leningrad in 1967, followed by a theological dialogue in Trento, Italy in 1975. When the World Council of Churches met in New York in 1963, Pope John XXIII was openly praised by the Russian Orthodox delegate, Metropolitan Nikodim, for his realism and his interest in the well-being of all mankind. The Metropolitan even exhorted the Second Vatican Council to create a better feeling of brotherhood between the Russian Orthodox and the Roman Catholic churches. In 1968, two Russian Orthodox priests went to the Collegium Russicum, the pontifical college in Rome, to do post-graduate studies.[27] The Vatican followed that up by inviting Orthodox observers to the second session of the Second Vatican Council held after the death of Pope John XXIII, headed by Paul VI his successor. At both church and state levels, exchanges and visits were carried out after the Kremlin found that the church contacts were satisfactory. Then on

[25] Stehle, *Eastern Politics*, p. 307.
[26] Babris, *Silent Church*, p. 430.
[27] *New York Times*, 31 April 1963.

the occasion of Pope Paul VI's visit to the United Nations, in October 1965, Gromyko, the Soviet Foreign Minister, met the Pontiff, and then paid a visit to the Vatican in June 1975. Gromyko's visit was timed to take place on the eve of the Helsinki Conference. This meeting with the Pope lasted about an hour, covering a wide range of topics, including the Catholic church in the Soviet Union, peace, disarmament, the Middle East, and the forthcoming conference on European security and co-operation.[28] Prior to that conference, a meeting had taken place between the Pope and the Soviet President Podgorny, at which they discussed world affairs including the Catholics in the USSR. This created much international interest. In spite of the fact that no agreement was reached both sides promised to continue the discussion at a later stage. *Pravda*, the Soviet official newspaper reported the colloquy on the front page.[29] The Kremlin made use of the goodwill of the Vatican to present a favourable image to the world before the Helsinki Conference in mid 1975 on peaceful co-existence. In this sense the Vatican became an instrument of the Soviet's United Front policy. There were many other significant meetings between the Vatican, Soviet and east European official representatives in the course of Ostpolitik.

The more significant agreements concluded were those with the Hungarian government of 15 September 1964, and with the Yugoslav government in June 1966. By these accords these Communist governments recognised the canonical jurisdiction of the Pope over the Catholic church in their territories, while the Vatican for its part acknowledged and endorsed the principle of loyalty towards a Communist state.[30] The agreements, however, saved the Catholic church of these two states from the danger of being detached from the Holy See as had happened in China under strong pressure from the government. Some scholars have argued that these diplomatic arrangements did not solve the urgent everyday problems of the local church in eastern Europe, but the contacts and arrangements hold out prospects for a better future.[31] Before passing an opinion on this we must briefly consider how the Catholic church lived under

---

[28] *Radio Rome*, 28 June 1975.

[29] *Pravda*, 31 January 1967. *Radio Vatican*, 31 January 1967. *l'Osservatore Romano*, 31 January 1967.

[30] H. Stehle, 'Vatican policy towards eastern Europe', *Survey* 66 (January 1968).

[31] Gerhard Simon, 'The Catholic church and the Communist states in the Soviet Union and eastern Europe', in B. Bociurkiw *et al.* (eds.), *Religion and Atheism in the USSR and Eastern*

the eastern European Communist parties. Even though all these countries adhered to Marxism–Leninism as their official ideology, the extent to which they were actually able to enforce it differed greatly.

The Catholic church in eastern Europe

In general, the treatment meted out to the Catholic church in the USSR and Albania was extremely harsh, reducing public church activities to a minimum. Albania went so far as to proclaim itself to be 'the first atheist state in the world'. As against this, the church in Poland and eastern Germany enjoyed considerable rights and privileges, and could be considered to enjoy some degree of freedom and independence from the government, even to the extent of being allowed to speak for itself in public.[32] A mid-way position prevailed in Hungary, Czechoslovakia, Romania and Bulgaria. Yugoslavia which was outside Soviet control adopted very special tactics to deal with the Catholic Croats and Slovenes. Instead of repression or terror, Tito obtained their loyalty by following a remarkably tolerant policy towards the Catholic church. In fact, Croatia and Slovenia suffered the least interference from the state of any of the east European countries. In 1918 Lenin decreed the separation of religion from the state, yet in reality the separation of church and state did not take place in many eastern European states, not even in the USSR and in Poland. In Czechoslovakia, for example, there was a complete dependence of the church on the state. The decrees on church–state relations were issued at the climax of the Stalinist period in eastern Europe. The governments of these Communist countries had three objectives: first, to eliminate the influence of the church in society, second, to control its activities and finally to compel the leaders of the church to be loyal to the Communist authority.[33]

The Soviet Union and Albania reduced and even stopped their financial support to the church so as to undermine it. In Poland, however, the church cautiously but firmly rejected any government aid which might eventually tie it to the dictates of the government,

Europe (London: Macmillan, 1975), pp. 190–221 (hereafter cited as Simon, 'The Catholic church and the Communist states').

[32] Ibid., p. 190.
[33] Ibid., p. 196.

because the church in Poland had sufficient support from believers to sustain itself without state funds. In this sense the financial assistance to the church by the government was a means to regulate church activities, but different churches in different states were able to respond to this in different ways. Another important means of controlling the Catholic church was the prevention of contacts by the local hierarchy with the Vatican. The one exception was Romania, where the church was allowed to have contacts with religious bodies abroad, through the Ministry of Foreign Affairs. The bishops of eastern Europe protested very strongly and took these laws as infringements of the church's autonomy and a violation of their constitutional rights.[34] Yet they could be regarded as fortunate not to have been forced to establish independence from the Holy See as happened in China after 1949 and in Albania. On the administrative level, following the Soviet model, a Department of Religious Affairs was founded in all those states, under the Council of Ministers (or the local equivalent), to implement church laws and supervise ecclesiastical activities including personnel matters, the recruitment of clergymen, teachers and employees of theological institutes and all matters connected with religious instruction of the youth. This office also was entrusted with the censoring of church publications and the publishing of official periodicals for the clergy.

To reinforce the control of the state over religion, all the eastern European governments made an effort to ensure the loyalty of the clergy to the state. In general the clergy were obliged to swear an oath of loyalty to the state. In Czechoslovakia and Poland, the Catholic bishops pledged irrevocable loyalty to a militantly atheist government only after very heavy pressure and terror had been exercised against them.

After the Second World War, all the east European governments launched land reforms and the nationalisation of private and church schools as the Soviet Union had done earlier. The church in Hungary was hit most seriously since it owned vast acreages of land through which it financed its charitable and educational works. The nationalisation of church land in June 1948, led to a series of

---

34 See the petition of the Czechoslovak episcopate to the government in 21 October 1949 in Gosovski (ed.), *Church and State Behind the Iron Curtain*, New York, 1955, and the memorandum of Cardinal Wyszynski, Primate of Poland of 8 May 1953 (Galter: Kotbuch der verfolgten Kirche, Recklinghausen, 1957), quoted in Gerhard Simon, 'The Catholic church and the Communist states', p. 197.

dramatic conflicts between the Hungarian Primate, Cardinal Mindszenty, and the government.

The situation regarding religious instruction varied from state to state. Czechoslovakia, Hungary and East Germany permitted closely controlled religious instruction in classrooms, but only as an extra-curricular activity. In Poland, Romania and Yugoslavia the catechism was taught on church premises and at special catechism centres. That was a satisfactory outcome for the church, even though private and unregistered religious instruction was prohibited. In the USSR, Albania and Bulgaria it was forbidden to give religious instruction to anyone under eighteen. The number of youths attending catechism classes declined in all countries drastically due to determined state efforts at secularisation and to the political pressure on believers and on the churches. Most seminaries and theological institutes were closed down at the peak of Stalin's persecution. In Hungary only six seminaries were left, while thirteen seminaries and theological institutes of different religious orders had been closed, and the numbers of theological students had declined from 1,079 in 1948 to 303 in 1965. The situation was similar in Czechoslovakia where seminaries had been reduced to two from seven.[35] While those countries had a great shortage of priests, it was announced that only one priest in each diocese could be ordained each year. The church press was under tight censorship, and lay Catholic organisations were dissolved. In Hungary, 4,000 Catholic associations were dissolved and the entire lay movement was extinguished. Similar steps were taken in the other countries. The church press and church libraries were confiscated in Czechoslovakia. In the USSR, the Catholic church, which had a flock of 3 million, was not able to publish any periodicals, although a Lithuanian missal was printed in 1968 in the detente period. Hostility was shown to religious orders. In 1949 and 1950, religious orders in Czechoslovakia, Romania and Hungary suffered immense hardships when all the convents and monasteries were closed down and some of them were turned into concentration camps. In Hungary alone, more than 10,000 monks and nuns were compelled to return to lay life since religious life was regarded as 'being used to shelter hostile agents, spies and even murderers ... and many monasteries served as bases for espionage and disruptive activities'.[36] Then in 1946 in Romania as well as in

35 G. Simon, 'The Catholic church and Communist states', p. 200.
36 Ibid., p. 202.

the Soviet Union, the Uniate Catholic church and the Greek Catholic church, were forced by the government to unite with the Orthodox church because these Communist governments thought it was easier to manage them that way; because of this many of these Catholics turned underground. Discrimination against the faithful in society was a common feature of Communist church policy. This kind of discrimination prevailed even in the detente period, except in Yugoslavia where discrimination was limited to party posts and state apparatus.

Understandably the Communists patronised only those priests and laity who were willing to co-operate with the government and the party, trying to split the church from within. Attempts were made to separate the local churches from the Vatican, but generally these attempts were not successful. In Albania in 1951 a general assembly of the Catholic clergy discontinued all relations with the Vatican and declared itself to be an independent national church, but this was the only such instance. An effort was made in Poland in 1946 to achieve the same with little success. The split within the priesthood was accelerated by the attempts to separate the church from the Holy See and the famous 'Pax' movement among progressive priests was established. The Pax society, like the Chinese Catholic Patriotic Association in China, became the home of those willing to compromise with the party whilst others refused to yield to the demands of the Communists. The Pax movement consisted of only a small percentage of clergy and was declared illegal by the church hierarchy and condemned by the Vatican. Yet this group exerted a considerable influence within the church. It helped to bring about the view that currently prevails in most churches that some sort of *modus vivendi* with the Communist state has to be attained, since the church cannot sustain a confrontation forever.

Ostpolitik: summit diplomacy or dialogue of opposing ideologies

In the 1960s the severe measures applied to the Catholic church in the USSR and in eastern Europe were relaxed to some extent in the day-to-day religious activites. Despite Khrushchev's anti-reform campaign, from 1959 onwards in the Soviet Union itself the treaty signed between the Holy See and Yugoslavia has been regarded as the greatest success of Ostpolitik. Under it the Catholic bishops in Yugoslavia have to swear loyalty to the country's constitution. This treaty had a long background, for Tito had sent emissaries to Rome some ten years earlier. In Yugoslavia, the Catholic church was well placed to play the role of mediator in the linguistic dispute with nationalist overtones between the Croatians and the Slovenes, whom Tito wanted to pacify in order to consolidate his multinational state. Also Tito's intention to be free from Soviet domination moved him to turn to Italy and the USA for help, and he knew that the establishment of good terms with the Vatican would put him in good stead with these countries. Though the treaty did not allow religious instruction to be conducted in schools, the Catholics could still send their children to parish priests for that purpose. Furthermore, a Catholic press was allowed. For some time the Yugoslavian government hierarchy observed the treaty faithfully. Since the Tito constitution proclaimed the division of state and church, the relations established between the Vatican and Belgrade were official. However, the Vatican was not entirely satisfied as it recognised that the Catholics in Yugoslavia did not enjoy the amount of religious freedom given in the west. The treaty with Yugoslavia was considered by the Vatican as a model that could be offered to other countries in eastern Europe as a basis for co-existence between church and state. In the hope that similar treaties might be formulated with other countries behind the Iron Curtain the Vatican intensified its contacts with Hungary, Czechoslovakia and especially Poland, whose population is over 90 per cent Catholic and where the Catholic church is identified with Polish culture and nationalism.

Despite the high degree of success claimed by the supporters of Ostpolitik, in reality the problems of the church, especially in the pastoral field, have far from been solved. The Yugoslav regime has continued to attack religion, particularly if there was any hint of church support or involvement in the Croatian and Slovenian nationalist movements.[37] In 1975–6 there was growing tension over the drafting of new religious laws, and the Catholic press has been subject to censorship. Nevertheless, the marked influence of Catholicism amongst the youth, a development that challenges the people's belief in the party and its ideology, has caused the authorities great concern.[38] Notwithstanding the existence of a signed agreement

---

[37] *Radio Belgrade*, 28 April 1976; *Tanjug News Agency*, 6 March 1978.
[38] Antic, 'Attacks continue against the Catholic church in Yugoslavia', *Radio Free Europe*, pp. 222–3.

between the state and the church, the latter has been able to exercise much influence in Yugoslavia and, as a result, it appears to be agreed by other Communist governments in eastern Europe that it would not be a good idea for them if they followed the Yugoslav example and allowed the church to pose a threat to their governments too.

Despite the fact that the Polish church suffered from various kinds of discrimination and persecution it was strong enough to have the power to bargain with the Polish Communist party without any help from diplomatic negotiations. Church and state negotiation in Poland did not actually begin until the 1970s. In 1971 the Primate of Poland had a long talk with the Polish Premier, P. Jaroszewicz, on the question of granting permits for building churches, on the promised grants to the church, on the ownership of ecclesiastical buildings and real estate in the former German lands, on permitting an independent church press, on the return of the charitable institutions of the church, and on the reopening of the church's cultural and religious associations.[39] The relaxation of tension in Polish church and state relations was apparently not due to the diplomacy of Ostpolitik. On the contrary, the Polish hierarchy were anxious about the talks between the Vatican and the Polish government. They were concerned that they would not be consulted, despite the fact that they had the best knowledge of the real situation in the church in Poland and of its relations with the atheist government. With evidence mounting that Vatican and Polish ties might become normal, the Polish bishops sought and received assurance from the Vatican that no Vatican–Polish government decision would be made without consulting the Polish episcopate.[40]

It is well known that the Polish church is the most influential in eastern Europe, since Catholicism is identified with nationalism and Polish culture. This made the Polish Cardinal Wyszynski one of the most powerful men in the country. In fact the church in Poland has also experienced subtle forms of discrimination, but in times of dispute between government and the mass of the people, the church has always been called upon as mediator. In 1976, in the famous price riots, the government turned to the church asking for co-operation. The bishops responded with an appeal to the people to work for the good of the country, while at the same time they

[39] *Radio Warsaw*, 3 March 1971, 5 March 1971; *New York Times*, 4 March 1971, 6 March 1971.
[40] *New York Times*, 4 May 1974.

demanded that the government release those workers who had been jailed for their strike activities.[41] Maybe the Polish episcopal conference considered that compromise brought about by Ostpolitik would de-moralise the high morale of the Polish Catholic church, or perhaps Ostpolitik was not the means they preferred to save the church, and they simply did not want the Vatican's architects of Ostpolitik to be too actively engaged with the Polish Communist authorities. It seems that they were convinced that the solution to the Polish church–state conflicts did not lie in making too many compromises. Schopflin observed that the church in Poland was being quite successful in strengthening the Christian faith and revitalising itself. The church's involvement in the workers Solidarity movement and its stance over the murder of Father Popieluszko in 1984, and the support it received from the Solidarity workers are indicators that it is strong enough to stand on its own and that there should not be any interference from Ostpolitik.

In the case of Hungary, the signing of the agreement in 1964 between Casaroli and the chairman of the State Office of Religious Affairs did not turn the tide in church–state relations or give any breathing space to the Catholic church in Hungary, neither did it reverse the anti-religious policy of the state. In March 1965, the party leader stated at a Central Committee Plenum that co-operation with the church was welcome, but the Communists must continue to criticise the political stand and activites of the church when these reflected resistance to Communist policies.[42] In reality two tactics were launched by the atheist government to defend itself from any possible increase in Catholic influence as a result of the 1964 agreement. First, the Hungarian government tried to bolster up atheist teaching and, secondly, in the spirit of the 1964 agreement, it attempted to suppress, by administrative means, clergy and believers who openly practised their faith. In June 1964 several priests were sent to jail for alleged activities against the state, marking the beginning of a campaign of periodical arrests of religious leaders who were charged with conspiracy.[43] In spite of the tragedy of Cardinal Mindszenty, who stubbornly refused to co-operate with the Communists, the Vatican and the Hungarian

[41] B. Szajkowski, *Next to God . . . Poland*, (London: Francis Puter, 1983), chapters 2 and 3.
[42] Laszlo, 'Towards normalisation', in Bociurkiw *et al*, *Religion and Atheism in USSR and Eastern Europe*, p. 292. Beeson, *Discretion and Valour*, (London, 1974), p. 240.
[43] *New York Times*, 9 July 1965; *L'Osservatore Romano*, 17 July 1965.

government reached a second agreement in 1974 and 1975 on the appointment of bishops to fill the vacant dioceses in Hungary. It was agreed that the bishop candidates were to come from priests from the Pax movement, making the church leadership acceptable to the government and co-operative with its atheist authority. When the Vatican consented to have Pax priests made bishops, the government in return made a lesser concession by legalising the teaching of the catechism in churches and other places of worship.

Ostpolitik: a cost-benefit evaluation

One can look at the 1974–5 Vatican–Hungary Agreement as a point of departure from which to begin the evaluation of Ostpolitik. Some scholars, namely Stehle, have remarked that the Vatican's diplomacy did not appear to be as clever, moral and far-sighted as many of its admirers had thought, but also not as sly, opportunistic and short-sighted as many of its detractors had insinuated.[44] We rather concur with the following view of Ostpolitik. The consent of the Vatican for the appointment of bishops with the approval of the government, and the fact that the bishop candidates were to be accepted by the government, had the result of filling the vacant dioceses in Hungary. But since the bishops were to be selected from the Pax movement they would neither be trusted nor accepted by the faithful as most of them had a record of having betrayed their fellow priests who went underground rather than comply with the demands of the government. Through these devices the Communist party actually tried to drive a wedge between the church leaders and the mass of believers, in order to disintegrate the church from within. These bishops could not do anything truly for the benefit of the church, nor could they stand up to teach the faithful on controversial issues of morality and doctrine, because they were compromised by the fact that they could only say something approved by the government. Take Archbishop Lekai for example, the successor of Mindszenty, who repeatedly made too many concessions to the government. He had a difficult time with the Catholics in Hungary.

If the Vatican considered that the main goal of Ostpolitik was to fill the empty sees in the USSR and in eastern Europe, then those agreements and negotiations did succeed in providing bishops for the tens of millions of Catholics behind the Iron Curtain. In this sense

---

[44] Dr. Hansjakob Stehle's German work *Die Ostpolitik des Vatikans 1917–75* was translated into English by S. Smith and published by Ohio University Press 1979.

the Ostpolitik did its job perfectly. But success in providing a good number of bishops is quite different from having good bishops who could carry out their pastoral duty in the local churches. Unless the bishops are free to teach the faithful and keep the church alive they can be no more than mere figureheads, rather than true shepherds of their flocks and real leaders of the local church. In the case of Lekai, his endless compromises might be a way to ensure the survival of the Hungarian church, but by the same token they prevent him from functioning as a bishop ought to function. Mere survival without a proper teacher of morality and truth will soon lead to the church becoming neglected and losing many of its faithful. It looks as if Ostpolitik only promotes the existence of the church as an institution, but that it fails to strengthen it, to extend its rights, and to assist those who struggle for religious freedom and human rights. George Schopflin, an expert in eastern European political affairs, remarked that in Ostpolitik, the Vatican confused the means with the ends, and the policy itself lacks a long-term objective. It is merely expediency after expediency. Instead of cracking the hard nut of the church and Communist conflict, the Vatican continuously went out of its way to improve its relations with the Communist states.[45]

It is true that the general trend of the Ostpolitik put too much emphasis on summit diplomacy, while failing to see that on the local level church discipline was being eroded as the result of persecution. Ostpolitik itself failed to do anything to arrest this or to make any improvements such as reviving the vitality of the church, to help it to withstand political oppression and to perform a new mission as the Polish church is able to do despite the difficult conditions under which it has to perform.

We have reason to think that up to now the Ostpolitik has been able to achieve very little for the pastoral work of the Catholic church in eastern Europe and in the USSR. One might ask what did the Vatican gain from detente in general and Ostpolitik in particular other than the episcopal appointments, diocesan boundary changes and limited church–state agreement? Even if these are considered as gains, were they not obtained at too high a price, that of keeping a kind of discreet silence about the restrictive practices

45 George Schopflin, of the Department of Government at the London School of Economics who specialises in east European political institutions, expressed this view to the writer on 17 March 1986.

carried out in the Communist states? The case of Cardinal Slipyi is a typical example. The silence required by the Soviet government was a condition for his release so that he would not be 'exploited as anti-Communist propaganda'. This silence prevented the suffering church behind the Iron Curtain from getting help from the Christians in the west. The same silence indirectly allowed more injustices and violations of human rights to be inflicted on the church under the totalitarian regimes precisely because all of this was kept hidden from the rest of the world. The Vatican, for the sake of negotiating with the Communists, agreed to a kind of silence, which eventually could diminish its moral power, instead of exercising its responsibility to speak up openly about the violations of justice and human rights which it knows to be taking place. Once the moral power of the church is eroded, the result is the loss of true substance just as 'the salt looses its taste', as the Bible says.[46] Furthermore it is surprising that the Vatican with its long history of diplomacy with major world powers should plunge into a losing battle by negotiating with the Communists in good faith while the Communists retain their goal of destroying religion. This view has received reinforcement from the ranks of exiled Soviet dissidents. Alexander Solzhenitsyn, who criticised the west for maintaining good contacts with the Soviet Union, has been equally critical of the Vatican for doing the same.[47] The compromise made by the Vatican with the Soviet Union has encouraged the Soviet authorities to take a more cynical and contemptuous attitude towards religion. Leviyin-Krasnov, one of the founders of the religious SAMIZDAT in the Soviet Union has noted that the Soviet government has not complied with one single command put forth by the Vatican. He thought that, if the church were to take up a fundamentalist position, its authority would increase immediately.

In Yugoslavia, Hungary, Poland and East Germany many obstacles to church and state dialogue have been removed, but how far can Ostpolitik go from here? Casaroli has made enormous concessions and compromises in working out the first stage of Papal–Communist relations in eastern Europe. He signed the agreements, made the first visits, and even consecrated the first group of bishops, so that church and state relations should be normal enough to discuss their differences in various countries and to work out a solution acceptable to both sides. It will be more difficult in the

---

[46] *Luke* 14: 31–2; *Matthew* 5: 11–12.
[47] Peter Babris, *Silent Church*, p. 431.

future for Casaroli to handle concrete matters in church–state relations except by even more compromise, since compromise appeared to be the key solution to the whole issue.

It is easier to make the initial visit and establish a diplomatic contact than to bargain and argue with one's opponent about the rights of the local church. Probably Casaroli will continue to make the initial contacts and start the ball rolling in church–state relations in the Communist ruled territories, and leave the bargaining part to the local bishops. If this proves true, one has reason to worry how many bishops chosen from the Pax movement would lay down their lives and be totally dedicated to the well-being of the church when part of their loyalty has been given to the party as required by the Pax movement.

Is Ostpolitik for China?

To discuss Ostpolitik in relation to the Sino-Catholic problem does not imply that religious problems in eastern Europe are the same as in China when there are tremendous differences in culture, politics and in the economies. Thus, it would be unrealistic to imagine that the Ostpolitik in its original design could fit into China without any modifications.

For example, if one looks at the development of communism, China and eastern Europe had their own particular paths. China's Communists had to have recourse to revolution before a Communist regime could replace the KMT rule. The new regime gained the support of the Chinese people. Most Communist governments in eastern Europe were set up by Soviet occupation after the Second World War, and consequently have enjoyed relatively little popular support. On the other hand, the churches there have been able to retain widespread support in spite of official persecution, and have sometimes become the foci for patriotic resistance to Russian domination. This is a far cry from the place of Christianity in Chinese society. In terms of the size and strength of the Catholic churches in eastern Europe and in China, the differences were even greater. With a high Catholic population (average 55 per cent in eastern Europe but only 0.8 per cent in China) and the long history of the church with its close relations with the people, especially in the case of Poland, the east European church is very patriotic while in China the Catholic church is named the 'foreign religion' (yang jiao), an unpatriotic religious organisation in the eye of the Communists.

In fact the Ostpolitik suggested dialogue and compromise as the Vatican's strategy for dealing with European Communist regimes in the hope of fostering less hostile church–state relations so as to provide a breathing space for the Catholic church. In other words, the Ostpolitik has been a diplomatic means, mobilised by the Vatican to deal with Communist states for the last twenty years. In the 1970s the architect of the Ostpolitik followed the same trend when dealing with Chinese Communists. One has already witnessed that the same Ostpolitik, applied to various states in eastern Europe, yielded success of different shades. How much more different would be the result when it was applied to China. One would expect that a considerable degree of adaptation and modification is needed before the European-oriented Ostpolitik can be applied to the East, in the context of the People's Republic of China.

Just recently in 1985 small signs have revealed that the Vatican is turning away a little from summit diplomacy towards inter-church contacts in dealing with church–state relations with some Communist countries. In the case of China, the Polish Pope John Paul II has expressed the view that he is not too anxious to normalise Sino-Vatican relations if he cannot have contact with the church in China.[48] This implied that diplomatic contact with the Chinese officials alone is far from being the aim for the normalisation of Sino-Vatican relations. What is needed is not only to preserve the Chinese church hierarchy, but to revitalise the dormant Chinese church. This Polish Pope has great experience of church and state relations in Poland and he must know how far Ostpolitik has gone in eastern Europe. In the audience he gave to Gromyko in 1979 he made it clear to the Soviet Foreign Minister that he knew how to distinguish patriotism from nationalism, strength of principles from intolerance, and that he saw that human rights including religious freedom could be preserved only in a peaceful world, not in a world torn by conflicts. Rumours from the Vatican suggest that Cardinal Casaroli is no longer at the peak of his political power because the Polish Pope in many ways holds different opinions from his, including on Ostpolitik. Casaroli's request to resign might be taken as a sign that Ostpolitik is to be treated otherwise, and compromise will not be so easily obtained from the strong hands of this Polish Pontiff.

[48] The Pope expressed his opinion in 1985, to the Jesuits who are in charge of Jesuits' China Affairs.

CHAPTER 4

The CCP and the Catholic church before and after 1949

ENCOUNTERS BEFORE 1949

In its early years (1921–7), the party was based principly in the cities where the links between Christianity and the foreign imperialist presence was most evident. Even the new CCP leaders who emerged in the course of the period in the countryside (1927–49) had also had experience of religious orders in the Treaty Ports.

The CCP and Catholics encountered in France

Many of the young Chinese Communists, including some of the later leaders, who went to France for part-time study of Marxism-Leninism through the Paris-based left-wing Fédération Franco-Chinoise d'études, never forgot their encounter with Father F. Lebbe, a Belgian missionary in China who afterwards worked for overseas Chinese students in France from 1920–7.[1] They must have had good evidence that this veteran missionary was trying to assist overseas Chinese students in all ways possible. One of the founders of the Federation, Liu Gai, and some other members were converted. A struggle took place between Father Lebbe and the atheist CCP in France, in the course of which Father Lebbe was criticised and attacked in the publications of the Fédération. Yet, at a time of crisis, Father Lebbe extended a helping hand and gave financial aid to the left-wing Chinese students when the government stopped paying for their scholarships and the bank in which the scholarship money was stored went bankrupt. It seems that Zhou Enlai and Xu Dili and some other CCP leaders got financial help from Lebbe. Zhou

---

[1] Ziyau Taipingyang Yuekanshe, *Lei Mingyuan Shenfu Zhuan* [The biography of Father F. Lebbe] (Saigon: Yuenan Ziyau Taipingyang Xiehui, 1963), pp. 320–59 (hereafter cited as Ziyau Taipingyang, *Biography*), for a detailed description of Fr. Lebbe's work in France.

73

obtained a few days living expenses from this poor missionary, who, knowing the small amount of money he could give was not enough, also gave Zhou his family heirloom, a gold watch, which had been handed down to him from his parents.[2]

The CCP met Father Lebbe in northern China

Later, in 1933, when the CCP planned to occupy some religious buildings in Anguo County, Hebei, as their base, one of the party members objected to the occupation of the religious house of the little Brothers of St John the Baptist, founded by Father Lebbe, on the grounds that these monks were not capitalists, they did not exploit the people and their good works attracted the support of the masses. This cadre suggested that it would go against the principles of the party if they did harm to this group of religious brothers, and would lead to loss of support from the proletariat with whom these Brothers identified. A similar incident took place in Shaanxi later in 1935. Before the place was occupied by the Red Army, Communist informants were sent out to enquire about the situation there. They reported that the people had a high opinion of this same group of religious Brothers of St John.

During the Second United Front period amidst the Japanese invasion, Father Lebbe changed his nationality to Chinese, and manifested his patriotic sentiments by organising the Chinese Catholic North China Battlefield Mass Service Group. He personally went out with an ambulance team staffed by Catholic intellectuals to work in the front line of battle, not only to help the wounded, but also to mobilise the local civilians to assist the Chinese army in combat. The Service Group enlisted forty members in its first recruiting drive. Through the work of this Service Group, Lebbe had the opportunity to meet Zhu De, commander of the 115th and 120th Armies.

In 1936, at Hongtong, Shaanxi, Zhu De gave Fr Lebbe $100 to offer a Requiem Mass for the repose of the deceased soldiers. Zhu himself and some other members of the Politburo participated in the Mass. After the Service, Zhu in a very delighted mood greeted Lebbe in a friendly manner and promised further assistance if needed. This may have been no more than customary Chinese

[2] Ibid., p. 506. Cao Lishan, *Chunfeng Shinian* [Ten years in the Spring Bliss] (Taichung, Taiwan: Sheng Fa Monthly, 1977), pp. 447–8.

politeness on Zhu's part, but Lebbe was impressed. He thought it wonderful that two communities with incompatible ideologies should co-operate in the great endeavour of combating the Japanese. At that stage Lebbe noticed the CCP really observed religious freedom, imposing no restrictions on religious believers; and even soldiers in the Red Army were allowed to believe in religion. Thus he thought that there was a possibility of co-operation in future.[3]

Lebbe recognised that the Catholics and the CCP were each patriotic in their own ways, the Catholics approached the problem by following the teaching of the Gospel and employed a rather moderate way, while the CCP followed the Marxist-Leninist approach and followed a hard line.[4]

Indications of the coming rift between the KMT and the CCP were first felt by the Catholic service group, before the defeat of the Japanese. The arrest of service group members who were sent to the Red area in Hebei to purchase grain,[5] the killing of twelve religious Brothers of Father Lebbe's congregation,[6] and the detention of Lebbe himself by the New Fourth Army commanded by Liu Baicheng in March 1940 at Yiuchuan, Hebei,[7] marked the breakdown of relations between the CCP and the Catholic service group which by that time was under the patronage of Chiang Kai Shek himself.

Father Lebbe's political involvement was very unusual for a Chinese Catholic priest at that time. In fact many foreign bishops in China did not agree with his campaign for national salvation. Bishop Rouchouse of Chengdu, and Bishop Vanni of Xian, for example, refused to receive Father Lebbe for fear of being involved in Chinese domestic political problems. Their attitude was perhaps typical of the general feelings of the Chinese Catholic church, which was much under foreign influence. A CCP member whose life was saved by the Catholic Ambulance Team and who was convalescing in one of Lebbe's religious houses remarked that Father Lebbe and his people were quite different from other Catholics.

---

3 Ziyau Taipingyang, *Biography*, pp. 509–11. Zhao Yabo, *Lei Mingyuan Yu Zhongguo* [Father Lebbe and China] (Taichung, Taiwan: Weidao Middle School, 1985), pp. 62–3 (hereafter cited as Zhao Yabo, *Father Lebbe*).

4 Ziyau Taipingyang, *Biography*, p. 519.

5 Ibid., p. 512.

6 Zhao Yabo, *Father Lebbe*, pp. 74–5. Ziyau Taipingyang, *Biography*, p. 523.

7 Ziyau Taipingyang, *Biography*, pp. 515–24 has a very detailed description on Lebbe's detention.

Through years of contact with the Catholic church and its foreign missionaries in China, CCP cadres might have formed negative as well as positive views of the Catholic church, yet at the establishment of the PRC, the director of the Religious Affairs Bureau of the State Council, He Chengxiang, repeatedly asked the cadres in his department to imitate the idealistic foreign missionaries in dedicating themselves to their work. He held the opinion that the efforts of numerous foreign missionaries in China would not be in vain, for such men had often lived long years in remote areas in extreme poverty, or at the least quietly spent their whole lives in this foreign and backward country to sow the seed of religion. The Protestant and Catholic churches had been able to establish themselves in China, according to He, mainly thanks to the tireless endeavour of the foreign missionaries.[8]

The CCP burnt down the oldest monastery in the Far East

The second major encounter of the CCP and Catholics in China occurred in the same province of Hebei soon after the end of the Japanese war. For reasons of tactical security during the battle of Shijiazhuang, the regional government and the Eighth Route Army under the leadership of Zhu De and He Long ordered the burning down of a Catholic village and the oldest monastery in the Far East. More than one hundred monks of the contemplative Cistercian Order were forced by the Red Army to march out in the direction of Shijiazhuang; some of the old monks could not endure the hardship and died on the road, while some of those in responsible positions in the monastery were tried by the People's Court of the Yenan government and sentenced to jail, six of them being shot and some put to death by the Red Army in a very brutal way. Altogether thirty-three martyrs gave up their lives in this episode.[9] The martyrdom of large numbers of religious believers was often reported in the Hong Kong Catholic press at that time, with the explanation

---

[8] Xiao Feng, 'Zonggong Zenyang Dueidai Jiaohui he Zongjiao Tu' [How did the CCP treat the church and religious believers]. *Zhishi Fengi* (Xianggang) 65 (16 November 1970): 13–14 part 1, 66 (16 December 1970): 21–4 part 2, 67 (16 January 1971): 30–2 part 3, 68 (16 February 1971): 29–30 part 4. The author spent 1949–59 working as a senior cadre in a provincial Religious Affairs Bureau in South China. This article showed religious policy in China from an unconventional angle. Hereafter cited as Xiao Feng, 'How did the CCP'.

[9] The details were reported by an eye witness, Fr. Stanlaus Jen, in his work *The History of Our Lady of Consolation Yang Kia Ping* (Hong Kong: Our lady of Joy Monastery, 1978), pp. 94–107.

that these things were done by the atheist CCP which had a deep-seated hatred of religion.[10]

The brutality of the Communists towards this Catholic monastery could however be explained by security reasons during the civil war. This Cistercian monastery with French connections since 1883 was located in the north-west of the Hebei province in the midst of one hundred square miles of cultivated land on a narrow plateau called Yangjiaping near the Taihangshan mountain range in the corridor between the two important towns of Zhangjiako and Shijiazhuang. As a matter of fact, Yangjiaping was very near the suburbs of Zhoulu county town, which was on a traditionally important strategic route from interior China to the outer part of the Great Wall; moreover it was eighty-five miles west of Beijing at the border of the Red occupied area. The sensitive situation of this monastery drew the attention of the Communist Yenan government, especially since the big monastery with its semi-French architectural style was surrounded by three high walls, its land covered over one hundred square miles, and it was run by a French abbot in charge of more than a hundred Chinese monks. The monastery was self-sufficient in its fortifications and food supplies (the monks grew their own food and cash crops and rendered protection to the people in the nearby villages). Several thousand Chinese Catholics from the nearby villages came there for religious services several times a year. During the Japanese war, when the nearby peasant Catholics were attacked and looted by the Japanese, they fled to the monastery for protection; so then for the sake of defence from the Japanese and local bandits, fortifications were built and arms were kept by the monks.[11]

Even without the deep-seated anti-foreignism and anti-imperialism of the CCP,[12] the Yenan government could not but frown on this 'imperium in imperio' and soon after the retreat of the Japanese when this region came into its domains, it subjected it to close observation and investigation for more than two years.

Civil war broke out between the CCP and the KMT soon after the defeat of the Japanese. The Red Army, sent by the coalition

[10] In nearly every issue of the Hong Kong Catholic weekly, *Kung Kao Po*, between 1946–57, news of this kind of persecution was reported.
[11] This was told by the eye witness of these events, Fr. Stanislau Jen.
[12] K. S. Liao, *Anti-foreignism and Modernisation in China 1860–1980* (Hong Kong: Hong Kong Chinese University Press, 1984), chapters 4 and 6.

government to wage guerrilla warfare in the Japanese occupied areas of North China, seized control of these territories on the defeat of the Japanese before the arrival of the KMT army. That was how many places in North China fell into the hands of the CCP, and the Nanjing government sent General Fu Zuoyi and his New Third Army to try to regain control of the area. In October 1947, a division of the Eighth Route Army was routed by the New Third Army led by General Fu Zuoyi and had to leave Zhoulu. It then went to Shijiazhuang, joining the other division of the Eighth Route Army to fight the big battle of Shijiazhuang.[13] At this critical point in this strategically important area, the CCP could not observe its previous policies of respecting religion and not touching religious institutes. Such a big religious house as this Cistercian monastery could be used as a fortress by the KMT, especially in view of its French connections at a time when the French and the nationalist governments were on friendly terms. Therefore the CCP decided to raze the monastery to the ground, leaving no trace of it, and leaving nobody behind who might give information to the KMT troops. This explained why they forced all the monks to flee with them under supervision. They broke into the cloister and made a thorough search, not for valuable religious items or food stuff but for ammunition, which they had been informed the monks had stored during the Japanese war. They harboured the belief that the monks had hidden most of their fire-arms in a secret cache and were refusing to surrender them, even though the monks had surrendered to them six old muskets and a small amount of bullets and claimed that this was all they had. Disappointed in their expectations, the Eighth Route Army, which was very short of ammunition, turned against the monks and tortured them in the hope of extracting the weapons and ammunition they believed should be there. The monks were tried by the People's Court in the nearby village of Tangjiayu, and were shot when no more ammunition could be obtained. A handful of these monks arrived in Hong Kong in the 1950s, and later in the 1980s they prepared to beatify the thirty-three martyrs from the destruction of the earliest founded and largest Catholic monastery in China and in the Far East, claiming that the monks died for a religious cause. From the point of view of the CCP, these same monks were considered as alien elements to the revolution, and they were

[13] The Battle of Shijiazhuang was recorded in Zhu De's writing and the date coincided with the monk's record, cf. *Selected Works of Zhu De* (Beijing: People's Press, 1983), p. 211.

suspicious elements, yet if the Japanese had behaved like this we would call it a war crime. The treatment of the monks was totally contrary to Mao's own instructions on the treatment even of KMT soldiers who were captured in battle.

One might wonder if the Red Army would have treated a mosque as it did this monastery. In all possibility, it might have been different, since the Muslims were the majority inhabitants of that area, and in a comparable situation would certainly have put their cavalry and ammunition to good use, keeping to their longstanding tradition of fighting for their survival. In any event, the CCP would have had to respect their religious susceptibilities. On the other hand, those who represented the Catholic church aroused much suspicion in the CCP because of their connections with the French, and locally they were exposed to many attacks because of their minority position as well as lack of support from the populace as a whole.

Let us now quote the teaching of Chairman Mao on the treatment of religious believers, in order to understand the difference between the theory and practice of the religious freedom policy before 1949.

In the problem of racial minorities, the CCP is in complete accord with Dr. Sun's racial policy ... to assist the broad mass of the racial minorities, including their leaders who have connections with the people, to fight for their political, economic, and cultural emancipation and development, as well as for the establishment of their armed forces that protect the interest of the masses. Their languages, customs and religious beliefs should be respected ...

All religions are permitted in China's liberated areas, in accordance with the principle of freedom of religious belief. All believers in Protestantism, Catholicism, Islam and other faiths enjoy the protection of the people's government as long as they abide by its laws. Everyone is free to believe or not to believe; neither compulsion nor discrimination is permitted.[14]

The Vatican in the foreign policy of the PRC in the 1950s

In Mao's era, the development of China's foreign relations had its own pattern according to its own needs at various stages, but consistently applied the principles of contradictions of dialectical materialism as a concrete method to deal with existential situations.

[14] D. MacInnis, *Religious Policy and Practice in Communist China* (New York: Macmillian Press, 1973), p. 14 (hereafter cited as MacInnis, *Religious Policy*).

In 1949–62 the CCP regarded the principal contradiction of the contemporary world situation to be the contradiction between US imperialism and its lackeys (the Western European countries) on one hand and the Soviet Union and the Soviet bloc on the other. In the 1950s China leaned heavily on the Soviet Union for aids and support, and took the Capitalist bloc as its enemies.

The Vatican after the Second World War, in the reign of Pope Pius XII, had warm relations with the west. As a matter of fact Pope Pius XII himself was from a well-known family in Rome, even before he was ordained as a priest. Ever since he was the Papal Nuncio to Germany, he had been well known for his anti-Communist attitude.[15] When he was made the Secretary of State to the Vatican, his personality and his family connections enabled him to have warm relations with right-wing leaders in Italian political circles and he had a considerable amount of influence in general elections. Above all, the American Cardinal Spellman was a close friend of Pope Pius XII, and through Spellman the Roman Curia got a great amount of financial support from the Catholic church of America. Given this political background, one has no difficulty in understanding why Mao Zedong took the Vatican as one of the imperialists when the US and its associates were regarded as the 'great imperialists and lackeys'.

The Korean War was a turning point in Sino-Vatican relations. The posting of the US Seventh Fleet in the Taiwan Strait makes the unification of Taiwan impossible even until the present time. At the end of 1950 when the White House decided to freeze Chinese assets in the USA, strong anti-American feeling was aroused. Zhou Enlai demanded all Christian churches and organisations terminate immediately all relations with American Mission boards. Foreign missionaries including the Papal Nuncio were expelled. Around this time the Vatican and the Catholic church were treated harshly. The Religious Affairs Bureau was set up in 1957 to control religious matters and the Catholic Patriotic Association was set up to implement the 'Three Selfs' policy in order to do away with the so-called 'interference' of the Vatican in church matters. But what irritated the Vatican most was the consecration of Chinese bishops without the consent of the Pope and the demand that the Catholic church in China be independent from the Holy See.

15 H. Stehle, *Eastern Politics of the Vatican 1917–79*, trans. by Sandra Smith, Ohio University Press,1981, chapter 7.

Non-conformists in the eyes of the CCP

As early as the May Fourth Movement, non-conformist Chinese intellectuals, such as Chen Duxiu and Li Dazhao, had contributed much to the building up of the CCP. In Mao's talk in Yenan, he admitted Chinese intellectuals had an important role to play in the struggle for a Democratic Revolution.[16] The main function of the intellectual in the political realm was to influence public opinion to accept or overthrow the ideology on which power is based. Mao himself was also aware that the first group of CCP leaders were intellectuals who had been so attracted by the utopian teachings of Marxism–Leninism that they risked their lives in support of these ideals. In other words the intellectuals can help to build a regime as well as overthrow an old regime. It all depends how one makes use of them. After the establishment of the PRC, the party used various campaigns to indoctrinate the intellectuals and forced them to follow closely the ever-changing political line. Through reforms in the 1950s such as the Hundred Flowers campaign and the Anti-Rightist campaign in 1957, intellectuals as well as non-conformist religious leaders, such as Bishop Gong Pinmei, Bishop Deng Yiming and Shanghai Jesuits led by Vincent Zhu S. J. were purged, then either thrown into jail or sent to labour camps. This reflected that Mao did not allow pluralism in ideology among intellectuals as well as among religious believers. Intellectuals and religious believers seek the truth in their own ways, other than from the teachings of Marxism–Leninism and Mao Zedong thought. The CPA was set up in 1957 with the purpose of putting the Catholic church under the control of the party instead of allowing it to follow the spiritual leadership of the Holy See. This again reflected how much the party wanted to manipulate, refusing to share with others, every non-conformist element within its domain which wished to retain its own teaching hierarchy. Given this background to the ideological differences between the CCP and Catholics and the intolerance of the CCP at that time, it is not suprising that the church–state conflict was at its peak.

---

[16] 'Talk on the Yenan forum on Literature and Art', *Selected Reading from Mao Zedong*, (Beijing: Foreign Language Press).

Religious policy immediately after the 1949 revolution

Since all religions present world views in conflict with the ideology of
Marxism–Leninism, the CCP from the beginning had no intention
of accepting any religious belief whatsoever. Later, as an after-
thought, it was decided to form a United Front for political purposes
with certain idealists and even with religious believers – a skilful
device to deal with these phenomena. On a theoretical level, the
party theoreticians divided religious questions into two categories –
religious beliefs and religious organisations – and so dealt with them
separately.[17] The party granted freedom in matters of religious
belief, since the CCP claimed belief or non-belief in religion was a
personal matter with which the party would not concern itself. On
the other hand religious organisations involve religious activities to
which the party could not remain indifferent. Infiltration, regulation and direction of religious activities were undertaken by the
party in a moderate or militant manner depending on the political
needs and social temperature at various stages. In the immediate
aftermath of the establishment of the PRC, a moderate approach
was taken in several aspects of social life, in order to create an
acceptable image abroad and unite all the people of China regardless of their ideology. A moderate line was also taken in dealing with
religious people. But, after some years in power, the CCP began to
promote a more orthodox Marxism–Leninism, and therefore
changed to a more militant line both in practice and theory.

After the 1949 Revolution, Li Weihan, the head of the United
Front Department, projected the party's official view on religion by
asserting that religion and theism are the negative and utterly
ignorant reactions of men to the natural phenomena of the universe.
Li emphasised that religion has its history of change and development. In the past, religious development and change was based on
the changing class relations in society. The ruling class made use of
religion to suit their interests as an instrument to control the people,
while the oppressed class found religion a binding force to gain unity
in resisting oppression, or a refuge from suffering.[18] Knowing the
political impact of religion, the CCP formed a United Front with

[17] Li Weihan, *Tongyi Zhanxian Wenti Yu Minzu Wenti* [Questions of the United Front and
national minorities] (Beijing: Renmin 1981), pp. 506–7 (hereafter cited as Li Weihan,
Questions on the United Front).
[18] Ibid., p. 173. *Renmin Ribao*, 18 May 1959.

religious people for political purposes.[19] Li also explained why the policy of religious freedom was basic to the party. Religious policies were used to encourage religious believers to work together with high motivation for the liberation of the whole nation, for social reconstruction, and ironically even for the withering of the roots of religion.[20] In one of the national meetings on United Front work Li Weihan explicitly explained that, in spite of the ideological discrepancies between the Communists and followers of religions, religious freedom was still allowed. He earnestly pleaded with the cadres to co-operate with him in implementing the religious freedom policy correctly, because it was the right way to eradicate the very root of religion.[21] In other words the party's ultimate aim in allowing religious freedom was eventually to eradicate religion itself, because it firmly believed that religious belief was untrue and, as it belonged to the superstructure of society,[22] it would disappear as exploitation disappeared. Since it will take a long time to eradicate exploitation from the human arena, it will also take an equally long period to kill religion.[23]

For the party religious freedom is a device to kill two birds with one stone. On the one hand, it aims at the extinction of religion in the long run, and on the other hand, it enables religion to be used in the United Front policy. This was the approach which the party adopted on the basis of its pre-1949 experience until such time as it was to call for more vigorous measures.

Religious policy in China from 1949 to the cultural revolution

According to Marxist–Leninist theory the existence or extinction of religion was a product of the particular stage of historical development that a given society was undergoing. In China, the CCP leaders defined the early years as those of the pre-socialist new democratic stage that had applied since at least the early 1940s. It was not until 1956 that the party claimed that China had reached the stage of Socialism. In theory greater tolerance for foreign religion

---

[19] MacInnis, *Religious Policy*, p. 12.
[20] Li Weihan, *Questions of United Front*, p. 174.
[21] Ibid., p. 174.
[22] Zhou Enlai told the Chinese Christian in the Christian Share to Revolution (1950). See MacInnis, *Religious Policy*, p. 24.
[23] *Renmin Ribao*, 18 May 1959. Ya Hanzheng, 'Lun Zongjiao Xinyang Ziyau' [On religious freedom] *Hongqi* 28 (16 July 1959).

would apply in the new democratic as opposed to the Socialist stage. In practice this was complicated by several factors: first, the issue of patriotism and the concern of the CCP to extirpate western cultural influences and foreign religious links; secondly, the issue of establishing a United Front between social groups and between the Han and the national minorities (which were often based on religious as well as ethnic ties); thirdly the issue of leftism or rightism within the CCP itself – the former being less tolerant and the latter being more accommodating. Thus both within the period of new democracy and the subsequent Socialist period the CCP's religious policies have lacked consistency.

Article 5 of the Common Programme as laid down by the Chinese People's Political Consultative Conference (CPPCC) in 1949, stated that the people of the PRC are entitled to enjoy freedom of thought, speech, publication, assembly, association, correspondence, person, domicile, change of domicile, religious belief, and the freedom to hold processions and demonstrations. From 1949 to 1951, as recalled by an ex-cadre in religious affairs the central government did not issue any comprehensive guidelines to officials of religious affairs, at provincial, municipal and county levels on how to implement the religious freedom policy written down in the Common Programme. Within the party itself no rules and principles were given to the central administration on how to deal with religious affairs. Only a simple explanation was given by the central party authorities as to the meaning of 'religious freedom', which was said to give people freedom to believe in religion or not, freedom to be anti-religious (however anti-religious propaganda among religious believers was forbidden at that time by specific order of the party) and freedom to change from one religion to another.[24] In practice, all religious activities were confined to religious buildings such as churches, mosques and temples, but not allowed in public places where there might be many non-believers. Thus the government on the one hand had to protect religious activities from the non-believer; and on the other to protect non-believers from being disturbed by the activities of believers. The task of dealing with religious affairs at that stage was entrusted to the Social Communities Section of the Internal Affairs Bureau, which was a combination of the departments of Internal Affairs and Social Affairs Bureaux of the former regime.[25]

[24] Xiao Feng, 'How did the CCP', part 1.
[25] Ibid.

This Social Communities Section was under the supervision of the Nationalities Commission.

After two years experience in dealing with the religious question without sufficient guidelines from the central government, it was probably found to be far more complicated than the party expected. Two years later (1951), a Religious Affairs Bureau under the Higher Education Department of the State Council was created to deal with the Muslims and it was linked with the Religious Affairs Section of the Nationalities Affairs Commission. Later the central government decided to extend the functions of the Religious Affairs Bureau to cover all world religions and place it directly under the State Council, removing it from the Nationalities Commission. Still later the Religious Affairs Bureau became independent from the Higher Education Department, remaining directly under the State Council.

At that time the Propaganda Department of the central government issued a directive advising the party cadres that at the provincial and municipal levels they should be extremely careful in dealing with religious affairs, since these involved many aspects of society and went beyond the domestic realm to the international sphere. The guidelines given to religious affairs cadres after 1951 were neither to prohibit nor to assist the development of religion but actively to lead religious personnel to engage themselves in the Three Selfs Reform Movement as a means to reduce the influence of religion.[26] The tone and explanations of these guidelines suggested that they were directed mainly at the Christian churches, while having some application to Islam and Buddhism as well. Generally this has been regarded as a moderate line that lasted until the Great Leap Forward. The appearance of a more militant approach based on classical Marxism–Leninism came in 1958 when Mao thrust the whole nation into the Great Leap Forward.

Application of China's religious policy 1949–58

The political leaders of the CCP usually advocated dialectical methods in dealing with religious questions – while they proclaimed the moderate line so as to unite the people under the banner of the United Front, at the same time they followed a more militant line so as to eliminate those in religious circles who opposed collaboration

[26] Ibid.

and to rid the Christian church in China of foreign influences. Only later when it was proclaimed that China had reached the stage of Socialism was more attention paid to ideological purity within the party itself, when harsh measures were applied to all religious personnel.

From 1949, controlling, infiltrating and regulating devices were applied to Catholic and Protestant churches. From the outset in 1949, foreign missionaries who were suspected of being spies were arrested and many expelled for reasons of national security. Many religious organisations and associations such as the Legion of Mary were disbanded.[27] During the Korean War when the Chinese armies fought the American-dominated UN forces beginning in late 1950, there were strong feelings of anti-foreignism and anti-US Imperialism. Missionary institutions funded by foreign money were closed down and all foreign missionaries expelled, amongst them the Internuncio of the Pope, Archbishop Riberi. National associations were established on government orders to control all the major religions operating in China. These were the Chinese Buddhist Association, Chinese Daoist Association, Chinese Islam Association, the Chinese Christian Three Selfs Movement Association and the Catholic Patriotic Association. With government chosen religious leaders to head them, these associations have never served as the main channel of communication between the government and the various religions. These associations were put under the Religious Affairs Bureau of the State Council to ensure smooth supervision by the government. The demand to cut off foreign relations did not apply to Buddhism simply because its international links did not extend to western countries. The devices of confiscating church properties, churches and temples and the sending home of both Christian and Buddhist monks and nuns on the principle (or pretext) that people are free to change from one religion to another and to cease to believe at all, revealed that the CCP hoped to change the character of religious organisations and to reduce considerably the impact of religion on Chinese society. It also tried to refuse to acknowledge that Islam was the particular religious custom of the Hui, and refused to admit that the Hui was an Islamic nationality. In 1952, the Islamic Hui in Beijing were organised as a racial minority and not as a religious group of Chinese Muslims. This

---

[27] *Suiyuen Daily*, 6 January 1952. *Renmin Ribao*, 20 November 1950, 21 August 1951, 6 September 1951.

policy towards the Hui who have the reputation of being fearless fighters and separatists was not new, since it had been stated by the Yenan government in 1941, when the Japanese instigated an independence movement among the Hui in North China.[28] Therefore the CCP took the line that the religious practices of the Hui were cultural customs and tried to eliminate their sentiment of religion in order to diminish the possibility of foreign links between them and their fellow Muslims abroad. The Buddhists by contrast were treated differently. For the sake of promoting friendship with Asian countries, who were not blacklisted as the 'lackeys of US imperialism' and in order to demonstrate that in new China religious freedom prevailed and religion was respected, the government, in June 1952, sent a Buddhist delegation to participate in an international religious conference on world peace, and the Sri Lankan Buddhist delegates were invited to visit China on their way home after the conference.[29]

Exceptions to the CCP's moderate treatment of religions: opposition under the cloak of religion

Although the CCP's religious policy towards both the Hui and others resembled the mechanisms of applied Marxist dialectics, it was applied in terms of both moderate and militant lines. When it came to the crunch, in incidents such as the Hui revolt, the CCP suppressed those rebellions mercilessly, while at the same time continuing to apply tactical leniency in its dealings with the rest of the Hui. The CCP treated these religious leaders of Muslim uprisings as harshly as any other reactionaries and counter-revolutionaries. It was reported that the Muslim leaders in the Ningxia, Urumchi and Kachi areas of Xinjiang were killed in the 1950, 1952 and 1958 revolts. It was also reported that in the period of the Hundred Flowers the Hui leaders expressed their discontent with CCP policy openly on the grounds that it was undermining the state constitution and was attempting to sabotage religion. The result was that they were arrested in 1957 and condemned to prison as 'reactionary'.[30]

---

[28] Gansu Institute of Nationalities Studies (ed.), *Yisilanjiao Zai Zhongguo* (Ningxia: Renmin, 1982), pp. 105–7.
[29] *Ta Kung Pao* (Hong Kong), 21 October 1952.
[30] Wang Zhangling, *Malie Zhuyi Yu Zhongjiao Zhi Chongtu* [Conflict between Marxism-Leninism and religion] (Taibei: Yeu Shi Press, 1982), pp. 75–6.

The Tibetan revolt in 1959 against the social reforms imposed after the 'peaceful liberation' of the region in 1951, leading to the escape to India of its political and religious leader, the Dalai Lama, was another case that illustrated the explosive mixture of politics and religion that could arise in CCP dealings with national minorities that had a long history separate from that of the Han People and that had strong claims for genuine autonomy if not independence. Paradoxically the revolt in Tibet was a very extreme case. It may seem strange that Tibet should cause the party such major embarrassment, despite having been blessed with exemption from class struggle, the anti-rightist campaign and the Great Leap Forward, and where traditional customs and the position of the traditional elite had been little changed. Though the party had promised to allow Tibetan society to remain virtually intact for the time being and, at least according to its own perception, had tried very hard to keep to this promise, yet the presence of party cadres, army units and bureaux in Tibet could not avoid disrupting the traditional society. The need for labour for the construction of roads and public buildings upset the local economy and conflicted with the serfs' duties to their masters. Even though a modest cadre training effort provided an alternative channel of social mobility to the monastic career, the deep-rooted feudal sentiments of society found this offensive. This and the church leaders' reaction to the rhetoric of the Great Leap Forward were the destablising elements in the precarious equilibrium. So the revolt broke out and was crushed, and consequently the Sino-Tibetan agreement of 1951 came to an end and a much more vigorous propaganda and training programme was introduced.[31]

The CCP's dealings with the Catholic church was another special case, precisely due to the church's strong teachings on Communism before Communism was employed as the means to transform the poverty of China. Pope Pius XI's encyclical 'Divini Redemptoris' of March 1937, denouncing atheist Communism, laid the foundation of anti-Communism in the Chinese Catholic church, before the CCP became the ruling party of China. The denunciation in this Papal encyclical was based on religious and moral reasons concerned with the ideology of Communism, rather than with recognition of the possible political implications. The view expressed was taken as the

[31] Dreyer, *China's Forty Millions* (Cambridge, Mass.: Harvard University Press, 1974), pp. 167–9.

stand of the church towards Communist ideology and was required to be accepted by all Catholics.

The Catholic church as is well-known has a highly hierarchical structure with its headquarters in the Vatican – a city state with the Pope as its head to administer the 700 million Catholic believers all round the world. Because the Vatican enjoys an independent political status in international law so as to enable it to exercise its spiritual and ecclesiastical authority without being bound to any sovereign state, in particular those nations which have an anti-religious ideology tend to regard the Catholic church as inevitably involved in political matters. The Chinese Communist leaders who, on their Communist principles, do not believe in religion, would logically disapprove of the idea of 3.8 million Chinese Catholics holding allegiance to the Pope, which in their reasoning would mean allegiance to a foreign state.

Three papal encyclicals were issued in response to the rough treatment given to the Chinese Catholic church in the 1950s. The first encyclical 'Cupimus Imprimus' expressed the Pope's reaction to the attacks and hardships imposed on church personnel by the CCP.[32] The nationalisation of church institutions and the confiscation of church property in north China – in the land reform campaign of the 1940s – were oppressive measures. In fact a great deal of land was held by Confucian institutes, Daoist temples and the like which were intimately linked with the traditional landowning class in the Chinese countryside. They were an integral part of the land holding system and social structure that the CCP was determined to change in the land reform programme. A similar view was taken of land holdings by Christian churches and monasteries. Thus the acquisition of land by the Catholic church for financial self-support and independence from foreign aid was interpreted as exploitation akin to that of other landlords. Accordingly the landless tenants, the so-called exploited, were instigated to purge the exploiting reaction-aries and snatch the land away from them. It was reported in many places in north China that provincial Religious Affairs Bureaux arranged meetings and assemblies to discuss how the Land Reform might be supported by getting rid of the Legion of Mary – an organisation of Catholics to promote evangelisation. Since the word 'legion' has the connotation of an army, orders were given to

---

[32] Elmer Wurth (ed.), *Papal Documents Related to the New China* (New York: Orbis Books, 1985), p. 33 (hereafter cited as Wurth, *Papal Documents*).

disband this Catholic organisation and its related activities. It was further remarked by the authorities through the media that 'by doing this, the freedom of religion can be correctly implemented and relations with imperialism severed'.[33]

In the spirit of religious freedom as recommended in Article 88 of the Common Programme, *Renmin Ribao* published an article entitled 'The Correct Understanding of the Questions of the Protestant and Catholic churches', in which guidance regarding the religious freedom policy towards these churches was given. It read as follows:

1. Religious freedom should be the principle for treating the Catholic and Protestant churches; but within church circles, all influence from imperialism should be eliminated, while patriotism should be promoted and developed, keeping the Catholic and Protestant churches away from foreign interference, making them become social activities of our own Chinese people. 2. The church cannot carry out evangelism outside church areas, while non-religious organisations should not go to churches to make anti-religious propaganda ... since church activities could affect the progress of land reform, therefore before land reform is completed and land redistributed, both internal and external religious activities in those areas should come to a halt (this includes Bible studies and prayer services). 3. The government of course is suppressing literature which borrows the name of religion but whose contents are full of slanders against the people's democracy. Punishment will be inflicted on the publishers of such literature.[34]

From the time of liberation till the 1957 anti-rightist campaign, the activities of the Catholic church were greatly crippled by harsh treatment by the government, which closed down church institutions in education, social service and medical work, and expelled a great number of foreign missionaries in China, who constituted more than half of the church workers.

The expulsion of foreign missionaries was carried out by the Foreign Section of the Public Security Bureau. The first to be expelled were the US citizens, and they were soon followed by other western people. It was ordered that the US missionaries should receive very severe treatment, while the rest should be treated more leniently.[35] According to an ex-cadre in religious affairs, the procedure was as follows: trial and jail sentences were given to those who were guilty of serious anti-government or anti-revolutionary action.

[33] *Siuyuen Ribao*, 6 January 1952.
[34] *Remin Ribao*, 20 November 1950.
[35] Xiao Feng, 'How did the CCP', part 1.

Then public assemblies were called to denounce those who had committed minor offences, and they were expelled. If any US missionaries were proved to have committed no offence, a deadline of leaving the country on a 'voluntary' basis was served. Other non-US missionaries were put under close supervision and observation. By May 1952, 90 per cent of the foreign missionaries had been expelled.

The charge of murdering infants was admitted to have been a trap by the same ex-cadre who was himself involved in such a case. The Foreign Section of the Public Security Bureau was alerted by the discovery that there was a burial ground for deceased babies at the back of an orphanage run by the Canadian missionaries of the Immaculate Conception in Guangzhou. A spy was sent deliberately to work in that orphanage in order to observe the general situation and see what charges could be made. Then a false record of the deceased infants was compiled and handed to the Public Security Bureau as evidence with which to accuse the missionary sisters. This device served the purpose of disgracing the church and expelling the foreign missionaries at the same time.[36] Those with better sense would realise that an appalling natural death rate amongst those infants was highly possible, since infant mortality was extremely high in China at that time. Although some parents did send their children to orphanages because they were too poor or too short of food to provide for them, most parents did not hand over their babies to the orphanage unless their infants were seriously ill without hope of recovery. The existence of the burial ground only proved a high mortality rate within the orphanage which was founded for abandoned infants. Neither the burial ground nor the forged record could prove that the infants were murdered by the missionaries as claimed by the Communists.

The accusations that other missionaries were spies, such as the case of Bishop Ford (US citizen) of Meixian in Guangdong Province, and the accusations that Fr Alf Bonningue, the superior of the Jesuits in Tianjin, and other French priests teaching in the Catholic university of Tianjin were spies for foreign governments were highly debatable.[37] They were accused of keeping radios and teleprinters and other instruments for illegal communications. Pictures of these

[36] Ibid.
[37] *Diguozhuyi Zenyang Liyong Zongjiao Qinlue Zhongguo* [How did imperialists make use of religion to encroach in China]. Xinhua shishi Congkan no. 92 [Xinhua series on current affairs no. 92] (Beijing: Renmin, 1951), pp. 89–91.

instruments were shown in the court to convince people of the alleged crime the missionaries had committed. No real objects could be produced before the court as evidence, nor had anyone seen the teleprinters and radios that were presumed to be in the residences of these missionaries. Since it was the state plan to expel foreign missionaries, the Communists had to find excuses to get rid of them. From the start the foreign missionaries were ill-treated not for religious reasons but as scapegoats for the United States. The purge of religious personnel brought to light the true nature of the United Front policy. The CCP began to regard religious people as their enemies, although one of the targets of the religious affairs policy was to win the religious leaders to the side of the government, while mobilising religious believers to participate actively in social reconstruction. The external factor of tension with the USA affected the treatment of the Catholic church.

But the worst thing inflicted on the Catholics was the demand they be independent from the Holy See, and against Canon Law consecrate their bishops without the consent of the Vatican. The grave matter of independence from the Pope is the key question of the Sino-Vatican dispute which has not been solved to date, and it still remains a highly sensitive problem in international relations. This is the first time since the Reformation in sixteenth-century Europe that this issue of total independence has come up in church-state relations. The independence movement started with the suggestion of so-called 'reform' at Guangyuan in Sichuan Province in November 1950 which led on to the formation of the Chinese Catholic Patriotic Association (CPA), entailing the schism amongst the Catholics in China. Joining the CPA was seen as a mark of yielding to the demands of the government by those who were still loyal to the Bishop of Rome. The agony of splitting was aggravated by the government's 'divide and rule' method of conferring special privileges on those who joined the CPA and denounced their fellow non-conforming Catholics in public trials, and betrayed the underground Catholics in every conceivable way.

The second Papal encyclical, 'Ad Sinarum Gentem' issued in 1954, employed even stronger words to describe the worsened situation of the Chinese church.[38] The third encyclical 'Ad Apostolorum Principis' issued in 1958 expressed the almost unbearable

[38] Wurth, *Papal Documents*, pp. 39–45.

resentment of the Vatican by using much harsher terms to denounce the CPA, and condemn those who spoke on church matters in China outside the orthodox teaching of the church for their 'deceitful and cunning endeavour' to preach false doctrine.[39] Then the Vatican condemned those candidates who had accepted illicit consecration without the consent of the Holy See as 'ipso facto' excommunicated from the church.

The case of consecration was a highly controversial one. On 21 March 1958, Father Dong Guangqing and Father Yuan were selected by the CPA as the bishop designates of Hankow and Wuchang respectively. The Vatican was informed and the permission of the Holy See on the consecration of these two bishops was sought. In its reply, the Holy See refused to recognise the legitimacy of the episcopal elections and recalled – in terms of the decree of the Holy Office of 1951 – the penalties of excommunication which the consecrating bishops and the two elected bishops would incur if the consecrations were to take place in spite of Rome's explicit wish to the contrary. The lack of personal contact between the Holy See and the bishop designates, Father Dong and Father Yuan, as well as the lack of communication between these two priests and their own religious congregations clearly was a great obstacle to the Vatican's dealing with this case. Both these priests were under strict surveillance by the Communist authorities and could not communicate freely. The Vatican had no way of knowing how great a pressure these two bishop candidates faced at that time from the authoritarian government. So the lack of understanding pushed these two men to the opposite camp. As both designates belonged to the Order of Franciscan Minor, their Minister General addressed two telegrams directly to them reminding them of the rule of absolute submission to the Holy See, and the penalties of expulsion from the Religious Order; also of the very special excommunication they would incur if the consecration took place. Apparently the 'ipso facto' excommunication of the consecration troubled their consciences.[40] These two candidates had hoped to gain support and guidance from the administrative body of the Catholic church when facing this unprecedented situation without any preparation, yet they got condemnation and threats in return.

The hard-liners in the Catholic church condemned them on the

39 Wurth, *Papal Documents*, pp. 51–9.
40 Triviere, *The Catholic Church in Mainland China* (n.p. n.d.), p. 68.

grounds that these were priests who had been properly trained. They knew their church history; they knew about false popes and schismatic bishops; they knew their duty under the Canon Law; yet unlike so many other priests and large numbers of ordinary laymen, they obeyed the demand of the state. They may have acted out of fear, in which case their culpability was reduced; but out of justice to those who faced prison or death for their loyalty to Rome, these weak priests had to be condemned.

This kind of condemnation only rubbed more salt into the bleeding wounds of the Chinese Catholics, who were by that time facing such untold suffering as to make them bitter towards the Vatican which even made enemies of its own priests. The purges during the political campaigns in the 1950s were aimed at the religious non-conformists, intellectuals and Catholic leaders who were influenced by a different ideology and who, if tamed, might be used to indoctrinate the faithful as the party wished. The wound once inflicted on the Chinese Catholic church seems not to have healed. The basic problem of the conflict of authority inherent in the appointment of Chinese bishops has yet to be solved. In the 1980s the universal church advocates reconciliation and it faces the question as to whether it will relent in its demand for the exclusive right of appointments in order to seek reconciliation in the form of normalisation of Sino-Vatican relations. This will be examined in subsequent chapters of the book.

The CCP's treatment of religion after the Great Leap Forward

The moderate policy was continued until 1958, when great changes took place. In that year the political attitude of the whole nation switched to the left in the Great Leap Forward. Already in the latter half of 1957, China's political leaders began to argue that the conflict between Socialism and Capitalism had sharpened, but in 1958 they claimed that the country had advanced further down the Socialist road towards the advent of Communism. As a result a much harsher line was taken towards what were regarded as the remaining vestiges of feudalism and Capitalism. Less tolerance was displayed towards the national minorities. Religion was seen as a clearly unwelcome survivor from the past. It now had to be suppressed more effectively than before. Given the fact that ideological zeal was prized above professionalism and that more administrative power devolved away from the state sector in favour of the party organisation and its cadres, the new policy directions were applied with perhaps greater vigour and less perceptional understanding than might otherwise have been the case.

In dealing with the Hui, China changed its relatively moderate approach and the slow paced programme of reform for a more radical one from 1958 onwards. This involved class struggle, ending co-operation with the traditional upper strata, increasing reliance on newly trained minority cadres and abolishing on a large scale the minorities' customs and special privileges. The party attacked the autonomous area system and forced the immediate adoption of the Han Chinese Communist economic and social model. These measures resulted in economic hardship, indeed they increased awareness of ethnic differences, and in complications in foreign policy. These latter were particularly noticeable in relations with India and the USSR. They also drove away many Muslims from Xinjiang who moved to the Soviet Union with their herds. In 1959, the stringent policy was relaxed a little till 1961. Buddhism however was not much affected by the 1958 change.[41] As early as 1955, the CCP in an internally circulated document had admitted that Buddhism did not have a compact structure nor a well-organised ideological system. It was thought too that the party had drawn out the hidden KMT elements from its midst. Thus the CCP did not do much to crush the hard core of Buddhist monks and nuns who refused to laicise, but tried to lead them to study patriotism and made them work for their livelihood.[42] Since Buddhism had been crushed before the Great Leap Forward and other later political campaigns no significant further hardships were imposed on this half-broken sector of religion.

The Protestant and Catholic churches were regarded by the CCP as having connections with the imperialist enemy and as being a form of cultural exploitation by the latter. The Catholic church was considered far more united and conservative in its approach, and was regarded as so much more reactionary from the political point of view. The Protestant church, on the other hand, having so many denominations, some contradictory to each other, was easier for the CCP to control. The heads of the Provincial Religious Affairs Bureau of Guangdong and Shanghai were criticised in a meeting

[41] Xiao Feng, 'How did the CCP', part 3.
[42] Ibid.

because they could not manage to deal with the resistance posed by the Catholic church under the strong leadership of Bishop Dominic Deng Yiming in Guangzhou and Bishop Gong Pinmei in Shanghai.[43]

The pre-1949 experience of the CCP in dealing with religion (mainly Islam) no doubt provided a broad guideline for religious policy when it became the ruling party. The Communists were also influenced by the Soviet example and their own Yan'an experience in dealing with matters relating to conflicting ideologies. Their limited experience of dealing with Muslims alone was not enough to equip them to deal with the complexity of the other religions, nor was Soviet Marxism–Leninism a sufficiently flexible guide. Later, when Catholics launched a strong resistance to the state policy of creating an independent Chinese Catholic church, and of cutting off relations with the Vatican, the attention of the Religious Affairs Bureau mainly centred on the Christian churches especially the Catholics. In the name of patriotism, the Chinese Catholic Patriotic Association (CPA) was created and the Chinese Catholics were placed in the dilemma of either appearing to be unpatriotic and refusing to join the CPA or being cut off from the Pope, their supreme leader. Having staged resistance for a number of years in their respective dioceses, Bishop Deng and Bishop Gong were finally put on trial at the peak of the Anti-Rightist campaign and sent to jail. That effectively brought to an end the major resistance that had been offered by religious bodies in China. Many Catholics, together with intellectuals and those trained in mission schools, were disgraced during these campaigns of 1957 and 1958.

The change in religious policy was supported by theoretical work which was published some time after the policy had been actually put into practice. It may be helpful to try to find a clue to explain the change in policy.

An article on religious questions in the party's mouth-piece *Hongqi* provided detailed theoretical explanations and guidance on religious policy for private study by the party cadres. On 16 July, 1959, in issue no. 28 of *Hongqi*, Ya Hanzheng, one of the moderate theoreticians, presented an article 'On Freedom in Religious Belief'. In this article, Ya Hanzheng also used the classic Marxist definition of religion as a 'wrong and inaccurate understanding of nature and the

43 Ibid.

universe', 'it is the opiate of people', 'the instrument employed by the ruling class to oppress and exploit the proletariat'. 'Therefore, religion will ultimately disappear when class oppression is extinguished with the development of science and production.' But at the same time, he emphasised that religion is an ideological question, so the party should apply the policy of religious freedom in such a way as to unite all believers and leave every individual free to decide on his own religious belief without any interference of compulsion. Ya also wished the cadres to educate non-believers to respect the religous beliefs of others.[44] This moderate and respectful attitude was fundamentally different from the militant attitude of the theoreticians of religious belief to be discussed below. On 26 February 1964 an article was published entitled 'On Correctly Understanding and Dealing with Religion', by Yao Xian and Liu Jenwang. This article, as has been remarked upon by some scholars, took a much more militant view of religion than the moderate line generally held by the United Front cadres, headed by Li Weihan and supported by Liu Shaoqi and Deng Xiaoping.[45] Yao and Liu argued that religion had been poisoning hundreds of thousands of the proletariat, becoming an instrument to numb their minds and dissolve their will to struggle, and it had been used by the exploiting class as an instrument to rule the proletariat. Therefore religious questions could no longer be tolerated as personal or private matters, but they constituted an important socio-political problem. The view of religion as having a socio-political dimension was in sharp contrast to the moderate line that it was no more than a personal dimension, and that its problems were not of the character of antagonistic irreconcilable class struggles but rather belonged in Marxist terms to the category of the internal contradictions among the people. Lau and Liu's essay held the opinion that, from the viewpoint of class struggle, religion should be put in the category of 'enemy No. 1' since the ruling class makes use of religion to protect its own interests which conflict with those of the proletariat. They also argued that among the proletariat, the world view of religious believers is in fundamental conflict with that of Marxists. Therefore even patriotic and democratic religious believers, in the light of politics, could be called capitalists and be in sharp contradiction

[44] Ya Hanzheng, 'On freedom on religion', *Hongqi* 28.
[45] MacInnis, *Religious Policy*, p. 36.

with the proletariat.[46] In analysing the class nature of religions the writers held the view that all big world religions have been the instruments of the reactionary classes for many ages. They even quoted examples showing that before Liberation the Catholic and Protestant churches were manipulated by imperialism, while Buddhism, Islam and Taoism were controlled by reactionaries. After Liberation the controlling powers had not been completely eliminated from the religions in China. Thus the religions were full of 'reactionaries hiding under the cloak of religion'. In other words, religion itself was saturated with poisonous reactionary elements. (The moderates on the other hand did not regard religion as reactionary and anti-revolutionary.) It was reported in the article that 'at the request of some religious believers, the CCP is leading the masses of religious believers to struggle against feudalist oppression and exploitation within the religious system'.[47] The writer suggested that the peaceful United Front approach should follow the line of unifying and struggling at the same time. The reason given for this was that one of the duties of a Marxist party in handling the religious question is to develop a revolutionary spirit and to give continual education to the masses, continuously emphasising the ideological education of religious believers as a means to gradually diminish the power of religion amongst the masses and accelerate its death. Although the Communist party made use of the policies of the United Front and the religious freedom policy, this never meant that it could assume a neutral attitude towards religion, nor could it afford to see the masses bound by religion and do nothing about it.[48] The two writers drew heavily on classic orthodox Marxist sources in support of their opinions.

It appears that the two polarised lines in religious policy continued right up to the dawn of the Cultural Revolution, when all moderate lines were suppressed. But from 1961 to 1966 an increasingly militant attitude was taken towards religious personnel. Those who were imprisoned at this time found later on that it was a blessing in disguise, because only the iron bars of the jails were strong enough to protect them from the hooliganism of the Red

---

[46] Yao Xian *et al.*, 'Zhengque Renshi He Chuli Zongjiao Wenti' [Correctly understand and deal with religion], *Hongqi* 138 (26 February 1964).
[47] Ibid.
[48] Ibid

Guards. This was claimed by Bishop Deng after he was released in 1979.[49]

Religion in the Cultural Revolution

All the evidence shows that the Red Guards were the worst enemies of religion. These hundreds of thousands of revolutionary teenagers were often hooligans in western terms. Not only did the non-CPA Catholics have a difficult time, but even CPA Catholics were purged. The CPA was disbanded and its last meeting was held in 1962 after which there were no more until 1980. Catholic churches together with other places of worship were desecrated and religious articles and literature were destroyed by the Red Guards in August 1966 at the peak of their frenzy. They set out to destroy the 'Four Old Practices' (old ideas, old culture, old customs and old habits of the exploiting classes) in order, as they claimed, that new practices could be established. Religion, being part of the old world, was mercilessly purged, and religious activities were ordered to come to an end.

In 1966 up to August, six groups of Chinese Muslims were sent to visit Iraq, Sudan, Syria and Lebanon to cultivate friendly relations with these Islamic countries. Two groups of Japanese Buddhists were invited to visit Beijing in June and July 1966 under the sponsorship of the Chinese Buddhist Association. After this, not only were religious activities forbidden, but the ignorant Red Guards inflicted great hardship on Muslim and Catholic religious personnel.

First of all, the Red Guards of the 'East Is Red' Commune in Beijing sent on 25 August 1966 a so-called 'Ultimatum' to the Muslims of that district using very rude and rough language, demanding that the Muslims commit an act which utterly outraged their religious feelings and cultural heritage:[50] they were ordered to eat pork. Their mosques were then demolished, Muslim organisations were disbanded, the ban on intermarriage with non-Muslims was nullified by the Red Guards, and the Koran was burned. They were forbidden to pray, the Red Guards declared it was a waste of time. Then the Muslims were not allowed to use the Arabic language for religious matters. In Beijing the biggest mosque on Ox Street was

---

[49] Remarked by Bishop Deng in a talk to the writer in July 1985.
[50] Li Jinwei, *Hongweibing Shilu* [Facts About Red Guards] (Xianggang: Shijia Huaqiao, 1967), p. 230.

turned into the headquarters of the Red Guards for their anti-Muslim activities.[51] The aged mullahs were publicly beaten up and humiliated.[52] The Muslims and even the Buddhists in the north-west beyond the Great Wall were not treated any better than those in intramural China. Many religious places of worship were destroyed, including both mosques and Buddhist temples. Many of these desecrated temples in the remote areas of Tibet and north-west China remained ruined even some ten years after the Cultural Revolution. The activities of the Red Guards thrust a wedge between the Han and the minorities, and wiped out all the work done by the veterans of the CCP, who had tried to defuse the racial problems.

Another villainy done by the Red Guards in Beijing in the Catholic field was the expulsion of the eight remaining foreign Catholic missionaries. Eight nuns belonging to the Franciscan Missionaries of Mary were the only foreign religious personnel allowed to stay in China after all the rest were expelled in the late 1950s. These nuns were asked to run a convent school for the children of foreign diplomats. In the midst of the chaotic vandalism by the Red Guards, the Municipal People's Council in Beijing was requested to take over this convent school on 26 August 1966. Then the eight foreign religious women were dragged out of the school and put on trial and treated with great humiliation and contempt.[53] On 31 August 1966, they were deported. One of them, an Irish missionary, died on 1 September, just a few hours after arriving in Hong Kong, as a result of the stress and hardship suffered at the hands of the Red Guards. This news received world-wide publicity, and caused additional damage to China's international image.

In general, the religious atmosphere in China during this period can be summarised in a poem by Guo Morou, a much-admired writer at the time, a friend of Chairman Mao and the head of the Chinese Academy of Science. Guo's poem was an inscription on a painting of the monk in the novel *Water Margin* written in December 1977. The poem reads as follows:

> Gods and Buddhas are all false.
> Who can believe in them?
> Break through the temple gates:

[51] Ibid., p. 231.
[52] Ibid., p. 231.
[53] *Renmin Ribao*, 1 September 1966.

Take a stick: wade through them all.
On seeing Buddhas, I lash out,
On seeing God, I curse,
Cursing the myriads of Gods and Buddhas.
Smashing them into mud.
The Abbots' staff is of great use:
Fostering modernization,
And spreading the flowers of Dazhai everywhere.[54]

CONCLUSIONS

Some church researchers have argued that China's religious policy does not specifically aim at the extinction of religion.[55] In spite of the fact that Marxism–Leninism is incompatible with Catholicism on the theoretical level, yet only on some rare occasions did such leading figures in the United Front Department, as Li Weihan, for example, admit that it was the wish of the party to implement the religious freedom policy and cause the death of religion.[56] But the wish of the party to dissemble its intentions in this matter was confirmed by an ex-cadre who recalled the instructions he had received on this subject. All the religious cadres were instructed that strong, harsh measures could not solve religious problems, but, on the contrary would gain China a very bad reputation internationally. Therefore the external forms of religion in terms of its organisations and activities were to be kept under control of the government, so as to infiltrate Marxism–Leninism into religious teaching, and make religion an instrument to serve Marxism–Leninism. Even in confidential documents circulated among senior cadres, such sensitive phrases as 'extinction of religion' were not to be used; some milder terms were substituted to allude to the death of religion when this was unavoidable in some theoretical articles.[57]

Splitting apart the Chinese Catholics over the question of loyalty to the Pope caused a great deal of harm to the Chinese Catholic church. It soon proved embarrassing however to the Chinese government when it became known worldwide that the non-conforming Catholics in China were being persecuted for reasons of

---

[54] *Renmin Ribao*, 29 January 1979, quoted in 'On Religion', *China News Analysis*, No. 1156.
[55] See *YI* (Hong Kong: Yi Editorial Committee), *China and Ourselves* (Toronto: Canadian Council of Churches); Tripod (Hong Kong: Holy Spirit Study Centre).
[56] Li Weihan, *Questions on the United Front*, pp. 12, 174.
[57] Xiao Feng, 'How did the CCP', part 1.

religion. China could be seen as violating human rights. The CCP, out of its ignorance about religion, was the only Communist party in the world to commit this sort of political faux pas. The behaviour of the authorities in Vietnam and Burma shows what they thought about this practice. In Vietnam, many restrictions have been imposed on the Catholics. Before the Sino-Vietnamese dispute began, the Vietnamese Communists studied every aspect of the Chinese Communist experience, and state control in religious matters was tightened in many ways. A Patriotic Association was formed along Chinese lines in 1954 right after Hanoi was liberated, but it did not function too well until the 1980s under the control of pro-government laymen. Yet there was no move either from the Patriotic Association or from the government to ask the Vietnamese Catholic church to be independent from the Pope.[58] The Burmese government did not allow any foreign missionaries to remain and seldom granted permission to its Catholic bishops to have 'ad liminia' visits to Rome, but it did not demand that its Catholics be independent from the Pope.

Generally, in modern times it has proved to be embarrassing for a sovereign state to persecute its citizens on religious grounds. The imprisonment of Bishop Gong and Bishop Deng in the long run had to be a setback to China's reputation. These two old bishops were not released before their long sentences were served and that coincided with major efforts by China's leaders to improve their country's image in international gatherings.

When the political atmosphere during the Great Leap Forward emphasised ideological zeal rather than professional expertise, the moderate approach in religion was suppressed and even the head of the United Front Department, Li Weihan, disappeared without trace in the early 60s. Later, *China News Analysis* reported that Li had been put under investigation in 1962, and that in 1964 he was purged and the whole department was criticised. Organisations affiliated to the United Front Department, and related personnel including religious personnel were purged.[59] The report on the meeting of the revived United Front Department in 1979, presented by its head Ulanfu, spoke of the great achievements of the Department before it met its ignominious end in the Cultural Revolution.

---

58 This writer was told this by a Jesuit priest, Father Celines who had spent more than 20 years in Vietnam after being expelled from China in the 1950s and who also knew Burma well.
59 'Religious policy', *China News Analysis*, Hong Kong, No. 1156.

This gives a good summary of the treatment of religion up to the Great Leap Forward. Ulanfu reported:

Our Party fully implemented the policy of freedom of religious belief, combining it with education of the masses of believers and patriotic persons in the matter of religion. An anti-imperialist patriotic movement was created. All ties between churches and imperialism were cut, democratic reforms were carried out in religious organisations, and feudal privileges, oppression and exploitation were eliminated.[60]

The Chinese Communist government's policy towards religion from 1958 to the end of the Cultural Revolution left it with a rather different balance-sheet.

[60] *Renmin Ribao*, 19 March 1979.

CHAPTER 5

The religious policy of China in the modernisation era

Introduction

The Third Plenum of the Central Committee of the CCP in December 1978 is generally regarded as a watershed in the history of China, this being the occasion when Deng Xiaoping established his ascendancy and the party launched the policies of reform and the Open Door. Great changes have taken place in Chinese social life since then. The economic reforms which are transforming China coupled with a limited degree of relaxation in ideology have provided room for the revival of religious activities in China. At the same time the new policies have also had unintended effects – such as a relaxation in moral attitudes. Throughout all the changes there has stood out the fact that the CCP's own authority, which had carried a good deal of weight before the Cultural Revolution, has no longer been a force that has commanded the nation's respect. Thus, the scope for alternative outlooks and philosophies including religious doctrines has been enlarged. All these things have contributed to the revival of religious freedom.

This chapter will firstly survey the government's policy on religion; and attention will be paid to its evolution in the ten-year period from the death of Mao to 1986. Secondly the reasons for the relaxation of control over religion by the government will be discussed in detail.

In the second part of this chapter, discussion will focus on the Catholic church in China since the condition of Chinese Catholics is a primary concern of the Holy Father and the Roman Curia in any attempt to improve Sino-Vatican Relations. Their concern extends to both sections of the Catholic church in China – the official church and the unofficial church, both of them demanding consideration.

The last part of this chapter will discuss the reasons for granting greater tolerance in religious activities.

NEW DEVELOPMENT IN THE NEW ERA

Relaxation of ideological control

At the 3rd Plenum of the Central Committee of the CCP in December 1978, a United Front policy was launched in internal affairs and an Open Door policy in foreign affairs. These subsequently transformed the Chinese scene. To some extent, the changes wrought were specifically sought by the CCP. On the other hand, the new policies have also had unintended effects – such as a relaxation in moral attitudes.[1] It is important to recognise that even before the 3rd Plenum it had become plain that the CCP's authority had been greatly eroded by the events of the Cultural Revolution, and the reforms exacerbated this tendency – at least in the short run.[2] Religion, therefore, benefited from this.

At least since the party's 7th Congress in April 1945, Mao had always been the Primal Leader and had the command of the party almost all the time.[3] Any challenges he perceived as adverse to his authority were ruthlessly put down. Even in the later years of his rule, when doubts about the party in general and Mao in particular began to ferment in the hearts of the young people, this could not find any means of expression because of Mao's suppression.[4] The

---

[1] The relaxation of moral attitudes is revealed by the authorities' call to youth not to be concerned for money alone but to care for the future of the nation. Also from the complaints about the lapse of morality. See for example, *Renmin Ribao*, 3 March 1982, *Sichuan Ribao*, 18 December 1981, and much later material. The lack of social norms and moral values have been felt for some time at the grass root level, but it was brought up by Professor Kenneth Lieberthal in *The first Electronic Seminar on U.S.-PRC Relations*, 18 October 1988, United States Consulate General, Hong Kong.

[2] The crisis of faith in the party is best illustrated by Hu Yaobang's report to the 12th Party Congress, 1 September 1982. See *Renmin Ribao*, 2 September 1982. There is no subsequent evidence that it has lessened.

[3] In this congress Mao's political report 'On the united government' was presented and his thoughts were adopted as the orthodox ideology, and this was confirmed by the Constitution of the CCP. See *Zhongguo Gongchandang Lici Zhongyao Huiyi Ji* [Important Meetings of the CCP], vol. 1 (Shanghai: Renmin Press, 1982), pp. 235–47.

[4] Huang Kacheng, a high official in the Central Disciplinary Committee of the CCP in his talk 'Quanyu Dangfeng Wenti' [On the party's discipline], in November 1980 admitted that. See *Renmin Ribao*, 28 February 1981. For western accounts of Mao's denouncement, see R. MacFarquhar, *The Hundred Flowers Campaign and the Chinese Intellectual* (New York: Octagon Books, 1974). R. MacFarquhar, *Origins of the Cultural Revolution*, vol. 1 (New York: Columbia University Press, 1974).

Tiananmen Incident on 5 April 1976, was the tip of the iceberg regarding this crisis of faith in Mao as the leader of the CCP. As reflected in the subsequent 'Literature of the Wounded',[5] the young people in the 1970s felt that they had been deceived, and that they had fallen victim to the power struggle among the political leaders. The depth of the crisis of faith was revealed only after Mao's death in 1976. Having lost the confidence and the trust of the people, the CCP has been finding it very difficult to regain as such. The paramount leader, Deng Xiaoping does not dominate his colleagues nor does he exercise the kind of authority over the Chinese people as Mao once did.

The policies of reform and the Open Door, begun in late 1978, have been accompanied by a revitalisation of intellectual life and the relaxation of many social policies. As a result, the scope for the development of alternative outlooks and philosophies, including religious doctrines, has been enlarged. An unintended effect of the new policies has been the surfacing of the crisis of faith in and within the CCP. The formation of the Inspection and Discipline Committee of the CCP in 1979 spoke for itself in that the disciplinary problems amongst party members called for the attention of the Chinese political leaders.[6] Further loosening of ideological ties and the escalation in economic crime among party members, as admitted by the top leaders, caused tremendous weakening of the party's morale and its ideological credibility.[7]

In the academic field, modern western philosophies, such as Existentialism, were introduced into the universities of China for the first time since 1949. Young people studied them with enthusiasm.[8] The relaxation in attitudes towards sex both in theory and in practice has not only caught on with the young people but also worried the authorities.[9] The development of greater religious

5 The 'Literature of the wounded' or the 'Literature of the scared', is a new name for the Chinese realist literature in the period after the Cultural Revolution. It mainly depicted the frustration and suffering of the masses during the Cultural Revolution.
6 Tang Yunchiao, Huang Kacheng, *Guanyu Dangfeng Wenti De Jianghua* [Talks on the party discipline] (Beijing: Renmin Press, 1981). Also see Hu Yaobang's talk on celebrating the 60th anniversary of the CCP. See Hu Yaobang, 'Zai Qingzhu Zhongguo Gongchandang Chengli Liushe Zhounian Dahui Shang De Jianghua' [A talk on the celebration of the 60th anniversary of the CCP] *Renmin*, 2 July 1981.
7 Tang and Huang, ibid., p. 5.
8 Jin Zhihua *et al.* (eds.), *Qingnian Rensheng Zhexue* [Philosophy of life for the youth] (Beijing: Zhongguo Qingnian, 1986), pp. 30–3.
9 Ibid., pp. 198–202.

freedom was mainly an unintended result of this relaxation in ideological control. It would be reasonable to suggest that when central control loosens more freedom in religion obtains, but when ideological control gets strict religious freedom is so much the more circumscribed. When religion sought chances to revive amidst the blossoming of unorthodox ideologies, the Chinese government thought it best for domestic and external reasons, not to suppress it as hitherto. For religion can help, although to a limited degree, towards modernisation. Thus, rather than suppressing, the government tried by directives to ensure that religious activities should be under the control of the party and not flourish in an undue manner.

Revival of religious activities: applying Maoism after Mao's death

It seemed as if religion had been extinguished amongst the Chinese people after the great persecution during the Cultural Revolution. Yet religious policies had already been moderated, though on a very limited scale, before the fall of the Gang of Four,[10] mostly to impress foreign visitors as well as to signal the beginning of a new foreign policy by giving permission for religious worship by foreigners. For example, one Catholic church in Beijing was opened for a religious service for the Catholic Spanish King Juan Carlos who visited China in 1972. Foreign diplomats in Beijing found that they could have Sunday religious services in the Catholic church and other Christian churches there in the same year.

At the beginning of the modernisation era in 1979 and 1980, various articles appeared in *Guangming Ribao* and *Renmin Ribao* giving guidelines and reasons for granting greater religious freedom.[11] Right after the 3rd Plenum of the Eleventh CCP Central Committee, when the religious freedom policy was launched, many party members were surprised to see that churches, temples and mosques were being re-opened at public expense, and that the Islamic and Buddhist Associations as well as the Catholic Patriotic Association

---

[10] They were Jiang Qing, Wang Hungwen, Zhang Chunchiao, and Yao Wenyuen. They were commonly branded as ultra-leftists and blamed for extremist activities during the Cultural Revolution by the post-Mao leadership. They met their downfall in October 1976.

[11] 'Xinyang Ziyou Shi Dang Zai Zongjiao Wenti Shang De Yixiang Genben Zhengce' [Religious freedom is the party's basic policy on religious questions], *Guangming Ribao*, 30 November 1980 (hereafter cited as *Guangming Ribao*, 30 November 1980). Xiao Yinfa, 'Zhengque Lijie He Guanche Dang De Zongjiao Xinyang Ziyou Zhengce' [Correctly understand and implement the party's religious freedom policy), *Renmin Ribao*, 14 June 1980. Xiao Yinfa was the director of the Religious Affairs Bureau of the State Council.

and the Protestant Christian Three Selfs Association began to be much more active than ever before.[12] All this was quite contrary to the previous practice of persecuting religion, which had started in the fifties and reached its climax in the Cultural Revolution. Inevitably, some cadres were suspicious about the new party policy, and some were haunted by lingering fears that the resumption of public religious worship would commit them again to the so-called error of being 'rightists'. Some still looked on the religious problem from the 'leftist' point of view because it was clear in their minds that the party as well as the central government should be following Marxism–Leninism and Mao Zedong thought, which, as previously interpreted, were ideologically incompatible with any religious belief.[13] Yet the central government's policy of allowing the revival of religious activities was taken as a practice of 'burning incense to attract the ghost' giving semblance to a revival of what they looked on as superstition.[14] The central government therefore tried to explain further the religious question to these cadres through an article by a 'Special Commentator' entitled 'Religious Freedom is the Party's Basic Policy on Religious Questions' in *Guangming Ribao* of 30 November 1980.[15] The government's standpoint on religion expressed in this article confirmed that the party still holds the orthodox Marxist belief that religion is conservative, backward and basically opposed to science and Marxist thought.

We emphasise that to implement a religious policy does not mean that we have changed our understanding of the intrinsic nature of religion. Religion intrinsically is conservative and backward, and basically opposed to science and Marxist thought. We Communists are atheists ... However, our party's policy of religious freedom has been drafted with regard to Marxist religious theory and in accordance with the practical situation in China ... Since religion is a problem of ideology one must use democratic means, and

---

[12] Religious activities of Islam, Buddhism and Christian churches were reported in the periodical publications of the patriotic associations of these religions. These are *Tian-feng* (Beijing: Chinese Christian Three Selfs Association), *Zhong-guo Tianzhujiao* [Catholic Church in China] (Beijing: The Chinese Catholic Patriotic Association), *Fayin* [Dhama Ghosa] (Beijing: Chinese Buddhist Association) and *Zhongguo Yisilanjiao* [Islam in China] (Beijing: The Chinese Islamic Association).

[13] Special Commentator, *Guangming Ribao*, 30 November 1980.

[14] Ibid.

[15] In China, an article on a prominent page of a newspaper in a different type of print and written by a 'special commentator' usually bears the same weight as an editorial and conveys a message from the party or the government.

persuasive education to positively lead the people. One cannot use force, commands, violent pressure or administrative measures . . .[16]

This suggested that the religious policy of this period was not intrinsically new. The CCP was trying in this article to emphasise that the party had not lost its way so far as to accept religious faith, but that it had to follow the Marxist way of treating religion as appropriate to China's stage of social development. After putting religion in the context of Marxism, the writer of this article admitted that religion can still exist after its supporting root and economic system vanish.[17] It would be a long, long time before religion would disappear. Therefore the party had to chart out a long-term strategy to deal with it, since it has a complicated and long-lasting role to play in the brave new world that China was confronting. In this way, the article tried to show that the new policy was, in fact, a return to orthodoxy – it was Mao's way of treating ideological problems.

As a matter of fact, in 1957, Mao in his famous article 'On the Correct Handling of Contradictions' laid down explicitly the strategy to deal with ideological questions. He emphasised,

We in no way mean that coercive measures should be taken to settle ideological questions or questions involving the distinction between right and wrong among the people. All attempts to use administrative pressures or coercive measures to settle ideological questions of right and wrong are not only ineffective but harmful. We cannot abolish religion by a decree of administration or by forbidding people to believe in it. We cannot compel people to give up idealism . . . The only way to settle questions of an ideological nature or of a controversial nature among the people is a recourse to the democratic method, the method of discussion, of criticism, of persuasion and education, and not by coercion or repression.[18]

The party specifically pointed out that coercion and repression should not be applied to religious questions but that Mao's strategy of the 'democratic method' should be employed.[19]

In his lifetime, Mao allowed twists and turns in the implementation of his own teaching on religious matters to such an extent that

[16] Special Commentator, *Guangming Ribao*, 30 November 1980.
[17] 'On religion', *Complete Works of Marx and Engels*, 23: 96–7. Quoted by Special Commentator, *Guangming Ribao*, 30 November 1980.
[18] Mao Zedong, 'On the correct handling of contradiction', *Selected Works of Mao Zedong*, vol. 5 (Beijing: Foreign Language Press, 1977), p. 389.
[19] Special Commentator, *Guangming Ribao*, 30 November 1980.

the 'democratic method' was replaced by persecution. By establishing the CPA, by throwing religious dissidents into jail, and by
driving the unyielding believers underground Mao tried to 'cast God
in a Communist image'.[20] Ironically, it was not until after Mao's
death that the party could apply these 1957 principles to religious
matters. There are many reasons which could be given to explain
this phenomenon: one of them might be that religion in general in
China suffered as a result of the Anti-Rightist Movement's attempt
in the Great Leap Forward to accelerate the unfolding of the socialist
stage towards Communism. There was a brief relaxation in the early
1960s before all religions actively came under attack during the
Cultural Revolution because of the focus on class-struggle against a
feared capitalist restoration. Another reason might be that: organised religion such as Catholicism posed too great an ideological
threat to Maoism: for example many of the Chinese Catholics in
particular refused to abandon their religious faith and to embrace
Maoism. The ten years' resistance staged by Shanghai Catholics,
and many other Catholics in other places to a lesser degree, all
suggested to Mao that, since the democratic method would not work
at this stage, then persecution had to be applied after all.

In the early 1950s, the party directives on the Catholics and
Protestants were very clear. Li Weihan, the director of the United
Front Department of the CCP, ordered that in the Protestant and
Catholic communities, the CCP should

through their progressive and patriotic members try to win over the ones
who stood in the middle as well as the mass of believers, whilst isolating the
minority who served the 'imperialists and their running dogs'. Then the
democratic awakening movement could be expanded within the religious
communities. Eventually one could make them truly cut off political and
economic relations with the aggressive imperialist and reactionary forces,
becoming self-governing, self-supporting and self-propagating religious
communities.[21]

But this line was followed later, as we have noted, by the outright
persecution of the Cultural Revolution period.

Apart from those years when all religious practices were sup-

[20] 'Casting God in a Communist image', *Universe*, 31 July 1987.
[21] Li Weihan, 'Renmin Minzhu Tongyi Zhanxian de Xinyingsi Yu Xinyinwu' [The new
situation and responsibility of the Chinese People's Democratic United Front'], *Tongyi
Zhanxian Yu Minzhu Wenti* [Questions on the United Front and nationalities], (Beijing:
Renmin, 1981), pp. 9–10.

pressed as being incompatible with the stage of Socialism that China had allegedly reached, CCP policy towards Chinese Catholics has been remarkably constrained. Since the party's directive of 1950 the policy has aimed at establishing an independent Catholic church, and this has been reiterated over and over again. When Jiang Ping, the vice-director of the Central United Front Department, spoke at the celebration of the 25th anniversary of the establishment of the CPA in April 1983, he not only reminded the Chinese Catholics that they should continue their independence of Rome but that they should also uphold the Four Principles, e.g. to uphold Socialism, the People's Democratic Dictatorship, the leadership of the CCP and Marxism–Leninism and Mao Zedong Thought, as a common political foundation while contributing themselves towards the modernisation of the country.[22] When the 4th Conference of the CPA was held on November 1986, its president Bishop Zong Huaide repeated the same regarding the policy of independence and upholding of the Four Principles.[23] The CCP did not deny that Marxism and any religious doctrine were totally opposed as far as their world views were concerned; but, since China was at an early stage of socialist development, the party not only had to be more tolerant, but it was also anxious to unite the religious believers through a united front under the party leadership to work for social reconstruction.[24]

Though Mao disappeared from the Chinese political scene in 1976, his teaching still carries a great amount of weight in the CCP. Now that his successors face the new task of modernisation and reform, they have to follow Mao's teaching skilfully and carefully in order not to rouse any criticism from the opposition for being too lax in ideology. On the other hand, the application of democratic methods and subtle means of persuasion, education and discussion might gain itself popularity by indirectly negating the stance of the Cultural Revolution and the Gang of Four. This way of dealing with divergence in ideological matters is strict and conservative enough to make good the claim that religious policy is being implemented within the framework of Marxism and Maoism, whilst it is also relaxed enough to convince the ideological non-conformists in

[22] *Zhongguo Tianzhujiao* [Catholic church in China] (Beijing) 7 (August 1985): 22–5 (hereafter cited as *Catholic church in China*).
[23] *Catholic Church in China*, 18 (March 1987): 7–12.
[24] Ibid., p. 23.

general and the religious believers in particular that more tolerance in ideological matters is being given.

Then after a couple of years of the new religious policy, the party summarised its experience and put it into a systematic code in an article in *Hongqi* entitled 'The Basic Policy of Our Party on Religious Questions in this Period of Socialism' as a brief for party members on religious matters.[25] Also in an internally circulated party document called 'Document 19', the party instructed high-level and middle-level cadres in a more specific and systematic way how to implement religious freedom as stated in Article 36 of the 1982 Constitution. 'Document 19' also followed the same pattern of acknowledging its allegiance to Marxism and Maoism before laying down concrete guidelines for tackling the problems which arose after the re-application of the religious freedom policy in this new era. These problems were: which places to designate for religious services, how to handle patriotic religious associations, what provisions to make for the training of young religious personnel, how to manage the CCP's relations with the ethnic minorities who are religious believers, what constituted illegal activities in the religious sphere and how to manage those aspects of foreign relations that touch on religious issues.

Although the different aspects of the religious question in Chinese society were reviewed within the framework of Marxism–Leninism, a very pragmatic approach was followed. 'Document 19' reaffirmed that simply making use of coercive measures to deal with peoples' ideological questions and spiritual matters would not only produce no results, but would also be extremely harmful.[26] The Central Committee document asserted that at the present stage of affairs, the difference between the mass of believers and non-believers was to be regarded as purely a secondary matter,[27] as the general policy of the state and the party no longer centred upon class struggle but on primary social reconstruction and modernisation. The Central

---

[25] 'Women Dang Zai Shehui Zhuyi Shiqi Zongjiao Wenti Sheng De Jiben Zhengce' [The basic policy on religious questions of our party in this period of socialism], *Hongqi* 12 (16 June 1982): 2–8.

[26] 'Zhonggong Zhongyang "Guangyu Woguo Shehui Zhuyi shiqi Zongjiao Wenti De Jiben Guandian He Jiben Zhengce"' (Wenjian no. 19: 1982) [Document 19 Issued by CCP Central Committee in 1982 – Regarding our nation's basic viewpoints and policies towards religion in Socialist Stage], *Zhonggong Yanjiu* [Studies on Chinese Communism] (Taibei) 3 (15 March 1983) (hereafter cited as 'Document 19'). For its English translation see Appendix I.

[27] 'Document 19', para. 4.

Committee through Document 19 reaffirmed its standpoint on the policy of religious freedom, namely, that, although the government and the CCP were committed to atheism, the basic starting point and foundation for handling the religious question and implementing the policy of religious freedom was:

to unite the mass of believers and non-believers and enable them to centre all their will and strength on this goal common to all: to build a modern, powerful socialist state. Any action or speech that deviates in the least from this basic line is completely erroneous, and must be firmly resisted and opposed by both the party and the people.[28]

Nevertheless, the implementation of religious policy depends very much on local conditions. This is mainly because the CCP policy evolved in a complex way. It was not spelt out specifically in terms of what was allowed on a day-to-day practical basis. It did not take full account of the vastly different problems that existed in, say, Muslim areas, where special food and pollution rules had to be observed, and in Catholic villages where restoration of church property was a minor problem compared with the conflict between CPA clergy and pro-Rome clergy. Shanghai, for example, has been relatively tough on religion, regardless of the general outlook of the CCP cadres running the city, not because Shanghai is 'leftist' but because of the local political realities. It is understandable that religious life in Shanghai should suffer from greater restrictions, and that the resumption of religious activities in this area should occur relatively later than in the other major cities in China.[29] In spite of the fact that Shanghai is more 'sophisticated' compared with most parts of China, and its population less 'superstitious', it is less under pressure to tolerate religious practices than more 'backward' places. This is partly because the ten years' struggle in the 1950s against Rome which was particularly centred in Shanghai has left a well-indoctrinated CCP structure hostile to religion as 'an agent of imperialism' to a degree not found elsewhere. It is also partly because Shanghai's unofficial church leader Bishop Gong has continued to protest against his sentence, and his influence is very much felt among Catholics both inside and outside China.

[28] 'Document 19', para. 4.
[29] Beijing and Guangzhou had Catholic churches re-opened in 1979, while Shanghai religious activities did not resume before 1982.

The party's further theoretical work on religion

Two years after launching its religious policy, the party in 1986 tried to justify the growing relaxation of restrictions on religious activities by re-interpreting religion in the context of Marxism in a much more positive tone.

As a matter of fact it was Deng Xiaoping, on the occasion of the 100th anniversary of the death of Karl Marx, who requested Chinese Marxist theorists to handle the basic theory of Marx in the context of the new reality in order to harmonise the relations between the believers and socialism. A Chinese scholar of religious studies, the deputy head of the Chinese Social Science Academy, Zhao Fusan, a former Protestant pastor, tried to respond to the call of Deng Xiaoping and reinterpret religion, especially Christianity, in a new perspective with a more positive outlook towards it, to indicate that there might be a more positive acceptance of religion in future.[30]

First of all, Zhao's article 'How to Comprehend the Nature of Religion' which appeared in the 3rd issue of *Chinese Social Science* in 1986, published by the Chinese Social Science Academy, reinterpreted Marx's famous saying that 'religion is the opium of the people'.[31] Zhao suggested that in the original German text of Marx's work the above-mentioned phrase is 'das Opiate des Volks'. He points out that the Chinese translation says 'religion is the emasculating opium of the people'. It was the translator who added the word 'emasculating' to the original text to illustrate the nature of religion in the historical context of the pre-liberation period in China.[32] According to Zhao, in Marx's time opium was a kind of expensive tranquilliser or pain-killer. In Marx's view, the poor could not afford opium to kill pain but sought religion – the cheap opium – which cannot physically alleviate suffering. Marx only implied that religion fails to cure people's problems and that it only helps to relieve the pain they suffer from class oppression. In China since the notorious Opium War, opium has had a negative connotation as a poison, and an emasculating poison. Therefore, he argued that the Chinese translation, 'religion is the emasculating opium of the people' brings a different connotation to the nature of religion from

[30] Zhao Fusan, 'Jiujin Zenyan Renshe Zongjiao De Benzhi' [How to comprehend the nature of religion], *Zhongguo Shihui Kexue* [Chinese Social Science] (Beijing) 3 (1986): 3–19.
[31] Ibid., pp. 5–6.
[32] Ibid., pp. 4–5.

that of Karl Marx.[33] Then he also argued that, according to Marx, religion is the outcome of the self-awareness and the self-consciousness of those people who are unable to control their own fate. Zhao remarks that this is the general nature of all religions in all ages.[34] He also points out that in China it is the prevailing 'leftist', or the hard-line, ideology which hinders the correct understanding of the positive nature of religion. Religion has played a role as a catalyst to stimulate change and development in society. For example, during the peasant wars both in China and in medieval Europe religion became the symbol that incited the peasants to revolt.

Zhao further cast doubt on the debilitating function of religion, by pointing out that, if it were true that religion would debilitate people, then a society without religious belief should be more progressive than a society with religious belief. In fact, in many cases the social performance of religious believers is better than that of non-believers. He quoted the example of the Catholic priests who died in peoples' guerrilla warfare in Latin America, and that of Johnson, the Dean of Canterbury, who accused the United States of using chemical weapons in the Korean War. Similarly, the struggles led by Archbishop Desmond Tutu in South Africa against apartheid are a positive contribution by religion in modern society. He also noted the numerous cases of religious believers who despite their sufferings during the Cultural Revolution still stuck to their principles of keeping the law and being patriotic, engaging themselves in hard work while directing their concern to the needy.[35] Finally he remarked that the religious values of righteousness, justice, and concern for social welfare are in opposition to selfishness, profit-orientation and egocentrism, and those religious values are in keeping with the morality of Socialism in China, and the spiritual civilisation of Socialism.[36]

Zhao's article appears to be the first theoretical one in contemporary China to take such a positive view of religion and in a pragmatic way to look into its nature and the contribution it makes. So moderately biased a discussion of the impact of the moral power of religion on people could hardly have been possible unless the writer either had a deep understanding of the inner lives of religious

---

[33] Ibid.
[34] Ibid., pp. 6–7.
[35] Ibid., p. 16.
[36] Ibid., p. 16.

believers or he himself had experience of religion. Zhao was able to
do this because he had been a religious believer and a pastor of the
Anglican church. It is too early to expect that his view would be
accepted by the more conservative and orthodox Maoists. But,
according to a reliable source, his positive re-interpretation of
religion, especially of Christianity, had the blessing of Deng Xiaoping. So it should carry some weight and give a lead in the political
policy on religion whilst Deng remains in power.[37] But the acceptance of his theory in the long run will depend less on Zhao than on
the future political trends. In spite of the launching of the anti-
Bourgeois Liberalism Campaign at the beginning of 1987 after the
downfall of Hu Yaobang and Zhao Ziyang, the new Secretary
General of the CCP has not used a strong hand to suppress religious
freedom, because recently all the discussions and directives on
religious matters do not take a left turn, but most of them try to
interpret 'Document 19' from a rather liberal point of view while
acting cautiously to remind people not to go back to the 'leftist'
directive nor to be so liberal as to depart from the framework set up
by the party, while some echoed Zhao Fusan's interpretations of
Christianity.[38]

RELIGION IN CHINA AFTER MAO

Places of worship

In Document 19 it is remarked that, at the establishment of the PRC
in 1949, there were about 100,000 places of religious worship, which
included Buddhist and Taoist temples, Catholic and Protestant
churches and Muslim mosques, and that about one third of them
have been re-opened.[39] There are various reasons for the restoration

---

[37] Opinion of Professor Wang Yao from the Department of Tibetan Studies of the Central
Institute for National Minorities.
[38] Some articles appeared in journals on religious studies in China discussing these matters. See
Yu Benyuan, 'Zongjiao Xinyang Ziyou Yu Wushenlun Xuanchuan' [Religious freedom
and propagation of atheism], *Shijie Zongjiao Yanjiu* (Beijing) 3 (1986): 131–9. Yu Chiaoqing,
'Zaitan Zongjiao De Benzhe De Shehui Zuoyong' [Further discussion on the nature of
religion and its social function], *Shijie Zongjiao Yanjiu* 3 (1987): 121–6. Gong Xuezeng,
'Guanyu Woguo Shehui Zhuyi Shiqi Zongjiao Fangmian De Jige Wenti' [On a few
religious questions in the social period of our state], *Shijie Zongjiao Yanjiu*, 1 (1986): 134–42.
Jiang Wenxuan, 'Tan Tan Wodang Chuli Zongjiao Wenti De Fan "Zuo" de Fang You',
Shijie Zongjiao Yanjiu 1 (1987): 104–12.
[39] 'Document 19', para. 6.

of places of worship.[40] In the countryside generally peasants sacrifice a great amount of money to construct new temples and restore old places of worship. At the same time the government distinguishes between 'superstition' and religion, and it would not tolerate temple building whose expenses are from the peasants' money. For this reason the government instructs its cadres about the priorities in the restoration of religious places and the priorities in conducting foreign visitors to such places.

Among the tens of thousands of overseas visitors who have streamed to China on visits, there have been dignitaries of various religions and sects: Catholic cardinals, the Archbishop of Canterbury and other Protestant leaders, Buddhist leaders from Japan and south-east Asia and Muslim leaders from the Islamic world. All these were naturally eager to visit places of interest relating to their own religions. In certain specific instances, the government by way of Document 19 complained that in some places of cultural and historical importance temples were still closed and this stood in the way of attracting foreign tourists and their foreign currency. Thus it is for very practical political and economic reasons, rather than for any religious motives, that the central government has instructed that the restoration of places of religious worship must be carried out systematically. These instructions have involved the restoration of a number of Buddhist and Taoist temples and churches in some average-sized cities, and in historically famous religious places, or in ethnic minority areas. The state ordered that the famous Buddhist and Taoist temples which enjoy both international and national prestige for their intrinsic cultural and historic value are to be restored as soon as possible.[41] In the absence of large numbers of believers and in view of the widespread demolition of temples the government has indicated that state funds should be used thriftily in the restoration work.[42] Its insistence in the same document that the surroundings of such places of worship should be kept clean, attractive and suitable for tourism is a further indication of its priorities.[43]

In the process of re-opening places of worship, the religious cadres

[40] *Guangming Ribao*, 8 September 1980. *Renmin Ribao*, 27 March 1986, 9 September 1980. *Fujian Ribao*, 8 January 1982. *Nanfang Ribao*, 20 April 1982.
[41] 'Document 19', para. 6.
[42] Ibid.
[43] Ibid.

were instructed that no money from the state nor from the collectives should be given for this purpose without state permission. Special precautions should be taken to prevent temples being built in villages. Cadres were instructed to refuse the rebuilding of places of worship if the request came from believers, even if the latter were able to collect donations for this purpose. Moreover, building and re-building of places of worship must never be allowed on such a scale as to hinder the promotion of socialist civilisation and values.[44]

Patriotic religious associations

There are at least eight patriotic religious associations established by the Chinese government to manage religious affairs. These are the Chinese Buddhist Association, the Chinese Taoist Association, the Chinese Islamic Association, the Chinese Catholic Patriotic Association, the Chinese Catholic Religious Affairs Committee, the Chinese Catholic Bishops' Conference, the Chinese Protestant Three Selfs Patriotic Movements and the Chinese Protestant Association. The government expects these associations to implement religious policy with due regard to the party, and there are party cadres on their staff. Document 19 specifically points out that these cadres were entrusted with the task of assisting the broad mass of religious believers and personages in religious circles to induce their awareness of patriotism and socialism, and all patriotic religious organisations ought to follow the party's and government's leadership.[45]

As we have seen three out of eight national religious patriotic associations were set up to deal with the religious affairs of the Catholic church. At present it is officially claimed that China has 10–15 million Muslims, 3 million Protestants and 3.8 million official Catholics.[46] The number of official Chinese Catholics is more or less the same as that of the Chinese Protestants and only one third of the Muslims. As far as professional religious personnel are concerned the Catholics have 3,400, the Protestants have 5,900 and the Muslims have 20,000.[47] One sees that the Catholics have the second smallest number of adherents in China and have the lowest number of religious personnel. Yet the government created three patriotic

[44] 'Document 19', para. 6.
[45] para. 3.
[46] para. 2.
[47] para. 2.

religious associations to deal with their affairs. The other religions have only one each. This may reveal the complexity of dealing with Catholics, who appear to need more governmental supervision than other religious believers.

The Chinese Catholic church in the 1980s

As already noted, the official figure for the number of Chinese Catholics in 1984 was 3.8 million.[48] At the time the Communists took over, there were 3 million Catholics, (one Catholic to 140 Chinese people). Shanghai alone had 140,000 Catholics.[49] Yet at Masses in the official church of Shanghai, there have recently been about 2,000. Perhaps some 2 per cent to 3 per cent of Catholics practise the 'patriotic' variety of their faith, according to the observation of a Catholic sinologist.[50] He also noticed that the government has been able to appoint forty-eight bishops, eleven of them married, for the 134 dioceses. Many of the state appointees are of advanced age.[51] There are several categories of people who identify themselves as 'Catholics'. There are those Catholics who joined the CPA and whose leaders are in effect salaried employees of the state. There are some professed CPA Catholics who secretly owe their real allegiance to Rome. Then there are Catholics who have never forsaken Rome and are outside the CPA. The official figure of 3.8 million must refer to those who joined the CPA and those who attend services in the open churches run by the CPA. As noted, Document 19 gives the figure of 3,400 priests. Since there are no official statistics on the geographical distribution of the Catholic population since 1949, one has no alternative but to refer back to the pre-Communist figures which were as below. It is probable that the geographical distribution has not drastically changed its pattern since 1949.

Apparently the largest number of Catholics resided in Hebei province, then came Shangdong and Jiangsu, with Manchuria and Hubei third. Shanxi and Inner Mongolia had a high proportion of Catholics in their relatively low total population. Most of the

---

[48] Wang Ganyi's article in *China Daily*, 6 July 1984. He gives the numbers of Catholics as 3.8 million, of Buddhists about 4 million.

[49] *Annuaire de L'Eglise Catholique en Chine. 1949*, table 'B', pp. 13–14.

[50] *Universe*, 31 July 1987, p. 2 (The Catholic Weekly in England).

[51] 'Casting God in Communist Image', *Universe*, 31 July 1987.

Table 5.1 *Distribution of Catholics in China in 1949ᵃ*

Province	Population in millions	Catholic population
Inner Mongolia	03.4	145,761
Manchuria	39.8	203,880
Hebei	39.7	759,689ᵇ
Shangdong	34.9	323,615
Shanxi	13.1	140,520
Shaanxi	11.1	98,341
Gansu	12.2	34,018
Anhui	24.0	132,664
Jiangsu	35.8	310,844ᶜ
Henan	30.2	171,788
Sichuan	53.7	161,593
Hubei	24.4	200,352
Hunan	31.3	57,962
Jiangxi	17.0	99,292
Zhejiang	22.3	94,242
Fujian	12.5	103,943
Guangdong	38.9	142,145
Guangxi	12.6	25,336
Guizhou	11.4	42,167
Yunnan	14.0	26,588

Notes: ᵃ From *Annuaire de L'Eglise Catholique en China 1949*. Table B-15
ᵇ This figure included 215,918 in Beijing and 50,000 in Tianjin
ᶜ This figure included 147,516 in Shanghai

Catholics were in rural areas except those in major big cities like Beijing, Tianjin and Shanghai.

The official Catholic church

As early as 1979, the gradual revival of religious activities was observed. The Chinese Catholic magazine *Zhongguo Tianzhujiao* [*Catholic church in China*] no. 5 1982, revealed that, since 1981, more than 300 churches in the cities and thousands of 'meeting points' for religious purposes in rural areas were in operation; and many churches were in the process of renovation. It was also reported that there were fourteen dioceses where bishops had been independently elected and consecrated (which means the process was carried out without the permission of the Holy See). A number of dioceses like Xian, Shijiazhuang, Hanzhong, Leshan and so forth had new priests ordained. In addition to the National Catholic Seminary which began to operate in Beijing in September 1983, regional seminaries also appeared in Shanghai, Wuhan, Xian, Shenyang and Chengdu and a diocesan one in Beijing.[52] It was reported that there were eleven theological seminaries.[53] The same magazine also reported that the Catholic Patriotic Association at national and provincial levels was busily engaged in negotiations between the government and church circles on aspects of religious affairs. The Chinese Bishops' Conference and the Chinese Catholic Administrative Committee have been arranging internal religious affairs. Bibles, prayer books and a limited number of basic religious books were reprinted for the needs of the faithful. Groups of Catholic representatives were sent abroad for international meetings and visits begining in 1981, with the purpose of formulating international contacts of 'equality, friendliness, mutual respect', as laid down by the government.[54] Amongst the numerous Catholics of the hundreds of thousands of overseas visitors who came to China there were three Catholic cardinals, including Cardinal Sin, the Prelate of the Philippines. Mother Teresa, the Nobel Prize winner, also paid a visit to the Catholic church in China in 1984. Bishop J. B. Wu of Hong Kong made a couple of trips to China at the invitation of the Chinese government, in March 1985 and February 1986, and his spokesman announced that one of these trips would help to pave the way for a diplomatic connection between China and the Vatican.[55]

The Catholic Patriotic Association in the 1980s

The Catholic Patriotic Association, like other patriotic organisations, is a semi-governmental organisation created by the government as early as 1957. It promotes the religious policy of the party under the direct leadership of the party. To be precise, it is the officials of the United Front Department, rather than the religious leaders at national religious meetings who set the tasks for the CPA. Its structure and purpose are clearly defined in the CPA Constitution. Article 2 states:

The Catholic Patriotic Association is a mass organisation made up of patriotic and church-loving clergy and laity. Its aim is to unite clergy and

---

[52] *Catholic Church in China*, 5 (30 September 1982): 34.
[53] It was reported by Bishop Dong Guangqing, Bishop of Wuhan who told the delegates of the Major Superiors of the Women's Religious Association of Hong Kong in November 1987.
[54] *Catholic Church in China* 7 (August 1983): 5–12.
[55] 'Jaime Cardinal Sin's Visit to China', *Tripod* 24 (December 1984): 50–6.

1 Receiving guests at a parlour in a Catholic church in China. This spartan life-style of these aged priests cannot be easily found in any Catholic parish in the west. *Source:* Author's private collection.

2 Zhao Fushan, the Deputy Director of the Chinese Social Science Academy, a Marxist theorist on religious studies (right) at an international conference in Montreal (1981). It was reported that Zhao defected to the west and asked for political assylum in France after the Beijing Massacre on 4 June 1989. *Source:* Author's private collection.

laity throughout the country and under the leadership of the party and the People's government, to develop the spirit of patriotism,

by observing the laws and policies of the country,

actively taking part in building up the socialist state,

promoting friendly relationship with Catholics on the international level,

opposing imperialism and hegemonism,

defending world peace,

helping the government to implement its policy of freedom of religious belief.[56]

On 23 April 1980, at the Third Representative Meeting of the CPA (the first of such meetings since the early 1960s), a speech was made by Xiao Xianfa, the head of the Religious Affairs Bureau (a position enjoying ministerial status). His official position and presence at this meeting underlined the importance of what he had to say

[56] *Catholic Church in China* 1 (March 1980): 12–13.

3 Bishop Tu Shihua (left), the rector of the National Catholic Beijing Seminary, Bishop Michael Fu Tieshan (next to Tu) of Beijing and Bishop Yang Geojian (2nd from the right), the vice-president of the CPA. *Source:* Author's private collection.

to the participants. Xiao laid down the government's policy on religion and the role of the CPA, declaring as follows:

This is also the very necessary and important task of the Catholic church as she continues to maintain her independence and autonomy in managing her own church affairs and as she assists the government in implementing its policy of freedom of religious belief. In order to do this she must unite the mass of clergy and laity so that they maintain order and unity and do their best to carry out the Four Modernisations as well as to oppose hegemonism and defend world peace.[57]

His speech then set out the government's position and policy in the new era regarding religious questions in general and the role of the CPA in particular. In fact all the others who spoke at that meeting in one way or another faithfully reflected this official policy.[58] At the same CPA meeting, its chairman, Bishop Zong Huaide, echoed Xiao's speech and requested all the clergy and laity

[57] *Catholic Church in China* 1 (March 1980): 4–5.
[58] Ibid. (November 1980) covered almost all the important speeches including Xiao Xianfa's.

of the Chinese Catholic church to love the motherland, to support the party leadership and toe the party line of Socialism. From the politicised speech of Bishop Zong, one was led to wonder whether the meeting itself was held for political purposes or for religious reasons. There is also reason to question whether Bishop Zong was exercising his church authority as a bishop for political ends. Yet, if one views it from another angle one can see Bishop Zong's difficulty. The CPA was recovering from the suppression and persecution of the Cultural Revolution. Yet it was as much tied to the party as before; and the party was turning to the new religious policies. Therefore, it was not unreasonable for him to urge support for party policies if these in turn were allowing the CPA to hold religious activities once again. At this meeting, Bishop Zong, after more than ten years of silence, was able for the first time to exercise his ecclesiastical power instructing the congregation, when he said as follows:

Our unswerving pledges are: ardently to love our country, whole-heartedly to support the Party leadership, firmly to walk along the Socialist road . . . Our fundamental welfare is exactly the same as that of the whole nation. With an ardent love for our motherland, all should positively take part in the work of the four Modernisations. This is the task common to the whole nation and it is the duty we clergy and laity must fulfil as well.[59]

At provincial level, the chairman of the CPA in Guangzhou echoed the same policy. At a religious meeting this leader kept on reminding the participants at grass roots level that the CPA was 'a mass movement to unite the clergy and laity to foster the enterprise of loving the church and loving one's motherland. It is a bridge to link the government and the church.' He further confirmed the government policy by saying that 'it was necessary and right to run the Catholic church independently, and to help the government to propagate and implement the policy of religious freedom'.[60]

Xiao Xianfa's speech to the CPA confirmed that the state policy towards the Catholic church was consistent with that developed during the formation of the PRC. The emphasis on independence from the Holy See was still there. The government's position in this question had not softened because of the relaxation in this modernisation era. In fact, through the CPA, the government tried to divide and keep under control the activities of the Catholic church in

[59] *Catholic Church in China*, 1 (March 1980): 7–12.
[60] Ibid., 5 (September 1982): 31.

China. Officially the CPA from the beginning of its establishment had to follow the official policy. In reality, however the CPA has not been a monolithic body. Its members have applied government policies in different ways in different parts of the country. There were actually places where they favoured and made it possible for the faithful to carry out the integral practice of the Catholic faith; whilst in others some CPA members practically became the state's policemen against the pro-Vatican Catholics, having received an assignment from the authorities to report on their movements. It is said that there are some CPA bishops who are acceptable to the Holy See. These bishops put their own men to be the heads of the local CPA of their dioceses. Thus, these church leaders endeavour through pastoral work to build up the lcoal church without paying much attention to political matters. In this way the influence of CPA gradually diminishes so much so that the Chinese bishops in the last Bishops' Conference from 24–8 April 1989, demanded that the Bishops' Conference not the CPA must be the first in making decisions regarding church affairs, and the CPA should be at the service of the Bishops' Conference.

The unofficial Catholic church

The Chinese government and the party require that religious activities be carried out by religious personnel or the faithful through the organisation of the various religious patriotic associations, with rituals performed at locations permitted by the patriotic associations.[61] Otherwise all religious activities are regarded as illegal and can only be practised underground. It is known for a fact that there are religious activities performed outside the sphere of the official supervision of the CCP, but it is difficult to get a complete picture or full statistics of the unofficial church members. One thing is certain, that those Catholics who are loyal to Rome are penalised by the government on the grounds that they are 'carrying out destructive espionage'.[62] The government has ordered that

if the former religious professionals, once their term of imprisonment is over and they have been released, go back once again to engage in these criminal activities, then they will be punished again in accordance with the law. All these reactionary secret societies, together with sorcerers and witches, who were banned but then started up again because of the relaxation on

[61] 'Document 19', para. 6.
[62] Ibid., para. 11.

religious practice, without exception will not be permitted to resume their activities.[63]

It is therefore surprising that the unofficial Catholics have been able to keep their religion alive, though in a clandestine way.

One cannot deny that the religious activities in open city churches are easily visible to visitors and journalists, who can photograph the churches and the faithful at religious services. In the countryside where the silent church or unofficial church is located the situation is reported to be quite different. The official press does not publish its activities nor are foreign visitors openly received by it. Nevertheless evidence has come out from China to prove that this sector of religious life does exist. For reports have been brought out by Chinese priests, and by religious and Catholic laity who living abroad and holding foreign travel documents have returned to their native villages to visit their relatives.[64] According to their reports they have discovered a new world, a living church of extraordinary vitality, even in places where there are no priests, strangely enough, and even more where the local priests after serving a long term of prison and forced labour have been sent back to be peasants in their own villages. In such villages, where the population is almost entirely Christian, Christian life flourishes.[65] These religious visitors have been deeply moved because they have witnessed an incredible depth of faith, kept intact through twenty to thirty years of hardship, and they have heard many stories of how the Christians suffered because of their faith. But this type of religious activity is so clandestine that even the same visiting Chinese religious person or priest may go to some other region of China where he has no personal connections and would not be able to trace the Catholics there. Such behaviour is typical of a clandestine organisation, and since a dark cloud is always hanging over the unofficial Christians they will identify themselves only to those whom they themselves or their families know.[66] The fear of betrayal is so great that priests in one region do not know what has happened to their fellow church personnel in other parts of the country. After collecting much

[63] Ibid., para. 10.
[64] L. Ladany, 'The church in China seen in December 1980' (Hong Kong: by the author, *China News Analysis* Office, GPO Box 3225), 1981. (The writer was the editor of *China News Analysis* 1957–83.)
[65] Ibid. Also J. Heyndrickx, 'A visit to Catholic church in China, May 13–June 2, 1985', pp. 24–6, 33–7. (A private report). Hereafter cited as 'Heyndrickx's Report'.
[66] Heyndrickx's Report, pp. 24–6, 33–7.

information on this part of the Catholic church the veteran sinologist, Father L. Ladany, summarised the situation as follows:

Our knowledge of the real life of the Christians, therefore, remains
fragmentary. We know that Christian life flourishes in many villages and
that it is not absent in the labour camps and among the ex-inmates of
labour. Many learnt about the faith in the camps. Catholics, priests and
laymen, are usually good workers and their honesty and devotion to others
shine and attract people, who then want to learn what gives them strength
in hardship. Many priests in labour camps throughout the years have
formed their parishes, invisible parishes in which people help each other
and live by faith.[67]

From private sources it has been learnt that in labour camps the
Catholic priests and laymen's lives are so outstanding that they
attract young people to join the priesthood and religious life.
Noviciates of men's and women's religious congregations do actually
exist in the labour camps.[68] Recently one of the seminaries and
noviciates of the underground church was discovered, and novices
and seminarians were arrested in September, 1986, and the young
novice nuns were sexually assaulted as well.[69] Religious broadcasts
from abroad have enabled these isolated Catholics in China to have
communication with Christians in the west, though probably only
on a one-way basis. Letters have been written by the unofficial
Catholics in remote areas to Radio Veritas, the Catholic broadcast-
ing station in the Philippines. This may illustrate how the Chinese
Catholics respond to the Christian message.[70] Much has been
published about them outside China even in book form, but except
for those who died martyrs' deaths, those mentioned in these
narratives are referred to under pseudonyms for obvious reasons.[71]

Both in principle and practice it is most unreasonable of the
Beijing government to categorise all the religious activities performed outside church buildings and party supervision as illegal and

---

[67] L. Ladany, 'The church in China seen in December 1980'.

[68] This was reported in the internally circulated news of the Jesuits on China published by the
Jesuits, see *Correspondence* (Manila: Provincial Office for the Chinese Apostolate) 5 (September–October 1982) (hereafter cited as *Correspondence*.) Heyndrickx's Report, p. 35.

[69] The source came from Agence France Presse, and it was reported by Hong Kong *South China
Morning Post* (Hong Kong), 23 September 1986, and *Sing Tao Jih Po* (European edn) 24
September 1986.

[70] See Appendix II, The English translation of 'A letter from a Catholic in Qinghai'.

[71] *The Silent Church* (n.p., n.d.). *If the Grain of Wheat Dies . . . Fr. Francis Xavier Chu Shu-tek S.J.*,
(n.p., n.d.). [It was privately circulated six months after the death of Fr. Francis Xavier Zhu
(Chu).]

abnormal.[72] Bishop K. H. Ting of the Anglican church, the president of the Christian Three Selfs Movement, and a Committee member of the CPPCC, openly admitted this in a conference. He said:

The implementation of the religious policy meets with many obstacles. Few churches have been reopened and most of the Christians hold their prayer meetings in private homes ... I, as one of the leaders of the Three Selfs Patriotic Association should not like to say that such home meetings are illegal. One cannot interpret the Constitution in the sense that there is freedom of belief in a church building and not in families. We should not have a Three Self Patriotic Movement merely for a small number of people. All must be united.[73]

In spite of that the government is still very cautious about the development of the unofficial Catholics in China and tries to curb it by various measures through the patriotic religious organisations. Thus, in the name of the Chinese Catholic Bishops' Conference and the Chinese Catholic Church Administrative Commission a set of regulations concerning the administering of the sacraments by the clergy was issued in 1986. The following are meant to restrict the unofficial clergy from administering sacraments.

1 Every clergyman's authority to administer the sacraments must come through the permission of the properly authorised bishop or diocesan head. It must also be reported to the proper church administrative commission at the provincial, city or autonomous region level. If a clergyman goes to another diocese he must carry an introductory letter from his own bishop or diocesan head before administering the sacraments or saying Mass.[74]

2 A clergyman who has been punished and stripped of his political rights due to violating the law immediately and automatically loses his authority to administer the sacraments. For the above mentioned clergyman to have his authority to administer the sacraments restored it must be approved by the local church administrative commission (provincial, city or autonomous region.) Afterwards, the properly authorised bishop or diocesan head of the place will again bestow the authority upon him.[75]

Obviously these regulations are meant to eliminate the rights of

[72] 'Document 19', para. 10.
[73] *Renmin Ribao*, 11 September 1982.
[74] *Catholic Church in China* 1 (March 1987): 24–5.
[75] Ibid.

the unofficial clergy who secretly perform their pastoral duties, while at the same time they are under pressure to subordinate themselves to the CPA bishops and the official church organisations. The second regulation is more apparently for the dissident clergy who fearlessly resume their pastoral work after they have been released from jail or from the labour camps.

The Chinese Bishops' Conference in the 1980s

On 2 May 1980, more than 200 Catholic delegates gathered in Beijing to participate in the joint conference held by the third national meeting of the Chinese Catholic Patriotic Association and the General Meeting of Chinese Catholics. In this joint conference it was decided that a Chinese Bishop's Conference and a Catholic Administrative Committee should be set up to deal with administration within the Catholic church in China. This mode of administration changed the role of the CPA from running the church administration to the liaison agent between the church and state as well as the party. From that time onwards, most external dealings, such as entertaining foreign religious visitors, negotiating with government on the return of church property, are entrusted to the care of the CPA, while pastoral activities and church's internal administration are the sphere of concern of bishops, priests and religious sisters.

The government sanctioned Bishop of Shanghai, Zhang Jiashu, was the first president of the Chinese Bishops' Conference which has thirty-three members and seven vice presidents. The Conference was not very active at the beginning of its establishment. However, the ice began to break when they set up three committees at the second meeting of the Conference in 1986. These committees are the Seminary Education Committee (headed by Bishop Louis Jin of Shanghai), the Liturgical Reform committee (headed by Dong Guangqing of Wuhan, Wubei Province) and the Theological Research Committee (headed by Bishop Tu Sihua, the Rector of the Beijing national Seminary). It has been recently said that these commitee heads are making moves on behalf of their committees.

As far as the Catholic Administrative Committee was concerned, both its membership and its functions were confused with those of the Chinese Bishops' Conference, because most of the members of the Chinese Bishops' Conference were members of the Catholic Administration Committee. The Chinese' Bishops Conference in China is a national organisation with no regional subdivisions. This is in contrast to the Administrative Committee which is organised on the provincial, county and even municipal levels.

As a matter of fact, the Bishops' Conference has been more active and has taken the initiative in church matters. For the sake of unity and formality, when the Bishops' Conference made any declaration, it was issued in the joint names of these two highest-ranking Catholic organisations. The Chinese Bishops' Conference provided a platform for the Chinese bishops to express their views and to get support from one another so much so that in the Conference bishops were able to take the initiative to discuss sensitive issues like how to be in communion with the universal church, their relationship with the Pope and so forth. At the Bishops' Conference held in April 1989, the Conference made a resolution that they support the position and authority of Pope John Paul II as the supreme pontiff.[76] This was an important step to take in the matter of doctrine enabling the Chinese Bishops' Conference to move closer to the universal church. Without the Conference as a platform, this step would have been unthinkable.[77]

At the same Conference, it was decided that the Chinese Bishops' Conference should have the final say on church administrative matters while the CPA only implement the decision of the Conference, not the other way round.

However there are Chinese bishops who do not belong to the government-sanctioned Chinese Bishops' Conference and they have been carrying out their pastoral duties outside the sphere of the CPA. Their episcopal ordinations were done clandestinely. Their appointments were approved by the Vatican but not by the Chinese government. Though these bishops have little contact with the ones in the Conference, they have a common goal of exercising pastoral duties in various ways. It was reported that a meeting of some of these non-governmental appointed bishops was convened on 21 November 1989 at Zhangerce, a village in Sanyuan district north of Xian, the capital of Shaanxi province in north-west China. The meeting decided to establish their own Bishops conference. The meeting also chose three Vatican approved bishops who did not attend the meeting as the episcopal conference officers. Bishop Fan Xueyan of Baoding, aged eighty-two who was reported missing, was

---

[76] Catholic Life Weekly (1 June 1989).
[77] Antony Lam, 'The Chinese Bishops' Conference in Beijing' *Tripod 56 (April 1990): 51–6.*

named as the president. Two honorary presidents were nominated. They were Archbishop Deng Yiming of Guangzhou, who is staying in Hong Kong, and Bishop Gong Pinmei of Shanghai, now living in the United States. The participants of this meeting had in mind not only to set up a bishops conference for those who were loyal to the Pope but one which eventually would incorporate the whole Chinese church.[78] Shortly after the Zhangerce meeting, all the participants were arrested by China's Security Officers, and after more arrests took place, it was reported that more than thirty Catholics were apprehended by the authorities after the meeting.[79] The arrests reflect that the government could not tolerate the growing influence of the non-official sector of the Catholic church. The establishment of their own hierarchy meant that they had taken a big step ahead to institutionalise their 'uncontrollable' religious activities.

The Vatican reacted very cautiously to this new bishops conference and the arrests. In the first place the Vatican was caught between the establishment of this new Chinese bishops conference to which it could not give its approval. On the other hand the Vatican could not ask it to be disbanded. First of all these were a group of church leaders who had been suffering persecution for no other reason than their loyalty to the Pope. Now they had organised themselves and institutionalised their loyalty, the Vatican in principle should welcome it with open arms. Unfortunately it was very bad timing; the Vatican was at the beginning of the long procedure of negotiating with the China. But the setting up of the conference had been mainly stimulated by the negotiations. The non-official sector of the Chinese church was afraid that the Sino-Vatican rapprochement would take place at their expense. Therefore they organised themselves and claimed that they were the authentic Chinese bishops conference.

Through some channels, the Vatican indirectly gave its negative opinions on this matter, by alluding to the set up as imprudent and hastily timed. It was reported that a middle-ranking Vatican official, Fr. Paul Pang, the head of Overseas Chinese Apostolate of the Sacred Congregation (SCEP), revealed that the SCEP even asked the Zhangerce organisers not to set up a conference.[80]

[78] *Asia Focus*, 17 March 1990.
[79] Ibid.
[80] Ibid., 31 March 1990.

At this juncture, the identities of these non-government approved bishops was revealed; it remains to be seen whether they can continue to exercise their pastoral duties as before without the interference of the Chinese government. How to solve the problem of the newly established Bishops Conference is yet another headache for the Vatican which already has too many problems to deal with in its relations with China.

REASONS FOR THE GREATER TOLERANCE IN RELIGIOUS POLICY

The United Front policy

From 1978, political leaders in China focused their attention on modernisation, and every state policy both internal and external was geared in this direction. It was realised that religion should have a role to play in promoting modernisation, and whilst the party acknowledged that the religious question could raise problems, it was also linked to the questions of the national minorities and international relations. The government instructed its cadres that the religious question must be pragmatically and carefully handled.[81] The reason for granting religious relaxation can be understood in the light of the famous United Front policy of the CCP.

As early as the days of combat with the Japanese in the 1930s Mao with great certainty admitted that

It also means that our eighteen years of experience have taught us that the United Front, armed struggle and party-building are the Chinese Communist party's three magic weapons for defeating the enemy in the Chinese revolution.[82]

Making use of the contradictions amongst the masses, Mao's strategy aimed at winning the majority to his side and uniting every possible element that could be united, in order to isolate the enemy and destroy him.[83] In 1983, the veteran director of the United Front Department, Yang Jingren, explained the new application of the

---

[81] 'Document 19', para. 11.
[82] 'Introducing a Communist', *Selected Works of Mao Zedong*, vol. 2 (Beijing: Foreign Languages Press, 1975), pp. 285–96.
[83] Li Weihan, 'Mao Zedong Sixiang Zhidao Xia De Zhongguo Tongyi Zhanxian' [The Chinese United Front policy under the guidance of Mao Zedong thought], *Renmin Ribao*, 17 December 1983. *Hongqi* 24 (16 December 1983): 14–23.

United Front policy in the era of modernisation. It was aimed at uniting every possible force, mobilising every possible element, and transforming negative elements into positive power to work for modernisation. He mentioned specifically the categories of people whom Hu Yaobang had named as the target to be won over by the United Front policy. They were non-Communist intellectuals, patriotic religious leaders and leaders of national minorities, members of the democratic parties, non-party prominent figures, former industrialists, Chinese in Hong Kong, Macau and Taiwan and returned overseas Chinese, etc.[84] Reading through the categories listed by Hu Yaobang one obtained the impression that now the CCP was even trying to be friendly with those who should have been regarded as class enemies because of their sharply contradictory ideology.

Surprisingly, as days passed, a still greater relaxation in this regard was accorded by the United Front. *Renmin Ribao* of 20 February 1986 contained an article called 'Tongyi Zhanxian De Xin Fazhan' [The New Development of the United Front], pointing out that the United Front of this era is a patriotic one. Patriotism has become the political demarcation line. The article states,

We are not mindful of the difference in nationalities, class qualities, party division, religious faith, nor ideological and political attitudes. Even those who have done something to oppose the people before, now so long as they support the unification of our motherland we shall unite them under the banner of patriotism ... In other words, the international structure of the United Front under this new definition has undergone a basic change, and now that the great majority of the exploiting class has been reformed into proletariat the intellectuals have already become part of the proletariat.[85]

It appears that the CCP is trying to lose no time in mobilising the religious believers as well as intellectuals as part of the reservoir of manpower for the development of the nation. It is interesting to note that religious groups have suddenly become a valuable target for the CCP to win over instead of to attack. However, this does not mean that all the religious believers are intellectuals who can contribute their brain-power and technological know-how for modernisation. But the intellectuals and the religious believers, especially the religious leaders, belong to the same category of ideological non-

[84] Yang Jingren, 'Xinshichi De Tongyi Zhanxian' [The United Front of this new era], *Hongqi* 7 (1983): 2–7.
[85] Chen Andong, 'Tongyi Zhanxian De Xin Fazhang' [The new development of the United Front], *Renmin Ribao* (overseas edn), 20 February 1986.

conformists in the eyes of the CCP.[86] The intellectuals would feel uneasy and lose their confidence in the government and the party, even if they were enjoying a certain amount of freedom, if their non-conforming religious partners were subjected to repression. They would think that the freedom that they were enjoying might be short-lived. If intolerance were shown to other sectors of non-conformists, under some pretext or other, sooner or later it could be shown to the intellectuals as a whole too. Freedom in religious activities is one of the essential parts of the whole package deal of tolerance and relaxation which is vital in attracting intellectuals to participate in modernisation. Intolerance towards any sector of non-conformists would have negative effects on all the categories which the CCP hopes to draw into the United Front. For example, the Chinese Muslims might not believe in the central government if the Chinese Catholics were persecuted for religious reasons. Therefore granting religious freedom to believers of all world religions could be one of China's strategies to mobilise the Patriotic United Front for the purpose of modernisation.

Also the relaxation of ideological control enables the Patriotic Front to broaden its contacts and appeal for help from the overseas Chinese, and Chinese in Hong Kong, Macau and Taiwan for their support in modernisation. The loosening of the grip in ideological discipline would be always welcome to this group of people who have knowledge and personal experience of freedom of belief in the west. The national minorities, that is, the Muslims in Xinjiang, Ningxia and Gansu, etc. as well as Buddhists in Tibet, suffered a great deal in the Cultural Revolution when their customs were greatly undermined. Now the Chinese government is eager to terminate this ill-feeling and unite them on the basis of equality, solidarity, mutual assistance and fraternity, as emphasised by Zhao Ziyang in his report on the government at the Sixth NPC, 6 June 1983. Religious freedom can be taken as one of the best tactics to demonstrate the respect shown by the central government, especially when religion is known to be one of the important elements in cultural life.[87]

[86] For a detailed comparison of intellectuals of integrity and religious believers as ideological non-conformists, the two categories of people the Communist leaders have little liking for and show little favour to, see Beatrice Leung, *Sino-Vatican Conflict* (1976–1982) (unpublished M.A. Dissertation, University of Hong Kong, 1983), pp. 71–86.

[87] Zhao Ziyang, 'Report on the work of the government', *Beijing Review* 27 (4 July 1983): II–XXIV.

The break-away from the Cultural Revolution

Although many China observers hold the opinion that religious policies were eased initially as part of the United Front, yet one has reason to argue that this trend started as part of the general need to break away from the Cultural Revolution. Catholics, for example, like many intellectuals, had suffered so much that they were no longer afraid of the CCP. The CCP after Mao was admitting to having condemned so many persons and so many ideas quite wrongly that Catholics and others who had been criticised in the past could present themselves as having been falsely accused. And what could the CCP say to that? One could see the United Front as a CCP formula or strategy to get over this. In other words, the CCP was no longer believed when it denounced people as 'anti-party' or 'reactionary', since, after all, practically all the best people including Deng himself, had been accused of such a crime. So Catholics could throw off their dunce's caps and be rehabilitated. In fact, the Jesuits and some other unofficial Catholics have been so fearless in openly receiving foreigners, discussing religion and reviving their religious activities as to cause the re-arrest of some in 1981. It is a good example of this kind of fearlessness.[88] Since they could neither be attacked nor dominated so easily, the CCP decided to try to draw these non-conformist religious believers into an alliance, the United Front. The tactic has been used throughout the CCP's history, as in dealing with the KMT, for instance. But some of them had gone beyond the prescribed limit of the party, therefore they were re-arrested, although the act of arrest was an act counter to the United Front policy.

Contribution of religious believers to modernisation

In the more relaxed social milieu of China in the 1980s individuals are entitled to keep their religious beliefs in private; and religious believers in principle are not purged wholesale as 'rightists' and 'reactionaries' as in the time of the Cultural Revolution. The religious believers should have an easier life. In a firm or in a working unit religious believers are allowed to keep their own type of belief in God no matter who their fellow colleagues and their

[88] *Sunday Examiner* (Hong Kong), 21 August 1981, 11 December 1981.

superiors are, so long as they can contribute to modernisation. In fact, some religious believers are reported to make outstanding contributions, partly due to their religious convictions and partly for other reasons. Some have been acclaimed as outstanding teachers, model nurses, red-banner women, pace setters; and some Christian families themselves have become model families while some Christians have been elected as labour heroes. In Shanghai, for example, it was reported that more than 300 Protestant Christians had won titles of honour because they had contributed to the national development in various ways. A Catholic village in Zhangjiakou, Hebei Province, was given recognition as a progressive village for its production success. Compared with the total Chinese population of one billion, of which 3.8 million are Catholics and three million Protestants, 300 is a very small minority, and one village is an insignificant entity amongst the vast numbers of villages. But these cases have been often quoted in international meetings by religious leaders both from the Catholic and Protestant churches to demonstrate how Christians can be patriotic and at the same time carry out their religious activities.[89] These cases are good examples to illustrate the attitude of the Chinese government, in that it allows Chinese citizens to embrace religion as a private matter. In so doing, it expects the religious believers to be motivated by their religious belief and so share the responsibility for promoting national development, as shown in the above instances. However, in terms of costs and benefits, while the Chinese government grants freedom of worship, which is only one aspect of Catholic life, it also jealously guards the other two essential aspects, such as religious doctrine and hierarchical structure. These remain untouched. In granting the first aspect the authorities expect to receive support from within as well as assistance from abroad in terms of technological know-how and financial aid. By 1986 China had succeeded in getting help from the Hong Kong Caritas and the Caritas of Switzerland, and other overseas Catholic social service institutions, in the training of managers for the hotel and tourist industry and in the establishment of medical and welfare services for handicapped children in Guang-

---

[89] Michael Fu, 'Zhongguo Tianzhujiao Shenzhi Jiaoyou Wei Jiduo Zuo Jiancheng' [The Catholic laity and clergy witnessed for Christ], *Catholic Church in China* 4 (March 1982): 30–2. Shen Yifen, 'Some theological reflections on being a local pastor in New China', *China Study Project Bulletin* (Kent, UK) 29 (January 1986): 11–17.

dong, Sichuan and Fujian provinces, as well as in Shanghai city. For these projects the German Miserior, a Catholic funding agency, gave H.K.$ 2 million (£200,000); and the Swiss Caritas spent H.K.$180,000 (£18,000).[90] The overseas Protestants' donations for social projects have been channelled through the Amity Foundation.[91] The Muslims in China try to raise funds from their fellow Muslims abroad for social developments in certain areas where Muslims are clustered. Through the generosity of Christian universities in the west scholarships have been offered for the further education abroad of Chinese students regardless of their religious beliefs.[92]

CONCLUSION

The revival of religious activities in China in the modernisation era is due to the effects of relaxation of ideological control. Both for domestic and external reasons the government does not find it opportune to exercise as strong a grip on religion as it had before. Therefore the revival of the religious freedom policy has been announced and guidelines have been drawn up to ensure that religious activities are carried out within stated limits. Moreover, scholars of religion were asked to provide appropriate explanations in Marxist theory for the new policy.

At this stage, many Chinese Catholics continuously refuse to carry out the state's demand to cut off ties with the Holy See. Nevertheless, there is a limited revival of Catholic life both in the official and unofficial sectors of the Chinese Catholic church. Yet, no Communist state can allow any organisation to exist in its domain without attempting to exercise its full authority over it. Therefore, constraints are imposed on the unofficial Catholics through the CPA which in turn has no alternative but to carry out its duties assigned by the government. In fact it would be unrealistic to expect no governmental limits to the freedom granted to the Chinese Catho-

90 *Annual Report on Hong Kong-Caritas 1984–85.* p. 16; Ibid. *1985–86.* pp. 69–75.
91 Peter Barry, 'Amity: Christian outreach in China', *Tripod* 27 (June 1985): 35–45. In *Tripod* 23 (October 1984): 97, it was reported that in August 1984 Muslims from Ningxia visited Hong Kong with the hope to promote economic and religious ties between Hong Kong and Ningxia.
92 The F. Verbiest Foundation of the Catholic Louven University in Belgium offers scholarships to Chinese students regardless of their religious beliefs.

lics. The problem for the party is to ensure that religion in general and Catholicism in particular should remain under its supervision, while at the same time trying to create an image world-wide that religious freedom is prevailing in China. Thus, great care is required by the party in handling the religious question.

CHAPTER 6

Constraints on the freedom of the Catholic religion

Introduction

The Chinese government presents its policy as one of 'Religious Freedom' or 'Freedom in Religion'. The term 'religious freedom' itself is debatable. Every official document issued from Beijing that discusses the tolerance displayed towards religious believers explains it with reference to the state's current practice of the policy of freedom of religious worship. A question arises as to why the greater freedom, though it is laudable, relates only to religious worship, but not to all aspects of religious life, for the Catholic church especially. The new freedom operates with regard to only the first of the three aspects that together constitute organised Catholic religion, namely: worship, doctrine and religious hierarchy.

To give freedom to the external and visible part of religion in order to cater to the needs of foreign diplomats may impress foreign visitors and satisfy the needs of believers, but by reserving the right to keep tight control over the substantial and basic part of the religion China's government may be said to display the true character of its religious policy towards the Catholic church.

Let us consider the question of doctrine: the Second Vatican Council (1963–5) changed the presentation of doctrine with the aim of invigorating the Catholic faith by making it more relevant to the modern world.[1] Not only were the Chinese church leaders not allowed to participate in the Second Vatican Council, but also a state order was issued forbidding the postal entry to China of any religious material concerning the Council.[2] It is no wonder that both the liturgy and the development of doctrine in the Chinese

[1] 'Lumen Gentium' and 'Gaudium et Spes', *The Documents of Vatican II* (London: Geoffrey Chapman, 1966), pp. 14–101, 199–308.
[2] *Xinhua News*, 27 January 1981. *Wen Wei Po* (Xianggang) 28 January 1981.

Catholic church has remained so archaic, with Latin Mass celebrated by a priest facing the wall. Yet, strangely, there is evidence to
suggest that Chinese Catholics prefer the traditional ritual, probably
because they see it as a return to true orthodoxy after the winter of
the Cultural Revolution.

Chinese Catholics are deprived of the right to have a spiritual link
with the Holy See and they are refused the right to acknowledge the
Pope as the supreme leader of the universal church inclusive of the
Chinese Catholic church. Thus, although much has been done by
the Chinese government for various reasons in making religious
expression so much more vigorous than before, yet there can be no
doubt that religion is still under constraint. In this chapter various
incidents will be discussed in order to throw some light on the degree
to which the Catholics operate under constraint in China. These
questions will be surveyed from the legal, political and religious
points of view, and particular emphasis will be given to the crucial
problem relating to the independence from the Holy See.

CONSTRAINTS

Religious freedom and the constitution

Zhao Ziyang in his government report to the Sixth National
Congress in 1983 announced that the state was trying to put more
emphasis on the legal system, and that henceforth people of every
walk of life including officials in urban and rural areas would be
expected to base their social, political actions on law.[3] Article 36 of
the 1982 Constitution states clearly that citizens of the People's
Republic of China enjoy freedom of religious belief.[4]

China's political leaders have made it clear that the State
Constitution will carry more weight in the days to come in every
aspect of life, not only because of the need to restore legal procedures, but also because of their concern to establish order in society
and especially order in production.[5] Nevertheless, this oft-quoted
term 'freedom of religion' cannot be regarded in isolation, but must

[3] Zhao Ziyang, 'Report on the work of the Government', *Beijing Review* 27 (4 July 1983):
ii–xxiv.
[4] *The Constitution of the People's Republic of China 1982* (Beijing: Foreign Languages Press, 1982),
art. 36.
[5] Zhao Ziyang, 'Report on the work of government', *Beijing Review* 27 (4 July 1983):
ii–xxiv.

be examined within the context of the constitutional and administrative law of a Communist party state as a whole. It cannot be understood by reference to the constitutions of liberal democratic states.

S. A. de Smith defines the nature of Constitutional Law stating that the constitution and the related administrative law are primarily concerned with political authority and power – that is the location, confirment, distribution, exercise and limitation of authority and power among the organs of a state. It is concerned with matters of procedure as well as substance. It also includes explicit guarantee of rights and freedom of individuals, and incorporates ideological pronouncements and statements of the citizens' duties.[6] In a democratic society the concept of 'rule of law' implies that the rulers as well as the governed should be subject to law. Recently, J. Triska, a scholar of Comparative Law, defined the distinction between the constitution of a Communist party state and a traditional western democratic government. His comparison might throw some light on our understanding of the CCP's concept of freedom of religion and its way of interpreting it. He remarked that, in the tradition of western democratic society, constitutionalism is a venerated concept. It defines a political structure in which law rather than man is supreme. Political authority is exercised according to law which is obeyed by all, including those who govern. By definition a constitutional government is a limited government deliberately adopted by the people governed by it. The constitution limits the powers of the constituent organs; its authority and sanction is the highest in the political system. The constitution is thus endowed with a superior, moral, binding force. As it reflects the will of the people, the constitution therefore receives broad social support.[7]

Triska argues that the Communist party state constitutions do not limit the respective governments, instead they are themselves limited by the ruling party's principal decision-makers. Man is supreme, not law. Hence Communist state constitutions are not symbols of freedom as are those in western democracies. They have no great moral force nor are they necessarily broadly supported. As the major instrumentalities of the rulers, they are obeyed, but they are not

---

[6] S. A. de Smith, *Constitutional and Administrative Law*, 3rd edn (London: Penguin Books, 1977), p. 18.
[7] Jan. J. Triska (ed.), *Constitutions of the Communist Party States* (Stanford University, The Hoover Institute of War, Revolution and Peace, 1968), Preface.

cherished. Moreover, because they serve the rulers, rather than limiting them, the norms which they contain are interpreted from the sole point of view of the interest of the state as determined by the rulers.[8] This kind of constitution of a single party state is apt to be something of a political manifesto. In such constitutions, however, lip service may still be paid to basic freedoms of the individual, as remarked by S. A. de Smith.[9]

At this point, one starts to wonder how the implementation of freedom of religion can take place as it should when the notion of God is incompatible with atheist ideology. Furthermore, freedom of speech and expression, freedom of assembly and association, and freedom of religion and conscience are intimately related, as further noted by S. A. de Smith. If serious encroachments are made on any of them, some or all will diminish. He argued that the most precarious freedom is the right to express one's opinion and to associate with like-minded persons for the purpose of opposing the government.[10] Could the CCP allow this to happen in China? Hu Yaobang, Secretary General of the CCP, gave his answer, in his article 'Guanyu Dang De Xinwen Gongjiao' [On the Journalistic Work of the Party] in *Hongqi* no. 8, 1985 where he stated in no uncertain terms that journalists should be the mouthpiece of the party and literary writers should necessarily have to toe the party line.[11] Even though Hu personally had to resign as General Secretary of the party in January 1987 for allegedly being too soft on 'bourgeois liberalism', his speech to the journalists in 1985 showed that even he was no liberal and may be taken as representing mainline CCP attitudes. How about religious matters? It is also a fact that the freedom of religion cannot be fully guaranteed unless the freedom of expression about one's belief is granted as well. Therefore even in principle it is only a limited form of freedom of religion that has been given and by prescribing the details of religious activites that may be carried out the party has retained the right to exercise constraints. It has also explained the purpose of that freedom in instrumental terms.

It is true that in China freedom is promised by the Constitution,

[8] Ibid.
[9] S. A. de Smith, *Constitutional and Administrative Law*, p. 30.
[10] Ibid.
[11] Hu Yaobang, 'Guanyu Dang De Xinwen Gongjiao' [On the journalist work of the party], *Hongqi* 8 (1985): 1–4.

but in reality the Communist party has the right to refuse to give protection to that freedom. In fact, when law is practised in a Communist state the individual takes second place to the state. Personal freedom is always subject to the convenience of the state.[12] Therefore when one surveys the other provisions in the Constitution about the need to uphold the socialist order, all these qualify Article 36 the article on religious freedom. Take the following articles in the Chinese Constitution of 1982 for example:

Article 15
Disturbance of the orderly functioning of the social economy or disruption of the state economic plan by any organisation or individual is prohibited.

Article 25
The state promotes family planning so that the population growth may fit the plan for economic and social development.

So if Chinese Catholics do not follow the state's recommendations of seeking abortion and artificial birth control and fail to promote family planning they commit an act of violation of Article 25 of the State's Constitution.

Article 28
The State maintains public order and suppresses treasonable and other counter-revolutionary activities.

As usual any dissident, including any religious dissident who has communication with the outside world, could be accused of carrying out treasonable counter-revolutionary activity, releasing state secrets to foreigners. China keeps on treating those who refuse to cut off their spiritual ties with the Vatican as dissenters. Many of them have been put into prison, and they are accused of acting against the Constitution and of being 'counter-revolutionary'.[13] Chinese officials hold the opinion that there are two groups of Catholics, that is: 'one blindly follows the Roman Curia and betrays its own nation

[12] Zhang Youyu, 'Yige Bixu Renzheng Yanjiu Tansuo De Wenti' [A problem which must be researched seriously], *Zhongguo Faxue* 2 (1987): 1–10.
[13] Gong Pinmei, 'Shengsu Shu' [The Letter of Appeal] in Beatrice Leung, 'Sino-Vatican relations: problems in conflicting authority (1976–1986)', unpublished Ph.D. dissertation, University of London 1988, pp. 419–52. Hereafter cited as Gong, 'The Letter of Appeal'. *Xinwen Ribao* (Shanghai), 9 September 1955. On that day Gong was arrested together with twenty-seven priests and 300 lay Catholics, as anti-revolutionary, because they all supported the Legion of Mary, and Bishop Gong had excommunicated Catholics who belonged to the CPA. Also see *Jiefang Ribao* (Shanghai), 9 September 1955, 10 September 1955, 14 September 1955, 16 September 1955; the Editorials in *Renmin Ribao*, 10 December 1955, 11 December 1955.

and engages in counter-revolutionary activites, whilst the other follows the Commandments of God, fervently loves its own nation, upholds the purity of the church, and accepts the policy of independently managing church affairs'.[14] It is clear that those who are attached to the Holy See are to be regarded as counter-revolutionary. Further, their action is said to violate the Chinese Constitution which demands punishment for counter-revolutionary acts.[15]

All the Chinese Constitutions have claimed to guarantee religious freedom. The articles on religious belief contained in all the past Constitutions of the PRC, inclusive of the latest one published in 1982, run as follows:

1954 Constitution Article 88
Citizens of the People's Republic of China enjoy freedom of religious belief.

1975 Constitution Article 28
Citizens enjoy freedom of speech, correspondence, the press, assembly, association, demonstration, the freedom to strike, and enjoy freedom to believe in religion and freedom not to believe in religion and to propagate atheism.

1978 Constitution Article 46
Citizens enjoy freedom to believe in religion and freedom not to believe in religion and to propagate atheism.

1982 Constitution Article 36
Citizens of the People's Republic of China enjoy freedom of religious belief. No organs of state, public organisations or individuals shall compel citizens to believe in religion or disbelieve in religion, nor shall they discriminate against citizens who believe or do not believe in religion.
The state protects legitimate religious activities. No one may use religion to carry out counter-revolutionary activities or activities that disrupt public order, harm the health of citizens or obstruct the educational systems of the state. No religious affairs may be dominated by any foreign country.

The assertion of religious freedom is not an innovation brought into the 1982 constitution. It has been proclaimed by the government since the 1954 Constitution. However there is a new paragraph in the 1982 Constitution, stating: 'No religious affairs may be dominated by any foreign country.' Needless to say, this is aimed directly at the Vatican as well as potentially at other religions such as Islam and the Tibetan Buddhists. It may be seen as a strong

---

[14] *Catholic Church in China* 5 (September 1982) reported the speech of Tong Lidiao, the Secretary General of the CPA, on this theme.
[15] Lei Zhenchang, 'Dang Dui Zongjiao Wenti De Jiben Zhengce' [The basic policy of the party on religion], *Guangming Ribao*, 27 June 1982.

reaction against the Pope's 'interference', i.e. the appointment of the Archbishop of Guangzhou.

However, the Chinese government gives a very clear definition of the meaning of the provision for freedom of religious belief enjoyed by Chinese citizens. That is that 'citizens enjoy the freedom to believe or not believe this or that religion. Within one religion, citizens are free to believe in this or that denomination. Citizens also enjoy the freedom to change from one religion to another or change from believing religion to not believing religion.'[16] In short the Constitution protects the citizens' rights to believe in any religion.[17] However, if one looks carefully into the demand of the government of the Chinese Catholics since the establishment of the PRC, one may see the other side of the coin. Those who aim at retaining a religious relationship with the Holy See are committing, in the eyes of the Chinese government, an act of violation of the Constitution itself.

One of the essential parts of the Catholic faith is the communion with the Holy See, the Vicar of Christ. Any local church which cuts away from the Holy See can no longer be called a member of the Catholic church, but it could still regard itself as a denomination of Christianity. The Catholic church in England, for example, at the time of King Henry VIII, adhered in liturgy and doctrine very closely to the Roman Catholic church; yet when the English Catholics, whether under political pressure from the king or not, declared their independence from Rome, and made the head of the state the head of their church, they were no longer adherents of the Catholic church and became adherents of a new Christian denomination known as the Church of England.

When the Chinese government through Zhou Enlai in the early 1950s requested the Chinese Catholics to cut off political and economic relations with the Holy See, the Chinese Catholics headed by Bishop Gong of Shanghai accepted the demand, provided they were allowed to retain spiritual ties with the Pope.[18] But those who executed religious policy in the 1950s insisted that the Catholics had to cut every tie with Rome, disregarding Zhou's promise to allow the spiritual tie to be kept.[19] Even so the government in the 1950s had

[16] Ibid.
[17] Ibid.
[18] Gong, 'The Letter of Appeal', para. 4.
[19] Ibid.

no difficulty in finding an excuse to carry out religious persecution of the Catholics, especially as the Constitution of 1954 had not laid down so clearly as the later Constitution of 1982 that no organs of state should compel citizens to believe in religion or disbelieve in religion. Therefore one has reason to think that the act of compelling Chinese Catholics to cut off relations with the Pope *ipso facto* is going against the Chinese Constitution, especially the new constitution of 1982, which so clearly states in great detail that the government protects religious freedom. The Chinese government looks at the whole thing from political and cultural points of view and would regard acknowledging that mainly the moral and to some degree the temporal authority rested with a foreign state – i.e. the Vatican – as an act of counter-revolution, because the Chinese political leaders would not allow their authority to be shared with a religious leader such as the Pope. Anyway, whether it is a question of temporal or moral authority, the line is less clear-cut. If it were a question of moral authority alone, religion itself would be forbidden altogether. However the CCP responded at several levels simultaneously to this question: (i) as national Communists who demand the cutting of ties with western 'imperialist' cultural institutions, (ii) as Chinese who sought to re-establish an authentic Chinese culture (of a new form), (iii) as political leaders who wished to stamp out alternative sources of political authority. As a matter of fact, the distinction between spiritual and temporal authority is unknown in the Chinese tradition and it is not very clear in the west either. Finally, the analysis of the CCP's tolerance must take into account the leaders' ideological views about the stage of historical development in which China was thought to be at any given time. For example, in the Great Leap Forward and the Cultural Revolution China was defined as being in a relatively advanced period of Socialism which restricted very severely the tolerance for religion of any kind, but since 1981 the official view has been that China is in the preliminary stage of Socialism; that means more ideological tolerance is allowed.

The arrest of catholics

It is not within the scope of this book to discuss the reasons which led the Chinese government to carry out the arrests of Catholics in the 1950s such as the arrest in the Shanghai area of Bishop Gong, twenty-seven priests and 300 Catholic laity in September 1955, and the putting behind bars of Bishop Deng and another group of clergy and laity in South China.[20] Yet here one must inevitably ask why in Deng's modernisation period, after the launching of the religious freedom policy in 1979, when churches began to re-open, and religious delegates were sent abroad to cultivate friendship with other Christians, were some Protestant and Catholic dissenters arrested, including Shanghai Catholics headed by the Jesuit Father Vincent Zhu? In 1955, Zhu himself had been jailed together with other Shanghai Catholics and Bishop Gong. Zhu and the other priests, some of them over sixty, had spent twenty and more years in labour camps, and then were paroled from indefinite sentences in the period of liberalisation. Father Zhu had often been quoted by foreign and Chinese visitors as saying that he believed his contacts with them were within the letter of the law as he understood it, after the opening of China's current modernisation programme. However, he was also quoted as saying that he was being watched and occasionally harassed by security agents. In fact these Jesuits kept on refusing to cut off their religious ties with the Holy See, and received many foreign visitors, and it was for this reason that they were re-arrested and sent back to labour camps.[21] Father Zhu did not leave the city area of Shanghai from the time of his release from the camp in 1979 until his re-arrest in 1981, but visitors kept on streaming to see him. In fact he communicated with a broad range of foreigners, including diplomats and journalists stationed in China as well as visitors from abroad, amongst whom were some officials from US Catholic universities.

Other groups of priests were arrested in Wuzhou, Guangxi Province, on the day before a funeral service for a ninety-year-old priest on 22 July 1981. Eyewitnesses reported that seventy security police were involved in the raid and that the police searched the house and took away vestments, food and money. It was reported that the authorities gave no reason for the action. The funeral was planned to honour the memory of the old priest Father Tang, who was widely known and respected in the city for his pastoral care and the traditional Chinese medical assistance he gave many people in the area. It was also reported that the Catholics there were

[20] *Kung Kao Po*, 1 October 1952. 'Brief outline of the life of Bishop Gong Pinmei', *Tripod* 26 (April 1985): 58.
[21] *Ming Pao*, 21 August 1981. *Sunday Examiner* (Hong Kong), 21 August 1981, 11 December 1981. *Kung Kao Po* (Xianggang), 18 September 1981.

dismayed, and said 'The priests are doing nothing illegal since freedom of religion is guaranteed by China's Constitution as amended in 1978.'[22]

All these arrests took place after the row between China and the Vatican over the appointment of the Archbishop of Guangzhou, and when increasing pressure was being put on Chinese dissidents of all kinds – writers and artists as well as religious non-conformists – not to have contacts with foreigners.[23] The above cases were only the tip of the iceberg, and there were reports of arrests in remote areas which could not easily be authenticated.

Bishop Fan Xueyan was one of the last Chinese bishops consecrated by the Vatican in 1951 before the PRC demanded that Chinese Catholics sever ties with Rome. First arrested in 1958, he was then sentenced to fifteen years' imprisonment. He was later reported to have been placed under house arrest in a neighbouring village after the completion of his sentence, because the authorities continued to be suspicious of his popularity and influence in the diocese. Although under house arrest, Bishop Fan apparently engaged in religious activities independently of the official CPA, and even ordained priests. This is believed to have led to his second formal arrest during Summer 1983, when he was sentenced to ten years' imprisonment. Reports indicated that Bishop Fan's health had not been good for some time. It has recently been suggested not only that his health is deteriorating, but also that he does not have access to adequate medical care. Amnesty International believes that Bishop Fan is currently imprisoned in Shijiazhuang, the provincial capital of Hebei.[24]

It is definite that those being arrested are the ones who refused to join the CPA, and subsequently refused to be cut off from the Holy See. Such arrests and subjection to being watched and harassed by security agents could be illegal, since the Chinese Constitution guarantees freedom to believe in any kind of religion, including that of the authentic Roman Catholic church which requires its believers to have religious ties with the Pope, the Vicar of Christ. Yet the question of ties with the Pope is for the Chinese political leaders not a religious question but a political issue.

[22] *Sunday Examiner*, 25 September 1981.
[23] Ibid., 11 December 1981.
[24] Amnesty International, 'Health concern. People's Republic of China: Fan Xueyan', ASA 17/04/87 (4 June 1987).

Religious activities permitted by the government

There is a long official list of religious activities officially permitted by the government, such as worshipping the Buddha, chanting the scriptures, burning incense, praying, explaining the scriptures, preaching, saying Mass, baptising, initiating monks and nuns, fasting, celebrating religious festivals, annointing the sick, holding requiem services and so forth. Implicitly this indicates that any kind of religious activity not officially listed and approved by the government is not to be practised. It seems that the CCP tries to exercise its authority in deciding for different religions on matters that relate to religious practice. Probably the Chinese authorities intended to eliminate the prevalence of what they regard as superstition among peasants, who fail to differentiate between so-called 'superstitious practice' and 'religious worship'. But concerning religious doctrines, the practice is still more stringent. It is only with the approval of the relevant government department, that Buddhist and Taoist temples and Christian churches can sell a certain quantity of prayer books, Bibles, religious literature, religious articles and religious works of art. It is to be observed that prayers for the Pope are deleted from Catholic prayer books. This shows that the Chinese Catholics are not free even to pray for the Holy Father.

There are official religious publications issued by the patriotic religious associations of various religions, reporting religious activities and some sermons on some feast days. In these publications, the directives from the government to religious believers are faithfully reported at full length. But, judging from the number of copies printed, one is led to question whether the religious literature is sufficient by any stretch of the imagination to reach the general mass of the faithful. The *Zhongguo Tianzhujiao* [Catholic church in China] for example, is the official but irregular publication issued by the Chinese Catholic Patriotic Association. Each issue printed is barely 10,000 copies, yet there are 3.8 million Catholics in China. The 10,000 copies include those to be sent abroad for propaganda purposes.[25] The inadequate supply of religious reading material and of the Bible has led to the smuggling of Bibles into China. This in turn led to a hot debate among Christians abroad whether overseas

---

[25] In September 1984, the writer was told by religious cadres of the CPA in Beijing that not more than 10,000 copies of *Catholic Church in China* were printed of each issue. The chairman of the CPA, Bishop Zong Huaide reported that only 7,000 copies of *Catholic Church in China* were printed of each issue. See *Catholic Church in China* 7 (15 August 1983): 8.

Christians should or should not 'interfere' in China's internal religious affairs.[26] At one time, the Xinhua News Agency issued a list of customs regulations regarding parcels and mail sent to China. The list of prohibited objects included printed matter about missionaries, together with publications which offend the leaders of the Chinese Communist party and the country, those which attack the social system, or propagate obscenity, pornography, horror and violence.[27] In practice religious books sent from abroad were not allowed to pass through the Chinese customs, although occasionally they were permitted to be directed via the Religious Affairs Bureau or the CPA. It is deduced from the above regulations that religious literature meant to explain religious doctrine is in the eyes of the CCP something gravely offensive to the party leaders, who equate it with works that attack the social system, or propagate obscenity, pornography, horror and violence.

Party members and religious cadres

The central government made it clear in Document 19 that the policy on religion is directed towards the ordinary citizens, but is not applicable to the party members.[28] It was not a new declaration by the CCP, since the CCP is a Marxist party and all its members must profess atheism, which is naturally incompatible with religious beliefs.

In the cities, as well as in rural areas among the Han people, the staff of the Religious Affairs Bureau and the various religious patriotic associations pose some problems for the religious believers as well as for the government. The atheist party officials of the Bureau operating at various levels of the organisation cannot carry out the religious policy smoothly, mainly because they themselves are not religious believers and cannot understand and see religious questions as believers do. They also tend to find it difficult to follow the development of religious affairs at the international level. Bishop Wu reported that, during his visit to Guangdong, he asked the officials in the Religious Affairs Bureau not to look at the Catholic church of today as if it was still the same as it was in 1950. He

---

[26] See the following Hong Kong local newspapers and their comments on this issue: *Hong Kong Standard*, 8 November 1981, 17 January 1983. *Ming Pao*, 3 October 1981, 15 October 1981, 3 January 1982, 4 January 1982. *Wah Kui Yat Po*, 8 November 1981, 17 January 1983. *Wen Wei Pao*, 15 October 1981.

[27] *Xinhua News*, 27 January 1981. *Wen Wei Pao* (Xianggang), 28 January 1981.

[28] 'Document 19', para. 9.

told the Guangdong religious officials that the Catholic church has gone through great changes and has given greater autonomy to local bishops than before. Bishop Wu was able to speak out openly to these religious officials regarding their ignorance of religion since they originated from the same district as he does – Meixian, so the Bishop was in a familiar milieu. His words could carry weight because of his standing in the Catholic hierarchy as well as his knowledge of the greater autonomy of bishops since the Second Vatican Council.

The CCP allotted posts in the CPA to priests on whom the state authorities could rely but who were, unfortunately, not well placed to win the respect of Catholics, since they had actively denounced fellow-clerics and laity, or married. This also raised another problem, that of confidentiality. State religious policy may not be carried out smoothly by religious personnel once they have betrayed their faith. Finally, in every religious sect, with the partial exception of the Quakers, and up to now even in the west, believers tend to prefer professional religious personnel as their religious leaders, rather than laymen in religious offices. The conflicts, over role-playing in these religious offices, also pose a problem to the government. Who are to be regarded as the real leaders in the church, the temple and the mosque – the priest, pastor, monk, imam or the religious cadres? While the religious believers prefer their religious professionals, the government understandably has its own preference for its own appointed cadres.

The training of professional religious personnel

As a rule the training of professional personnel is a crucial factor in the life of any religion. The Chinese government follows the Soviet practice of separating education from religion. Even though there is no specific injunction in the Constitution about the separation of religion from education, and matters to do with state administration and legislation, it is made clear in party documents that party members must ensure that religion remains a personal matter, and that it should have nothing to do with education.[29] Thus the Chinese government is placed in a very delicate situation on the

[29] 'Women Dang Zai Shehui Zhuyi shiqi Zongjiao Wenti De Jiben Zhengce' [The basic policy on religious questions of our party in this period of Socialism], *Hongqi* 12 (16 June 1982): 2–8. 'Document 19', para. 4.

question of the education of future religious personnel. It realises that the training and education of the younger generation of patriotic religious personnel will decisively influence the future image of the religious organisations, especially at this time of social reconstruction. So the Beijing government aims at fostering in each religion a large number of fervent patriots who will accept the leadership of the party and the government, and walk firmly on the road of socialism and safeguard national and ethnic unity. They are expected to be learned in religious matters and capable of keeping close links with representatives of the religious masses.[30] While their education cannot be totally entrusted to any religious group, neither can it be totally taken over by the atheist party, because the believers would never accept the party as the authentic transmitter of their faith from one generation to another. As against this the party cannot be so naive as to entrust this important task entirely to non-party hands. For this reason, interference by the party is very subtle, aiming in the long run at bringing about the natural death of religion. Accordingly, the government defined the purpose and ultimate goal of religious education in China as follows:

We should not only continue to win over, unite and educate the present generation of persons in religious circles, but we should also help each religious organisation to set up religious seminaries to train new professionals. All these young professional religious personnel should continually heighten their awareness of patriotism and socialism.

We should help each religion. The task of these seminaries is to create a contingent of young patriotic religious personnel who from the political aspect, fervently love their motherland and support the party's leadership and the socialist system, and possess furthermore sufficient religious knowledge. These seminaries should hold entrance examinations and admit as students those youths who are patriotic, and who wish to devote themselves to this religious profession . . .[31]

Generally speaking, religious education should be a programme which embraces the spiritual, intellectual and disciplinary aspects of a religion. For example, the Decree of Priestly Formation in the Catholic church sets the purpose and ultimate goal of religious training in the following words:

Major seminaries are necessary for priestly formation. In them the whole training of students ought to provide for the development of true shepherds

[30] 'Document 19', para. 5.
[31] Ibid., para. 8.

of souls after the model of Our Lord, Jesus Christ, who was teacher, priest and shepherd ... Therefore every programme of instruction, whether spiritual, intellectual or disciplinary, should be joined with practical implementation and directed towards the afore-mentioned pastoral goal.[32]

The emphases put on the formation of religious personnel in China are different. The religious aspects of formation have been very much soft-pedalled in the Chinese programme, and stress has been placed on the political aspects to safeguard patriotism, the party leadership and socialism in religious circles.

Comparing the above guidelines on the formation of religious leaders, one has no difficulty in distinguishing their differing nature and goals. The formation guideline of the Catholic church is very religious in its approach and orientation, and aims at having a Christian leader after the model of Jesus Christ (in spite of the fact that very few could reach near so high a degree of perfection); it seeks for a virtuous spiritual leader in moral and intellectual accomplishment. Therefore, in the tradition of the Catholic church, one has to be 'called by God' to embrace the priesthood before the commencement of one's training, and take it as a 'vocation' which requires life-long dedication and commitment. It should not be regarded as a 'profession' or 'career' as it is called by the CCP. If the Chinese seminaries are operated according to the directives of the government, which aims at training new professionals in religious affairs with a high awareness of patriotism, socialism and a willingness to uphold the party leadership, as well as with sufficient religious knowledge, one can foresee that the end-product of the formation would be a religious cadre acting as an intermediary between the party and the church. The training would be far from adequate to produce future religious leaders. Since religious doctrine and spirituality are not emphasised in the programme of formation, one has reason to fear that in terms of both doctrine and spirituality the future religious personnel will not be in a position to wield real moral leadership among the religious believers; and so religion as such will fail to carry moral weight in Chinese society. Thus the immediate result will be to deprive the Catholic church of true leaders able to uphold the authentic Catholic faith.

Those who enter the seminaries do not all have the same motives. Unquestionably there are some sent there as government agents,

[32] 'Decree on priestly formation', Walter Abbott (ed.), *The Documents of Vatican II* (London: Geoffrey Chapman, 1967), p. 442.

who after their training will be assigned to responsible posts. Could it be that during their training with other seminarians they will give secret reports to the party on those staff and students who are loyal to Rome? There will always be the suspicion that beneath the surface of normal seminary life, politics may be being played ruthlessly.

International relations

The fact that the major world religions, such as Buddhism, Islam, Protestantism and Catholicism, all have a universal nature and world-wide links has served to draw the attention of the Chinese government to them as useful tools for the expansion of China's political influence.[33] The government seeks to improve its image abroad as part of its aim to develop economic and cultural relations with the west, and it recognises that Christianity has played an important role in western cultural heritage. At the same time it accepts that religious freedom constitutes an important aspect of human rights. Friendship with Buddhist-influenced Japan is desired by China's political leaders, who hope that economically developed Japan could be an important source of financial and advanced technological aid for China's modernisation. Now that the Islamic world is playing a considerably more important role in global as well as Middle Eastern affairs, China has to treat Muslims within its territories more gently if it wishes to win the favour of the rich oil-producing states in the Persian Gulf. In other words religion is an important aspect of China's attempt to develop a more global foreign policy. Tolerance and indeed the encouragement of the world religions is particularly important in view of the bad image created by the hooliganism of the Red Guard during the Cultural Revolution. 'Document 19' acknowledges that Buddhism, Islam, Catholicism and Protestantism hold a very strong position in the nationalism of some people. At the same time they are ranked among some of the most important world religions. China admits that 'all of these have extensive influence in their societies. Catholicism and Protestantism are widespread in Europe, North America and Latin America, as well as in other places. Buddhism is strong in Japan and south-east Asia while Islam is widespread in several

[33] 'Document 19', para. 11.

countries in Asia and Africa. Some of these religions are looked upon as state religions in a number of countries.'[34] Now that the Chinese government is seeking foreign aid, it hopes that religious believers abroad will supply help and donations to their fellow religious believers in China, even though they may all realise to what extent religious freedom in China is restricted.

Through their formal and informal contacts with China, many of the foreign religious believers can see that there is a different degree of understanding of religious freedom within and outside China. Yet their zeal for evangelism pushes them to do whatever is possible within their limited reach. The visit to Guangdong by the Chinese Bishop Wu of Hong Kong is a case in point. He was the first Chinese bishop born in China to be invited there as an official guest. The ostensible reason for the visit was the time-honoured one of visiting his eighty-five year old mother in his home town Wuhua in Guangdong province, in February 1986. He had been invited some time earlier by his priest teacher and an aged priest friend to celebrate Mass in Wuhua and Jiaoling counties respectively. But the Chinese government at the last minute refused to allow him to say any Mass there. He was most diplomatic at a press conference at the end of his trip, when, with the view of not embarrassing the Chinese government at that stage, he smoothed things over by making excuses that 'because they were both private invitations, whereas he was an official guest in China, the Chinese authorities felt it inconvenient and inappropriate for him to do so'.[35] At the same time he had to give reassurances to the anxious Hong Kong Catholics who after 1997 would be governed by this same Chinese government. So he advised Hong Kong people not to judge by Hong Kong or other like standards the degree and type of freedom enjoyed by the people in China, because there is a considerable difference between China's and Hong Kong's interpretations of religious freedom.[36]

At the same time the Chinese government is very concerned about the possible infiltration of the so-called 'imperialist religious forces' such as the Vatican and the Protestant foreign mission societies, who

[34] Ibid.

[35] See the Hong Kong local newspapers: *South China Morning Post*, 2 February 1986. *Hong Kong Standard*, 2 February 1986. *Wah Kiu Yat Po*, 2 February 1986, *Xianggang Zhibao* [Hong Kong Times, 2 February 1986].

[36] Ibid. Bishop Wu also confirmed his view on the difference in standards of religious freedom when he was interviewed by the writer on 14 February 1986.

strive earnestly to use every possible opportunity to establish contact
with the unofficial religious groups in China and to pass on their
strength and encouragement to those dissident and non-conformist
Catholics and Protestants.37 Meanwhile the Chinese Catholic Bishops' Conference and the Chinese Catholic Church Administrative
Commission, published an official document in 1986 to regulate the
practices of the clergy in their ministries. Its purpose was mainly to
prevent the 'infiltrations' through outside clergy who on their visits
might have 'unwanted' effects on the Catholics, such as arousing
their desire to follow the new Roman Liturgy in which the vernacu-
lar language is used. The new liturgy itself has been practised by
Catholics throughout the world since the Second Vatican Council in
the 1960s. However the new liturgy is a symbol of having communion with Rome because it was issued from the Vatican. The
regulation goes as follow:

A clergyman who is authorised to administer the sacraments and to say
Mass must, for the time being, observe the traditional ceremonies and
regulations of our Chinese church. Without permission of the Bishops'
Conference and the Church Administration Commission, no one may make
unauthorised changes in or simplifications of the ceremonies.38

The appearance of a pro-Rome clergyman to administer the
sacraments or to say Mass in a church run by the CPA would
contradict the religious work done by the government among the
Catholic laity, many of whom have no choice but to go to a CPA
church for sacraments, but deep down in their hearts are still linked
with the Holy See. The Catholics flocked to Cardinal Sin and Bishop
Wu for blessings when they were in Beijing Cathedral, and completely ignored the CPA bishops who were at the time accompanying
them. These incidents may be the tip of an iceberg in reflecting the
inner feelings of Chinese Catholics. The banning of the Masses of the
Bishop of Hong Kong in Guangdong villages, when he visited there
in February 1986, may be seen as reflecting the response of the civil
authorities to the possible manifestation of similar attitudes by local
Catholics.39 Therefore, the clergy from foreign countries, Hong

37 On China's concern, see 'Document 19', para. 11. On the contacts see J. Heyndrickx, 'A
 visit to the Catholic church in China, 13 May–2 June 1985' (A confidential report) pp. 24–
 6, 35–7.
38 *Catholic Church in China* 1 (March 1987): 24–5.
39 For the incident of the Bishop of Hong Kong being banned from saying Mass in
 Guangdong see chapter 7 of this book on 'Bishop Wu's second visit to China'.

Kong, Macao and Taiwan, who visit China, are circumscribed by a special regulation concerning their saying Mass:

In accordance with China's Constitution and the Chinese Catholic church's principle of the independent administration of the church, clergy from foreign countries, Hong Kong and Taiwan who come to China to travel or to visit relatives do not have the authority to administer the sacraments. If such a clergyman, for the sake of his own personal religious life, asks to say Mass, the properly authorised bishop of the place may grant special permission for private Mass to be said at a place designated by him . . .[40]

Meanwhile, official Chinese religious personnel are now even encouraged to engage in mutual visits and friendly contacts with religious persons in other countries, as well as developing exchanges in the fields of religious art and culture. In the year 1985 alone, eleven religious delegations were sent from China to Hong Kong, Japan, Europe and the Middle East, as part of the cultural exchange programme. Among these eleven religious groups two Catholic groups went to Hong Kong and Belgium.[41] Yet only those in the patriotic associations got a chance to go abroad on these visits; and the programmes of the visits were strictly supervised by the religious cadres who accompanied the delegations. China uses these privileges as rewards for people who are docile to the party, as well as using them as proof to the Chinese Catholics that 'patriotics' are recognised in foreign countries. Moreover, in their speeches the religious delegates had to parrot the guidelines of the government on current political as well as in religious policies. Those who had contact with these religious personnel from China got the impression that they are not free to express themselves even in religious affairs, but are expected to toe the party line everywhere.[42] On the other hand all foreign religious visitors to China are guided to visit the open churches and to meet the priests and laity who have joined the patriotic religious associations. Visitors are not allowed to meet any religious personnel who might cause embarrassment to the government. Cardinal Sin, during his visit to China in October 1984, kept on requesting to meet Bishop Gong Pinmei, the Bishop of Shanghai,

[40] *Catholic Church in China* 1 (March 1987): 24–5.
[41] See '1985 Nian Zhonggong Dueiwai Wenhua Tongzhan Huotong Gaikuang Diaocha' [A survey on the 1985 CCP cultural United Front activities], *Zhonggong Yanjiu* [Studies on Chinese Communism monthly] 231 (15 March 1986): 118–28.
[42] Some Hong Kong Catholics expressed this view after they had met the Shanghai Catholic delegation who visited Hong Kong in July 1985, led by Bishop Louis Jin Luxian.

who was put behind bars in 1955 because he refused to follow the party line and declare himself independent of the Holy See. Cardinal Sin's wish was not granted and in all documents relating to his visit to China his request was not even mentioned. The Bishop of Hong Kong also made the same request to see Bishop Gong on his first visit to China, but that too was refused.[43]

The party also set up norms for the international contacts of religious persons. Basically, the party demands that: 'They [the delegates] should adhere to the principle of maintaining an independent, self-governing autonomous church, and resolutely resist all reactionary religious forces from abroad who want once again to gain control over religion in our country.'[44] Apparently the party is anxious to develop friendly relationships with foreign religious groups and yet maintain China's policy of running independent autonomous churches. Interactions at the international level are always a mixed blessing both for the Beijing government and for the Catholic church. Foreign Catholics may always have an unwanted impact on the Catholics in China, especially on the question of independence from the Pope, and make it harder for the CCP to uphold the policy of independence. On the other hand, foreign Catholics may easily forget the question of communion with the universal church through Rome, and take the CPA Catholics as the only segment of the Catholic church in China, and ignore the sufferings of the unofficial Catholics.

The difference between religion and superstition

Apart from the unofficial Catholic church activities, the second type of illegal or abnormal religious activities which the Chinese government and the party try to combat is superstition. From the beginning of the religious freedom policy the government has tried to distinguish between religion and superstition, since many people, including religious cadres, fail to see the difference. According to the definition given by the party in an article in *Guangming Ribao*, 'Religion is certainly a kind of superstition, but not all superstitious activities bear the colour of religion. Religion is a belief with a formal

---

[43] Cardinal Sin's request to meet Bishop Gong Pinmei was revealed by his assistant, who went with the Cardinal to China. 'Letter from Bishop Wu after his return', *Tripod* 26 (April 1985): 75–6.

[44] 'Document 19', para. 11.

organisation, written doctrines and prescribed activities and liturgy. Feudalist superstition does not bear the significance of a world religion.'[45] The article goes on to say that religious activities are superstitious since they hinder production, and adversely affect national security. Therefore, they are not inducive to the fostering of national prosperity.

Government directives do not consistently distinguish between what is superstition and what is not. It is no wonder that there are reports of the revival of various kinds of superstition. Fortune-telling, geomancy and witchcraft are widely practised. Even local officials have organised elaborate ceremonies at funerals, marriages and many social events, especially in the countryside.

The building and rebuilding of Buddhist temples is another example. When the Fujian provincial government busied itself rebuilding Buddhist temples at scenic spots to attract tourists, some of the peasants got the impression that they could also build Buddhist temples in their own villages, and even use public money for this purpose. The provincial government has stated in the newspapers that the indiscriminate building of Buddhist temples for local deities is an act of superstition, that it is wasteful and should be stopped without delay.[46]

Some Hong Kong newspapers reported a serious incident of religious intolerance in December 1986. In a certain city in northern Henan Province, a crowd of 3,700 teenage secondary and primary school students totally destroyed twenty-eight Buddhist temples which had recently been opened. It was said that the local authorities had given their consent to the students' vandalism and wished to record this action of 'liberating' their citizens from temples. The city authorities were convinced that such an action was demanded by a recent resolution of the Communist party urging construction of a 'spiritual socialist state', and the destruction of 'feudal superstitions'. Such behaviour recalls that of the Cultural Revolution when the Red Guards destroyed numerous temples, mosques and churches.[47]

45 'Xinyang Ziyou Shi Dang Zai Zongjiao Wenti Shang De Yixiang Gengben Zhengce' [Religious freedom is the party's basic policy on religious questions], *Guangming Ribao*, 30 November 1980.

46 *Fujian Ribao*, 2 April 1981. *Nanfang Ribao*, 20 April 1982, 30 November 1982, 16 December 1982, 17 December 1982. *Sichuan Ribao*, 2 May 1982. *Zhejiang Ribao*, 24 March 1982, 15 March 1984. *Zhongguo Qingnian Bao* [Chinese youth daily], 20 November 1982, 25 November 1982.

47 *Correspondence* 25 (February 1987): 14.

Yet, while orders are given to stop building temples for local deities, the official stand with regard to the building of temples has not been clear from the start. Moreover, it is not clear what kind of deities deserve temple building, since most of the local deities in China are honoured by Buddhism and Taoism, which are listed by the government as religions in which Chinese are allowed to believe. The cadres in rural areas have been busy persuading the common people not to engage in so-called 'superstitious' activities, but they must be led to ask why Buddhist temples could be built in the scenic spots. If the government has the authority to decide even where to build temples, how much freedom can prevail in religious worship? In the provincial newspapers regular columns have been reserved to discuss the question of feudal superstition, in order to induce the people towards materialist atheism and scientific Marxism–Leninism in the hope that 'superstitious' practices would vanish into thin air.[48] This reveals that the party and the government are really bothered by the revitalisation of the so-called 'superstitious' activities among the masses. 'Document 19' provides some precise statements to guide the religious cadres to cope with this question. With no uncertainty it states:

We are determined to safeguard all normal religious activities. Included in this crack-down are all those superstitious practices which fall outside the scope of religion and are injurious to the national welfare as well as to the life and property of the people. We will severely punish according to law those counter-revolutionary elements as well as other criminal offenders who hide behind the facade of religion . . .

All reactionary secret societies, sorcerers and witches, are hereby banned, without exception and will not be permitted to resume their activities. All those who spread fallacies to deceive people and all those who hoodwink people of their money, will, without exception, be severely punished in accordance with the law. Party cadres who profit by these unlawful activities to accumulate wealth, will be dealt with all the more severely. Finally all those making their living by phenology, fortune-telling and geomancy should be educated, warned and helped to earn their living through their own labour, and not be allowed to engage in these superstitious practices which only deceive people.[49]

In theory, the Chinese government has drawn a line between superstition and religion. Yet in practice it is sometimes very difficult to differentiate between the two. Is it necessary in the people's

[48] *Fujian Ribao*, 8 January 1982. *Daizhun Ribao*, 27 January 1982. *Nanfang Ribao*, 20 April 1982.
[49] 'Document 19', para. 10.

interests to suppress all forms of superstitious activity? The above-mentioned case of temple building for local deities in Fujian Province does not look like superstition, although the religious cadres have stated it to be so. In Hong Kong, with its 90 per cent Chinese population, a fashion has developed during the last ten years among the business class of fortune-telling, phenology and astrology as a means of seeking guidance in their ventures. Although this kind of 'superstitious practice' has become fashionable in the social circle of the Hong Kong entrepreneur, there is no report that the prosperity and stability of Hong Kong have been jeopardised by it. In fact, Hong Kong people consider that phenology, astrology, geomancy and palm reading have helped them better themselves economically. Only that class of people who are relatively wealthy can afford to pay heavily for the services of the astrologists, phenologists, geomancers and fortune-tellers; the charges for their services come to a substantial amount. The Hong Kong government, whose high officials are mostly Christians and do not in principle practise superstition, does not issue any official document to put an end to this practice lest superstition jeopardise Hong Kong's prosperity and modernity. With their different political ideologies, the Hong Kong government and the Chinese government treat superstitious activities among Chinese in different ways, and only the Chinese who have had the experience of living under both governments can tell the world which style they would prefer.

Bishop Gong's appeal

In 1985, the Chinese government announced that Bishop Gong was to be released, since he had pleaded guilty to his 'counter-revolutionary crimes'. The bishop said he never admitted to such crimes.[50] In fact, since 1979 Bishop Gong had kept on sending letters of appeal to the People's Supreme Court both in Beijing and in Shanghai requesting a review of his case.[51] In Gong's Letter of Appeal, one can see clearly why the pro-Vatican Chinese Catholics cling firmly to Rome. Out of religious conviction they give no leeway on the question of severing ties with the Pope. However, the procedure of Gong's appeal revealed how the Chinese government put into practice the legal system in treating religious matters.

[50] *Amnesty International Report 1986* (London: Amnesty International, 1987), p. 216.
[51] Gong Pinmei, 'The Letter of Appeal'.

4 Bishop Gong Pinmei meets the Pope at the Vatican (12 May 1989). *Source:* Foto Felici.

First of all Gong in his long Letter of Appeal pointed out that its purpose was not to rehabilitate himself but rather to re-establish the good name of the church, and to request the right for the Catholic church to defend its integral faith under the protection of the Chinese Constitution.[52] Gong admitted that he was caught up in the church and state conflict. According to him, the focus of the dispute lay in the Three Selfs Movement launched by the govern-

[52] Ibid., para. 2.

ment, compelling the Chinese Catholics to become schismatic by severing relations with the Pope.[53] As the church leader of Shanghai, a big Catholic diocese in China, Bishop Gong had no objection to having Chinese bishops administer the Chinese dioceses, to having Chinese missionaries preach the gospel, and to having local Chinese Catholics contribute to the financial support of the church, as advocated by the Three Selfs Movement (self-governing, self-supporting and self-evangelising), but he could not support the Three Selfs Movement in its ultimate aim of cutting off the Chinese Catholics from the Pope.[54]

Gong also recalled that in 1950 when Zhou Enlai promised the Catholic leaders that the Catholics could retain their spiritual relations with the Holy See provided they sever political and economic relations with the Vatican, he supported the government's decision in this matter. But after he was arrested in 1955, on the eve of his being sentenced in Court in March 1960, the chief prosecutor of Shanghai met him in prison and suggested to him that he could have his freedom in exchange for his complete severance of any relations with the Pope, inclusive of spiritual relations.[55] He refused so vile an exchange, primarily on religious grounds. For him the denunciation would be a schismatic act abandoning the Roman Catholic faith and embracing another denomination of Christianity. Therefore, Gong in his appeal went on to ask whether the state has the right to force religious believers to change their religious faith and become schismatic? Gong recalled also Mao's teaching that the party could not eradicate religion by administrative order and could not compel people not to believe in religion, and remarked that in his case the government seemed not to carry out the teaching of Mao too well.[56] Candidly he went on to ask whether it were not against the state Constitution and the practice in international conventions regarding religious freedom that the state compel its citizens to alter the basic and integral part of their religious doctrine?

As far as his own sentence was concerned, he admitted that the government regarded his actions in leading the clergy to shun the schismatic Three Selfs Movement as: (a) leading a counter-revolutionary syndicate, (b) contacting the imperialists and (c) betraying

53 Ibid., para. 3.
54 Ibid., para. 3.
55 Ibid., para. 4.
56 Ibid., para. 5, section 2.

the motherland.[57] He then analysed his sentence and showed it to be disproportionately exaggerated. First of all, he asked the authorities to list the name, nature, constitution and members of the so-called 'syndicate'. He affirmed that, apart from joining the Catholic church, which is a legal organisation, he had never participated in any illegal syndicate. If the fifteen priests named by the government were regarded as a counter-revolutionary syndicate, he argued that in practice only five of them were under the jurisdiction of the Shanghai diocese; and he had no juridical right over the rest of them.[58] He did not admit to having contacted any imperialists because only after the 'foreign imperialists' had withdrawn from China, was he sent to fill the vacuum left by them. Neither did he meet them in person nor did he engage in any intrigues with them. He simply requested the government to name the imperialists whom he had allegedly contacted and pointed out what kind of contact he had made. He never admitted he had betrayed his motherland. He argued 'there is no way I could betray the motherland in which I was born and on whose soil I was brought up.'[59]

He also denied the accusation that there was a radio station and a store of firearms in the bishop's residence. In fact he revealed that only a wooden rifle butt without a barrel, trigger or bullets had been found. He also asked the government to name the place where they found the firearms and the quantity discovered, if any. He asked the government to display the equipment of the confiscated radio station and the firearms to prove that they had indeed found them.[60] In his sentence he was accused of having subverted the three campaigns, namely, on the Korean War, the Land Reform and the General Socialist Line. He admitted that he could shoulder part of the responsibility for the subversion but not the whole.[61] He revealed that the adviser on Canon Law in the diocese, a French priest, Father Lacretelle, or Ge Shouping in Chinese, handed him on 27 April 1951 a memorandum evaluating the current political movements. He admitted that this Canon Law adviser and he himself should take joint responsibility for dissuading the youth from enlisting in the army to fight in the Korean War. The reason was

[57] Ibid., para. 6.
[58] Ibid.
[59] Ibid.
[60] Ibid., para. 7.
[61] Ibid., para. 8.

that their Catholic faith would be at stake, since the army had to study the atheist Marxism–Leninism. He pointed out that in this memorandum the legal adviser only remarked that the Korean War was not a completely just war. (In French 'La guerre de Corée n'est pas absolument juste' as Gong quoted.) He argued that the court had wrongly twisted the statement from 'not completely just' to 'completely not just'. That was an exaggeration, Gong argued.[62] He remarked that the legal adviser had already been expelled some years ago, so Gong found that, at this juncture, it was unjust for him to take sole responsibility for everything.[63]

On the question of Land Reform, he admitted that seminars had been held among the clergy to discuss the land reform in the light of Catholic teaching. Although criticisms of the land distribution itself had been voiced in these seminars, it was not true that Rome and the Shanghai Catholic diocese tried to subvert the movement. Gong argued that it was groundless to accuse the Shanghai Catholic diocese of subverting the land reform. In fact the Catholic diocese in Shanghai had demonstrated its co-operation in land re-distribution by handing over all its land to the government one year earlier.[64]

As far as the subversion of the general line of Socialism went, he admitted that in one of his pastoral letters he used the phrase 'the line of the Heavenly kingdom' without any intention of staging a confrontation with the Socialist general line of the government.[65] He admitted that in using the expression he was not aware that it could stage a confrontation between the Catholics and the government.

Then Gong traced the treatment of the Catholic church from the 1950s down to the Cultural Revolution and re-affirmed his stand.[66] He also revealed that in 1956 he thought that the government was really implementing a religious freedom policy when he came to know that religious believers were being treated a little more gently than before. He thought that the hard line he had taken with the government was wrong. Therefore he showed his sincere repentance and his trust in the government by surrendering the mission foundation money left behind by the previous bishop, in the form of

[62] Ibid., para. 8.
[63] Ibid.
[64] Ibid.
[65] Ibid.
[66] Ibid.

首任國籍主教紀念
贊公天爵榮任上海教區
一九五〇年八月十三日

5 Bishop Ignatius Gong Pinmei, the first Chinese Bishop of Shanghai (13 August 1950). *Source:* Author's private collection.

1,830 taels of gold. But he recalled that in his wildest dreams he never thought that, after the government had been given this great amount of gold, it would in return demand of him to acknowledge that it was a subversive fund for counter-revolutionary activities. He refused to make this false statement. Unilaterally, the government then announced the finding of this 'fund for counter-revolutionary activities'. In his Letter of Appeal, Gong made it plain that he felt that he had been greatly let down by the government. He demanded that the current government review his case.[67]

In general, Bishop Gong tried to put the accusations into their proper perspectives refusing to admit to some of them while admitting some responsibility in others. In fact, his appeal painted a clear picture of the Sino-Vatican conflict in the 1950s. He tried to analyse

[67] Ibid., para. 8.

the focus of the conflict – the Three Selfs Movement and his refusal to sever ties with the Holy See. Of course Gong's argument is mainly from the religious point of view. Yet it enables one to see that China in the 1950s let ideological rhetoric and simplistic formulas overshadow its proper legal approach and did not demonstrate sophistication and realism in dealing with a complicated court case like this.

The legal process versus the appeal

In the beginning Gong hesitated to dredge up old matters, because he noticed that in prison, if anybody raised any suggestion of an appeal it was taken badly, such being regarded as a contestation of the sentence.[68] But in 1979 when the government began to promote legality in the national administration, many court cases were reviewed with the intention of rehabilitating the wrongly accused. This offered him a chance too.[69]

In his letter of appeal, sent to Jian Hua, the Director of the People's Supreme Court, on 18 January 1987, Gong revealed that in 1979 he had presented his first appeal, but he got no reply. In 1981 he submitted his appeal again. Even then there was no answer from the government. He had gone on submitting his appeal practically every year until 1985. Then an official came to see him. Gong gave this man all the relevant documents, for he promised that he would process the appeal for him. That was the last Gong saw of that official: nothing was done. Gong also protested that, when he appeared in court on 3 July 1985 for his parole, he was told that he could be free, yet up to 18 January 1987, the very day he submitted his last appeal, he was still under house arrest simply because he refused to sever relations with the Pope.[70]

In comparing the official announcement of Gong's release and the way in which his appeal had been treated, one sees the double-dealing to which this religious dissenter had been subjected. Whenever religious visitors asked about Bishop Gong the government would justify its treatment of an eighty-six year old prisoner of conscience, by repeatedly giving the reason that he would not admit his crime.[71]

---

[68] Ibid., para. 2.
[69] Ibid.
[70] Ibid., final part.
[71] The writer heard one of the religious cadres in Beijing pass this remark about Bishop Gong in 1984. Even before that the same opinion was current among the China observers of the Catholic church.

The government appeared very unlikely to review his case, in which there were some points deserving of reconsideration. So many foreign visitors, including prominent figures like Cardinal Sin and the Bishop of Hong Kong, had asked to meet him, that the government decided to move him from a prison cell to house arrest. There are many reasons to explain this extraordinary case. Putting a bishop in prison and keeping him under house arrest for religious reasons greatly disfigured the image of China, especially when it had proclaimed that religious freedom was being practised. Since the accusations against Gong were mostly false, China perhaps wants to hush up the sentence passed on him. This is contrary, however to its present practice of rehabilitating those wrongly accused and falsely imprisoned in the modernisation era. The main reason may be that Gong's loyalty to the Holy See cannot be accepted by the Chinese government and that his influence is very great among the unofficial Catholics.

CHURCH AND STATE RELATIONS AS VIEWED BY CHINA

The political role of Catholicism and of other religions in recent years

Since China's door has opened, the Chinese political leaders can hardly fail to see the political impact of religion on modern international relations. Through the special party newspapers for 'Internally Circulated Reference' they should be aware that the Iranians, armed with the idea of fighting an Islamic holy war, went fearlessly to the battle-field and gave their lives willingly as religious martyrs. Similarly, they are well aware of the black South African Archbishop Tutu's struggles against Pretoria's apartheid policy and that the highest spiritual leader of the Church of England, the Archbishop of Canterbury, Dr Runcie, is behind him, giving him encouragement and support. The same Dr Runcie's personal representative, Terry Waite, is kept hostage in the Middle East after making several missions on behalf of other hostages. Today's political history in the Philippines would not have happened as it did, had not the Archbishop of Manila, Cardinal Sin, influenced the people from behind the scenes in the overthrow of Marcos' corrupt regime. The Catholic church in Korea also played a positive role when the people demanded democratic elections under the dictatorial regime of President Chun.

No sensible political leader in China could deny the moral power of religion, as demonstrated in these outspoken Christian church leaders. Convinced of their Christian faith, they took action in the cause of justice and peace. China's leaders have publicly praised the struggles of Archbishop Tutu; and China has voiced opposition to apartheid. Indeed, it has long since been proclaiming itself a good friend of the Africans. The Chinese government officials have privately criticised Cardinal Sin for his involvement in the politics that overthrew Marcos' regime. The reason given is that, if Cardinal Sin is a religious leader, he should not have involved himself in the political struggle between Marcos and Aquino. This was a movement beyond the scope of religion.[72] In this case, the Chinese officials saw only the political involvement of a religious leader, but they did not consider the role true religion should play in fighting oppression. The private criticism of Cardinal Sin's interference in politics implies that China would not allow the Chinese bishops to follow suit in such matters.

The constant assistance given by the Catholic church to the Polish Solidarity Movement in strengthening its opposition to the Polish Communist regime did not escape the attention of the Chinese Communist leaders. In fact, such action could never be considered acceptable in China. Many religious believers as well as professional religious personnel have been indirectly helping Amnesty International, on both the local as well as the international levels, to work for the release of prisoners of conscience and to bring the torturing of political prisoners to an end.[73] It is a known fact that the arrest of the Shanghai Catholics in 1981 and the arrest of the Catholics in Hebei Province in 1986 were made known to the public as well as to Amnesty International by the Catholics in Hong Kong. Then Amnesty International adopted the arrested priests and laity as prisoners of conscience and pleaded for a fair public trial. The Chinese government was rightly bothered by the negative image

---

[72] Reported by a Catholic China observer who went to Shanghai in 1986 and casually discussed Cardinal Sin's involvement in Philippines' politics with the staff of the the CPA.

[73] In the Missionary of the Oblates of Mary Immaculate's regional report, presented to their General Chapter in September 1986, it was revealed that a couple of their priests were involved in the work of Amnesty International.

Amnesty International also got information very fast on the arrest of Catholics in China in the years 1980 and 1986, through the Catholics in Hong Kong. See 'Report of the European region to the chapter', and 'Report of the Latin America region to the chapter', Presented to the General Chapter of Missionary of the Oblates of Mary Immaculate, Rome, September, 1986.

created by the various media abroad. In spite of the embarrassment caused by such publicity, China could not as yet retaliate against the Catholics in Hong Kong or against Amnesty International but had to yield to their demands, arranging public trials of the detainees – quite contrary to the practice adopted during the Cultural Revolution and before that.[74]

China thenceforth became more aware of the calls for prayer by the Pope and his work for peace, since Beijing has repeatedly claimed that he was a leader of the imperialist forces.[75] In fact, the Pope's message at Assisi on the Day of Peace, 27 October 1986, pleading with the world for peace and reconciliation, was not only meant for his own Catholics and the 150 religious leaders present in Assisi that day, but for the IRA, PLO and the rest. He asked all violent men to lay down their arms and seek reconciliation rather as a means of solving their problems. In this symbolic gesture, representatives of all the major world religions, with three and a half billion followers, came together at the invitation of the Pope to pray for peace and to commit themselves to seeking a world where peace and brotherhood would prevail. The Pope stated at Assisi:

We have come together not for an inter-religious conference on peace but to make an invitation to the world to become aware that there exists another dimension of peace and another way of promoting it which is not a result of negotiations, political compromises or economic bargainings . . .'[76]

Through his message at the Peace Rally in Assisi, as Dr Runcie later put it, the Pope played the role of the spokesman on peace for all the Christians in the modern world.[77]

As far as the Vatican is concerned, although the Polish Pope, John Paul II, may appear conservative in matters of church doctrine, moral teaching and church discipline, he is not regarded as conservative in his political principles – which are to defend democracy, protect human rights and oppose all forms of oppression. China has reason to keep an eye on the Catholic church in Hong Kong as well as the Catholics in the mainland because its supreme head is now

---

[74] The public trial of the Shanghai Catholics was conducted a few months after their arrest and the verdicts were made public.

[75] Director of Religious Affairs Bureau, Qiao Liansheng's speech, and the Deputy Director of the United Front, Jiang Ping's speech, at the celebration of the 25th anniversary of the Chinese Catholic Patriotic Association, 21 April 1983. See their speeches in *Catholic Church in China* 7 (August 1983): 22–32.

[76] *The Universe*, 31 October 1986.

[77] BBC World Service, 'Radio News', 13 October 1986.

very active in advocating peace, non-violence, democracy, human rights and so forth. The Pope himself laid down the principle that Catholic church personnel should avoid party politics but should involve themselves in struggles for the above-mentioned principles by political means. For example, on the occasion of his visit to Chile in April 1987 to meet General Pinochet, the Catholic Chilean dictator, he courageously told the General that it is the church's duty to defend freedom as it did in the Philippines, and he called for respect for the rights of individuals. He spoke to the Chilean bishops on human rights in their country. His candid speech was so irritating to the Chilean authorities that they demanded that the state controlled television station cut out the live broadcast of his speech.[78] The Pope's political principles based on Christian teaching oppose the egoism and selfishness in Capitalism and the authoritarianism in Communism. He calls for the basic reform of society. His political outlook and his involvement in global political affairs, as in the Philippines, Poland and South America, is a further area where China may consider that the normalisation of Sino-Vatican relations might provide new chances for the church to interfere in Chinese internal affairs, such as in the sensitive and debatable issues of human rights, democracy and freedom.

Challenges from religions: to accept or repress?

It is possible that the authority of the Chinese leaders could be either directly or indirectly challenged by religious leaders who are able to generate moral power. If people of the calibre of Cardinal Sin, Dr Runcie and Archbishop Tutu were to arise in China and espouse some issues of great public concern, could they have similar repercussions on the Chinese leaders? Is the Chinese government willing to face moral challenges from religious leaders? How would it deal with them? In fact some doctrinal and moral issues, such as family planning, have become a big enough issue for China to accept the challenge if it wants to. China has promulgated the 'one child family' policy as the way to solve its population problem. So far the Chinese Bishops' Conference has now explicitly expressed its position to the government on the issue, which is backed up in the China context by abortion, sterilisation and artificial contraception – all

[78] BBC World Service, 'Radio News', 2 April 1987, 3 April 1987.

methods disapproved by the Catholic church. In Taiwan the Bishops' Conference and the Catholic publications have expressed the standpoint of the Catholic church leading the Catholics personally to respond to this church teaching positively.[79] The CPA and the Chinese Bishops' Conference of the PRC find it difficult to say anything on this controversial subject and therefore keep silent. On the one hand, they could not say 'no' to the government's policy, but, on the other, if they approved it, they would put themselves in a rather unfavourable position before the universal church. Apparently the party does not want to put its brainchild in such an unfavourable position at this time while the party is seeking international recognition through contacts with the bishops of the universal church. It would be unwise to make the official Catholics appear heretic by giving any semblance of disapproval of the church's teaching to please the Chinese government. But at provincial level, the Patriotic Association of Hebei Province, at a meeting for exchanging progressive Christian experiences in 1984, quoted examples of Catholics accepting the one child policy and persuading others to practise artificial birth control. The news was not published by any media, but became known through the newsletter of the provincial CPA.[80] It was reported that at a meeting of the Shanxi Provincial CPA in 1983 a resolution was passed calling upon priests of that province to persuade Catholics to carry out the government's policy on population control.[81] Of course the teaching staff of the national seminary has no choice but to follow the teaching of the government in this matter. Whether it was of his own accord or not, one professor of Moral Theology in a Chinese seminary, a Catholic priest, stated that he supported the state family-planning policy, because he admitted that it was correct, and religion should not interfere with state affairs.[82]

The silence of the Chinese Catholic priests and bishops on this

---

[79] *Jiaoyou Shenghuo* [The Catholic life] (The Catholic weekly of Taibei Catholic diocese) frequently contains articles and editorials conveying the messages of the Bishops' Conference.

[80] *Beijing Jiaoyao Tongxun* [The Catholic newsletter of Beijing diocese] (for internal circulation) 4 (1985): 37–8.

[81] *Catholic Church in China* 18 (March 1987): 42.

[82] This Catholic priest, whom the writer met in Beijing September 1984, was the professor of Moral Theology at the national seminary. In the course of our discussion, the question of family planning was brought up. It was difficult to ascertain whether the unorthodox Catholic teaching which he embraced was his own opinion or forced upon him under pressure. It appeared that he had no alternative but to echo the government's policy.

moral issue, also suggests that they are not free even to perform the teaching function of the Catholic church among the Catholic faithful in such a political environment. If Cardinal Sin, Dr Runcie and Archbishop Tutu were put in the same situation, one has reason to doubt whether they would be given the chance to be so provocative on behalf of truth, love, peace and justice. Even the Vatican itself, mindful of the delicate situation and hoping for the normalisation of its relations with China, has not yet made its position explicitly clear on China's population policy. The silence on this issue partly, on the part of the church, – so far as the Vatican is concerned – out of tact towards those with whom it seeks friendship and partly, on the part of the Chinese Catholics, out of fear since they are merely tolerated, is understandable. But, if the church hopes to impress with its moral weight, how long can it keep its silence? Yet the population problem in China has been a very difficult one, since it has to feed one billion people. Population control appears to be the most effective way to deal with this thorny question. It may be worth pointing out that there is room for compromise as there is no requirement in Chinese law for enforced abortion and the Catholic church is not opposed in principle to attempts to limit childbirth. Since the Catholic church approves the natural family planning method as a means to regulate the birth rate, the question arises as to whether the Chinese government could allow the Chinese Catholics to practise this method instead of seeking artificial contraception and abortion.

MOVING TOWARDS RECONCILIATION

The Vatican's directives in contacting China

In general, the Vatican encourages the Catholic clergy and laity to visit China and to establish warm fraternal relations with the Chinese Catholics, but the Vatican makes suggestions to the visitors, and through these suggestions manifests its views on the Chinese Catholics. There are some other signs to indicate that the Vatican is taking some steps that might eventually help to bridge the gap between the sector of Chinese Catholics who belong to the Patriotic Association, and those who remain underground. In March 1986, China observers in the Catholic church were summoned to Rome for a consultation on the recent developments in the church in China, especially on the ever growing contacts it has with the universal church.[83] It was expected that the Vatican would issue some directives on how to deal with the Catholics and the clergy related to the CPA in a proper way, aiming at a toleration broad enough not to exclude them but to take them as brothers in Christ, while at the same time being strict enough to keep church doctrine and discipline whole and intact.

In advance of the Vatican's official directive suggestions were offered to the foreign Catholics who planned to visit China, to manifest the Vatican's positions and views on Chinese Catholics. The following views were given by the Vatican as a very general guideline:

1 The Holy Father loves and cares for the church in China.
2 Communion with the See of Peter is an essential part of the Catholic faith.
3 The Holy See does not interfere in the internal affairs of any country: the Three Selfs are fully respected in the Holy See's activities.
4 The Holy See enjoys good relations with other Socialist countries and would be happy to have the same relations with China.
5 As Catholic clergy in communion with Rome, the visiting clergy in China would have no 'communicatio in sacris' with the CPA clergy.[84]

Following the March meeting, Catholic Sinologists tried to sum up the positions of the Holy See towards the Chinese government in general and the Chinese Catholics in particular. As a result, a more comprehensive directive has been given to those who will have contacts with China. The directive itself reflects the attitudes of the Vatican to China even though it was issued by the Catholic Sinologists. It reads as follows:

Reflections to keep in mind in our contacts with the faithful, the clergy and government officials of PRC

A There is a common agreement on the following facts:
1 The present religious policy of the Chinese government officially proclaims freedom of religion and in fact, allows, under certain restrictions, the public exercise of religious practice and assists in the establishment of a

---

[83] The consultation was arranged by the Cardinal head of the Propaganda Fide in March 1986. It was reported by an Italian church magazine. See Alberto Bobbio, 'Summit Segreto a Roma: IL Papa apre alla Cina?' [The secret summit in Rome: is the Pope open to China?], *Jesus* (Rome) (April 1986): 85.
[84] Bishop Mahon, the Auxiliary Bishop of Westminster, got these instructions on the position of the Vatican, which he consulted in person before he made his trip to China in March 1987. Also see Bishop Gerald Mahon, 'A visit to the People's Republic of China, Monday 23 March–Saturday 11 April 1978'. A private report.

number of religious institutions. Yet, it is a policy clearly inspired by the Communist ideology of atheistic materialism (see 'Document 19' issued in 1982).

2 The Catholic Patriotic Association (CPA) is in itself an official instrument of the government to divide and keep under control the activities of the Catholic church. In reality, however, the CPA is not a monolithic body. This means that its members act and apply government policies differently in different parts of the country. There are actually places where they favour and make possible for the faithful the integral practice of the Catholic faith.

3 It is a fact that, at present, the Catholics, generally speaking, enjoy greater freedom than ten years ago, and that it is easier to communicate with them. We are to respond to this privileged moment.

B How to proceed in concrete cases:

1 We should try to answer with generosity the various requests addressed to us by the Chinese faithful. Often, this has to be done through the CPA.

2 It is left to the conscience of the Chinese faithful the decision to participate in the Eucharist and to receive the sacraments in a church considered to be under the control of the CPA. More so if the priest who celebrates the Eucharist and administers the sacraments is, at present, considered by them a good pastor.

3 Relationships with the active members of the CPA must be cordial and sincere, but our actions should not convey an unqualified approval and recognition of their situation *vis-à-vis* the Holy See, and we should point out, whenever possible, that the integrity of our Catholic faith includes the acceptance of the Primacy of Peter and his successors. In other words, we must always act in 'truth and love'.

4 Visits to bishops and priests, even if they are members of the CPA, are useful. For they offer good opportunities for that kind of dialogue which is mutually enriching by the sharing of the expectations of our local churches and by searching together for the best ways to live the ecclesial communion with the successor of Peter. At the same time, we must stress the present understanding of the legitimate autonomy of each local church and how the fostering of unity in diversity and reconciliation is the very significant task of the church council.

5 If a priest in good standing is invited to join the faculty of seminaries administered by the CPA, the priest concerned must decide according to his best judgement on the situation and the rules of practical prudence. But if asked for advice, he should be encouraged to join the seminary staff in the hope that he may exert a positive influence in the sound and solid formation of the future priests of China.

6 Contacts with government officials are desirable. Friendly relationships with members of the church helps them to a better appreciation of the church and creates occasions to let them see the positive, non-threatening role of the church in most nations of the world.

7 The Catholics going to visit China should express their desire to go to Mass on Sundays and Feasts of obligation, and they must feel free to participate in the Eucharist unless there are reasons or circumstances which may advise otherwise.

The above reflections and guidelines are the results of reliable sources of information and of some recent authoritative exchanges.[85]

The Chinese Catholic Patriotic Association (CPA)

In the 1950s membership of the CPA formed a demarcation between those who were loyal to the Holy See and those who yielded to the demands of the government, but in the 1970s and 1980s this is not the case. The CPA today is not regarded as the embodiment of the Catholic church in China nor does it want to be a schismatic movement working towards a formal separation from the Holy See. Apart from some extremists and some over-zealous 'patriotic' elements, a number of leaders of the association give genuine pastoral care, displaying a concern for the integrity of their faith and giving clear signs of living inwardly in communion with the Pope. There are examples of admirable bishops, in mutually recognised communion with the Holy See, who have CPA Catholics in their dioceses, who they often manage to control, putting in their own men as heads of the local CPA. In this way, the CPA gradually becomes meaningless. It is interesting to note, that it was officially down graded in significance at the last Bishops' Conference held in Beijing from the 24–28 April 1989. In this Conference it was accepted that the Bishops' Conference not the CPA must be the first in making decisions regarding the affairs of the church. The bishops are the primary administrators of the diocese. The CPA must therefore become an organisation of the Catholics at the service of the Bishops' Conference.[86] That is why some overseas Catholic scholars are optimistic that some of their public statements reflecting the party line against the Vatican do not necessarily imply a formal rejection of the Petrine Office in the church.[87] It is true that for practical

[85] These points are printed in a pamphlet by the Catholic Sinologists to circulate among the Catholics who often visit China.

[86] This information came to the writer through private communications with the Chinese people.

[87] Jose M. Calle, 'Some thoughts to better understand the present situation of the Catholic church in China today', *Eastern Asian Pastoral Review* (Manila) 1 (1986): 89–93.

reasons many prefer to practise their religious life openly by allying themselves with the CPA and remain discreet in expressing their fidelity to the church in Rome. There are others who still practise their faith in the underground with great fervour and dedication. For doctrinal and canonical reasons they avoid contact and 'communicatio in sacris' with those whom they suspect are illegitimate representatives of the Catholic church. Because of the relaxation there are some who until very recently were in the underground, but who now publicly participate in liturgical services offered in the open churches sponsored by the CPA. There are some bishops and priests who have never been members of the CPA but who are now allowed to exercise their pastoral ministry publicly. A few years back this was not possible.[88] All this reveals that the party for the sake of modernisation has very much defused religious questions and has tried to down-play the contradiction between the atheists and religious believers. It is even so with the conflict between China and the Vatican. Yet, it seems that the ice has not yet been really broken. On more than one occasion in recent years China has insisted that the Catholic church in its territories should be independent from the Vatican.[89] In what ways do the historical background and the hierarchical structure of the Vatican have a bearing on their relations with the PRC?

The Vatican is also aware of the gradual change in the function and nature of the CPA. As stated above, some of the religious leaders in the CPA show authentic pastoral concern and display relatively great integrity of faith. It is reported that a number of bishops of the CPA deep down in their hearts are deeply pained by the separation from Rome. The authorities have told them that whatever their personal feelings may be they must openly refuse allegiance to the Holy See; yet there are some bishops in the CPA who never speak against Rome and are known in China for their pro-Rome attitude. They are in places remote from cities, in regions where party discipline is not so rigidly observed. Therefore, a careful investigation has been carried out in the Roman Curia into each bishop's

---

[88] These phenomena were reported after visits by foreign and overseas Chinese Catholics who went to make informal contacts in various places in China with the purpose of collecting some authentic information about the Catholic church there. Also see 'Profession of Faith of a Chinese Priest in Communion with Rome', *China Bulletin* (Rome) 3 (March 1986): 10–11.

[89] For instance, on the occasion of the 25th anniversary celebrations of the Chinese Catholic Patriotic Association, the director of the Religious Affairs Bureau, Chiao Niensheng, and the deputy director of the United Front Office, Jiang Ping, reiterated that it was the policy

case, to ascertain his marital status, his relations with Rome and the legitimacy of his consecration and so forth. Through intensive contact with those bishops it is hoped that some positive results may be obtained. For example, one of the first Chinese bishops, consecrated without the consent of the Holy See in the 1950s, was contacted several times between 1982–4. He was able to open his heart very frankly to a visitor from abroad, who was able to transmit a message from him to the religious congregation to which he originally belonged, and to the Holy See about the circumstances in which he accepted the election and consecration as bishop without the consent of Rome some thirty years ago. The talks were held not only without stress but also with great understanding. That bishop took it as a sign of acceptance from the Vatican. It was a very important step to win the hearts of such bishops, who immediately softened their anti-Vatican rhetoric and increased their pastoral zeal.

In fact many Chinese bishops in the CPA are said to have mellowed recently in their anti-Rome attitude. Perhaps it is the first sign of a bright future. But how much of this softening of approach can be tolerated by the party, and how long can the party tolerate this kind of informal communication between Rome and the Chinese Catholic leaders? How far does the party feel confident that it has the loyalty it wants, when, for example, some of the candidates for consecration as bishops get permission to use the old Latin rite, instead of the Chinese text where the candidate has to vow to be independent from the Holy See and be loyal to the nation?[90] The present Shanghai auxiliary bishop, Louis Jin Luxian, claims he himself is one of these. When he was released from jail after more than twenty years, he obtained an assurance from the party that he could make visits freely and receive visitors. His scholarship won him friends abroad and he was sent to visit Hong Kong and Germany as a representative of the Catholic church in China.

When the opinion of the Roman Curia was sought about the

of the Chinese government and the CCP to insist on the independence of the Chinese Catholic church from the Vatican. See *Catholic Church in China* 7 (15 August 1983).

[90] In the Chinese text of the liturgy of the consecration of bishops. A privately circulated booklet to be used in China on the occasion of consecration of bishops in which the candidates have to vow to denounce the Roman Curia. Compare the liturgical text used by the west on the same occasion, cf. 'Episcopal Ordination of the Right Reverend John Patrick Crowley', a liturgy of the consecration of the bishop of Westminster Catholic Diocese, England, on 8 December 1986.

reception to be given Catholic delegations from China by local church leaders, the Vatican made it plain that it wished them to be well received. Rome gave the instruction that, although there was to be no 'communicatio in sacris', other forms of joint prayers and friendly and even fraternal receptions were very much to be encouraged.[91]

Further reconciliatory gestures were made when the Pope requested the overseas Chinese Catholics to act as the bridge between the church in China and the universal church.[92] However, it is worth asking whether the overseas Catholics are more likely to cement the gap or drive a wedge at this juncture. Some incidents reveal that, with the support of overseas Catholics, some Chinese Catholics decline to be reconciled for various reasons, e.g. some married priests and bishops of the CPA are afraid to have reconciliation with the Vatican for fear of incurring church discipline. Some unofficial Catholics would be greatly disheartened if they were forgotten while the CPA were taken as the embodiment of the Chinese Catholic church.

The opportunity offered by the seminaries

Mention has already been made of the aims of the CCP in opening seminaries in China. Yet here the opportunities for the strengthening of Catholicism and the bettering of relations between the Holy See and China are as great as the dangers. Seven major Catholic seminaries have been established since 1979, headed by the National Catholic Seminary which opened in Beijing in September 1983. The other seminaries are the Beijing Diocesan Seminary, and five other regional ones in Shanghai, Wuhan, Xian, Shenyang and Chengdu respectively.[93] Up to summer 1987, it was reported that there were

91 The bishop of Hong Kong and German bishops received the same instructions from the Vatican when they sought the latter's advice on how to receive the visiting Chinese Catholic delegations in their own dioceses.

92 *Zhongyang Ribao* [The Central Daily] (Taiwan), 28 February 1984 reported the whole text of the Pope's speech to the Bishops of Taiwan on this matter. Also the Bishop of Hong Kong repeated the Pope's request in his pastoral letter to the Hong Kong Catholics, cf. *Ming Pao*, 9 November 1985. *Kung Kao Po*, 15 March 1985, 22 November 1985, 24 January 1986. For the English text see 'The Pope on Taiwan and the Chinese Diaspora: "Be a bridge-church"', in Wurth (ed.), *Papal Documents Related to New China*.

93 Yang Guojian, 'Zhongguo Tianzhujiao Jiaowu Weiyuanhui Lianlian Lai Gongjuo He Jinhou Yinwu De Baogao' [A bi-annual report of Chinese Catholic Administrative Council and its future responsibilities], *Catholic Church in China*, 7 (15 August 1983): 15.

altogether eleven seminaries.[94] The opening of the seminaries seems to be a positive sign given by the Chinese government to demonstrate its sincere intention to grant long-term religious freedom. Seminary training is a crucial factor in the life of the church, since it ensures that the Catholic doctrine is transmitted to the future priests who in turn will instruct the laity one day. The struggle between the CCP and the Chinese Catholics to gain the upper hand in the seminary training has been an existential one of a very gentle yet subtle nature. The religious cadres have tried to set the time-table, the text books and the curriculum, and they are responsible for recruiting the teaching staff and the admission of the candidates. Owing to the lack of teaching staff and up-to-date theological books, the CCP, though very reluctantly, have had to recruit as staff priests who were qualified but had long refused to join the Patriotic Association. It is said that in the Beijing Diocesan Seminary there is a one-hour class on politics each week as required by the government, but among the seminary staff there was nobody available to teach the subject. The seminary rector arranged things in such a way that the class has only been given twice a year. Moreover, the content of the class is just some history, and no examination is required for it.[95] Catholics abroad are more than eager to donate both reference and text books on theology and philosophy to the newly established seminaries once they come to know of the relatively poor collections of books in the libraries, and special permission has been given by the government for religious books to be received from any quarter.[96] Some Catholics in Hong Kong have even started a project to supply seminaries with large quantities of Chinese text books on various subjects in response to the call of the Pope for overseas Chinese Catholics to build a bridge between the Chinese Catholic church and the universal church.[97] The supplying of orthodox teaching material on church doctrine has long been the concern of the Vatican, which has been trying not to call the CPA schismatic, in the hope that this sector of the church will be reverting back to the main stream of the universal church.

[94] It was reported by Catholic visitors who got this information from Bishop Dong Guangqing, the Bishop of Wuhan in November 1987.

[95] J. Heyndrickx's report. pp. 14–18.

[96] Ibid.

[97] *Zhongyang Ribao* [The Central Daily] (Taiwan), 28 February 1984. The Bishop of Hong Kong's pastoral letter to the Hong Kong Catholics, cf. *Ming Pao*, 9 November 1985. *Kung Kao Po*, 15 March 1985, 22 November 1985, 24 January 1986.

CONCLUSIONS

Chinese Catholics and religious freedom

Relaxation of political control was needed to some extent if China wished to create an environment in which its people could contribute their best to modernisation. Yet, although a slight relaxing of the tense control was essential, the result has been a change in the social life in China (perhaps more far-reaching than the government intended), from which religion has also benefited. Part of the change was deliberately sought by the authorities, but the new policies have had unintended effects as well – such as the relaxation of moral attitudes.[98]

Throughout all the changes one significant fact has stood out: namely, the authority of the CCP which had previously not been challenged, now failed to command people's obedience. Thus, the scope for alternative outlooks and philosophies, including religious beliefs, was enlarged. On the other hand, government directives were issued to guide religious affairs in this period. By studying the religious policy as applied by religious cadres in different provinces, both in urban and rural sectors, one may perceive the goals the government has set itself in respect of religion.

First of all China has given much publicity to its religious freedom policy by showing to the whole world that more and more churches, temples, mosques and other places of worship have been opened. But on the other hand Buddhist temples built without official consent were forcibly pulled down.[99] Christians, both Catholics and Protestants, have been re-arrested, and it has been reported that an aged bishop in jail was left without sufficient medical supplies and that he was very sick.[100] Again much publicity was given to the release of Bishop Gong, but in fact he was merely moved from a prison cell to house arrest, and was not allowed to receive visitors without the consent of the government.[101]

In the seminaries, although party members are little qualified to

98 The government in fact complained about the relaxation of moral attitudes, for example freedom in sex. See Jin Zhihua *et al.* (ed.), *Qingnian Rensheng Zhexue* [Philosophy of life for the youth] (Beijing: Zhongguo Qingnian, 1986), pp. 198–202.
99 *Nanfang Ribao*, 5 January 1982.
100 Reported by Amnesty International on 4 June 1987. See Amnesty Internal, 'Health concern. People's Republic of China: Fan Xueyan' ASA 17/04/87 (4 June 1984): 1.
101 See, Gong Pinmei, 'The Letter of Appeal', p. 16. It was reported that he was released from house arrest in January (BBC World Service, 'Radio News', 6 January 1988).

organise religious education, the CCP has nevertheless tried by all means to influence the training programme of the future religious leaders in accordance with the intentions of the party. They hope that the future religious personnel will be subservient to the party instead of being faithful to their religious beliefs.

Although the state constitution, the ultimate legal authority of the nation, promises freedom in religion, it affords no guarantee. For Catholics have been pressurised to abandon their religion and take up a new branch of Christianity prescribed by the CCP. Indeed the CCP has been insisting that Catholics sever relations, including spiritual relations, with the Holy See.

The CCP has even gone to the extent of prescribing what kind of religious activities can be performed, and the party has the final word on who can conduct religious services and where religious services can be held. One cannot but see how much more interest the CCP displays in the more sensitive but essential aspects of Catholic religion: doctrine and hierarchy.

In a regime with Marxism-Leninism as the orthodox ideology, the religious believers and the intellectuals are two categories of people the Communist leaders have little liking for and show little favour to. In the USSR, the persecution of intellectuals, as described by Alexander Solzhenitsyn in his work *The Gulag Archipelago 1918–1956*, is one long revolting list of sufferings at the hands of Marxist regimes.[102] In China, the intermittent purgings of intellectuals in the 'Anti-Rightist Campaign', 'The Hundred Flowers Movement' and the recent 'Anti-Bourgeois Liberalism Movement', have all revealed that the degree of tolerance of divergent ideologies (as embraced by intellectuals as well as Catholics) depends on the mood of the CCP at that particular time. This has been and still remains a serious problem; the CCP leaders have always emphasised the four basic principles, but have periodically relaxed restrictions on religious practice and intellectual freedom. Both religious believers and intellectuals have confidence in truth and will search continuously for the truth each in their own way, explaining the truth systematic- ally as they see it without going to the party and accepting their tenets as the CCP expects. Catholics go to the church for teaching of truth; and the intellectuals seek guidance from their own consciences and thoughts and academic disciplines. Their truth may be quite

---

[102] Alexander Solzhenitsyn, *The Gulag Archipelago 1918–1956*, trans. by Thomas Whitney (London: Book Club Associates, 1974).

different from the explanations given by the party. Consequently, the intellectuals and Catholics are both held in suspicion by the CCP. The harsh treatment given to Bishop Gong, Bishop Deng and the Chinese Jesuits led by Father Vincent Zhu, suggests that the problem of belief and ideology is one of the factors explaining why the CCP leaders can not show much tolerance to the Catholic church. Although church buildings have been reopened to give people the impression that the government-sponsored church represents the essentials of religion, few outsiders realise that many essential teachings have been eliminated.[103] The main church doctrine being challenged is church unity: one Catholic church united with the universal church under the leadership of the Pope.

Seldom is the controlling hand of the party not seen in any area of religious matters in China. 'Document 19' and all the party directives that have appeared in the party media since the 3rd Plenum of the 11th Central Committee of the CCP, have declared to the whole world that religious freedom has been granted to the people. This was very laudable although in the west religious freedom is considered not as given by the governing body, but by God as a birthright.[104] So essentially how much freedom may be given, when it will be given, and how long it can be given all depends on the giver. There may be grounds for hope that, from the evidence of religious practice in China so far, even within the framework designed by the party freedom for religious activities may prevail.

At the end of December 1986 and the beginning of January 1987, some notable events took place in China – the student demonstrations in major cities. These started at Hefei University in Anhui Province, and then spread to Wuhan, Guangzhou, Beijing and Shanghai. The students asked for more political freedom through direct elections.[105] Some observers of China expected that the demonstrations would be the catalyst for the birth of democracy.[106] It turned out that they sparked off the dismissal of progressive intellectuals from the party membership,[107] the clamp-down on

---

[103] The writer was told by one of the National seminary teaching staff in Beijing in 1984 that they had begun to rewrite the seminary text books in terms of the situation in China.

[104] The CCP said that 'religious freedom is our basic policy . . .'. See *Hongqi* 12 (June 1982): 2; and 'Document 19'. This revealed that the Chinese leaders thought that the party was the one who granted religious freedom to people.

[105] *The Nineties* (January 1987): 17–20.

[106] Ibid.: 17–20.

[107] *Renmin Ribao*, 1 January 1987. *The Nineties* (January 1987) reported the student demonstration. One month later it devoted the whole issue in February 1987 to analysing the

'bourgeois liberalism' by tightening censorship, and the ousting of the CCP's Secretary General, Hu Yaobang.[108] The suppression of the democratic movement by Chinese officials illustrates that freedom is in the hands of the rulers, who will grant it to the people in their own time for their own reasons, and above all that they may take it back if they so wish. One must accept that this is the logic stemming from China's long indigenous political culture, in which freedom and democracy have been lacking. This is the mentality that governs the political behaviour of the Chinese leaders. This logic also applies to religious affairs. Not only may the limited freedom prescribed by the CCP be taken back if the general policy of the party reverts to tight ideological control once more but, indeed, if the CCP were to find a compelling reason at some time to seek closer Sino-Vatican relations, the long insisted-upon policy of 'independence' from the Vatican of the Chinese Catholics could be changed almost overnight! Does one not still remember how terrible a crime it was to attack the 'Three Banners' in the early 1960s? Yet, today the people's communes have gone, the Great Leap Forward is ridiculed. Is this not good evidence to prove that the CCP can change its mind on anything at any time?

The unsolved problems of Sino-Vatican relations

For an ordinary Catholic the Vatican has a religious significance, but for a political scientist or anyone versed in politics, the Vatican is a powerful and special political institution rooted in a tiny sovereign state in Rome, administered by a group of dedicated officials at the centre of a world-wide ecclesiastical network. China has been quite attentive to the political aspect of the Vatican, especially for the information it can obtain from there.[109] Is not the core of the Sino-Vatican conflict focused on the clash of authority between the

downfall of Hu, the student demonstration and the dismissal of leading intellectuals from the party. See *The Nineties* (February 1987): 9, 40–88.

[108] It was reported that from January to April 1987, eleven directives were issued criticising Hu Yaobang. It was reported that Directives No. 2, 3 and 8 openly criticised Hu allowing the growth of bourgeois liberalism. See *The Nineties* 6 (June 1987): 33–4.

[109] The left-wing Hong Kong newspaper *New Evening Post* on 11 June 1981 had an article on 'Qingbaowang Bianbu De Fandigang' [The Vatican with its intelligence networks]. The article discussed (1) the Vatican's efficient intelligence networks (2), its Ostpolitik, and (3) Pope Paul VI and Pope John Paul II's travelling missions. Also see: Yu Shouzhen trans., 'Waikan Ping Fandigang' [Remarks on the Vatican by foreign journals], *Shijie Zongjiao Ziliao* (Beijing) 2 (1986): 22–5.

Vatican and the Chinese government as to the ideological leadership of the 3 million Catholic population? Its resentment that the head of another sovereign state, the Vatican, should manage any religious affairs on Chinese soil is apparently unbearable to the Chinese government, especially at a time when it has successfully won power after a revolution and hates the USA for supporting Chiang Kai Shek and for sending the Seventh Fleet to the Taiwan Strait. Moreover, the insensitivity of some western missionaries in the past has left a legacy of suspicion in the minds of the Communist Chinese rulers. The Korean War and the US embargo drew China into an utterly anti-western stance, and the Vatican is one of the western states. The demand from the Chinese government that the Catholic church in China be independent from the Vatican might be considered a very natural outcome. China found it difficult to accept the fact that church affairs should be handled by the bureaucracy set up by the Vatican city state. The highly structured bureaucracy of the Vatican city state that governs the Catholic church with its 700 million believers scattered over the whole world may have aroused great suspicion in the newly established politburo, nearly all of whose members in 1949 had little experience of the outside world or knowledge of international relations.

This attitude may have been reinforced by the Chinese government's observation of the church–state relations operating in other countries, and possibly China took this lesson too much to heart. No state in modern history with 0.7 per cent of its population Catholic (3.8 million) has reacted to the supposed threat so strongly as to create an independent church in order to rid itself of the attentions of the Roman Curia. The Communist government in Vietnam and the Socialist Burmese government did not do this, neither did any state in eastern Europe. But these governments do forbid foreign missionaries to preach the Gospel in their territories. The result of creating an independent Chinese Catholic church has had the result of dividing the Catholic believers. The division itself might indeed have been the desired objective, since political purges and class struggle prevail in the party's repertoire, and it frequently makes non-conforming religious believers victims in its political purges. But now China is no longer willing to let the issue of ideological conformity stand in the way of its modernisation programme.[110] Some argue

[110] *Hongqi* 12 (16 June 1982): 2–8. 'Document 19', para. 2. *Guangming Ribao*, 30 November 1980.

that, since the policy of tolerance is also applied to Catholics, this indicates that the Communists in China are not particularly antagonistic towards the Catholics any more. In the past China has certainly ill-treated the non-conformists. Like the intellectuals, the Catholics were ill-treated because the Catholic clergy were non-conforming intellectuals: nor were the laity conformists, even if not intellectuals. In the 1950s the government ill-treated all religious believers: Buddhist monks and nuns, Protestant ministers and Muslim Imams, as well as Catholic priests and nuns; all were persecuted without exception. This shows that China is not necessarily particularly anti-Catholic. The continuous quarrel with the Vatican is due to the peculiar nature of the latter, which in the eyes of the Beijing government poses a special threat. The autocratic nature of the Vatican and the Catholic church, and the strict discipline demanded of the believers in general and its professional religious personnel in particular, have made Chinese political leaders feel the presence of the Vatican's authority in church matters within China.[111] Many Catholics before the 1949 Revolution sought advice from their clergy over their relations with the Communists as well as over social issues, instead of accepting the solutions offered by the CCP. For the Catholic church has its own attitudes and opinions on moral and political affairs. It is the unofficial Catholics' constant claim that the Church's teachings affect their political and moral attitudes. The reasoning given by Bishop Gong in his appeal is a good example of this kind. The CCP could cope with folk religion but must have felt it much more difficult to cope with the Catholic church with its long history of giving its own directives and teachings on every aspect of social life through a highly educated, disciplined body of priests and religious personnel. On the question of the appointment of local bishops, the Vatican has jealously guarded the right of appointing bishops exclusively for the Pope, leaving no room for the involvement of the local civil authority. It was this that sparked off the Sino-Vatican conflict.

From the Chinese government's point of view, the question of the

---

[111] Xiao Feng, 'Zhonggong Zenyang Duidai Zongjiao He Zongjiao Xindu' [How did the CCP deal with religion and religious believers], *Intellectual Semi-Monthly* (Hong Kong) 65, 66, 67, 68 (1970). The author had spent ten years as a leading cadre in religious affairs in the 1950s in one of the Chinese big cities. In the article he recalled how the Catholics in Shanghai and Guangzhou under the strong leadership of Bishop Gong and Bishop Deng refused to be separated from the Holy See and unquestionably accepted the right of teaching of the Catholic church through the clergy and religious leaders.

Catholic Patriotic Association and the unofficial church has to be solved somehow or other, China cannot destroy its brainchild – the CPA – by dissolving it in order to recognise the unofficial church which has remained loyal to the Holy See. China has a valid reason in helping the CPA Catholics who are docile to the demands of the party and help the party by discouraging the Chinese Catholics from being loyal to Rome. Another political reason which does not allow China to undermine the CPA is that at this stage of socialism in China, the political leaders seem to be bent on boosting patriotism in a united front.[112] With the unification of Taiwan and the return of Hong Kong and Macao in mind, the Catholic Patriotic Association can hardly be down-graded in the context of patriotism. On the other hand, the unofficial church is a thorn in China's side, even though because of the small percentage of the population belonging to it, it seems to be of a minor nature. Still for all that, China cannot totally suppress this sector of religion because that suppression would damage its reputation abroad and possibly undermine its policy of appealing to intellectuals at home. At the same time China is not willing to allow the existence of any organisation outside its control. Tolerance in religious affairs could be a way to bring to the surface members of the unofficial church and make it possible to encourage them to seek security in the open church. On the other hand, the simple Catholic folk do not understand the delicate, subtle relations between church and state, neither do they realise the intricacies of other unsolved problems. However, they continue to look to the Catholic church for pastoral care and the sacraments and some display a remarkable loyalty to Rome.

[112] Yang Jingren, 'Xinshiqui de Tongyi Zhanxian' [The United Front policy of the new era], *Xinshiqi Tongyi Zhanxian Wenxian Xuanbian* [Selected documents on the United Front policy of the new era] (Beijing: Zhonggong Zhongyang Dangxiao, 1985), pp. 281–95.

CHAPTER 7

Sino-Vatican relations in the modernisation era

Introduction

The Open Door Policy that was part of the modernisation programme initiated at the Party's Third Plenum in December 1978
provided the Vatican with a longed-for opportunity to find out
about the real situation in China. The long silence, especially during
the ten years of the Cultural Revolution, kept the Vatican from
making any accurate observation and contact. Even the correspondence of the Chinese Catholic laity, priests and religious women to
their relatives outside, revealed little more than scanty accounts of
the real situation in the Catholic church and of religious life in
general. For example, during times of harassment Catholics could
only make known their sufferings to their relatives abroad by using
indirect metaphorical language such as, 'the weather is very hot this
season; and we are greatly troubled by the mosquitoes'.[1] The
scarcity of news from China even tempted some China observers to
think that religion had been eradicated by the atheist government.[2]
Thus as late as 1981 despite the Vatican's access to various
channels of information by then, Pope John Paul II sadly admitted
that he did not have enough information on the Chinese Catholic
church.[3]

It was through this Roman Pontiff that the Vatican clearly and
openly made some important new gestures to woo China with the
intention of initiating a reconciliation with the Chinese Catholics as
well as with the Chinese government. The time was ripe, as China
was more open to the west than ever before. Prior to that, several
small trial balloons had been sent up by Pope Paul VI, a predecessor

---

[1] From a private correspondence of a priest in China to one of his relatives abroad.
[2] L. Ladany: 'The church in China seen in December 1980' (privately circulated article).
[3] 'The Pope speaks to Chinese Christians', *Sunday Examiner*, 27 February 1987.

of Pope John Paul II, in the 1960s with the purpose of establishing relations with China in one form or another. It led this Pontiff to visit Hong Kong and to direct a speech to the Chinese Catholics in 1959. But his word did not carry: China was then embroiled in the upheavals of the Great Leap Forward. China totally ignored all these gestures as if nothing had taken place. China in effect was cocooned in its own revolutionary isolation and it declined to have international interaction with the west in Mao's time except for strategic and limited economic purposes.

In the period between 1976 and 1986, the Vatican tried all possible means to establish contacts with China for the purpose of initiating a Sino-Vatican dialogue in order to thrash out their differences. It was hoped that a Sino-Vatican rapprochement could be developed now that China had begun to come out from its isolation and to involve itself in international affairs, both on global and regional levels. In the course of these ten years of interaction between the Vatican and China, several speeches were made by the Pope clearly demonstrating his intentions of initiating a friendly relationship with China. The first major speech was made in Manila in front of a group of overseas Chinese in February 1981, in the course of his first trip to Asia.[4] He openly expressed his wish to formulate a brotherhood with the Chinese, borrowing the Chinese proverb 'Amid the four seas, all men are brothers'.[5] A few days later, on 1 March 1981, another overture was made by Cardinal Casaroli, the Secretary of State in the Vatican and the chief architect of its Ostpolitik. With his experience in dealing with Communist states in eastern Europe, Cardinal Casaroli openly suggested more concrete measures to resolve the thorny questions of church and state relations between China and the Vatican, including Taiwan and the CPA Catholics. He held a press conference in Hong Kong together with Bishop Dominic Deng who had just been released by the Chinese government after twenty-two years of imprisonment.

Then, in May 1981, the Vatican took a further step to formulate a warmer relationship with China by conferring the Archbishopric of Guangzhou upon Bishop Dominic Deng, a man seemingly trusted by the Chinese government. But this overture turned out to be a real clash of authority between the Vatican and China. China's leaders objected strongly to this appointment made by an alien power

4 Wurth (ed.), *Papal Documents Related to the New China*, art. 14, p. 95.
5 Ibid.

without even informing them in advance. This unexpected setback in Sino-Vatican relations led the Vatican to take a new turn in its approach to China. It sought to mend the breach by developing a network of very low-key contacts on a large scale, including visits to Catholics at the grass roots level, and supplying material aid for government projects in religious work and social service. It appeared that the Vatican was making friendly gestures designed to demonstrate its good faith and, although the Chinese did not respond warmly, they did not reject the gestures.

However, in the course of establishing contacts, several significant personalities became involved. In the controversy over the appointment of the Archbishop of Guangzhou, Bishop Dominic Deng was the focus of the storm. But the visit of the two European Cardinals, Cardinal Etchegary of Marseilles and Cardinal Koenig of Vienna in 1980 (prior to that quarrel) was taken as an opportunity by China to demonstrate its interest in developing relations with the Vatican. China used the occasion to present its views on the Chinese Catholic church as well as to put forward conditions for rapprochement. This was followed by the visits of Cardinal Sin of Manila and Bishop Wu of Hong Kong who, when they reported back to the Vatican, outlined their views on the situation of the Catholic church in China. These visits further confirmed China's interest in establishing a dialogue with the Vatican. In addition to the visits of these eminent figures of the church, the interactions of ordinary Catholics in China including priests, religious women and laity, with Catholic visitors from abroad generally reaped positive results. They enabled the Vatican to obtain a truer and fuller picture of the situation of the church in China, and they contributed to a true image of the universal church to those inside China, thus helping to dispel fears and suspicions which are the major obstacles a rapprochement and reconciliation between the churches themselves. The Chinese authorities for their part allowed the Chinese Catholics under their control to develop foreign contacts in the hope of using these for the purpose of legitimising its brainchild, the CPA, and introducing it to Christians all over the world.

The contact between the Vatican and China was not conducted in a vacuum but across a bridge. The overseas Chinese in Hong Kong and Taiwan were the major bridge builders. In their own ways, they contributed whatever they could to make a reconciliation possible. But before one of the bridges, notably Hong Kong, could fulfil its mission and witness the normalisation of Sino-Vatican relations, Hong Kong itself suddenly became one of the major, though not the main concerns, of the Vatican and China: the 1984 Sino-British Agreement decreed that this crown colony would go back to China in 1997. The other bridge was not too safe either, for Beijing has been trying hard to lead Taibei to the negotiating table and decide on the unification of Taiwan with the motherland.

The aim of this chapter is to study how the clash of authority influenced the process of friendly gestures by the Vatican from 1976 to 1986, and how China responded to these gestures. At the same time it will explore how these goodwill gestures between the Vatican and China were exchanged so shortly after the apparent clash of authority.

THE VATICAN'S OVERTURES FOR RAPPROCHEMENT

Overtures in Mao's era

Ever since the death of Pope Pius XII in 1958, the Vatican for pastoral reasons has contemplated breaking the ice and developing warmer relations with China, a country that has 3.8 million Catholics and a huge population to evangelise. The Vatican had also to think of some compatible ways of settling the problem of the CPA, which after its birth in 1957 continuously declared itself to be independent from the Holy See. In fact many small gestures had already been made by previous popes, such as John XXIII and Paul VI. Thus in 1959, during the reign of Pope John XXIII, there was a meeting in Hong Kong of church experts on China affairs, under the Prefect of the Congregation of Propaganda, Cardinal Agaginaian. They came to the conclusion that the new Chinese bishops consecrated without the approval of the Pope should be regarded as valid but lacking in legitimacy. They argued that the Chinese Catholic church should not be treated as schismatic, cutting it off from the universal church, like the Anglican church in the time of Henry VIII.[6] This view became the basis for the principal guidelines of the Vatican on Chinese church affairs. Shortly after his election, the new Pontiff Paul VI sent a telegram to China to show his goodwill in June 1963. The Chinese side did not reply, probably inspired by

6   Ibid., art. 45, pp. 177–8.

political rather than religious considerations. For, in October of the same year, China hosted a big religious ceremony for its Japanese guests to celebrate the 1200th anniversary of the death of the Chinese Buddhist monk, Janzhen, who first brought Buddhism to Japan. This was the time when the tide of 'anti-US imperialism' was still running high; the Sino-Soviet rupture had taken place and China was claiming to be the centre of authentic Marxism–Leninism. Again, at the start of 1966, the same Pope Paul VI sent a New Year message to Chairman Mao. Still there was no reply. Pope Paul VI expressed his wish to begin some form of contact with China by appealing for freedom and peace in his homily on the feast of Epiphany, 6 January 1967. This was when the Chinese Catholics were being subjected to severe over cruel persecution due to the Cultural Revolution. The Pope's burning anxiety led him to look for every possible opportunity, religious or otherwise, to make contact. The release of an American missionary, Bishop James Walsh, from China in 1970 after twelve years of imprisonment, was for Pope Paul VI 'a sign of better days to come, days so long desired for the cause of freedom and religion, as well as for the honour and prosperity of that immense nation which the church has never ceased to love'.[7] Pope Paul VI, being the head of a sovereign state, came to realise that the release was one of the overtures to the United States by China to pave the way for Sino-US rapprochement in the 1970s, after the Sino-Soviet rupture in the early 60s. Evidently the Pope had seen religious implications in an action which was motivated entirely by political considerations.

Pope Paul VI's dramatic visit in December 1970 to Hong Kong, clearly illustrates more of his ever urgent desire to have some kind of contact with the silent Catholics in China. As this was his first trip to Asia and Oceania, Hong Kong would not normally have been on the itinerary. Had the Pontiff wished to show his friendship to England and usher in ecumenical relations between the Catholic church and the Church of England, he should have gone to London instead of going to a British colony in the Far East. But since China was closed to foreign visitors from the west and Taiwan would have been a faux pas indeed, Hong Kong was the only possibility left. Obviously the Pope's intention was to pass some friendly signals to China from Hong Kong for the sake of the Chinese Catholics. For

[7] Ibid., art. 23, p. 114.

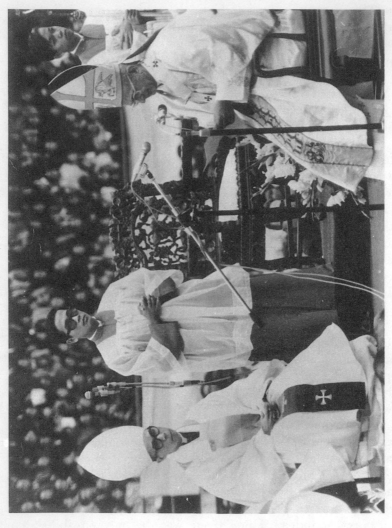

6 Pope Paul VI speaks to the Hong Kong Catholics on his short visit to Hong Kong (October 1969).
Source: Kung Kao Po (The Chinese Catholic Weekly).

political reasons, the British government had to be cautious in the welcome accorded to the Pope. Therefore the Acting Hong Kong Governor met the Pope while the Hong Kong Governor remained in England. At the same time, the Hong Kong government with Sir David Trench at its helm was in no mood to make any concession to Beijing. It was important of course that the Pope should not use Hong Kong to make political remarks that would embarrass Britain, especially as Britain had recognised Beijing, while the Vatican had not. The main problem was one of security. The return of the Governor for the Papal visit was much discussed. The Governor's presence would have seemed like giving a great deal of special attention to the Pope at a time when Britain itself had not established diplomatic relations with the Vatican; it was decided not to have him return. He needed the holiday anyway, for his health was not particularly good then.

The Pope decided to go there all the same. Then through the British Ambassador in Rome the government of Hong Kong urged Pope Paul VI to make no statement directed to Roman Catholics in Communist China, while Taiwan Catholics and bishops who hoped to meet the Pope in Hong Kong were refused visas by the Hong Kong government.[8] All these difficulties did not dampen his interest in speaking to the Chinese people. Although he could not explicitly direct himself to the Catholics in China, the Pontiff succeeded in hinting something to the Chinese Catholics in his formal and informal speeches made on his half-day visit there.[9]

The signals discharged from the Vatican did not receive positive responses from China. Even when Hua Guofeng visited Europe in November 1979 and met the Italian President in Rome, he refrained from going to the western part of that city to pay a friendly visit to the Pope at the Vatican. The reason given in response to questions by foreign journalists was that there were no diplomatic relations as yet between China and the Vatican. The PRC leaders indicated that they were not yet sufficiently well informed about the affairs of the Vatican. Signs of a slight change came about when the Chinese political leaders let it be known that they wanted to have a clearer understanding of the nature, history and recent development of the Vatican, including personal data on the new Polish Pope, John Paul

8   These things were not mentioned by the local media in Hong Kong but were reported by foreign newspapers. See *The New York Times*, 25 November 1970.
9   Wurth (ed.), *Papal documents Related to the New China*, pp. 120–2.

II. The more liberal Austrian Cardinal, Koenig of Vienna, revealed that, before he was invited to China by the Sino-Austrian Friendship Association, he had shown himself a friend to China by accepting the invitation for a long talk from the Chinese Ambassador to Austria, who was very interested in ascertaining some information about Pope John Paul II from him.[10] Interestingly, at the same time as the Vatican-related study groups began to be established in Hong Kong to investigate religious matters in China, the Chinese Academy of Social Sciences in Beijing added a much stronger team to their religious section for the purpose of making special studies of the Catholic church and the Vatican. These studies on both sides seemed to pave the way to some form of academic dialogue and encounter.[11]

Pope John Paul II's overtures

The Vatican took the release of Bishop Dominic Deng in June 1980 as a positive sign that some kind of dialogue between the Vatican and China would be possible.[12] The Chinese had made a positive public gesture of goodwill and an initiative for dialogue in allowing Bishop Deng to go to Hong Kong and Rome after his release. When Pope John Paul II took a trip to the Far East in February 1981, he decided to speak to the Chinese in a more explicit manner. This time, realising how much inconvenience and restriction the Hong Kong government had imposed on His holiness, Pope Paul VI, as regards directing a speech to the mainland, he did not choose Hong Kong. Manila, the capital of the neighbouring Philippines was the place he selected for the purpose, and on the occasion of receiving a group of overseas Chinese, resident in the Philippines, he delivered his famous speech to woo China for a dialogue, giving at the same time the strongest and most explicit statement of the Vatican's policy on China. Repeatedly he affirmed that a good Chinese Catholic should be a good Chinese citizen, and pleaded with China to let bygones be bygones, stating that he hoped to have a new beginning and establish new relations:

[10] Fox Butterfield, 'Cardinal in China', *The New York Times*, 14 March 1980.
[11] Many Catholic scholars including Cardinal Koenig were invited to lecture in the Chinese Social Science Academy in Beijing. In Hong Kong the Xinhua News Agency, the quasi-consulate of China, had been establishing various forms of contact with personnel in the Catholic study and research circles.
[12] *Kung Kao Po*, 12 September 1980.

But whatever difficulties there may have been, they belong to the past, and now it is the future that we have to look to.[13]

He also expressed at great length his esteem for China and its culture as well as its endeavours in modernisation. He continued:

Your country is great indeed, not only in terms of geographical extension and population, but especially because of its history, the wealth of its culture and the moral values that the people have cultivated all through the ages.

Your country is indeed devoting all its energies to the future. It wishes to ensure through scientific and technological development and through the industrious collaboration of all its people that its citizens can live in true happiness . . .[14]

He also assured the Chinese authorities that the Chinese Catholics would be good citizens who would work diligently for the progress of the nation. He stressed:

I am convinced that every Catholic within your frontiers will fully contribute to the building up of China, since a genuine and faithful Christian is also a genuine and good citizen.[15]

By saying this it seemed that the Pope was trying to lay down a clear guideline to improve Sino-Vatican relations, that should be acceptable to China: he claimed that a Chinese Christian should in religious matters be submissive to the authority of the supreme religious authority – the Pope, but in civil matters be submissive to the highest civil authority, the Constitution of the state. In other words, theoretically, the Pope advocated that in religious matters a Chinese Catholic might go to religious leaders for guidance, but he must obey the state law and civil leadership in civil affairs. It sounded clear and easy enough in theory, but in practice, it still left open the question as to who had the authority to decide which issue belonged to the civil and which to the religious realm. Here the Pope just touched the core of the problem, the clash of authority, and whether he knew it or not the speech of the Holy Father merely brought the nature of the conflict to the surface between the Vatican and China.

In the Gospel of St. Mark, Jesus Christ himself laid down the

[13] 'The Pope speaks to Chinese Christians', *Sunday Examiner*, 27 February 1981.
[14] Ibid.
[15] Ibid.

teachings on church and state relations by saying Christians should give to Caesar what belongs to Caesar, and to God what belongs to God.[16] But now it is not enough to distinguish between state and church affairs, which are so often interlocked in human life. It needs someone to give the final decision by declaring what belongs to Caesar and what to God, before taking up the problem according to its nature. In the course of European history there were numerous church and state conflicts, even wars, because the heads of the states and the heads of the church fought over the right to decide which was God's business and which was Caesar's. In China, this same old story repeats itself. When the Pope said that a good Christian would be a good citizen, had he clearly mapped out in his mind a blueprint as to who could give the definition of a good citizen and a good Chinese Christian?

The Pope ended his important speech by reiterating the mission of the church as being concerned with nothing but a religious purpose. 'It does not aim at a worldly mission with political or economic purpose', the Pope said: 'It [the church] wants to be, in China as in any other country, the herald of the Kingdom of God. It desires no privileges but asks that all those who follow Christ may be able to express their faith freely and publicly and live according to their consciences.'[17] Not only did the Pope explain clearly the mission of the Catholic church, but he also gave a reply to the repeated accusations by the Chinese in the past that the church was interfering in the internal affairs of the country, while the Chinese Constitution was demanding that religion should be a private affair. The state in practice has been using public money to reopen places of worship and to facilitate religious activities, and of course supervise religious affairs with its own cadres, although the state and party embrace the atheist Marxism–Leninism.

When the Pope was on this Far East trip, he rejected a proposed visit to Taiwan on his way between the Philippines and Japan to avoid the risk of annoying Beijing. He also brought along with him his assistant, the Secretary of State, Cardinal Casaroli, the famous architect of the Vatican's Ostpolitik, who had had long experience in the art of negotiating with Communist leaders of the eastern European Bloc. The Secretary of State of the Vatican left the Pope after the last stop of the Papal visit in Japan and made a private trip

16 The Gospel of St. Mark 12: 17.
17 'The Pope speaks to Chinese Christians', *Sunday Examiner*, 27 February 1981.

to Hong Kong, where he met Bishop Deng, and talked to the Apostolic Charge d'Affaires of Taiwan, then he summoned the Catholic China watchers to discuss the situation in China and the possibility of establishing a dialogue. Many took this as a big move by the Vatican towards a possible rapprochement. It was true that the Pope's speech in Manila only mapped out the general trend of his intention to seek reconciliation. The message at a press conference in Hong Kong jointly given by Casaroli and Bishop Deng specified the sensitive and concrete problems of Taiwan. Casaroli claimed that the Taiwan problem could be solved through diplomatic channels, and local churches could have many forms of independence.[18]

The Chinese leaders kept quiet before the Pope's Manila speech. They expressed their reaction through their sponsored bishop, Michael Fu, who showed a sudden change of attitude after the Papal speech in Manila and Casaroli's gesture. He stated that he would welcome friendly relations and hoped that Casaroli would play the role of Kissinger. But two days later his attitude hardened; in a hostile tone he declared that it would be meaningless for the Pope to visit China at that stage when the Vatican had caused contradictions among Chinese Catholics. He demanded that the Vatican should demonstrate the sincerity of its dialogue by deeds, such as cutting off diplomatic relations with Taiwan. Apparently the general feeling of the Chinese government at that stage was that Sino-Vatican relations would only be a liability, not an asset except in the question of isolating Taiwan. The shifting of Chinese official opinion as expressed through Bishop Fu suggests that there was a diversity of opinions in high political circles in China regarding religious matters. This would mean that it was difficult for the Chinese side to form a unified voice on this delicate matter.

Many observers were optimistic regarding the positive signals sent by the Vatican signifying that great concessions were being made on their side, and hoping that China would respond well.[19] The speech of Bishop Fu did not seem to carry much weight with the Vatican because of reports against his personal integrity. In fact, he was married. This was so according to some Catholic China observers. If this were the reason, it seems that the Vatican was being very short-sighted. The selection of the messenger may be of symbolic signifi-

---

[18] See *Hong Kong Standard, Sing Tao Yat Po, South China Morning Post,* 1 March 1981.
[19] *Wen Wei Po,* 22 February 1981. *Reuter News,* 21 February 1981.

cance, but ultimately it is the message that counts. While the Vatican was still waiting for a more favourable reply from China, the veteran Vatican diplomat Cardinal Casaroli read the signs and diagnosed that there were still too many obstacles in the way of a Sino-Vatican rapprochement; therefore, he remarked that he was neither optimistic nor pessimistic regarding the Sino-Vatican relations. He made this statement before he left Hong Kong for Rome after meeting Bishop Deng and other people concerned. This was long before the Vatican appointed the Archbishop of Guangzhou.[20]

China's response: the ripples from the appointment of Archbishop of Guangzhou

Some months after the controversy over this appointment, the Pope tried to discuss religious problems relating to the CPA, such as communion with the Holy See. In a very indirect way, he tried to dwell on the trials and the hardships of the unofficial church in China, discussing at the same time for the benefit of the CPA the question of union with the Holy See, from a theological and scriptural point of view, to show that the union is love and truth. The discussion was presented in the form of an open letter of 6 January 1982 to the bishops of the world asking for prayer for the church in China. This written message was so very strong in its religious tone that only those who were interested in religious questions would have had the patience to read it to the end.[21] Prejudice and misunderstanding came looming between Rome and Beijing. Beijing again tried to interpret the question from a political point of view, angry that Rome should allude to religious persecution in China. The Pope also mentioned that the 'brothers and sisters in China have been made to face difficult and prolonged trials in the past thirty years. In spite of those severe sufferings they have given proof of their fidelity to Christ and His church; comparing such courageous witness to that of the first centuries of the church.'[22] It must be said that this suggests 'clumsy diplomacy': it could not hope to forward any rapprochement, accusing Beijing of religious persecution and then saying one wanted good relations. This could

---

[20] When he visited Hong Kong on 28 February 1981, Cardinal Casaroli on a private occasion told one of the Catholic researchers that he was neither optimistic nor pessimistic about the development of Sino-Vatican relations.

[21] Wurth (ed.), *Papal Documents Related to the New China*, art. 36, pp. 146–9.

[22] Ibid., art. 36, p. 148.

only be interpreted as expecting the Chinese to apologise or change. Had not the Vatican urged that bygones be bygones?

Beijing responded by accusing the Vatican of vicious slander against the Catholic church in China.[23] On 21 March 1982, the Pope celebrated a special Mass for Chinese Catholics. He prayed that the Chinese Catholics would be able to 'practise their faith without hindrance, remaining united to the Catholic church of Rome'.[24] The following day, 22 March, a spokesman for the Chinese Foreign Ministry told the reporters: 'Chinese citizens have freedom of belief, which is protected by law. Any attempt to distort the facts is futile.'[25] The problem for the Vatican was how to speak to its own audience (the Chinese Catholics) without being heard by the other audience (the CCP) in the period when the news of the appointment still rankled grievously. At first glance the reaction from the Chinese appears to have been overly strong, but if one enters deep into their mentality it is not surprising that they should react in such a manner.

Whenever the Chinese political leaders made any reference to 'the Catholics in China', they meant only those Catholics who had joined the CPA and whose activities were sponsored by the government under the auspices of the CPA. Moreover, the Chinese government regarded any religious activities which were not held by approved personnel at approved locations to be illegal. The non-CPA Catholics refused to be independent of the Holy See and naturally they refused to be identified with the CPA. This group of clandestine Catholics were regarded by the government as religious dissidents. It was this group of religious dissidents that the Vatican was especially concerned about and prayed for, and it was this same group of dissidents who obtained no recognition from the Chinese authorities and were persecuted for disobedience to civil law and government orders in religious matters. That was why Bishop Yang Gaojian and the spokesman for the Chinese Foreign Ministry accused the Pope of vicious slander against the Catholics in China. Yang Gaojian expounded the activities sponsored by the CPA when the religious freedom policy was implemented. He stated that: 'in the past ten years national and diocesan administrative organisations have been set up; church affairs have gradually expanded, more than two

[23] *Xinhua News*, 20 March 1982.
[24] Wurth (ed.), *Papal Documents Related to the New China*, art. 37, pp. 151–3.
[25] *Wen Wei Po*, 23 March 1982.

hundred churches have been repaired and are open for Holy Mass and thousands of faithful Catholics attend church.'[26] What he said was very true, but he only portrayed the church life of the CPA. How about the persecuted non-CPA?

On the Chinese side, although it was a fact that the unofficial Catholic church was very active, China could only turn a blind eye to it and would not give it recognition. In order to give support and prestige to the CPA, the government had to accept the CPA Catholics as the only sector of the Catholic church in China, and refused to recognise the view taken by the Vatican that there was one Catholic church in China but it was divided into two sectors. Furthermore, the government gave the CPA the assignment of being the police of the non-CPA Catholics. When the Chinese government accused the Pope of vicious slander against the Chinese Catholic church, it was exercising its authority to decide on 'who is a Catholic in China' by telling the Vatican as well as the whole world two things: (1) only the CPA Catholics were Catholics in China, their church activities were accepted and they were not persecuted, (2) any religious believers were punished who violated Article 36 of the Constitution by voluntarily 'subjecting themselves to foreign domination'. They were outlawed religious dissidents and counter-revolutionaries hiding under the cloak of religion. China added that its patience was limited. It would launch a counter-attack if the Pope did not call a halt to his false testimonies and accusations. In other words if the Pope were to continue to call the attention of people to the religious dissidents, the underground non-CPA Catholics, China would exercise its civil authority and do something about it.

Despite the Chinese attitude, the Pope persisted. On the 25 October 1982, he requested to appear at the concluding session of the international Ricci Studies Congress on the occasion of the fourth centenary of the arrival of Matteo Ricci in China.[27] The Congress was organised by the University of Macerata, the Pontifical Gregorian University, and the Ricci Study Centre. At the end of his speech eulogising Matteo Ricci as the bridge of communication

---

[26] *Ta Kung Po* (English edition), 25 March 1982.

[27] According to the disclosure of Monsignore Celli, generally the Pope seldom speaks at any academic congress at length. In fact, it was Pope John Paul II who wanted to have such an elaborate celebration of the anniversary of Matteo Ricci and he himself suggested making his speech on this occasion, because he wanted to take every opportunity to resume the dialogue between China and the Vatican.

between the east and the west, he assiduously called for the revival of the fading dialogue between Rome and Beijing. He stated:

The tomb of Matteo Ricci in Beijing brings to mind the grain of wheat hidden in the heart of the earth in order to bear abundant fruit. It constitutes an eloquent appeal, both to Rome and Beijing, to resume that dialogue begun by him four hundred years ago with so much love and with so much success.[28]

The encounters through eminent personalities

China had perceived the need to include religious believers in its United Front strategy and so develop a more positive image among religious organisations outside China. The purpose was to enhance the modernisation and the open door policies. This explains the invitation to the two European Cardinals to visit China through the Sino-Austrian Friendship Association and Sino-French Friendship Association in 1980. Cardinal Etchegaray of Marseilles and Cardinal Koenig of Vienna accepted the invitation to be the state guests of China as distinguished French and Austrian individuals, but not in their capacity as dignitaries of the Catholic church or as officials of the Vatican. Nevertheless it was expected that the visits would break the ice, for it was the first time since 1949 that such high-ranking church leaders had visited China.

It would not be too optimistic to take the visits of Cardinal Etchegaray, the President of the French National Bishops' Conference, and of Cardinal Koenig, the President of the Austrian National Bishops' Conference, as a sign of a breakthrough in Sino-Vatican relations. After a careful analysis of every aspect of the visits, it was confirmed to be a gesture of importance skilfully made by Beijing. These Cardinals were leaders of note in their local national churches, but were also 'Princes' of the Catholic church. Therefore discussions could be held that would not necessarily entail either side giving ground, but could pave the way for further developments.[29] First of all, these visits took place within one month of each other: in February and March of 1980. China took the initiative in extending the invitation to these European religious leaders of high positions in the hierarchy of the Catholic church. They were the best choice at

---

[28] Wurth (ed.), *Papal Documents Related to the New China*, art. 40, p. 166.
[29] *Ta Kung Pao*, 28 February 1980, 14 March 1980, 21 March 1980; *Wen Wei Po*, 28 February 1980.

the time. Beijing was not yet ready to approach the Vatican officials who were directly or indirectly related to the China Desk at the Secretariat of State or to the China Section at the Congregation for the Evangelisation of Peoples (Propaganda Fide) which is responsible for the China Mission in the Vatican. In spite of the fact that China had expressed its view that the time was premature to begin a dialogue with the Vatican because the latter was not prepared to cut off its diplomatic relations completely with Taiwan, the Chinese would have expected the Cardinals to have consulted with the Vatican. After all, they were VIPs of the church. It was an opportunity to test the ground without either side losing face. As in any negotiating process, at the start both sides could be expected to state their maximal conditions of principle. From the visits of the two Cardinals (as gathered from the people they were allowed to meet, and what could be learnt of their conversations which were not publicly disclosed), Beijing decided through these church dignitaries to reveal its religious policy to the west as well as to legitimise the CPA by introducing its officials to these western religious visitors. At the same time the Chinese hoped that these guests from the church would make use of their high position in the Vatican to convey to the Pope the conditions laid down by China if the Vatican wanted to initiate a dialogue.

The Cardinals were taken to meet China's top officials, notably Ulanfu, a Mongol member of the Politburo who had been working for many years in the United Front Department for the national minorities and was very familiar with religious questions relating to the minorities. Ulanfu explained the overall religious policy of China to the Cardinals. Then in their meeting with the director of the National Religious Affairs Bureau of the State Department, Xiao Xianfa, it was hoped that the Cardinals might be informed about the more concrete implementation of the state policy, particularly towards the Chinese Catholics.[30] The meeting with the church leaders of the CPA and its bishops, who had been newly consecrated without the approval of the Vatican, signified that it was this type of Catholic and hierarchy that was accepted by the government, and thus indirectly China tried to tell its guests that it was determined to have an independent Catholic church in China.[31] They were not allowed to meet any 'unofficial' Catholics. Nor were they taken to

[30] *Ta Kung Pao*, 14 March 1980.
[31] Ibid., 21 March 1980.

visit such bishops as Dominic Deng and Ignatius Gong who were still behind bars. Since these Cardinals were European and had no experience of dealing with Orientals, much less with the Chinese, they were probably expected to carry away with them a good impression of Catholic life in China as conveyed by government sources. Being unable to speak Chinese they got no chance to make contact with people at the grassroots level. With the visit of Cardinal Sin five years later, one could get a clearer picture of what China had expected from the visits of the European church leaders.

Cardinal Sin did not enjoy the same friendly treatment from China as the other dignitaries. Ostensibly his mission was primarily intended as a visit to his elder brother who was ill in Shanghai in 1985. In spite of the fact that this Philippine Cardinal holds the same high rank in the church hierarchy as Cardinal Etchegaray and Cardinal Koenig, yet being half Chinese with Fujian as his paternal home province his perception of the religious policy of China could be expected to be quite different from that of his two European colleagues. In the terms of China's United Front policy, Cardinal Sin belongs to the category of semi 'Tongbao' and therefore he should have been welcome to visit the motherland, especially as Sin is a very prominent figure in the Philippines and a progressive cleric with considerable political influence. He has good personal relations with the Chinese Embassy in Manila and he is careful not to be rude about Beijing. But in actual fact, his visa was not granted for a long time after his application had been submitted. Eventually when his brother had become gravely ill, and Cardinal Sin was anxious to see him before it was too late, it was only through the good offices of the Marcos' government in Manila that he was finally given a visa as a guest of the Sino-Philippine Friendship Association to visit China, and he actually received the visa after the death of his brother. The granting of a visa to this church official, who is believed to have had a special mandate from the Pope to do all he could to reach China in friendship was a further indication of China's intention to make contact, because Cardinal Sin would not have been able to make these visits without the approval of the Chinese authorities. He went to visit his own hometown and meet his own people in Shanghai. There he conversed with all the clergy he met both CPA and non-CPA in Latin, although this language, which prevailed in the Catholic church some thirty years ago, has now become rather obsolete in the west. Cardinal Sin also dared to make an embarrassing request to visit Bishop Gong who was still in jail. All this served the Vatican's purpose of fact finding, and indirectly indicated to China where the Vatican stood in the matter of religious problems. Sin's gestures were perfectly in line with protocol and went well towards fulfilling his purpose.

While the presence of Cardinal Etchegaray and Cardinal Koenig in China gave a chance to the Chinese government to demonstrate its authority in religious matters, the visit of Cardinal Sin passed on a message to China that the Vatican has the spiritual responsibility for Catholics over the whole world, including those in China. In fact, China did not regard Cardinal Sin as a good guest. While he was still in China, the Vice-President of the CPA remarked that the Vatican sent people to China in the guise of making a home visit to try to instigate anti-socialist sentiments and create disunity among Chinese Catholics.[32] Obviously this criticism was meant for Cardinal Sin. When Sin was in Shanghai, he was invited by the CPA of that city to come back in May 1985 for the reopening ceremony of the famous pilgrimage shrine of the Blessed Virgin – the Basilica of Zhishan. After Sin returned to Manila, he stated that he was prepared to attend on this occasion.[33] But he never turned up at the reopening ceremony of the Basilica of Zhishan. Apparently the Chinese government at the last minute did not send him the invitation. Perhaps there was a diversity of views in China again on this matter.

Cardinal Sin was not treated with the highest standards of courtesy or hospitality during his visit to China. One of the explanations lies probably in the fact that, despite being an overseas Chinese, his loyalty lay first with the Vatican. An additional complication, of course, is that he moved into opposition against Marcos' regime, while Beijing tended to support it until very late in the day. Beijing had not realised early enough how fragile Marcos' power base had become.

Cardinal Casaroli's concrete proposal

After 1977 numerous non-conformists were gradually being released from prisons and from labour camps as part of the new policies

[32] United Press News, Beijing, 31 October 1984. Quoted by *Witness* (Taiwan) 144 (January 1985): 66.
[33] *Kung Kao Po*, 4 January 1985.

7 Cardinal Wu, the Cardinal designate, at the auditorium Paul VI, receives a nomination letter from Cardinal Casaroli, the Secretary of State to the Vatican. Does the architect of the Vatican's Ostpolitik also implicitly request Wu to implement his strategies in China? *Source: Kung Kao Po*
(The Chinese Catholic Weekly).

towards intellectuals whose contributions were desperately needed for the tasks of modernisation. Many Catholic laity and clergy who were no threat to the government or to its control of religious life were released. The improved flow of information about Catholics in China began with their return home from the labour camps. At the same time, a number of people who had suffered politically in the Cultural Revolution and who had emigration rights (to Hong Kong and the USA mainly) started to leave the country. These migrants included some Catholics of importance, among them being the Bishop of Guangzhou, Dominic Deng. He was released on 5 June 1980 after more than twenty-two years of imprisonment. Three months later he was granted an exit permit to go to Hong Kong to receive medical treatment for an intestinal complaint.

The release of Bishop Dominic Deng and his going to Hong Kong, his birth place where he has the right to stay, might be taken as a trial balloon sent up by China to see the reaction of the universal Catholic church to its liberalisation policies. It could have been that it was thought that it would be expedient for at least one church leader to be released in order to make the outside world believe that religious freedom prevailed in the land. It was known in the west that there were two prominent church leaders still in jail because of their resistance to the Chinese government over their religious beliefs. These men were the Bishop of Shanghai, Ignatius Gong Pinmei, and the Bishop of Guangzhou, Dominic Deng Yiming. In the eyes of the Chinese government, Bishop Gong was the more formidable because of his ten years of resistance in the Shanghai area in the 50s. Not until the bishop was gaoled together with more than fifty other Jesuits[34] from the neighbouring counties, was the CCP able to exercise complete control of religious affairs in the area around Shanghai. Since there was no more resistance in evidence in the Guangzhou area in the 70s, the release of Bishop Dominic Deng, unlike that of Gong Pinmei did not pose immediate threats to state security. Since Bishop Deng was sandwiched between China and the Vatican, China could not give him a free hand to run religious affairs unless he had been tested, tried and proved to be worthy of trust by the Chinese government. Bishop Gong Pinmei would have had his turn later, had China not suspected that he might be named a cardinal bishop by Pope John Paul II, who in the Consistory held on 30 June 1979 conferred red hats on a group of candidates, creating them Princes of the Church. After announcing the list of candidates to the public, the Pope said in a very solemn tone in Latin 'Praeter hos, qui nominati sunt, adlegere in Collegium vestrum decrevimus alium, quem tamen in pectore reservamus et quandocumque arbitrio nostro renuntiabimus'[35] (besides these, who have been named, we have determined to appoint to your College another, whom however we keep in our heart [i.e. secret] and at some future time, of our own choice, we shall make the same public). It revealed that one on the list of candidates assembled at St. Peter's Basilica in Rome to receive the red cap was absent. He was named as 'in petto' – that

---

34 *Correspondence*, 18 (September 1984): 2. (The Jesuits' internally circulated materials on China. Issued from the Delegate's office for the Chinese Apostolate, Manila.)
35 *Acta Apostolicae Sedis. Vol. LXXI*, City State of the Vatican, p. 898.

means the name of this cardinal was close to the heart of the Holy Father and known to him only. Those who were close to John Paul II notably the Prelate of Cologne, West Germany, hinted that the Cardinal 'in petto' was Bishop Ignatius Gong Pinmei. This could not have escaped the attention of the Chinese government. On the occasion of participating in a church conference in Montreal, in October 1981, K. H. Ting, a Chinese Protestant bishop, the head of the Chinese delegation to the conference, who is close to the Chinese government, asked one of the contact persons of the Vatican whether the Pope might consider conferring the title of cardinal on Bishop Gong if Gong were released.[36] Ting also remarked that the conferring of the Cardinal's red hat on this religious prisoner would embarrass China. Partly because Gong had been relentlessly manifesting his attitude of non-conformity, protesting in letters of appeal to the government that he was innocently condemned[37] and that the Chinese government delayed his release, because of the suspicion that he would receive the red hat. In 1985, however, Bishop Gong was released from jail but was immediately put under house arrest and was not allowed to receive any religious visitors.

Thinking that he might in some way bridge the gap between the Vatican and China and help towards effecting a reconciliation, Deng remained cautious in his speech when talking about China. In the press conference he gave jointly with Cardinal Casaroli, who made a detour to see him during his visit to Asia with the Pope in February 1981, Deng even reiterated that the views of the Catholics in China and of the Chinese government on the church's 'self rule' were similar, because 'self-rule' was not equivalent to 'independence'. The Catholic church in China with self-rule could have connections with the Pope.[38] It sounded as if the Vatican was seriously contemplating a direct contact with China, and Dominic Deng appeared to be the man who would be a go-between, as indicated in the statement Casaroli issued at the press conference. It read:

The Holy Father wished to express his very special, personal interest in, and esteem for Bishop Deng and what Bishop Deng represents – the Church and people of China. During our brief meeting, Bishop Deng and I have talked

---

[36] The writer by chance was on the spot when Bishop K. H. Ting conducted the conversation with the Vatican's contact person.
[37] Appendix II. Gong, 'The Letter of Appeal'.
[38] See *Hong Kong Standard, Sing Tao Yat Po, South China Morning Post*, 1 March 1981.

about matters of interest to us, related to the Holy See and the Catholic church in China.[39]

To play his role as the bridge and the middle man, Bishop Deng kept in touch with the Chinese government via the Hong Kong branch of Xinhua News Agency. He even went so far as to give the semblance of toeing the party line in dealing with religious affairs, by advising the overseas Catholics that if anyone was going to help Catholics in China he should first of all appear to be a sincere friend of China. He told western reporters in one of the interviews 'Take this (friendly) attitude or you will meet with many difficulties. If you want to help, do it openly. Go through the official channels of the government.'[40] Even though he had been jailed as a religious dissident, he very diplomatically demonstrated his conformist's attitude in certain religious matters with the intention of creating closer links between the Vatican and China.

In the mind of Cardinal Casaroli at this stage there was a blue-print for dealing with the questions of independence as understood by the Vatican. He once talked of a special 'Chinese rite' that would give the church in China an administrative autonomy but keep it in communion with the Pope. There are similar arrangements that link the Ukranian, Greek, Armenian and Maronite Catholic churches with the Vatican.[41] This proposed arrangement had not been much discussed by those Catholic theologians who were familiar with church studies as well as Chinese affairs, probably because nearly all the Chinese Catholic theologians in the Far East, such as in Hong Kong and Taiwan, belong to the Catholic Latin rites and they were rather unfamiliar with other Catholics of other national rites. As far as the question of Taiwan was concerned, the newly established Sino-American relations are based on Kissinger's model. This is acknowledging with the Chinese on both sides of the Taiwan Strait that 'there is one China and Taiwan is a Chinese province'. Kissinger's model might be contemplated too by the Vatican, who was accused by China of interfering in its sovereignty by recognising Taiwan. Cardinal Casaroli in untangling this thorny question would

---

39 'Statement of Cardinal Agustino Casaroli, Vatican Secretary of State', Press release on the press conference jointly held by Cardinal Casaroli and Bishop Dominic Deng in Hong Kong, 28 February 1981.

40 *Sunday Examiner*, 7 November 1980.

41 Michael Parks, the *Times*' staff writer in an article 'Feud among Chinese Catholics sours hopes for Vatican ties', in *Los Angelos Times*, 24 April 1982, revealed Casaroli's proposal of a 'special Chinese rite'.

8 Bishop Wu of Hong Kong (middle) and Bishop De Costa of Macau (right) meet
Bishop Dominic Deng Yiming on his first visit to Hong Kong after twenty-two years
of imprisonment (1980). *Source: Kung Kao Po* (The Chinese Catholic Weekly).

not necessarily follow the American model and apply it to the
Vatican's relations with Taiwan, but he did suggest that 'within
different cultures in the world, the church has an enormous number
of variations. Some form of connection could be worked out . . .'[42]

Inaccurate calculations

It remains a big question why the Vatican failed to de-code the
signals sent by China in response to the overtures made by the Pope
and then by Cardinal Casaroli from Hong Kong. First of all the
Chinese government asserted total indifference in public by ignoring
the Pontiff's remarks and the Cardinal's overtures by allowing no
Chinese newspaper, radio or television to cover the Pope's Far East
trip. Nor had the official media even mentioned the Pope's address
to the people of China. When it was asked how Beijing would

[42] Casaroli answered the questions raised by some journalists at the press conference held in
Hong Kong, 28 February 1981. The writer was also at the conference.

respond to the Pope's 'longing' to visit China, the government-sponsored CPA spokesman said very indifferently that 'At present we have no relations with the Vatican' and he continued to blame the Papacy for the Sino-Vatican rift of the past twenty and more years.[43] The Vatican might have thought that the indifference on the part of China was due to concern about the psychological set-back that this might cause the clergy of the CPA. Since for various reasons the clergy had joined the CPA and were cut off from the Pope, the proposed rapprochement might have some negative impact on this group of apostate Catholics. In the event of a rapprochement, the fear of facing church discipline might be an added reason for their continuing to advocate the Sino-Vatican rift in their lifetime. The signals given by the spokesman of the CPA were not received with sufficient care by the Vatican which construed the statement as probably a reflection of their guilt-laden consciences. The Vatican probably expected to have a more formal reply from higher levels in the Chinese political hierarchy. Since the overtures were openly sent out by the head of the Vatican and the Secretary of State, the Vatican might have thought that only a reply from the Religious Affairs Bureau or some department of equivalent status could bear weight as an official reply from China. But the silence from this direction was not 'loud' enough for the Vatican to get the message correctly. The rather negative gestures on the part of China about the proposed rapprochement did not cool off the over-enthusiastic zeal on the part of the Vatican – for it decided to appoint Bishop Dominic Deng as the Archbishop of Guangzhou. It was precisely this ill-advised and hasty step by the Vatican that brought about the adverse consequence of widening the rift.

The appointment of Dominic Deng as the Archbishop of Guangzhou: a real clash of authority

On 26 April 1981, Bishop Deng went to Rome to pay an 'ad limina' visit to the Pope in his capacity of Apostolic Administrator of Guangzhou. When he was received by the Pope in a private audience, he was asked by the Pontiff how he would react if he were appointed the Archbishop of Guangzhou. Apparently the Pope could not make up his mind whether to engage himself in such a

43 *Hong Kong Standard*, 20 February 1981, 2 March 1981.

9 Archbishop Dominic Deng Yiming – an official picture taken in exile. *Source:* Private collection of Archbishop Deng.

10 Bishop Dominic Deng of Guangzhou meets Pope John Paul II on his first 'ad Limina' visit to the Holy See (26 April 1981). *Source:* Private collection of Archbishop Deng.

move to display a gesture of honour and encouragement to the church in China on the one hand and to make a step towards improving relations between the Holy See and Beijing on the other.

At the time Pope Pius XII appointed Father Dominic Deng as Bishop and Apostolic Administrator of Guangzhou in 1950, the Archbishop of Guangzhou Monsignor Pierre-Jean Fourquet was living in France convalescing from illness. And from the day of his consecration, Dominic Deng began to administer the church affairs of Guangzhou Archdiocese under the title of Apostolic Administrator. In the Roman Catholic tradition, when the bishop or archbishop of a given place has not been able formally to administer

11 St Peter's Basilica, the symbol of the Roman Catholic church, and Archbishop Deng. *Source:* Private collection of Archbishop Deng.

the diocese or the archdiocese effectively for various reasons, a bishop is appointed to administer with the title of an apostolic administrator. In this case, therefore, when Dominic Deng was consecrated a bishop in 1950, he was only the apostolic administrator of the Archdiocese of Guangzhou. (It is again a general practice in the Roman Catholic church that the diocese of a provincial capital is called an archdiocese while an ordinary town or city is called a diocese.) The last Archbishop of Guangzhou died in France in February 1952. In other words, there was no archbishop in Guangzhou from 1952–81, and, in the normal circumstances, since Guangzhou had been made an archdiocese in 1946, and since the last archbishop had died long since, the naming of an archbishop

12 Archbishop Deng explains himself to the Press Conference on the Papal
appointment to the Archbishop of Guangzhou (June 1981).
Source: Private collection of Archbishop Deng.

was expected. Although in theory there should have been nothing
provocative in the appointment, in actual practice it proved to be
otherwise. When the Pope was in two minds whether to make the
appointment or not, he consulted Dominic Deng and Deng's Italian
advisor, Father F. Belfiori. In the 1970s Father Belfiori had served
the Taibei Apostolic Nunciature for some years. He did not see the
wisdom of making the appointment. Deng however agreed with the
Pope's suggestion. It was unfortunate that the Pope and Bishop
Deng were not sensitive enough to anticipate the hostility and bitter
denunciations which were to be the result from Beijing's political
leaders. Deng took the appointment as an honour and as encouragement to his country and his brothers and sisters in the church, and
hoped thereby to improve relations between China and the Vatican.[44] The CCP in Beijing took it as an outrageous breach of their
sovereign right, an outrage to Marxist thought.

At that crucial moment when consultation was sought from

44 'Translation of Statement of Monsignor Dominic Deng Yiming', given out at the press
conference in Hong Kong, 23 June 1981.

Bishop Deng, both the Holy Father and Bishop Deng had miscalculated the Chinese Communists' reactions. First of all the Holy Father had mistakenly thought that if this aged bishop after long years of suffering could survive the political upheavals in China, he must have a good basis for understanding the Chinese Communists. On this assumption the Holy Father went ahead with the proposed appointment. It is regrettable that Bishop Deng himself did not have good knowledge of communist politics. The twenty-two years spent behind bars only offered him protection from the hooliganism of the Red Guards during the Cultural Revolution, but did not offer him the chance to follow closely the political development of China, and subsequently he did not learn from it. As it turned out his opinion was unsound, unlike that of Deng's Italian adviser who had rich experience in the diplomatic service in Taiwan and who had a good knowledge of Chinese international behaviour and attitudes.

Moreover, Deng appeared to be acceptable to the Chinese authorities, as he had been permitted to resume his episcopal title and had even been allowed legally to go to Hong Kong. It was the Chinese government who gave him the permission to stay in Hong Kong for one whole year, although Deng's exit permit was granted through a bribe in Guangzhou.[45] Further, the Chinese authorities did not realise apparently that the Hong Kong British administration would give him a passport to enable him to go abroad so easily.

The appointment was announced from the Vatican on 6 June 1981. Five days later, China demonstrated its hostile reaction. A statement of strong protest was issued by Bishop Yang Gaojian, Vice-Chairman of the CPA, Vice-Chairman of the Chinese Catholic Religious Affairs Committee and Vice-President of the Chinese Catholic Bishops' Conference. Yang's document sounded official in tone. Then meetings of the CPA at provincial and city levels were called specially to denounce the appointment.[46] The third issue of the bulletin of the CPA, *Catholic Church in China*, was wholly devoted to this controversy. Out of the forty-one articles in that issue, fifteen directly pointed an accusing finger at Bishop Deng, while reaffirm-

---

[45] One of Deng's close friends disclosed to the writer that Deng's exit permit was obtained through bribery.
[46] For the Guangdong Provincial CPA, see *Wen Wei Po*, 14 June 1981, *Nanfang Ribao*, 14 June 1981. For Beijing Provincial CPA, see *Beijing Ribao*, 17 June 1981. For Shanghai city CPA, see *Wenhui Bao*, 18 June 1981.

ing the standpoint of the CPA that it is independent of the Holy See
and that it will continue in its policy of autonomy.[47] In reading
through all these documents it is noteworthy how a more or less
identical formula is used to express the hostile official reaction to
Dominic Deng's appointment and the Pope's Manila speech. Often
the similarity is extended to identical phrases and terminology, and
to the character of the ideological rhetoric and sloganeering.[48]

It is very interesting to note that in the late 1970s after the
country's shift towards pragmatism, there was a general trend
towards professionalism among China's foreign affairs specialists, as
observed by some sinologists. One of the striking changes was a
dramatic decline in the use of ideological rhetoric and in the kind of
simplistic formulas that in earlier years dominated many Chinese
discussions of foreign issues. This was because the Chinese now saw
the need for sophistication and realism rather than sloganeering in
dealing with complex international problems.[49] In the case of
Deng's appointment, the Religious Affairs Bureau supported the
rejection of the Pope's appointment, repeating the sloganeering of
the CPA, which was contrary to the newly adopted sophistication
and realism in foreign relations. Was it because the appointment
itself so greatly aroused the indignation of the Chinese, at the
Vatican's interference in their internal affairs, that the Chinese
officials lost their grip and allowed the sloganeering and unpolished
language to overflow?

The indignation of the Chinese authorities

On the occasion of the appointment of Dominic Deng, a statement
was made by Bishop Yang Gaojian, who held responsible posts in all
the three Catholic associations. The Chinese political leaders
refrained from making any statement of their own but it is safe to
assume that the statement by Bishop Yang expressed their own
attitude. The Religious Affairs Bureau however stated that it

---

47 *Catholic Church in China* 3 (October 1981).
48 See *Catholic Church in China* 3 (October 1981), cf. the statement made by Bishop Yang
    Gaojian, the Vice Chairman of the CPA, 'An open letter to the clergy and laity', 'Joint
    resolutions' issued by the Standing Committee of the Chinese Catholic Patriotic Associ-
    ation, the Standing Committee of the Chinese Religious Administrative Committee and the
    Bishops' Conference (18 July 1981), and the protest of Bishop Ye Yinyun all shared the
    same ideological rhetoric and sloganeering. For the English translation see Appendix III.
49 Doak Barnett, *The Making of Foreign Policy in China* (London: Tauris, 1985), p. 91.

supported the rejection of the appointment, giving an impression to the whole world that religious matters should go to the Religious Affairs Bureau and be treated by it. The full statement ran as follows:[50]

A statement on the Roman Curia's appointment of Deng Yiming as Archbishop of Guangdong province[51]

Recently the Roman Curia has disregarded the sovereign rights of the Chinese Catholic church by appointing Deng Yiming as Archbishop of Guangdong. Because of this we make the following declaration:

The Roman Curia has consistently shown a hostile attitude to the Chinese people. Since the liberation it has pursued all kinds of subversive and destructive activities against the new China.

Therefore, our nation's clergy and laity, in order to defend our motherland's independence and dignity as well as to preserve the church's integrity, have firmly freed ourselves from the Roman Curia's control and have chosen the way of independence and autonomous self-administration for the church. This fully accords with Jesus' mind in founding the church and with the tradition coming from the apostolic mission. The present action of the Roman Curia in appointing Deng Yiming as archbishop of Guangdong is illegal and we voice our strong opposition to it.

We cannot tolerate this crude interference with the sovereign rights of the Chinese Catholic church on the part of the Roman Curia. Because Deng Yiming had shown his repentance, last June 5 (1980) the government magnanimously released him from prison. The Catholic clergy and the laity of Guangzhou restored to him his pastoral ministry as Bishop of Guangzhou diocese. This appointment also received no approval of the Chinese Catholic Religious Affairs Committee and the Chinese Bishops' Conference.

After a while, the government granted Deng's request to go to Hong Kong for a medical check-up and to visit his relatives. Yet he shamelessly went to the Roman Curia to receive his so-called pastoral office of Archbishop. He also travelled to several other places to carry out his activities.

In doing so, he besmirched his dignity both as a cleric of the Chinese Catholic church and as a Chinese citizen. He also violated the Chinese Catholic church's principle of independently and autonomously administering its own affairs. The mass of the Chinese clergy and laity cannot tolerate this kind of behaviour.

[50] The statement was translated from *Catholic Church in China*, 3 (October 1981): 1.
[51] The correct name of the archdiocese is Guangzhou, the provincial capital of Guangdong Province. Here it indicated that before clarifying the nature of the appointment and the related matters, the CPA had to follow the governmental line and attack the Roman Curia, the administrative body of the Holy See.

Therefore we once again proclaim here that the age in which the Roman Curia controlled the Chinese Catholic church is now past and will never return. The mass of clergy and laity of the Chinese Catholic church will definitely under the guidance of the Holy Spirit, continue along the road of independent, autonomous administration of their own affairs and they will do so with ever-increasing success.

The Chinese Catholic Patriotic Association
The Chinese Catholic Religious Affairs Committee
The Chinese Catholic Bishops' Conference

Yang Gaojian (in charge)
11th June, 1981.

Studying the statement itself one cannot deny that Communist China was extremely unhappy with the sabotage of the Chinese church's independence and autonomy, and the interference with the sovereign rights of the Chinese Catholic church on the part of the Vatican. The controversy over the appointment unfortunately touched the heart of the above mentioned key question and directly provoked the indignation of the Chinese political leaders. It is true that there was ideological rhetoric and sloganeering; as appeared in the resolution of many meetings of the CPA at provincial and city levels. Yet it is worthwhile paying some attention to the open letter to the laity and clergy, issued on 18 July, 1981, after the joint meetings of the three major Chinese Catholic associations. More specifically the open letter pinpointed the particular ways in which Red China views the Vatican's administration of the Chinese church as having a strong colour of an imperialist approach and an anti-socialist dimension.[52]

First of all it referred to the last century when the Vatican supported the colonial nature of missionary work as a continuing cause of resentment to the present Chinese political leaders. These were their remarks on the missionary work of the Catholic church before 1949: 'Before liberation, the Chinese church existed in a colonial status and for a long time it was manipulated by the Roman Curia and the foreign missionaries. It served the aggressive policies of the imperialists and so harmed our country in many ways.'[53] In a very subtle way this anti-foreign missionary sentiment was carried down to the Chinese leaders of this generation. Their anti-Catholic

---

[52] The text of this open letter has been translated and appears in Appendix III.
[53] Ibid.

sentiment found its expression in the feeling that their cultural heritage and national pride had suffered greatly as the result of foreign encroachment in the late Qing period. Then came the face-to-face confrontation between the PRC and the Vatican in the 1950s on the question of independence from the Holy See and the consecration of bishops without the approval of the Pope.

The CPA as well as the Chinese Communists tend to allude to scenes from the past when referring to the present situation in the Catholic church of the post-Second Vatican Council (1963–5) period. This tendency seemingly prevails from the top high-ranking officials to the local cadres. When Bishop Wu of Hong Kong met them in Guangdong during his visit in February 1986, after listening to the remarks of the Chinese officials on the practices of the Catholic church, he suggested that the officials depart from China and visit the universal Catholic church for themselves and witness the great changes in the Catholic church since the Second Vatican Council. Since then, for example, on the Catholic side, relations with Marxism–Leninism and Communist parties have altered drastically.[54] This Council has also changed the relationship between local churches and the Holy See, and there is far greater room for national cultures to find free expression both liturgically and institutionally.[55] Moreover many Catholic leaders in the 1950s had already shrugged off the colonial aspect of the church and had tried to blend Chinese culture, especially the teaching of Confucianism, with Christian doctrine. Take Bishop Gong for example, in his letter of appeal, he argued strongly on the point that he preferred to embrace the Catholic faith and that he suffered the consequences because he followed the teachings of Confucianism on loyalty: a patrician who should be prepared to sacrifice himself for the sake of the virtue of loyalty.[56] The fact that the Chinese Communists accused the Catholic church of a pre-Vatican II mentality shows that either they were ignorant about the Catholic church in China and in the outside world, or deliberately wished to shape an obsolete and fallacious image of the Catholic church for their own ends.

When diplomatic relations were established with Japan in 1972, the Chinese government was able to put aside memories of the brutal

---

[54] 'Gaudium et Spes', in Abbott (ed.), *The Documents of the Vatican II*, pp. 217–20.
[55] 'Lumen Gentium' and 'Sacrosanctum Concilum', in Abbott (ed.), *The Documents of the Vatican II*, pp. 43, 432.
[56] Gong, Pinmei, 'The Letter of Appeal'.

massacres by the Japanese, who killed hundreds of thousands of Chinese, looted an immense amount of Chinese wealth, rendered numerous Chinese homeless and raped many Chinese women in the course of the Sino-Japanese War of 1933–45. In fact the Chinese government now makes friends with the Japanese in the post-Mao Era, because China desperately needs Japanese economic investment and technological knowhow for its modernisation. There would appear to be an inconsistency in the way the Communist Chinese apply their high principled references to past grievances in foreign affairs.

Vatican: supporter of religious dissent

In the open letter the Vatican was blamed for 'stubborn opposition to the policies of new China, for publishing time and again reactionary "encyclicals" and "orders" inciting the Chinese clergy and laity to oppose every policy, law and decree of the People's government'.[57] In the early 1950s when the government decided to exercise its authority over every civil organisation, including the Catholic church, it insisted that the church be autonomous and independent of the Vatican. The question of independence from the supreme church leadership turned some Catholics underground as they felt that the communion with the Holy See constituted one of the essential parts of the Catholic faith which they would embrace even at the risk of their own lives. This is why the Vatican was accused of 'calling for a "bloody martyrdom" in support of its political machinations. It fouled up the whole atmosphere. Some people went so far as to commit crimes.' This directly revealed that the Vatican was unacceptable to the PRC, partly for security reasons, since it was accused of continual support of Chinese religious dissidents.

Indeed, supporting political dissent of whatever nature can be very embarrassing in international relations. As a consequence of its policy some thirty years ago China met the same embarrassment in its dealings with ASEAN. The Chinese Communist support for the armed revolutionary struggles of the Malay, Thai and Indonesian Communist parties in the 1950s and 1960s resulted in considerable suspicion being felt by the rulers of these countries in the 1970s, when

57 *Catholic Church in China* 3 (October 1981): 12–18.

China was very anxious to cultivate better relations with its southern neighbours because it was vulnerable to Soviet encirclement.

Yet the situation of religious dissidents is quite different from that of political dissidents. In fact, it seemed that China's failure in carrying out its policy was the main reason for the creation of religious dissidents. Bishop Gong in his letter of appeal revealed that, in the Spring of 1950, Zhou Enlai had promised at a meeting with religious leaders that even when they cut off their political and economic relations with the Pope, the Chinese Catholics would be allowed to maintain religious relations with the Holy See. Bishop Gong gave his full support to Zhou's policy and praised it as reasonable, prudent and right. Gong remarked that it was a great pity that China did not carry out Zhou's religious policy well.[58]

Subsequently, the Catholics who turned underground had done so on the grounds that they followed the example of their leader in cutting off political and economic relations with the Vatican while keeping the essential and particular part of the Catholic faith – the maintenance of spiritual relations with the Pope. According to the Catholic faith, once an adherent cuts himself off from religious relations with the Pope, while he could still claim to be a Christian, he could no longer be a Roman Catholic. The example of the emergence of the Church of England from the Roman Catholic church at the time of Henry VIII is a case in point. The act of demanding that the Catholics be independent from the Holy See in the religious sense was tantamount to demanding the establishment of a new church independent of the Roman Catholic church. Therefore by compelling Chinese Catholics to have no relations with the Holy See, the Chinese government can be considered to be in violation of its own state constitution. Article 36 of the 1982 Constitution clearly states that the citizen of the PRC has freedom of religion which includes the freedom to believe in this or that religion.[59]

Vatican's 'Interfering' in China's sovereign rights

Since its establishment in 1949, the People's Republic of China has continuously and very strongly put emphasis upon its sovereign

[58] Appendix II, Gong Pinmei, 'The Letter of Appeal', para. 4, pp. 4–5; ibid., pp. 4–5, section 4.

[59] *Xinhua News*, 10 May 1982. *Hongqi* 12 (16 June 1982): 4.

rights. In the first Chinese Constitution, the Common Program, it was stated that the foreign policy of the PRC is based on the principle of protection of sovereignty, independence, the freedom and integrity of its territory. The severence of relations with the nationalist government has been the condition for establishing diplomatic relations with the PRC. The Constitution states:

Article 54 of The Common Program
The foreign policy of the PRC is based on the principle of protection of the independence, freedom, integrity of territory and sovereignty of the country, upholding lasting international peace and friendly co-operation with the peoples of all countries, and opposing the imperialist policy of aggression and war.

China's changing relations with the Soviet Union and the United States (judged to be the principal sources of threat to Chinese security) can be said to be based upon that principle. Furthermore from the 1950s to the 1980s China's interstate relations have been based assertedly on the upholding of the five principles of mutual respect for sovereignty and integrity of territory, mutual non-aggression, non-interference in each other's internal affairs, equality and mutual benefit, and peaceful co-existence, while opposing imperialism, hegemonism and colonialism, as stated in the preamble of the 1982 Constitution.[60] Therefore one has sufficient reason to believe that in dealing with foreign affairs China has had a long tradition of carefully safeguarding its sovereign rights, and allowing no one to interfere in its internal affairs.

The Chinese took the incident of the appointment as interference with their sovereign rights; the appointment of a Chinese citizen to exercise religious authority within a designated part of Chinese territory was made by the head of a foreign state – the Vatican. The CPA Bishop of Beijing, Michael Fu, remarked that the appointment was the 'Second Chinese Rite'. Fu's remarks might well reflect the feelings of Chinese political leaders. The Vatican, a very peculiar state created to administer religious affairs, could for various reasons be regarded as a sovereign state and not as an administrative centre for a religion. Being a state embracing atheist Marxism–Leninism and Maoism, China has no reason to accept the Vatican as the sovereign state of a religious body.

According to normal practice, when the Pope intends to appoint a

60 *The Constitution of the People's Republic of China* (Beijing: Foreign Languages Press, 1983), pp. 3–8.

candidate to be bishop or archbishop in a particular country, an ambassador, if that country has diplomatic relations with the Vatican, is informed before the appointment is announced. If the Pope wants to consecrate someone as a bishop or archbishop of a place in a country which has formulated a concordat with the Holy See, according to the conditions laid down by the concordat either the Vatican nominates the candidates for the post and lets the government choose a suitable one from amongst them, or the Vatican itself makes the definite choice. The selection of the candidates is normally arranged through the diplomatic intermediary of the Prefecture: Nuncio or Internuncio of the Holy See to a given country. Where such diplomatic relationships are non-existent, a different procedure applies. The practices under a concordat were cited by the Chinese government in 'The Open Letter to the Clergy and Laity' seeking to justify the indignation of the Chinese political leaders. In this way, it alluded indirectly to the fact that China had not been asked to participate in the process of the appointment and selection of the bishop. The Open Letter stated:

The selection and appointment of bishops has very much to do with national interests and the political and religious life of the faithful. No government will allow anyone who rebels against its country's interests to usurp an ecclesiastical office. Hence many countries successively signed agreements with the Roman Curia.

These include, for example, Germany, Austria, France, Russia, Ecuador, Guatemala, Honduras, San Salvador, Haiti, Australia, Italy, Spain and others. These agreements or treaties state either that the country has the right to nominate bishops or that, before they are appointed, the opinion of the government is to be solicited. Some treaties state that when the bishop takes office, he must swear an oath of loyalty to the state.[61]

The Chinese government did not cite the thorny cases of the appointment of bishops in the East European Bloc, where many bishops' seats were vacant and the Vatican has had a difficult time to appoint any candidate unless they were hand-picked by the government.

A Puzzling Case

Here it looked as if China was furious that the appointment had been made without their being notified or their consent sought. The appointment was regarded as 'illegal'[62] because it went against the

---

[61] Appendix III, 'An open letter to the clergy and laity'.
[62] *Wen Wei Po*, 12 June 1981. The statement by Bishop Yang Gaojian.

normal practice in international relations in church and state affairs. It appears to be a puzzle to everyone in international relations studies as to whether the Vatican had notified the Chinese government before the announcement of the appointment. In spite of the complete silence from the Vatican in face of the angry repudiation and the many accusations by the Chinese, there is some evidence to suggest that it might have invited the Chinese to participate in the appointment directly or indirectly through formal or informal channels. First of all, being a sovereign state with a long history of dealing with various kinds of complications in European politics over many centuries, it is difficult to imagine that the Vatican would commit this fatal mistake by not carrying out so basic a procedure in the protocol of international relations. Many people who were close to the Vatican remarked that this appointment would not have been made without the tacit consent of Beijing.[63] An Associated Press reporter even quoted the name of the Vatican spokesman by saying 'The Rev. Romeo Paciroli, the Vatican spokesman, indicated that Beijing had been consulted and had agreed to the naming of the seventy-three year old prelate who was freed last year from twenty-two years in prison.'[64] According to some confidential information, before the announcement of the appointment some kind of documents about it had been sent back and forth between the Vatican and China through the French embassy in Rome. It is difficult to believe that, when some high ranking diplomats in France knew about the appointment before it was announced, China itself did not know anything about it. Yet Beijing claimed that Dominic Deng 'behind the back of the Chinese people and Chinese Catholics received the post as archbishop'.[65] In other words, China claims that it was not informed or consulted about the appointment before it was announced. Monsignor C. Celli however expressed the view that both before and after the appointment all correspondence sent from the Vatican to China, through the Italian, French, German and later the US embassies to the Holy See, was simply ignored and returned.[66] It might be that one of these letters returned to the Vatican from China had to do with such an appointment. If China

[63] *South China Morning Post*, 7 June 1981.
[64] 'Way open for Pope's possible visit to China', *Hong Kong Standard*, 9 June 1981.
[65] Appendix III, 'An open letter to the clergy and laity'.
[66] Monsignor C. Celli, the head of China Desk, Secretariat of State of the Vatican, disclosed the news when he was interviewed by the writer in March 1985.

ignored these letters it could not entirely blame the Vatican. Even so, is it possible that the Vatican should be so careless as to go ahead unilaterally without even the slightest understanding with its counterpart?

An Italian sinologist, A. Lazzarotto, has mentioned that a daily newspaper in Rome, *Il Messagero*, on 8 June 1981 reported details of some proposals that were said to have been part of the negotiations: the Holy See would approve the episcopal appointments already in China, while Chinese bishops would confirm their adherence to the universally accepted praxis that requires episcopal nominations to be approved by the Pope.[67]

Gathering all the clues stated above, a very controversial picture emerges as to whether China had been consulted or not before the announcement of the appointment. One thing is clear: no formal consultation had taken place with the Chinese political leaders, for China would not have reacted so strongly without the trump card of the fact that no official approach had been made to it. If the lack of consultation was due to the non-acceptance of the Vatican's correspondence on the part of China, then China must also be partly responsible for this. The evidence that the mediator knew about the appointment, makes it difficult to believe that China had not been informed. From some reliable sources it appears that the visit to the Chinese Embassy in Rome by Dominic Deng when he visited the Vatican strongly indicated that he had an informal and verbal consultation or interview with the Chinese officials there. But, if Deng did not get the chance to meet the Chinese Ambassador to Italy, would it be an excuse for China to say that it was not informed? If one believes that some informal negotiation had been going on and even conditions had been laid down to settle the disputes between the CPA and non-CPA Catholics, China would not be out of touch with the intention of the Vatican towards the Catholic church of China. It seems very possible that China through informal channels was informed about the appointment. Since there was a lack of ambassadorial contact which would constitute unmistakably formal and official communication, the Vatican could not do anything except go through informal channels – the only communication media available when the Sino-Vatican diplomatic relations had not yet been started.

[67] A. Lazzarotto, *The Catholic Church in Post-Mao China* (Hong Kong: Holy Spirit Study Centre, 1982), p. 134.

On the other hand if good evidence proves that informal channels had been established even to facilitate Sino-Vatican negotiations it might be that the Vatican took these as an acceptable medium through which to communicate with China in an unofficial and informal way. Later in 1985, Monsignor C. Celli, the head of the China Desk in the Secretariat of State of the Vatican, remarked that both the Vatican and China committed mistakes in the controversy of the appointment.[68] His statement might allude to the fact that the appointment was too hasty, without a request being transmitted to China in a more acceptable manner. Would Monsignor Celli also take overreacting and fact-twisting as mistakes by the Chinese during the process of informing or consulting, both before and after the appointment was announced? The Vatican did not know if the Chinese approved (why else should the Pope ask Deng and his advisers for their views?). Secondly, the Chinese must have had some knowledge that the appointment might be made, but made no effort to signal their opposition in advance. Finally, the Vatican nevertheless went ahead despite the fact that contacts with the Chinese were still at an early stage and no clear understanding had yet been reached. The documents of the Vatican archives will be disclosed in seventy-five years. Let the historians of the next generation search out the truth in this controversy, and in the year 2056 the puzzle will be solved.

However, Bishop Deng sought permission from the Chinese government to return to Guangzhou when the term of stay in Hong Kong allowed by his exit permit came to an end. The Chinese government first laid down the condition that he should renounce the title of 'Archbishop of Guangzhou' in exchange for his return. Although Deng was conscious that his role of mediator would vanish with this dispute, he did not want to let down the Pope and the Vatican. His renunciation of the title would not only throw mud in the face of the Holy Father, but also it would confirm that the appointment was a totally wrong act. The renunciation of the title would mean that in future the Pope would have no right to appoint any Chinese bishop. Deng realised that his personal future would be sacrificed because he was accused by the Chinese of being a lackey of the Vatican and his personal integrity was under attack, yet he made a decision to show his loyalty to the Pope and the Catholic church;

[68] This remark was made by Monsignor Celli in his interview in March 1985.

therefore, he retained the title. It did not mean that the title of an archbishop would do him much good, since he was in exile in Hong Kong. He considered the possible consequences for the Catholic church in general and the CPA in particular. Renunciation would possibly perpetuate the independence of the CPA from the Holy See and the Pope would possibly have no share in the appointment of Chinese bishops in future. Yet Deng tried to bargain with the Chinese government. He stated that, if he were allowed to return to his diocese, he would promise not to use the title on all occasions. China kept to its original plan and refused to accept the compromise as suggested by Deng.[69] Deng has had to live on in exile in Hong Kong. It is hoped that he will write his autobiography so that a clear portrayal of his treatment under the Communists and the general situation of the Guangzhou Diocese at the time of Communist take-over would then be recorded.

China dramatically put an end to the episode of the appointment with a religious ceremony for the consecration of bishops held on the morning of 25 July 1981. This was of a tit-for-tat character signifying defiance after the appointment of the Archbishop of Guangzhou.[70] In the same afternoon in the People's Hall, the Chinese religious leaders held a meeting and the vice-chairman of the State Council, Yang Jingren, spoke to the participants. Yang insisted that independence should continue to be the policy of the Catholic church in China in the days to come, because as he explicitly said China would not allow the Catholic church in China 'to kneel down before the Vatican'.[71] It was clear that China clung very tenaciously to its authority over anything within its domain, even in religious matters: for the Chinese government this is full of political implications. Any move by the Vatican to bypass the authority of the Chinese government has always been completely unacceptable to Beijing, even if such a move were the result of mistakes or misunderstandings.

Again it is necessary to establish why the Vatican remained silent and let the facts speak for themselves. The silence of the Vatican could be interpreted as the result of various factors. First, consider-ations of diplomacy: it would have been difficult for the Vatican to admit that it was mistaken in failing to consult China on the

---

[69] Deng revealed this incident when he was interviewed by the writer on 11 July 1987.
[70] *Hong Kong Standard*, 25 July 1981. *Ming Pao*, 24 July 1981. *South China Morning Post*, 26 July 1981.
[71] *Wen Wei Po*, 25 July 1981.

appointment formally and officially, without at the same time
revealing all the truth about the actual procedures of informal
contact. Although the true circumstances would then be known to
the whole world, the crude truth might embarrass the mediators as
well as China. At that stage the Vatican would not be so unwise as to
close the door to further dealings by revealing all the truth and thus
cause even greater indignation on the part of China. The silence
itself also reflected the nature of the Vatican diplomacy, which
always claims to be moral and spiritual in nature, aiming at the
spiritual welfare and religious life of the Catholics in China. The
Vatican, after evaluating the pros and cons, may well have preferred
to be silent while looking for a future opening in China. Its
experience of dealing with the Communist party states in eastern
Europe had also taught the Vatican the lesson that, whenever state
and church relations are tense, the grassroot Catholics there are the
ones who suffer most, government reactions being unleashed upon
them. All the deployments from the Vatican, including the appointments, aim at nothing else other than to enable those following
Christ to express their faith freely and publicly and to live according
to their conscience.[72] The disclosure of the whole truth at that stage
would not have been wise. The slightest imprudence by the Vatican
at this critical moment might have defeated its purpose, above all if
the door of China were to be closed once and for all. This would be
the last thing that the Vatican would wish to see happen.

The Vatican's strong desire to keep the possibility of communication with China open for a more opportune time in the future made
it hold silence before the furious repudiations of the Chinese. For
some years this silence did appear very embarrassing but it proved
very wise in the long run. First of all, the silence of the Vatican in the
face of strong repudiations of a very rude nature won the sympathy
as well as the acclaim of diplomatic circles. This was partly because
China had been long noted for its ideological rhetoric and simplistic
slogans (which dominated its discussions of foreign affairs), and for
refusing to show sophistication and realism in dealing with complicated problems of this nature. Furthermore, the silence paradoxically spoke louder for the spiritual and moral nature of the Vatican's
diplomacy. It was possibly because of this prudent silence that the
Vatican would retain its chances for a reconciliation, to assist the

72 'The Pope speaks to Chinese Christians', *Sunday Examiner*, 27 February 1981.

Chinese modernisation programme in various ways, to show its goodwill in action and to pave the way for dialogue and informal contacts in later years.

Taiwan–Vatican relations: an obstacle to Sino-Vatican relations

The PRC had long since laid down the condition that any nation wishing to establish diplomatic relations with it had to cut off relations with the ROC. Its intention was clearly stated in Article 56 of the Common Programme as early as 1949. This read:

With any foreign government which cuts off relations with the reactionary Nationalists and holds a friendly attitude towards the PRC, the Chinese government will establish diplomatic relationship on the grounds of equality and mutual respect of sovereignty.

Until 1978, the United States had been faced with the tricky problem of deciding what to do about its relations with Taiwan. China stuck to its unarguable tenet for normalisation: viz. the breaking of diplomatic relations between the United States and the ROC, the termination of the Mutual Security Treaty between the two governments and the withdrawal of all US military personnel from Taiwan.[73] In September 1978 the US solution to this problem led it to establish diplomatic relations with Beijing and to break off diplomatic relations with Taibei, but the US retained its extensive economic ties with the island and handled inter-governmental relations through an ostensibly private body staffed by government officials.[74] It was not the best solution for the PRC who aimed at incorporating this island into its sovereignty. Yet, it was the best that the US would offer. Beijing accepted it, because the normalisation of Sino-US diplomatic relations benefited both the PRC and the US in more than one way, both in the short and long term.[75] In the 1980s Chinese political leaders were not happy with the fact that neither the normalisation of Sino-US relations in late 1978 with the publication of its position on the reunification of Taiwan and the mainland

---

[73] R. Clough, *Island China* (Cambridge, Mass.: Harvard University Press, 1978), p. 4.
[74] Ibid.
[75] Ralph Clough in his work *Island China* analysed in detail the Taiwan problem in the light of US interest and its relations with PRC.

accompanied by all sorts of United Front strategies aimed at unification nor the termination of the US–Taiwan Mutual Defense Treaty was able to bring Taiwan to the negotiating table to talk about the future of that island. Furthermore, China was suspicious that the Reagan administration would upgrade US–Taiwan relations and re-activate something like a Two-China policy. The PRC was trying very hard to isolate Taiwan in foreign affairs. The Vatican being one of the twenty-three small or mini-sized states that still maintains formal diplomatic ties with Taiwan, the PRC laid down that one of the conditions for the Sino-Vatican dialogue as proposed by the Pope and Casaroli be that the Vatican cut off diplomatic relations with Taiwan, before any possible negotiations could begin.

Isolation of Taiwan: the PRC's strategy

It seemed that to isolate Taiwan in international affairs was one of the major concerns in Sino-Vatican relations on the part of the Chinese government. On more than one occasion, through bishop Michael Fu, the intention of Beijing was expressed in clear terms. Each time he was asked by journalists about Sino-Vatican relations he repeated China's policy on Taiwan, that of severing Taiwan relations as a prerequisite to any dialogue between the Vatican and China. As early as June 1980, shortly after he was consecrated Bishop of Beijing and in one of his earliest interviews with foreign journalists, Bishop Fu spoke to ANSA, the Italian news agency, and said that basically the government and the CPA were willing to talk with the Vatican. However there were two conditions: the Vatican must recognise the government of Beijing as the only legitimate government of China, including Taiwan, and the Vatican must recognise the bishops who had been consecrated without Rome's approval since 1958.[76] Then, when he was asked to speak on the Pope's speech in Manila inviting the normalisation of Sino-Vatican relations and the Pontiff's wish to visit China, the Bishop of Beijing repeatedly remarked that the Pope's visit was impossible since no diplomatic relations had existed between China and the Vatican since 1957. He said that the CPA opposed the Two-China policy, and the Vatican must cut off its diplomatic ties with Taiwan before

[76] *ANSA News*, 20 June 1980.

it could have any meaningful talks with China.[77] Until the great setback of the appointment, China did not seem to have any definite plans to gain further concessions or compromises from the Holy See on the question of Taiwan. Since October 1971 the Papal Nunciature in Taibei had been headed by a chargé-d'affaires ad interim. When the ROC was forced to give up its seat in the United Nations the Papal pronuncio in Taibei at that time, Archbishop Edward Cassidy, was appointed concurrently papal representative in Bangladesh and resided there while continuing to be accredited to Nationalist China. Then a few years later he became the Apostolic Delegate in Southern Africa. No pronuncio to the ROC had been named since them. Apparently the PRC wanted to isolate Taiwan further by insisting that the Vatican should cut diplomatic ties altogether with Taiwan. The downgrading of Vatican–Taiwan diplomatic relations was not enough because it was a unilateral action and Taiwan still had its ambassador to the Vatican all the same. The Vatican was the only European state where Taiwan had an embassy. Lots of intelligence could be collected not only from the diplomatic circles there but also through the connections with the headquarters of missionary societies in this mini-state. The downgrading of the diplomatic relations between the Vatican and Taiwan have seemingly not served the aim of the PRC to isolate Taiwan politically.

Taiwan: church allied with state

Naturally the national government in Taibei was very nervous about the developments in the Vatican and its relations with the PRC. It was reported that on 3 March 1981, immediately after the Pope's speech in Manila, the Ambassador of the ROC to the Vatican, Mr Zhou Shukai, spoke with the Prefect of the Propaganda Fide, Cardinal Rossi, at the Vatican for more than thirty minutes on common questions relating to the two states. The meeting was requested by the Ambassador of the ROC. Then on 4 March 1981, the Foreign Ministry of Taiwan summoned Monsignor Giglio, the chargé-d'affaires in the Taibei Apostolic Nunciature, and requested him to explain once more the relations between Taiwan and the

[77] This was the answer given by Michael Fu when he was asked about the Pope's Manila speech and the Pope's longing to visit China.

Holy See.[78] The Taiwan government openly admitted that they were closely watching the developments in the relations between the Vatican and mainland China. In these circumstances the best course the Taiwan government could take was to ally itself with the local Catholic church for mutual support.

The church in Taiwan consisted of 300,000 Catholics in seven dioceses, most of the Catholics being migrants from the mainland in 1949, and almost all the Taiwan bishops having been born on the mainland. The Taiwan Catholic church did not share the same views on the Sino-Taiwan relationship as its government. The Pope's proposal for rapprochement with mainland China met with no opposition or nervousness, because the Taiwan Catholics understood that the motivation behind the Vatican's gesture was pastoral, for the sake of the Catholics in China. They saw that the attempt made by the Pope to open dialogue with the PRC was for the sake of the church on the mainland, and that the downgrading of the relations with the Taiwan church was to release the pressure by the government on the Catholics on the mainland.[79] In spite of the fact that the Taiwan government strictly refused to have even any social contact with the PRC before 1987, and that Taiwan residents were not granted exit permits to visit mainland China, nevertheless many of the Taiwan clergy and laity did manage to visit China through Hong Kong and south-east Asia. In particular they paid visits to their old homes and their fellow-Catholics there, largely for nostalgic reasons. It was this group of overseas Chinese Catholics that had connections with the unofficial church and who identified themselves with it because of their common anti-Communist sentiments and their shared loyalty to the Holy See. Because of these sentiments some Taiwan Catholics could be manipulated by the nationalist government into becoming junior allies in safeguarding Taiwan's interests in Sino-Vatican relations. As a matter of fact the church leaders in Taiwan knew very well that the ecclesiastical position of the Taiwan Catholic church would not be jeopardised by the downgrading of diplomatic relations between Taiwan and the Vatican, because the spiritual relations between the local bishops with the successor of Peter would not be affected by the presence or

78 *Ta Kung Po*, 9 March 1981.
79 'Luen Zhongguo Jiaohui – Yimu Yizhan' [On the Chinese church – one flock and one shepherd]. A pastoral letter issued by the Taiwan Chinese Bishops Conference. *Jiaoyou Shenghuo* [Catholic Life Weekly] (Taipei), 27 September 1984.

absence of diplomatic relations between the Vatican and any particular state. Take Poland for example, the Vatican has no diplomatic relations with the Polish government, yet the religious links of the Polish church and the Vatican have been much closer than those of other local churches.

Nevertheless the Taiwan church leaders had to oblige the government which had the means to subtly exert pressure on the church if the latter refused to stand by its side. The church and state alliance in Taiwan was uneasy for the Taiwan Catholic church. In responding to the call of the Pope 'to build a bridge' between the Catholics on the mainland and the universal church, the Taiwan church ran the risk of going against the political trend of the nationalist government which demanded no contact by any section of its people with the mainland. Through Hong Kong, Taiwan Catholics nevertheless supplied books on theology and philosophy to the seminaries run by the CPA, thereby signifying that their attitude towards the CPA was less hostile than before.

The junior ally acted for its senior partner

The Taiwan Catholic church as well as the Taiwan government felt very uneasy when suggestions were made to the Vatican, in the wake of the issue of the appointment of the Archbishop of Guangzhou, to the effect that the Vatican sever diplomatic ties with Taiwan in order to initiate contact with China. That implied that the Vatican would have to close the Papal Nunciature in Taiwan, while the Taiwan Chinese ambassador in the Vatican would have to be recalled, and be replaced by a special papal delegate of non-diplomatic nature in Taibei. Under pressure from the Taiwan government, the Catholic church in Taiwan tried to lobby the Vatican officials not to sacrifice the church of Taiwan for the sake of the church on the mainland. The cardinal and the bishops had to do something about that. First of all the Vice-Prefect of the Propaganda Fide, Cardinal Loudusamy, was invited to visit Taiwan for the celebration of the 400th anniversary of the arrival of Matteo Ricci in China in 1983. Then the President of the Pontifical Commission of Justice and Peace, Cardinal Gantin, was asked to visit Taiwan on 17 February 1984 so that the Taiwan bishops could voice their discontent about the possible move of the Vatican towards the PRC. This provided an occasion for them to express their anxiety at being betrayed if the normalisation of Vatican–China relations were to be made at their expense. They hoped Cardinal Gantin would be sympathetic towards them and view the severing of diplomatic ties from their standpoint of justice and peace.

Eventually all the seven members of the Taiwan Chinese Bishops' Conference headed by its President, Archbishop Lokuong, were able to go to the Vatican on February 1984 to have a 'dialogue' with the Pope and the high-ranking Vatican officials, including the Under-Secretary of State, Martinez Solmalo, and the Foreign Minister, Cardinal A. Silvestrini. In several sessions, they had long discussions with the Vatican officials and with the Pope on their grudges about the Vatican's policy towards mainland China. They challenged the views of the Vatican on the possible severing of diplomatic ties with Taiwan and remarked that this would be a great blow to the morale of Taiwan Catholics. Their fear of being victimised by the Vatican in its wooing of mainland China was also explained. They requested to be kept directly informed of the Vatican's future moves towards mainland China. In this encounter and dialogue, which was loaded with tension, the Vatican was able skilfully to reassure these seven anguished bishops, backed up by their own government, that the normalisation of Sino-Vatican relations would not be at their expense. The Vatican gave them a promise that in future if there were to be any move by it towards the PRC or the Catholic church in China, the Taiwan Chinese Bishops' Conference would be the first to be told. Then the Pope tried to recruit the Taiwan church to help him with China, by inviting it as well as all overseas Chinese Catholics to be the bridge between the Chinese Catholic church and the universal church.[80] In so doing, the Vatican completely won over the Taiwan bishops, by giving them the high honour and privilege of reuniting their fellow Catholics on the mainland with the universal church. National, ethnic and cultural affinity had made reunion with their relatives on the mainland a strong attraction for every Chinese Catholic. In Chinese history division and civil war invariably ended up in reunification. Throughout the long history of China no territories inhabited by Han Chinese ever broke away permanently from the mainland.[81] In their hearts no Chinese were willing to see separation. For the Taiwan Catholic church it was an

---

[80] Wurth, (ed.), *Papal Documents Related to the New China*, art. 45, pp. 177–9. *L'Osservatore Romano* (English edn), 12 March 1984.
[81] Clough, *Island China*, pp. 123–4.

honour and a privilege as well as a moral responsibility to play the role of bridge-builder, so that the Chinese Catholics astray on the mainland could be reunited in the orthodoxy of the Catholic church. Archbishop Lokuong, the President of the Taiwan Chinese Bishops' Conference seriously took the lead in the enterprise by taking up the work of blending Chinese culture with Christianity and hopefully later to have the acculturated Christian message brought to the mainland. With much pride and honour he accepted that the Taiwan church should be the bastion for the revival of the mainland church through cultural adaptation, and called upon the Catholics in Taiwan to shoulder this grave responsibility entrusted to them by the Pope.[82]

The cultural bridge: the Taiwan Catholic church

Owing to political conditions, the Taiwan Catholic church was not free to be the mediator or to facilitate any informal political interaction between the Vatican and the PRC. This was because the nationalist government found it difficult to tolerate any attitude which was sympathetic to Communism, especially as it had to deal with the political United Front tactics coming from the other side of the Taiwan Straits. At the same time there was a great need to indigenise Christianity and translate the Gospel teaching into a message relevant to the modern Chinese. The Catholic church in Taiwan had been engaging itself in this kind of cultural work for quite some time, since it had a Catholic university with is theologate and a couple of other centres for cultural and theological studies and research which had attracted a cluster of Catholic scholars. No doubt compared with Hong Kong and other overseas Chinese communities, Taiwan was the most qualified for this task. In fact, there was really no alternative left, because Hong Kong was too westernised in its cultural outlook. In the theological dialogue with the Chinese Communists, there was a small group of theologians appointed by the Taiwan church authorities who met the Catholic scholars appointed by the Hong Kong bishop regularly, not only to update their knowledge of the development of the Catholic church in mainland China, but also to enable them to exchange political and theological views on this question among themselves. The

[82] The Homily of Archbishop Lokuong, delivered on 22 March 1984. See *Witness* 137 (April 1984): pp. 2–4.

interactions of Catholic scholars from these two sides, in a modest way, provided some positive advice for the church authorities, on the questions of church and Communist relations in the Chinese context. Evidence indicates slow but positive developments, and their scholarly publications suggest grounds for confidence that they are conscientiously carrying out their mission of building a cultural bridge.

In dealing with the whole question of the relationship with Taiwan, one can also note another interesting instance of the PRC's rejection of the Vatican. Beijing is very anxious to use United Front tactics to penetrate Taiwan society. The Catholics, with the Vatican's encouragement, have been very brave in making contact with the mainland, mainly, though not exclusively, through Hong Kong. The mainland does not seem to be as warm and encouraging to the Taiwan Catholics as it would be to writers or businessmen from Taiwan, for example. The overall impression seems to be that the mainland side distrusts the Catholic church of Taiwan, and this is not simply because it has some senior clergy who are known as KMT supporters but it is because the Taiwan Catholics are suspected of being loyal to the Vatican and their activities guided by the interests of the Vatican especially as far as the mainland is concerned. All of this may be regarded as contrary to normal United Front tactics which usually welcome all types of contacts with the opposition.

THE POLITICAL BRIDGE: HONG KONG

The Hong Kong Catholic church: a church established in a British colony

The Catholic church in Hong Kong is a comparatively young church because its history does not go back beyond 150 years. Out of a total population of 5.5 millions in 1984 the Catholic population was only 270,000, more than 90% of these being Chinese. There is no doubt that it is the largest Chinese Catholic diocese not only in terms of membership but also in terms of the number of local church personnel.[83] It was called upon by the Pope to be the bridge probably not only because of its nature as a young, promising and well-structured local church, but primarily for geo-political reasons.

Viewed geographically, Hong Kong is about seventy miles south-

---

[83] *International Fide News Service*, 7 May 1986; quoted by *Tripod* 33 (June 1986): 42–52.

east of the southern Chinese city of Guangzhou. It acquired its importance only in the middle of the last century as the result of the growing trade with South China. The Opium War resulted in the Nanjing Treaty of 1842 by which this small trading port was ceded to Britain. British-administered Hong Kong is about 404 square miles in extent, and the population was only 1,500 in 1840. Then after 1945 due to the civil war in China refugees began to flow in, making the population grow from 600,000 in 1945 to 2.3 million in 1949. With the help of capital and cheap labour pouring in from China as well as the general development of the world economy, Hong Kong experienced a period of unprecedented growth. Its population had grown to 5.5 million by 1984.[84] The overall population density of about 12,500 per square mile makes it one of the most densely populated spots in the world. From the outset the British government did not regard Hong Kong as a political possession like its other colonies. From the beginning the main interest of the British in Hong Kong was in the volume of trade passing through the territory, as an entrepot in which British law prevailed. By 1984 the people of Hong Kong had reached a high standard of living, with a per capita income of about US$4000, almost fifteen times that of the PRC.[85] Despite a lack of democracy, British law obtained, backed up by the democracy in London, and the right of legal appeal to the Privy Council. As a result various types of freedom have prevailed in this colony, especially economic freedom. With manpower and managerial skill provided by the Chinese refugees and their descendants, together with the *laissez-faire* policy of the British Hong Kong government, the Hong Kong people began to enjoy a much higher living standard than most others in Asia, about equal for example to Taiwan and Korea, while somewhat less than Singapore. Its container port ranks third in the world in size and second in terms of tonnage. After London and New York, Hong Kong is one of the world's leading commercial, manufacturing and communication centres. All this is very impressive for a territory without any natural resources.[86] Economically, Hong Kong had been a bridge to China for quite some time, since it supplied 40 per

[84] Edmond Tang, 'Hong Kong 1997: A Historical challenge for the Churches', *Pro Mundi Vita: Dossiers*, 1 January 1985, Asia–Australiasia Dossier no. 32. *Hong Kong 1985*, Hong Kong Government, 1986, p. 249.
[85] Chu Hungdah (ed.), *Symposium on Hong Kong 1997* (University of Maryland, School of Law, 1986), p. 3.
[86] Secondo Einaudi, 'The Catholic Church in Hong Kong', *Tripod* 25 (February 1895): 55.

cent of China's foreign exchange through its annual trade with the PRC.[87] Hong Kong also offered a highly convenient and efficient source of capital funds, market information, managerial expertise and technological innovation for China's modernisation.

Four types of 'bridges' in Hong Kong

The Catholics in Hong Kong began in 1978 to take the initiative in contacting Catholics in China. Hong Kong Chinese Catholics touring China sparked off grassroot contacts. Then foreign missionary societies that had formerly worked in China also sent their members to Hong Kong before and after they went on fact-finding trips in China. After 1978 not only did local Hong Kong Catholics stream in to visit China, because of their sense of patriotism and feelings of national identity, but they also formed a small group of young clergy and laity with ulterior apostolic interests in China. In addition to conducting visits, they held discussions and reflected China's policy of religious freedom, arising out of what they had seen of the religious revival and re-opening of churches in China. Furthermore their progressive political outlook, their consciousness of their own national identity and their romantic patriotism, led them to sympathise with the CPA in so many ways that they gave it strong support and agreed with the CPA on almost every stand that it took. Therefore they formed very warm relations with the CPA, which desperately needed overseas supporters to make itself acceptable to the universal church. This radical group was made known to the public through their publication called *Yi (Messenger)*. It was a Catholic publication that reported news about China – mainly about the activities of the Three Selfs movement of the Protestant church and the CPA activities on the Chinese Catholic side. This group really played the role of a messenger or a bridge to make the CPA known to the Hong Kong Catholics as well as to the overseas Catholics. Since *Yi* was the first publication to appear immediately after the relaxation of religious control, when religious news was very scanty and had even been completely absent during the time of the Cultural Revolution, it had a limited circulation among the common people. In spite of the fact that the viewpoint of this group of Catholics was a little removed from the traditional

87 Chu, *Symposium on Hong Kong: 1997*, p. 3.

Catholic teaching, and appeared to be too pro-CPA, they nevertheless received support from a small group of younger people because of the character of their nationalistic appeal, which was based on cultural ties and Chinese national identity. The Vatican as well as the head of the Hong Kong Catholic diocese always frowned on them, and refused to acknowledge *Yi* as an official publication of the diocese. The *Yi* group for their part were happy that they were given a free hand to work outside the grip of the Catholic hierarchy. The leader of this progressive group requested neither funds nor manpower from the diocese. He had some financial aid from overseas and some funds from unknown sources. The Hong Kong Catholic diocese on the one hand had to tolerate this group because the leader happened to be a priest and the group were Catholics. They were also in good standing with the CPA both at national and provincial levels. The church authorities on the other hand would not identify themselves with this radical group, but had to render some protection to them when they were attacked by the more conservative clergy, in order to keep unity among the church personnel. Long before the 1984 Hong Kong Agreement was signed, the bishop already knew very well that this group would be a good bridge if the diocese should need any connection with Chinese officials or the CPA, especially since the Hong Kong Catholic diocese had rarely had any contact with the Communists before.

Nevertheless in 1980 when the diocese was asked by the Vatican to make some studies, and establish research and personal contacts with China, no one from this group was chosen by the Hong Kong bishop to initiate this important project. The bishop picked Father John Tong, the director of the diocesan research centre on China, to be his contact man with China, and not Father Anthony Chang, the leader of *Yi*. Tong was a new hand in this field; before he started the research centre in 1980 he had no experience at all of China and the Chinese Catholics there. His merit in the view of the Vatican was that he had been trained in Rome, that he had a reasonable theological background and had had the time and opportunity already to do semi-academic work because of the seminary post he held. Tong managed to get Chang's assistance in obtaining introductions to Chinese Communist circles, notably the Chinese quasi-embassy, the Xinhua News Agency, Hong Kong Branch, but from the beginning bureaucratic rivalry was found between these two bridging groups. After the initial introductions Tong kept a safe

13 The Anglican Bishop K. H. Ting (right), Steering Committee Member of the National Peoples' Congress, visits the Hong Kong Catholic Diocesan Research Centre on China (1982). *Source:* Author's private collection.

distance from Chang, and made himself the official liaison between China, the Hong Kong Catholic church and the Vatican. He may be said to have done his introductory work well. Then the situation became more complicated when the third and fourth types of bridge emerged.

The third type of bridge was built by the missionary societies who still had their own Chinese religious priests and nuns in China. The missionary societies had for very many years lacked contact with their own Chinese members, but once the situation eased they sent fact-finding missions to seek them out, and investigations were made especially in some controversial cases, such as the marital status of the priests and bishops of their own orders, the motivation of priests in joining the CPA and their willingness to be ordained as bishops, etc. Some religious congregations, the Jesuits for example, had a great number of their members sent for long-term prison sentences or to labour camps, and as early as the 1950s they had come to know the whereabouts of these Jesuits and how many of them had been released and how many of them had died, or were still alive in jail. This third type of bridge had a completely different orientation and approach that arose out of their previous experience with China. Their contact with Chinese Catholics was not due to romantic patriotism, but was based on their desire to find out the bare facts about those Chinese Catholics, clergy and laity, after they had refused to be cut off from the Holy See. They also wanted to discover the true accounts of those who had joined the CPA. It was through this type of contact that the situation of the unofficial church was made known. Usually these visits were quietly made to both the CPA and non-CPA Catholics. Aside from confidential reports to the high-ranking religious leaders of the responsible religious societies and to the Vatican, some reports of valour were made known to the public, using fictitious names of persons and places in order to protect the people who were still in China. This type of bridge was resented by the Chinese authorities; it was regarded as a group of 'hostile religious forces from the outside designed to set up underground churches and other illegal organisations'.[88]

The fourth type of bridge like the third type was built by foreign missionary societies who had carried out mission work in China before 1949, but unlike the previous type they practically had no Chinese religious members of their own in China. They initiated a new type of mission, not by directly sending their missionaries to China proper as they had done before, but by trying to work for the Catholic church in China in the spirit of reconciliation which they felt the Chinese church needed most. In their own way they played the role of a bridge in contacting the CPA, with a very sympathetic attitude and approach. Informally they invited the CPA to send its members abroad for visits, with the aim of softening the antagonistic attitude of the CPA to the Vatican and of breaking the isolation of the CPA by giving it a chance to come out of its shell and see for itself that the local churches in Hong Kong, Germany, the Philippines and US operated with a great amount of freedom and autonomy while keeping their essential spiritual union with the Holy See.[89] At the same time this group of people through their international connections were able to offer material assistance to the CPA in the form of donations of books to seminaries, and scholarships and

---

[88] 'Document 19', para. 11.
[89] S. Einaudi, 'The Catholic Church in Hong Kong', *Tripod* 25 (February 1985): 53–69.

grants for Chinese students to study abroad, as well as financial assistance in many other ways.

Generally speaking, the third and fourth types of bridges were built mainly by foreigners from the international missionary societies and with some co-operation from local Catholics. The stance taken by these four 'church bridges', in terms of their views on the CPA and the non-CPA not only had a bearing on the type of work they did, but also complicated the attainment of unity among the people working on these four bridges. Above all the divisions between the bridge groups perpetuated the divisions between the CPA and non-CPA. Not only did they keep a safe distance from one another, but also for ideological reasons as well as from bureaucratic rivalry they were so greatly divided that the Vicar General of the Hong Kong Diocese found it necessary to call for unity among the church leaders on the occasion of a Jesuit workshop on China on 26 November 1984.[90]

The bridge on fire: the Hong Kong Catholic church facing the challenge of 1997

Long before the Pope called on the Taiwan and the Chinese diaspora to be the bridge between China and the universal church, the bridge in Hong Kong had already been built and only waited for the Holy Father to name it as such in February 1984. Fortunately or unfortunately, in the same year, one of the bridge churches, the church in Hong Kong, had to face an historic challenge caused by the Sino-British Agreement to return the sovereignty of Hong Kong to China. Talks between China and Great Britain over the future of Hong Kong began in 1982. After two years of secret negotiations without the participation of any representatives of the Hong Kong people, the two governments reached an agreement. In September 1984, the United Kingdom and the People's Republic of China made a Joint Declaration on the Future of Hong Kong.[91]

In the Joint Declaration it was stated that the Chinese govern-

---

[90] On Bishop Louis Jin's visit to the Philippines, see *Correspondence* 21 (October 1985). On Jin's visit to Hong Kong, see *Tripod* 28 (August 1985): 46–9. On Jin's visit to Germany, see *Tripod* 33 (June 1986): 79–80. On Bishop Michael Fu's visit to the USA, see *Tripod*, 36 (December 1986): 75–9.

[91] *A Draft Agreement between the government of the United Kingdom of Great Britain and Northern Ireland and the Government of the People's Republic of China on the Future of Hong Kong*, a White Paper, Her Majesty's Government in London, 26/9/1984 (hereafter called *The Joint Agreement*).

ment had decided to resume the exercise of sovereignty over Hong Kong with effect from 1 July 1997, and the British would restore Hong Kong to China on the same day.[92] The declaration was accompanied by three Annexes which further specified China's basic policies for the territory, which will become a special Administrative Region under China's sovereignty. The Sino-British Agreement signified the end of an era, and the beginning of a new age. Beijing had pledged a charter guaranteeing an unprecedented degree of self-government to the people of Hong Kong. There is no doubt that China's main interests in Hong Kong are economic and to give an example of peaceful reunification to attract Taiwan. Detailed guarantees were put into the Joint Declaration and the Annexes, promising to maintain the trading and financial structures of the territory. By comparison the social and political sectors were treated rather vaguely. Some of the problems were left unresolved on the day of the signing of the Joint Agreement, to be dealt with at a later period. These were the future nationality of Hong Kong citizens, the basic law, the guarantees for a free political process, etc. Understandably the people of Hong Kong received the Joint Agreement without enthusiasm, but they had no alternative but to accept it. The lack of confidence they showed was mainly because of China's record with its own people and its disrespect for human rights. Hong Kong people, especially the millions of refugees from China, could not forget that in the last thirty-five years China had travelled a zig-zag road of development, reneging on its own declared policies and promises almost overnight to suit its own interests as interpreted by senior leaders.

The deep concern of the Catholic church in Hong Kong over its future after 1997 could be seen reflected in the actions of its Catholic bishop. During the period of turmoil when various groups of Hong Kong citizens were fighting for a chance to express their ideas on the future of Hong Kong on various occasions through various media, the Hong Kong bishop, John Wu, wrote to the British government and the Chinese government expressing his deep concern about the prospects for religious freedom in Hong Kong after 1997. Six months prior to the issuing of the Joint Declaration on the future of Hong Kong, in February 1984, he consulted his advisers and Catholic leaders from all walks of life and after careful reflection and

92 *The Joint Agreement*, p. 11.

discussion he prepared a manifesto which was to be issued on 15 August 1984. In the manifesto he specified the type of religious freedom which the Hong Kong Catholics had been enjoying and particularly pointed out that the Catholics needed to be united with the universal church through union with the Pope.[93] About the same time, he wrote to the British Foreign Secretary, Sir Geoffrey Howe, and to Cardinal Hume of England to express his concern over the future of Hong Kong, and appealed to Sir Geoffrey Howe to provide a clear legal guarantee in the Sino-British agreement to give 'full and effective recognition to all the rights and freedoms hitherto enjoyed by all religious associations and their members in Hong Kong and to preserve all such rights and freedoms beyond 1997'.[94]

The bishop's letter aroused some criticism from the more progressive Catholic leaders because the latter considered the letter to be of an over-suspicious tone in the light of the repeated assurances made by the Chinese authorities.[95] Some considered it to be a diplomatic 'faux pas' that the letter was not written to the Chinese government but to the outgoing colonial government. It was argued that it would be difficult to refute future criticism that the Catholic church is foreign and colonial in nature.[96] Even some overseas Catholic China observers agreed with this criticism and noted that it produced some change in the thinking of the Catholic leadership, particularly when another manifesto was drafted after the signing of the Sino-British Agreement; beginning in a more positive tone:

As Chinese we are proud of our heritage ... As people of Hong Kong we want to work in solidarity with all fellow-members of the community ... .[97]

When one views the criticism and the letter of the bishop from a different angle one may see that the criticism was not well grounded. First of all, if the bishop had expressed his concern for the religious freedom of the Hong Kong Catholics merely to the outgoing

93 Bishop John Wu, 'Statement on the Catholic church and the future of Hong Kong', press letter, 23 August 1984, released by Catholic Information Service.
94 *The Tablet* (London), 19 May 1984, p. 471.
95 The Deputy Director of Xinhua News Agency, H. K. branch, gave a lunch to Italian Senior V. Colombo (one of the contact men between the Vatican and China), reassuring him that after 1997 Hong Kong would enjoy the same amount of freedom as before, cf. *Kung Kao Po*, 23 December 1983 and the cautious reactions from some Catholic leaders to the reassurances. *South China Morning Post*, 4 January 1984.
96 Edmond Tang, 'Hong Kong 1997: a historical challenge for the churches', *Pro Mundi Vitae: Dossier* (July 1985): 16.
97 Ibid.

government and not to the incoming one, one might have reason to take this action as a diplomatic 'faux pas'. But he expressed the same concern for religious freedom in Hong Kong after 1997 to the British government as well as the Chinese government. In fact one could say that the bishop showed a very high diplomatic skill in approaching different governments in different ways, each according to its own style and in languages that they would respectively understand. Again if one reads the manifesto carefully between the lines, one can clearly gather that the thinking of the Catholic leadership had not changed to a more positive approach. The bishop was still weighed with the same concern for religious freedom. In fact he only said that he was proud of the Chinese heritage. He did not say that he was proud of the atheist government with its one-party dictatorship, which the Chinese Catholics had encountered with so much difficulty in the past and which would cause them immense headaches in the days to come. If one listened to what the bishop did not say in his manifesto, considering at the same time how carefully and minutely he listed the type of religious freedom Hong Kong is enjoying, one could understand his anxiety and concern that the rights and freedoms which the Hong Kong Catholics have enjoyed so far may not be preserved after 1997.[98] His statement in the manifesto on religious freedom went as follows:

Religious freedom as we enjoy it in Hong Kong includes the following rights:
a The right to have or to adopt a religion or belief of one's choice, and to manifest it in worship, observance, practice and teaching.
b The right of the individual to worship in private and public, alone and with fellow-believers.
c The right to make one's religion known to others, and to instruct those who are interested in this religion by the spoken and the written word.
d The right of parents to provide religious instruction in bringing up their children.
e The right of religious communities and associations to hold meetings and to promote educational, cultural, charitable and social activities.
f The right to appoint personnel, to train them and to send them abroad for specialised studies and at the same time the right to utilise, if and when necessary, the services of personnel from abroad.
g The right to erect and/or use buildings for religious purposes and to acquire such property if necessary.

[98] Bishop John Wu, 'Statement on the Catholic church and the future of Hong Kong', press letter, 23 Autust 1984, released by Catholic Information Service, art. 6.

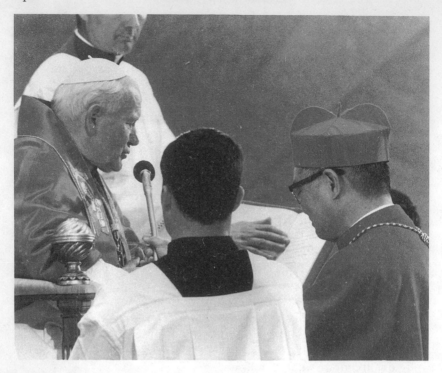

14 In the Consistory, Pope John Paul II confers the zucchetto (skull cap) and the Beretta to Cardinal Wu of Hong Kong (28 June 1988). *Source: Kung Kao Po* (The Chinese Catholic Weekly).

h For the Catholics, in particular, the right to maintain their existing links and their existing unity with the universal church, through union with the Pope and also with the Bishops and Catholic communities in other parts of the world. This unity is basic to the Catholic church's belief.

Obviously the bishop knew very well that the religious freedom Hong Kong Catholics enjoyed was quite different from that in China because of his own personal background.[99]

His two visits to China as a guest of the state, which had involved the refusal of his requests to meet the jailed Bishop Gong of Shanghai and to be allowed to say Masses in public, provided him with sufficient facts to prove that the quality of the religious freedom provided and supervised by the party differed considerably from that which prevails in Hong Kong.

[99] He was born in Wuhua, Guangdong Province, and was ordained in Hong Kong in 1952. He has worked outside China proper since then but his family is living in Wuhua.

15 Bishop of Hong Kong, Bishop John Baptist Wu (now Cardinal Wu) and his companions meet the press before their departure for the first official visit to Beijing (25 March 1985). *Source: Kung Kao Po* (The Chinese Catholic Weekly).

Bishop of Hong Kong's first visit to China

Bishop Wu's visit to China was entirely initiated by the Chinese government. Knowing the delicacy of his position as the prelate of the Hong Kong Catholic church, which has close relations not only with the Vatican but with the Catholic church throughout the whole world including the Catholic church in Taiwan, he carefully maintained a discreet distance from the Chinese Catholic church and the CPA so as to avoid unnecessary misunderstandings and misinterpretations. But he himself was very well informed on all the developments in church and state relations in China down to the last detail. After the signing of the Joint Agreement on the future of Hong Kong, Bishop Wu knew that he could not avoid contact with his Chinese CPA counterpart any longer. Prior to his own visit to China, he had sent only his representatives to be the official guests at the ceremony of the signing of the Sino-British Agreement on the future of Hong Kong on 24 September 1984. Then the Chinese government invited many prominent Hong Kong figures to Beijing to celebrate the National Day on 1 October 1984. The Chinese bishop of the Anglican church of Hong Kong and the heads of other

Christian denominations were present on that occasion, which Deng Xiaoping wished to celebrate with particular ceremony with regard to the settling of the question of Hong Kong through an unconventional means, 'one state and two systems'. The Catholic churches of Hong Kong and Macau only sent their Vicars General. When the invitation came to Bishop Wu of Hong Kong asking him to visit China after these two big occasions, he knew that he had no alternative left, and he had to accept the invitation which was a challenge for him. In spite of the fact that the bulk of the agenda for his discussions was focused on the religious matters that would affect Hong Kong after 1997, it was clear that none of these questions could be treated independently of Sino-Vatican relations. In Beijing, he met the chief officials of the Religious Affairs Bureau, of the United Front Department and of the Hong Kong and Macau Affairs Office. In Shanghai, he met the chief officials of the Shanghai Religious Affairs Bureau and of the Shanghai Municipal government. In both Beijing and Shanghai, he met the leaders of the Chinese Catholic Patriotic Association.

In his meetings with the officials, he posed some very challenging questions to the Chinese government as to how the Catholic church could contribute to the modernisation programme. His questions as recorded by one of his followers on the trip were as follows:

As the Catholic bishop of a diocese and as a member of the worldwide college of Catholic bishops, I would like to inquire further about three matters: First, regarding the great task of reunification of the motherland, what type of bridge-role can the Hong Kong Catholic church play? How can we make more foreign friends for China and increase her international reputation? Secondly, faced with a changing situation in Hong Kong, besides the present work, what further contribution can the Hong Kong Catholic church make to promote the integral development of society as a whole (including its material, spiritual and religious aspects)? And thirdly, under the principle of the 'three mutualities',[100] how can we increase contacts between Catholics inside and outside China? And within our present relationship, and in communion with the universal Catholic church, how can we best work in building up a better society for the benefit of all mankind?[101]

One could not expect an immediate reply from China to these

[100] 'Three mutualities' is a short form of 'non-subordination, non-interference and mutual respect': the three principles laid down by the Chinese government regarding the relationship between the Hong Kong Catholics and the Catholics in China after 1997.
[101] John Tong, 'With Bishop Wu on his historic visit to China' *Tripod* 26 (April 1985): 50–1.

questions. However, this gesture can be taken as a further condition laid down by the Vatican through this bishop, who has a very close relationship with the Vatican, and whose high officials were consulted before he accepted the invitation for this trip.[102]

When Bishop Wu touched on the question of the Sino-Vatican dialogue, he made a very significant remark which might well demonstrate the attitude of the Vatican on the Sino-Vatican dialogue at that particular period of time. He briefly and frankly pointed out:

To engage in dialogue does not mean that one side be required to abandon principles. On the contrary, it is precisely because each side's viewpoint is different that dialogue becomes necessary. Nor does dialogue mean that the parties involved must arrive at a position pre-judged before the dialogue opens. To set certain conditions that must be fulfilled before one is even willing to engage in dialogue, is not a method used today in any kind of fruitful international negotiations. Such a stance, on its face value, may be judged as lacking in sincerity, and could also result in one's views not being taken too seriously in international circles. As for how and when a dialogue between China and the Vatican might take place, that is for the two sides to work out between themselves. Any frank and direct dialogue is bound to lead to better mutual understanding, a lessening of unnecessary misunderstanding and a working towards everyone's betterment.[103]

Unmistakably the bishop echoed the Vatican's response to the condition laid down by the Chinese, namely that the Vatican must cut off relations with Taiwan before a dialogue could even be begun. At the same time the Vatican took the opportunity to inform China through the bishop what kind of dialogue the Vatican had in mind. For the Vatican, a dialogue could provide the chance to talk and understand and above all to remove their differences rather than provide a guarantee that a concession would be made by Rome in advance.

However, Bishop Wu's request to visit the jailed Bishop Gong of Shanghai might throw some light on the still sour Sino-Vatican relations. Bishop Wu made his request through the Xinhua News Agency Hong Kong Branch one month before his trip. Recognising the sensitivity of his request, Bishop Wu outlined his reasons: it was only meant as a fraternal visit to a Christian brother. Wu also

[102] This was acknowledged by Mgr. Celli, the director of China Desk, Secretariat of State of the Vatican.
[103] John Tong, 'With Bishop Wu on his historic visit to China', *Tripod* 26 (April 1985): 53–4.

suggested that if the authorities felt it inconvenient for the whole delegation to enter the prison, then the bishop could go just by himself in the company of someone selected for the task. He assured officials that his reasons were not of a personal nature, for he and Bishop Gong had no family ties other than being fellow-Christians. But, at the eleventh hour of his stay in Shanghai, the bishop was informed definitely that he could not meet Bishop Gong. Bishop Wu cancelled the rest of the scheduled activities in Shanghai, as a protest at the refusal, saying that he needed time to formulate some appropriate answers to Catholics in Hong Kong when they might ask about his meeting with Bishop Gong. The pro-Vatican bishop gently pursued this strong case – a significant visit to another pro-Vatican bishop in jail. The refusal of the Chinese government could be interpreted as a sign that China still resents the Vatican, especially as Gong was the key symbol of Chinese Catholic loyalty to the Holy See. This was not the first time that religious visitors were forbidden access to Gong. Cardinal Sin made the same request, and his request too was rejected. In any case, Cardinal Sin did not strongly pursue this issue. Sin did not protest nor did he mention it publicly. No public record of Sin's visit to China has ever mentioned his request to meet Bishop Gong. He mentioned it only verbally to those close around him in Manila.

Nevertheless, Bishop Wu's request for a visit to a religious dissident eighty-four years old put China's officials on the spot. Bishop Gong has been the symbol of defiance to China's insistence on the total independence of Chinese Catholics. Together with the famous leaders of the Chinese democratic movement, notably Wei Jingsheng, Fu Yuehua, Liu Qingsan and others, Bishop Gong was adopted as a prisoner of conscience by Amnesty International. Amnesty International appealed publicly for his release on humanitarian grounds, for it believes that he and the others have been detained for non-violently exercising their fundamental human rights.[104]

So China was embarrassed by Bishop Wu's request. No convincing reasons were given for the refusal to allow him to visit a frail prisoner of eighty-four years of age who had spent more than thirty years in jail, especially when the whole world was being told that freedom of religion prevailed in China after the fall of the Gang of

[104] Amnesty International, *China, Violations of Human Rights*, pp. 19–35.

Four, and more tolerance was being practiced in social and political life. In addition to China's resentment at Bishop Gong's unyielding loyalty to the Holy See, it appeared that his detention for religious reasons was unjustified.[105]

Later, when Bishop Wu came back to Hong Kong, he informed the Catholics there about the refusal of his request to meet Bishop Gong. He had to make known this news, because many Catholics had carefully observed their bishop's trip and took the gesture of visiting a pro-Vatican bishop in jail as a sign of Bishop Wu's allegiance to the Holy See. Bishop Wu's announcement was publicly given both at home and to the world outside. Naturally it caused much embarrassment to China and perhaps, as a result, Bishop Gong was transferred from a prison cell to be placed under house arrest. Nevertheless he was still not allowed to receive foreign visitors, except for a very few. Nor was he allowed to say Mass and conduct liturgical services in public. Bishop Gong's treatment speaks for itself about the depth of China's resentment at a person's loyalty to the Vatican.

Bishop Wu's second visit to China

Bishop Wu next visited China at the invitation of the Guongdong provincial Religious Affairs Bureau on 21 January 1986, and had a reunion with his eighty-five-year-old mother in his hometown, Wuhua County, Meixian, after a separation of forty years. He spent seven hours with his mother and was able to say a private Mass officially just with his family, but in fact it was also attended by a number of villagers.[106]

The following day, 24 January 1986, the bishop was scheduled to say Mass at the local Catholic church of Wuhua County at the invitation of the parish priest. This would have been the first Mass said by a Catholic bishop from outside China since 1949. More than one thousand people gathered for the occasion, some having travelled for more than an hour to attend it. At about 08:00 a.m. an official arrived to announce that the Mass would not be allowed.

[105] Gong, Pinmie 'The Letter of Appeal', Amnesty International, *China, Violations of Human Rights,* on Bishop Gong, pp. 19–21.
[106] *Sing Tao Jih Pao,* 15 January 1986, 22 January 1986. *Hong Kong Standard,* 22 January 1986. *Nanfang Ribao,* 22 January 1986. *South China Morning post,* 23 January 1986, 24 January 1986, 25 January 1986. *Wen Wei Po,* 23 January 1986, 24 January 1986, 25 January 1986.

The official reason given was that the invitation did not come from a bishop in China or from the CPA or the Religious Affairs Bureau. Most of those who expected to participate at this Mass were driven away by the officials. But more than two hundred villagers, mostly middle-aged and elderly, were allowed to stay when the Hong Kong bishop arrived six hours later than scheduled. The crowd was not allowed to meet the bishop at close range but only to greet him from afar. It was also discovered that the county's United Front Department did not allow the Mass to be said and the fire crackers bought by the church authorities to welcome the bishop were not allowed to be set off.[107]

On the following day, the bishop had again been scheduled to say Mass at a church in Jiaoling County, but was again prevented from doing so. This time the officials wanted to cancel his visit to Jiaoling altogether, but Bishop Wu pressed his case, and was allowed to make an appearance there. No official reaction was expressed by the bishop, although one Hong Kong delegate who accompanied him queried, 'What bad affect would the Mass have on the people and the government?'[108] The issue went beyond the mere fact of his celebrating a Mass; the appearance of a pro-Vatican bishop for the first time since 1949 would have been contrary to the Chinese policy of independence from Rome. The ban on Bishop Wu's Mass was only the tip of an ice-berg demonstrating that the Chinese government had not softened its stance on total separation from the Vatican. The incident might dispel the illusion that a closer relationship between the Chinese government and the Vatican had been established. Although the government did not make any public comment and even though the bishop did not openly criticise his hosts after his trip, a China analyst in Hong Kong who has close links with the church remarked that the situation was far from simple.[109] The ban could be interpreted as an indication of resentment towards a pro-Vatican bishop, whose appearance might have had a counter effect on the religious work done by the government.

These incidents themselves bring out the great difficulty that Catholics have in sympathising with China and its religious policies. One must remember that the bishop had been invited back to visit

[107] *South China Morning Post*, 26 January 1986.
[108] Ibid., 27 January 1986.
[109] Leo Goodstadt expressed this view in a communication to the writer whilst the latter was in London.

China. He has never made any provocative statements, and he is known to be non-political with no close relations even to the Hong Kong government. He travelled on a Hong Kong Certificate of Identity. Yet he was refused permission to say Mass twice in rather embarrassing circumstances. No one on the Chinese side seemed to care what Catholics in Hong Kong might think about the situation. The same point could be made about his being refused permission to see Bishop Gong. Could the reasons once again be that he is known to have one fundamental principle: loyalty to the Vatican? Nevertheless he was back a second time despite his having asked for something embarrasing from the PRC on his first visit. That suggests that the PRC was prepared to carry out its declared principles with a degree of flexibility and that it did not want to close the door on Rome altogether.

It is almost certain that the Catholic church in Hong Kong will face very great challenges as a result of the Chinese take-over of the colony. Yet the responses to the challenges and the changes cannot wait until 1997. In anticipation of the challenges to come, the Hong Kong Catholics and Protestants feel generally that they have to make efforts in three areas: to strengthen the church from within, to establish better relations with the populace in Hong Kong, and to be open to China.[110] The young and progressive Chinese priests in Hong Kong also follow this same trend of thought and try to translate these ideas into the Catholic context by proposing new developments in their ministry, including the study of Marxist Communism with an open attitude by responding to Pope John Paul's appeal, by endeavouring to contribute to a reconciliation with China, and by helping Hong Kong to participate faithfully in creating a new future.[111]

CONCLUSION

The modernisation era saw China and the Vatican head for a dialogue which could lead to a rapprochement. With both sides beginning to demonstrate their goodwill through contacts, the controversy of the appointment of the Archbishop of Guangzhou then erupted. It proved to be a regrettable stumbling block to

[110] This was the recommendation of the Hong Kong Christian Council. Quoted by Edmond Tang, 'Hong Kong 1997: a historical challenge for the churches', p. 22.
[111] *Yi* (Hong Kong), December 1982.

warmer relations. The ill-advised gesture of this appointment proved that it is extremely difficult for the two states to have a common understanding, since these two centres of authority have conflicting concepts of what constitutes the true source of authority. Asking for prayers for the Chinese Catholics is a good act in itself, but it was done at the wrong time. To have done this immediately after the controversy of the appointment caused unnecessary misunderstanding and misinterpretation. The wrong timing turned this good act into 'clumsy diplomacy'.

Despite the blunders resulting from the issue of the appointment and the asking for prayer, both sides did not waste much time before resuming grassroot contacts, mainly through the 'bridge-churches'. It was the Vatican who thought of turning to low-key contacts by assisting China's modernisation programme in many ways, yet it was China which revealed indications of wanting to reach out once more by accepting the material assistance offered by overseas Catholics. China could have made use of the appointment as an excuse to put an end to the contacts if it wanted. In fact China kept on responding to the gestures of the Vatican positively and looking for a better relationship in future.

CHAPTER 8

Negotiations and concerns

The Sino-Vatican conflict has been a regrettable fact in international relations for the past thirty years. Skilful diplomatic negotiations accompanied by concessions and compromise would be a feasible means to resolve this thorny problem. Yet before any negotiations can start there are many factors on both sides which demand careful consideration. There are common concerns which interest both sides in different ways, e.g. the Hong Kong problem. There are some factors which solely influence China and have very little to do with the Vatican and vice versa, for example bourgeois liberalism for China and the legal status of Chinese bishops for the Vatican. On the whole, in the relations between the two, China takes a political approach to the religious issues, while the Vatican claims that it wishes to deal only with religious matters, even though so many religious matters in China are full of political implications.

COMMON CONCERNS

The triangle of relations

Being a bridge for the Vatican to China, and a territory which in ten years' time will go back to China, Hong Kong (including its Catholic church) cannot escape the attention of both sides. Moreover, Hong Kong in its own right constitutes an important element in a triangular relationship with the Vatican and Beijing.

Indeed, the Vatican has been very concerned over the future of Hong Kong. Its officials always have detailed reports on the activities of the Catholics there. After the signing of the Sino-British Agreement in 1984, the Vatican's Sacred Congregation for the Evangelisation of Peoples (Propaganda Fide) and the Apostleship of Prayer took up this question for the month of July 1986. The

16 Ren Wuzhi, Director of Religious Affairs Bureau, State Council of PRC, visits the grave of Hong Kong's first Catholic missionary at the Catholic Cathedral of Hong Kong (1986). *Source: Kung Kao Po* (The Chinese Catholic Weekly).

monthly intentions for this are at times recommended by the Pope as an indication of his special pastoral concern.[1] At this stage, the Vatican must have thought it better for the question of normalising Sino-Vatican relations to be settled well before 1997, either through open or closed channels. The significance of this time factor was enhanced by the knowledge that already in Hong Kong progressive Catholics were seriously searching for a way to cope with their dual identities as 'Chinese' and 'Catholic'. It has been very easy for certain over-enthusiastic groups motivated by patriotism to exchange orthodox Catholicism for Chinese patriotism. In a more concrete context one could not exclude that they might yield to the temptation of exchanging preaching the gospel in China for yielding to the CPA and selling out their union with the Holy See. Instead of being a bridge to serve the Vatican's purpose of communicating with China, Hong Kong would itself become a problematic factor in its own right for the Vatican in its dealings with China. While the Vatican can contemplate the possibility that the many Hong Kong Catholic institutions in education, medicine and social services will be given up and handed over to the government after 1997, it seems much more difficult for it to envisage that the church in Hong Kong may be eroded by the CPA. Indeed around the time that the Sino-British Agreement was signed some young progressive priests expressed privately to the Chinese agency in Hong Kong that they did not mind starting a Hong Kong branch of the CPA. But, for the sake of public serenity in Hong Kong, the Chinese government gave a guarantee that there will be no CPA in Hong Kong, and the Hong Kong Catholic church will stay as it is.[2]

Indeed Hong Kong has been playing a considerably important role in the Sino-Vatican contacts. Whether the Chinese government accepts or rejects the eight-point request presented by the Hong Kong church, the impact of it will be felt only after Hong Kong's return to China in 1997. If the request is accepted, this would also help to solve the differences between the CPA and non-CPA Catholics.

[1] *Tripod*, 33 (June 1986): 42.
[2] Such guarantees have been given on many occasions, the most significant one was by the Director of the Chinese government's Religious Affairs Bureau, Ren Wuzhi, who was invited by six Hong Kong religious groups to visit the colony. Yet Ren could only give 'empty reassurance', for he could only state general broad principles but failed to provide specific safeguards and undertakings to clear the doubts on many sensitive issues. See *Hong Kong Standard*, 11 April 1986.

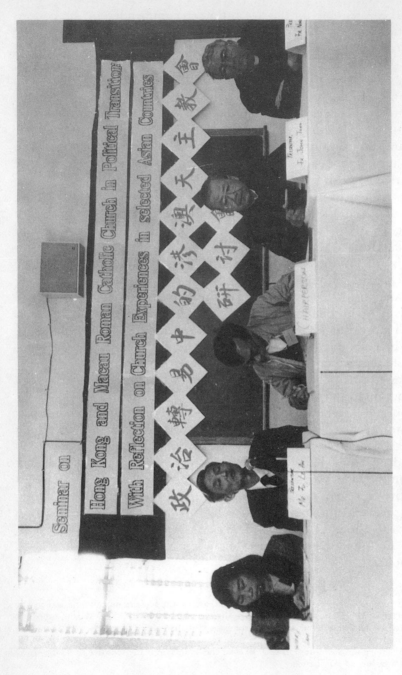

17 The Hong Kong and Macau Catholics held a seminar on church and state relations *vis-à-vis* the political transitions in 1997 and 1999 respectively (1988). *Source: Kung Kao Po* (The Chinese Catholic Weekly).

The activities of the Hong Kong Catholics in political issues, such as direct elections to the Legislative Council and the Daya Bay Nuclear Plant, in this sensitive transitional period will have a direct bearing on Beijing's policy towards the Chinese Catholic church in the days to come. In fact the Hong Kong Catholic bishop issued a pastoral letter to all the Catholics in his diocese encouraging them to exercise their duty as citizens by participating in the elections to the Legislative Council, which is moving toward direct public election of at least some of its members, with the aim of making the Council a more representative quasi parliamentary body in the western style before 1997. Deng Xiaoping eventually in April 1987 declared that he would not allow Hong Kong to have a western democratic parliamentary system as such.

A nuclear plant has been under construction by China at Daya Bay, which is located on the southern Chinese border only fifty miles away from Hong Kong city centre. The people of Hong Kong out of concern for their own safety, especially after the nuclear accident at Chernobyl, Ukraine in 1985, launched a movement to campaign against the Daya Bay nuclear plant. The Hong Kong Catholic Peace and Justice Commission and the Catholic Youth Council as well as other Catholic individuals and many other Christians joined the campaign by holding seminars and open forums, as well as distributing leaflets and literature to arouse the awareness of local people on this safety question. In spite of mass opposition from the general public, the Daya Bay nuclear plant was carried through all the same. Apparently the campaign caused much additional trouble and inconvenience to the Chinese government.

Although Bishop Wu on his first trip to Beijing in March 1985 demonstrated the willingness of the Catholic church to be co-operative by asking the officials in Beijing what could the Hong Kong Catholics do for modernisation, the Catholic church has its own principles on questions of respecting human life and the duties of a citizen. In the above-mentioned issues the Hong Kong Catholic church did take a stand which put it on the opposite side to the Chinese government. For this reason alone, Beijing will be more vigilant about the Catholics of Hong Kong in future.

Apart from that, the Catholic diocese of Hong Kong in 1985 began to launch a new project to educate the laity on the relations between religion and society in the context of Christian social doctrine, with the aim of training Catholic lay leaders to apply

18 Cardinal Wu not only encouraged his Catholics to be involved in local social and political issues, but also took the lead when casting a vote in a district election in Hong Kong in March 1985. *Source: Kung Kao Po* (The Chinese Catholic Weekly).

Christian principles to social affairs. The establishment of a Catholic Centre for Religion and Society was precisely for this purpose. The Centre, which allies with Hong Kong intellectuals to promote direct public elections to the Legislative Council as well as to encourage the public to respond more actively on the drafting of the Basic Laws for after 1997, is frowned upon by Beijing.[3] It appears that the Catholic church in Hong Kong has emerged from its traditional quiet and is involving itself in local political and social issues. The suggestion from the Drafting Committee of the Basic Law of Hong Kong to have the clause 'religion to be separated from politics' clearly written into the Hong Kong Basic Law was not made without reason.[4] Perhaps it is the first sign that Beijing does not want religious groups in Hong Kong to engage themselves in any activities which could embarrass the Chinese government in the name of democracy, freedom and human rights. The strategies and responses of Catholics in Hong Kong *vis-à-vis* this political challenge will form not only the basis for Hong Kong's future church–state relations with the Beijing government, but they will also have a strong impact on the treatment of the Catholic church on the mainland by Beijing. On the other hand, it would be unrealistic for China to imagine it will encounter a Catholic church of the pre-Vatican II type, not at all involved in political and social issues.

Indeed the Vatican has high hopes for the Hong Kong church because of its role in Sino-Vatican relations as well as because of its influence on the Catholic church in China. The political disunity amongst the Hong Kong church leaders is its Achilles' heel, and causes great concern to the Vatican. The local-born clergy who have no experience of Communist rule cherish a romantic patriotism, they might easily exchange their allegiance to the Holy See for the chance of evangelism. This is the same group of clergy who have been giving immense support and recognition to the CPA Catholics. The clergy and religious who came to Hong Kong from China in the 50s and 60s cannot easily forget the bitter experiences they themselves and their fellow Catholics endured at the hands of the Communists, and naturally they cast a suspicious look at Beijing's religious policy and its promise to Hong Kong through the Sino-British Agreement. Without waiting for anyone to drive a wedge

3 He Li, 'Jiaohui Jieru Zhengzhi Soudao Jinggao' [The Church was warned for Being Involved in Politics], *The Nineties* 206 (March 1987): 44. *Kung Kao Po*, 13 March 1987.
4 Ibid.

between them the leadership of the Catholic church in Hong Kong has already split to an extent that provokes the concern of its own bishop and the Vatican. In the political involvement of the Catholic church in Hong Kong, there is a contradiction between claiming that the Pope only wishes to exercise spiritual leadership and between asserting a political role for Catholics because of Catholic principles on which the Pope exercises leadership.

The Vatican's informal penetration

Learning from its experiences in dealing with the priests of the PAX Association in eastern Europe, the Vatican was able to deal with the CPA judiciously. The enthusiastic assistance given to the Chinese Catholic seminaries in donating text books and reference books as well as all kinds of other material aids is an excellent way of co-operating with the government projects in the religious field, whilst helping to preserve the orthodox Catholic doctrine for transmission to the priests-to-be. The donating of scholarships to Chinese students to further their studies in foreign Catholic universities, while requesting priests and university chaplains to look after the spiritual and material welfare of these young intellectuals, is a very subtle and long-term strategy to influence the Chinese leaders of the next generation. It is hoped that they will in the future have a positive opinion of the Catholic church. This plan has so far been carried out without major obstacles, partly because there is a considerable number of overseas Chinese and Chinese sympathisers involved in the various related projects. They are working against time because they never know how long it may be before the Chinese government policy changes again. Therefore, they are maximising this chance 'to make hay while the sun shines'. A foreign expert on China affairs noticed that the tendency within the Catholic church in China is to move slowly but surely towards Rome, with more willingness among the CPA bishops to think about ways of reconciling their position with the Vatican.[5] One might say that all the endeavours by the Vatican on China stem from the Ostpolitik with modifications. The Vatican was able to learn its weaknesses and its strengths in dealing with eastern Europe for more than forty years. At the present stage,

[5] Leo Goodstadt made this remark to the writer on 16 December 1986 after observing Catholic affairs in China for more than twenty years, and so far as is known he is still of this opinion.

the Ostpolitik in China shows greater momentum than in eastern Europe. This might be due to the fact that the Vatican has Hong Kong as its bridgehead and because the overseas Chinese Catholics, especially those in Hong Kong, Macau and Taiwan, out of national affinity, offer immense help which one could not find elsewhere. Although China has introduced some regulations to counteract the ideological 'penetration', how effectively have they worked? And how far can the penetration by the Vatican go with or without the normalisation of Sino-Vatican relations? Will the penetration help or jeopardise the rapprochement? All this deserves serious consideration.

The question of the CPA and non-CPA Catholics

Due to cultural and political encroachment by imperialists in the last century, China on grounds of nationalism and patriotism has reiterated that the Catholic church should be independent of any foreign control, a Chinese church self-governing and self-administrating, and has not allowed the supreme head of the Catholic church, the Pope, and the administrative body of the church, the Vatican, to have any relations whatsoever with the Chinese Catholics. In other words if the Chinese Catholic church with the backing of the Chinese government has full autonomy, only the Chinese government can exercise authority over the church. By arranging this Beijing intended to negate completely the very special feature of the Catholic church of having communion with its highest spiritual leader, whereby all the local churches of the Catholic denomination have various degrees of spiritual linkage with the See of Rome. The Vatican finds it difficult to accept a local church which is not willing to be called schismatic but refuses to have communion with the universal church through communion with the Holy See. In other words, if the Chinese Catholic church refuses to acknowledge the highest moral and doctrinal authority vested in the Pope, from a religious point of view, the Chinese Catholic church cannot be called 'Catholic' any more.

Both from religious and legal points of view, as Bishop Gong pointed out in his 'Letter of Appeal', communion with the universal church through the Pope is against the Chinese constitutional laws and the Chinese government persistently insists that the Chinese

Catholic church should be independent of Rome.[6] At this stage of historical development, one cannot put back the clock and ignore the CPA which is the brainchild of the CCP, created out of patriotism and opposition to imperialism with which the Vatican has been identified by the CCP. Moreover, the CCP had to put some emphasis on patriotism in its United Front tactics in the modernisation period, and this is another reason why it cannot abandon the CPA. On the other hand, if one takes a realistic look at the Catholic church in China, one also realises why the Vatican cannot give up its contacts with and support for the non-CPA Catholics who are mainly underground. Many signs reveal that this section of the Catholic church flourishes on a much larger scale than many people imagine.

Friendly visits of eminent personalities cannot get very far, more papal speeches may cause more misunderstandings, and the bridge churches' endeavour will have more limited scope, if the deep-seated resentment from both sides is still there. The early life experience of the Polish Pope, John Paul II, in dealing with the Communists in his own country, and his own experiences underground in his youth will encourage him to continue his support for the underground church. Should China come to accept that legitimate Chinese Catholics include not only those of the CPA, but the non-CPA members as well, for they are the two sides of the same coin, and if China should feel that it is time to make concessions and compromise on this issue as a means to resolve the conflict through negotiations, then the two sides could have a dialogue and thresh out their differences as first steps to solving these religio-political problems. The suggested pattern of reunion of the Anglican and Catholic churches might be a useful model for dealing with the CPA and non-CPA Catholics.

The Taiwan question

However, informal Sino-Vatican talks have taken place already. That indirectly indicates that China does not insist very much on the severance of Taiwan–Vatican relations as a precondition for the dialogue. When the time ripens for the normalisation of the Sino-Vatican relations, it would not be too late for the Holy Father to

---

[6] Gong Pinmei, 'The Letter of Appeal', para. 5.

transfer his Apostolic Nunciature from Taibei to Beijing, and send a papal delegate of non-diplomatic status to Taiwan but with a staff of Vatican officials.

CHURCH AND STATE RECONCILIATION

Both the Concordat and the plans for re-union by stages would remain on paper if there were no concrete actions to manifest the goodwill of both sides. If China should accept the above conditions and make a concordat with the Vatican, it would be the first Communist party state without a Christian cultural background to make this significant step in flexibility and openness. It would be an important breakthrough in church and state relations in the Communist world. On the other hand, China would have to risk its ideological reputation in international communist circles by being so open and relaxed towards religion. Even those Communist states which have long traditional and cultural links with Catholicism, such as Poland, have not yet established diplomatic relations with the Vatican. The Chinese would be open to criticism for having moved too far away from orthodox Marxism–Leninism, because a good follower of atheist Marxism should not legally formalise a long-term open-ended relationship with any religion. Its leaders might be vulnerable to criticism both at home and abroad because of such an action.

It is understandable that both sides would expect to obtain some concessions as well as to accede to some compromises before an agreement could be reached. How far either would be willing to go in terms of compromise and concession largely depends on how eager they are to normalise their relations. Great skill will be needed to make the necessary adjustments between these two, but even such a touchy issue as population control could lend itself to accommodation provided there was goodwill.

Take the issue of China's family-planning problem for example, the Beijing government has promulgated the 'one-child family' policy as the way to solve China's population problems. The policy has been backed up by abortion, sterilisation and artificial contraception, none of which is supported by the Catholic church. In principle, the state does not compel its citizens to employ the above-mentioned methods. Under law therefore the Chinese Catholics should have the opportunity to choose whatever method is acceptable to the church. Basically, the objection to the Chinese population policy is not just one of methods of family planning, but it is a conflict between two diametrically opposed philosophies of life. Even so, the crucial factor in this question is respect and understanding from both sides on this sensitive issue when it is implemented at the grasssroots. The practice in Great Britain in fighting against AIDS should be an inspiration for the Vatican and China. The British government in its campaign against AIDS makes suggestions to the people and advises them to use condoms during sexual intercourse to avoid infection. The Catholic church in England toes the line of the orthodox teaching of the Catholic church very closely and does not agree with the popular method of recourse to condoms, since it regards promiscuity and homosexuality as the two main channels of transmitting the virus. In spite of the opposite positions of the government and the church, the Catholic church in England and Wales led by Cardinal Hume has launched its own campaign against AIDS by teaching the English Catholics to observe some basic rules of morality: rule out sex before marriage, remain faithful in marriage and choose a life-long marriage partner who shares one's moral convictions.[7] Apparently the Catholic campaign and the government campaign are based on different philosophies, although both of them are focusing on the same problem. The government and the Catholic church in England have enough respect and understanding for each other's position and give ample freedom to each other to launch their own campaigns. It seems that it would be valuable if the Chinese government and the Chinese Catholic church could have the same degree of mutual respect and understanding in launching their respective population campaigns. Apart from that, a high degree of flexibility in the diplomatic negotiations between church and state representatives over this delicate question is also required.

If the Catholics at home as well as abroad would work more intensively and creatively, making outstanding contributions to the modernisation programme, China might exchange this for a concordat, and initiate a reconciliation with the Vatican. But would such a rapprochement accelerate the infiltration of 'leftist' ideology into the church? This is another major problem the Vatican must be considering.

---

[7] See the leaflets distributed to the Catholics in all the parish churches in the Catholic dioceses of England and Wales on combating AIDS in 1987.

It would be an important question for the Vatican whether it could afford the price of normalisation of Sino-Vatican relations by decentralising its authority and sharing it with the Chinese Catholic church. At least to grant some degree of autonomy to the CPA, allowing them to acknowledge the Pope as an 'uncle' instead of a father, would be better than making an enemy of them. By so doing, the Vatican could save the non-CPA Catholics as well as Hong Kong Catholics from being penalised by the Beijing government, should China agree to have a concordat with the Vatican on those terms and settle the thorny religious problem.

It is obvious from the complexity of Sino-Vatican relations, and the unique nature of the Vatican city state, that all the plans offered to solve the dispute could only be suggestions or points of reference, whether in connection with the US model for dealing with the Taiwan problem, the eastern Catholic Rite or the Anglican proposals for unifying the CPA and the non-CPA Catholics. These suggestions might not necessarily work well in such unique church and state relations. Take the US model for solving the dual relations with the PRC and ROC for example. From the point of view of Beijing, Kissinger's model might not be the best way of forcing Taiwan to the negotiating table, but it was the best that the US could offer. Beijing had to accept second best as the price to pay for the rapprochement with Washington which it needed after the Sino-Soviet rupture in the 1960s. China was very accommodating and flexible because the mere breaking of diplomatic relations with Taiwan by the US alone was unsatisfactory for Beijing, since US arms continued to be shipped to Taiwan and US–Taiwan trade continued to flourish. At the same time both the US and the PRC dared not press Taiwan too hard for fear it would declare independence. All these concessions and compromises were made by China just because it needed the US as its major ally in global and regional affairs. The improvement or deterioration in Sino-US relations would be of immediate concern to Beijing. Now there is no similarity whatsoever between the US and the Vatican in terms of their impact on China. On the other hand, China has also some other internal factors to consider before it can make up its mind on how to negotiate with the Vatican and on what it wants to obtain from these negotiations.

CHINA'S DOMESTIC CONCERNS

The reactions of other religions in China

In China, most of the Christian churches have already complied with the demands of the government even to the extent of amalgamating the various churches apart from the Catholic one. This non-denominational Christian church has not created so many problems as the Catholic church has done. In fact the Chinese Christian church not only has very smooth relations with the party but it also helps to facilitate financial and technological assistance to China in several ways. The Muslims in China are now more satisfied with their treatment by the state than before, and they are allowed to have loose contact with their fellow Muslims all over the world. If the CCP makes too many concessions to the Catholics and allows a type of Anglican–Catholic relationship to appear, would it stimulate the Anglican section of the non-denominational Chinese Christians to contemplate leaving the Chinese Christian church and seeking their own identity as Anglicans? If the Anglicans in China request, say, to have an alliance with the Archbishop of Canterbury and the Muslims in the north-west of China seek their communion with, say, Khomenie of Iran, would the Chinese government give them the same permission as given to the Chinese Catholics? Such requests are not likely to win favour with the CCP, because more foreign connections mean more foreign support, especially in times of crisis when believers are under oppression.

The anti-bourgeois liberalism campaign

One may remark that more concessions by China would be reciprocated with a greater willingness to participate in the modernisation programme by overseas Chinese and overseas Christians as well as by religious believers at home. Greater flexibility and openness in handling Sino-Vatican relations would give the Chinese a great reputation in the west as the first Communist state to be so liberal and understanding over religious freedom, since religion is diametrically opposed to its ideology. Yet China might have to face criticism at home and abroad from the Communist hard-liners for having given in too much in religious affairs, especially since at this stage in the ideological development of Marxism–Leninism China is facing a great challenge from its youth, who suffer a crisis of faith and many have not liked the recent change to a tighter ideological grip. The anti-bourgeois liberalism movement which is the Chinese version of Soviet anti-western liberalism began to loom at the end of 1986. Eventually it caused the downfall of Hu Yaobang, the progressive Secretary General of the CCP. This anti-bourgeois liberalism movement was the result of the ideological clash between progressives and conservatives within the Chinese top political circles. The resignation of Hu and the launching of the campaign signified that Chinese politics had begun to swing to greater ideological control even at the expense of economic gains through its open door policy. In other words, the orthodox Marxists were ready to pay the price of slowing down the pace of modernisation rather than lose ideological control. Although the campaign has since died down, it was evidence of enduring tension between orthodoxy and heterodoxy which is bound to erupt from time to time. In this political climate, in dealing with the Sino-Vatican dialogue, the Chinese political leaders are vulnerable to attack from their conservative colleagues who dislike western life styles including the western religion. In these circumstances, one should not be surprised if China is unable to make as many concessions as it should at this particular time.

The personality of Pope John Paul II

The Polish Pope John Paul II, may appear conservative on matters of church doctrine, moral questions and church discipline, but he is not conservative in his political principles – to defend democracy, protect human rights and oppose all forms of oppression. China has reason to keep an eye on the Catholic church in Hong Kong as well as on Catholics on the mainland, because its supreme head is now very active in advocating peace, non-violence, democracy, human rights and so forth. He himself laid down the principle that, while the Catholic church personnel should avoid party politics, they should involve themselves in the struggle for the above-mentioned principles by political means. For example, on his visit to Chile, a great majority of whose population is Catholic, when he met the dictator General Pinochet in April, he courageously told the General that it is the church's duty to defend freedom as it did in the Philippines, and he called for respect for the rights of individuals. He spoke to the Chilean bishops on human rights in Chile. His candid speech was so irritating to the Chilean authorities, they demanded that the state-controlled TV cut out the live broadcast of his speech.[8] His political principles based on Christian teaching oppose egoism and selfishness in Capitalism and the authoritarianism in Communism. He calls for a basic reform of society. His political outlook and his involvement in global political affairs, such as in the Philippines, Poland and South America, must give China's leaders food for thought when considering the pros and cons of normalising Sino-Vatican relations, since this could create new opportunities for the church to interfere in Chinese internal affairs over the sensitive and debatable issues of human rights, democracy and freedom. More-over in Christian circles Pope John Paul II's moral authority is felt more strongly than that of his predecessors Paul VI and John Paul I. Since the Chinese political leaders wish that moral authority rest in the party itself, the Pope could well be a threat to the CCP, especially when the latter is in the midst of a crisis of faith.

The Catholic church: a political factor in world politics

The Roman Catholic church today is more able than ever before to transfer resources from one local church to another, and China has witnessed how Catholics in the US, Canada, Germany, Belgium, UK and other places in Europe act for Rome in contributing resources for modernisation. Furthermore, China has to consider very carefully about possible future struggles with the Catholic church for moral leadership. Modern communication technology has greatly increased the feasibility of imposing a central strategy and subsequently has increased the challenge of the church to the state. Stanley Hoffmann has described how competition between states take place on several chessboards in addition to the tradi-tional military and diplomatic ones: for instance, the chessboards of world trade, of aid and technical assistance – and the chessboard of what has been called 'informal penetration'.[9] This sort of informal penetration is being felt in China not only through the Catholic church but through many other agents just because of its open-door policy. On the other hand, China cannot ignore the informal penetration which is closely related to the crisis of faith of the CCP.

[8] BBC World Service, 'Radio News', 2 April 1987, 3 April 1987.
[9] Stanley Hoffmann, 'International organisation and the international system', *International Organisation*, vol. 24, (Summer 1970.), 401.

In spite of the very low percentage of Chinese who are Catholics the status of the Vatican as a sovereign state with its transnational character is an irritation to the Chinese government. But, on the other hand, if China wishes to have more involvement in global affairs it cannot ignore the rules of the international political game and ignore the Vatican's overtures forever.

Modern political scientists suggest that negotiation is the mechanism to resolve conflict when co-operation is impossible, yet one cannot live with the problem and confrontation is not recommended, because the price paid for 'winning' direct confrontations is tremendous.[10] China is also finding that its gains from the thirty years of Sino-Vatican confrontation have been limited. Yet in the end the risks involved for China in negotiating a settlement with the Vatican may appear too great, and it may prefer to leave things as they are or drag out a negotiating process for a very long time. It may decide that living with the problem is the best solution.

THE VATICAN'S MAJOR CONCERNS

The autonomy of the Chinese Catholic church

Some experts have suggested that there are possible routes to the reunion of the CPA and the non-CPA Catholics as well as to resolving the question of the autonomy of the Chinese Catholic church (this will be discussed in detail later in this chapter). In spite of keeping the Pope as the spiritual leader, the acknowledgement of the autonomy of the local Chinese church might lead the Catholic church as a whole to face the risk of decentralisation of the powers of the Vatican, which is rather centralised and feudal in practice, especially because decentralisation has been sought by all local churches at various places in Europe and America in recent years. Thus the Vatican would have to consider very carefully the consequences that may arise from granting so large a degree of autonomy to the Chinese church and whether the present Roman Curia could cope with those changes. In fact the autonomisation of the Chinese church would be a further step towards reducing the importance and power of the Roman Curia. Yet, when the vertical link between the Vatican and local churches is weakened, the horizontal link

[10] Windham, 'Negotiation: conflict management', in Matthews *et al.*, *International Conflict and Conflict Management* (Scarborough: Prentice-Hall of Canada, 1985).

between the local churches would still be there and could be developed. Moreover, a certain degree of autonomy in the long run would be essential for the indigenisation of the Chinese Catholic church, and its acquisition of a stronger Chinese character.

China: a potential ground for future missions

One cannot deny that, in the second half of this century, the Catholic faith in Europe and in North America has suffered a decline,[11] if one takes the number of baptisms and number of vocations for the priesthood and religious life as the yardstick. On the other hand, the church in the third world has been flourishing and has become much more active and alive. It is understandable that the Vatican should place more hope on the church in the third world than in the affluent west. China, being a big country in the third world, in terms of its territory and population, could be a potential land for the spreading of Catholicism, since the great majority of the Chinese population are not Christians. The Vatican has reason to believe that the martyrdom of the non-CPA Catholics and also of some CPA Catholics in the Cultural Revolution may be the seed of the future growth of the Catholic faith. They each contributed their own share of religious martyrdom in China.[12] Moreover China is the second largest Communist country, and, if the Vatican can deal with China with success, it would be easier for it to deal with other Asian socialist states, e.g. Vietnam, Burma, Laos and Kampuchia.

The leftist infiltrations in the church

In spite of the fact that the Catholic church since as far back as the nineteenth century has been trying to deal with the threat of 'secular faiths', including Communism, through preaching, condemnation or papal pronouncements, the infiltration of leftist ideology into the church is marked. Catholics in Spain, Italy, Germany, Portugal and other parts of western Europe join local Communist parties, while

---

11 Cardinal Hume calls it 'the pastoral problem of urban decline'. See Cardinal Basil Hume, 'Letter to the editor', *The Times*, 5 December 1987. *Kung Kao Po*, 6 November 1987. Also *Kung Kao Po* has a detailed analysis of the statistics on the decrease of baptisms in Europe and North America and increase in Asia and Africa.
12 Influenced by the martyrdom of the Christians of the early church, it is widely believed in Catholic circles that the blood of the martyrs is the seed of the Catholic church.

the Catholics in Latin American even employ Marxist theory, and have a new interpretation of the gospel teaching called the Liberation Theology.[13] On the other hand, Marxist–Christian dialogue and co-operation is being carried out on local and international levels by local Catholic leaders.[14] Furthermore, the leftist movements in the Philippines church have been growing so much that they also employ Marxist dialectical praxis as the tool of analysis to pursue 'peace and justice'.[15] Above all, many progressive theologians in the third world have formed an Ecumenical Association of Third World Theologians (EATWOT), and claim to re-write theology in the third world context of oppression and exploitation. They are even conducting a dialogue with the traditional European theologians. Whether with formal approval from the Vatican or not, they go on all the same with these activities with a 'leftist' tinge. Would a rapprochement in Sino-Vatican relations add more momentum to this Marxist ideological penetration into the Catholic church? The Vatican must be making a careful cost and benefit analysis.

NEGOTIATIONS

Reconciliation between church and state, could no doubt be worked out according to principles laid down by both sides. In this process, the procedure is a very vital question requiring great understanding, prudence and diplomatic skill. The controversy over the appointment of the Archbishop of Guangzhou has no doubt served as a good lesson for both sides. The procedural steps must be observed with great care, as the slightest mistake, even with goodwill, would spoil the whole plan.

---

[13] The literature on Liberation Theology is enormous and still growing. The important sources include Gutierrez's *A Theology of Liberation* (Maryknoll, N.Y.: Orbis Books, 1973). Segundo, *Jesus of Nazareth, Yesterday and Today*, trans. by John Duray (Maryknoll, N.Y.: Orbis Books, 1984). E. D. Dussel, *Ethics and the Theology of Liberation*, trans. by Bernard McWilliams, (Maryknoll, N.Y.: Orbis Books, 1974).

[14] C. Torres, *Father Camilo Torres, Revolutionary Writings* (New York: Harper and Row. Colophon Books, 1972).

[15] There are numerous works in this field. The series published by the Socio-Pastoral Institute of Manila reflects its highly politicised Christian faith and the source of its inspiration in Liberation Theology. See *Readings on Faith and Ideology Vol. 1* (Manila: Socio-Pastoral Institute, 1986), *Theology in the Third World* (Manila: Socio-Pastoral Institute, 1983).

Reception of signals and the reactions

China cannot have unanimous reactions to the direct and indirect signals sent out by the Vatican when the latter seeks rapprochement. There is no homogeneous thinking among the Chinese political leaders; reformers and conservatives, depending on their different emphasis in state policy, would each have different interpretations of and reactions to the overtures. If the Chinese political scene is dominated by the conservatives, who put more emphasis on the elimination of ideological diversity and regard it as 'bourgeois liberalism', the chance of successful negotiations would be slim. Nevertheless, the new Party Secretary, General Zhao Ziyang, at the 13th Party Congress, in October 1987, reiterated that China is still at the early stage of Socialism which allows for greater toleration of pluralism and diversity in many social and economic aspects. This line would benefit negotiations over religious matters, because the well-being of the Chinese Catholics largely depends on the CCP's toleration of diversity.

In the Vatican, there are also different opinions and approaches in dealing with China. It is well known that the Secretariat of State of the Vatican, headed by Cardinal Casaroli a veteran of the Ostpolitik, would like to negotiate with Chinese communist leaders through diplomacy, with compromise and concessions. On the other hand, the head of the Congregation for the Evangelisation of Peoples (Propaganda Fide), Cardinal Tomko, a Czech by birth and a contemporary and good friend of the Polish Pontiff, would hold a hard line on China affairs and would be less inclined towards compromise and accommodation. In addition to his personal background as a Czech, his orthodoxy can also be explained by reference to the fact that Tomko has been in the Congregation of the Doctrine of Faith and has the determination to preserve the authenticity of the Catholic faith at all costs. Therefore it is important to note which congregation is assigned to work on the negotiations, or which office carries most weight in the negotiating team.

In China, if the Religious Affairs Bureau of the State Council takes up the negotiations, then greater emphasis will be placed on religious matters. But, if the Party's United Front Department intervenes too much in the negotiating then the Foreign Affairs Office will influence the whole approach with a strong political orientation, and regard it as a matter of a state to state affair with little concern for religion. Therefore for both sides bureaucratic as well as other factors will greatly influence the course of any negotiations.

Those close to the Vatican have disclosed that secret negotiations had begun to take place between Beijing and Rome before Cardinal Sin's second visit in November 1987. This signifies that after some thought China had decided to have a more formal dialogue over the Catholic-related problems.

It seems that Beijing and the Vatican have different interests in these same Sino-Vatican relations. For Beijing, the major concern appears to be to the severing of Taiwan–Vatican relations as a means to isolate Taiwan on the international diplomatic stage. For the Vatican its ultimate aim in dealing with Beijing is to search for a better political environment for the Chinese Catholics in which they can breathe more freely. Obviously the negotiations will be very complicated and difficult because both sides, although facing the same question, have different concerns and emphasis.

Good will mission

Before any form of negotiation could take place, some 'good will' missions had to be sent out by both sides for informal contact, to clarify some concepts and to exchange opinions so as to cultivate understanding. This process was exemplified by the meeting of Zhao Ziyang and Cardinal Sin, apart from contacts through third parties. The advisers from each side could then gather appropriate frames of reference with which to analyse the real situation, to form their strategies and to help put the problems in their own correct perspective. Through this kind of preliminary contact, each side can develop some kind of common understanding of the other's ideologies, which can be interpreted in many ways by the other side. For example terms such as 'spiritual leadership of the pope', 'religious ties of the Chinese Catholics to the Holy See', 'communion with the universal church through the communion with the Holy See' and so forth can be clarified by the Vatican, and the practice related to these concepts spelled out for China to consider. In return, the Vatican would come to know in detail the real meaning and application of the 'religious freedom policy' and some moral issues which cause it concern, such as population control and civil marriage. Such exploratory missions are particularly important, for these two sovereign states function on entirely different ideologies and very often they have different understandings of the same terminology.

Agenda and procedure

Usually the agenda and the procedure of negotiations reflect the negotiating parties' priority of concern. In the Sino-Vatican negotiations, obviously the Vatican would put the religious problem at the top of the agenda, e.g. communion with the Holy See, the appointment of bishops, the relationship between the CPA Catholics and the non-CPA Catholics and so forth. For China it would certainly be the Taiwan problem which would attract much of its interest, and it would wish the negotiations to take place in the light that Beijing will be acknowledged as the legitimate government of the sovereign state of China. The rest of the problems are low on China's priorities of concern.

Gathering suggestions

The Vatican has sought suggestions from all concerned persons for some time past. It began by summoning Catholic experts to a Consultation in March 1986.[16] The people who have been involved in building the 'bridge' are a good source from which advice can be obtained. The Catholics in Hong Kong, Macau and Taiwan, as well as those overseas who are concerned for the Catholics in China and who have been involved in informal contacts with the Chinese Catholics in many ways, cannot only convey the desires of the CPA and non-CPA Catholics but they must have their own way of looking at the whole issue as well. As these bridge-builders have different motivations for contacting China and different approaches they do in fact provide different perspectives. Even the opinions of the neighbouring churches, for example those from the Philippines, Korean and Vietnamese Catholics, have been taken into account in order to strengthen the church's hand. Of course the opinions from Taiwan have received special attention, because the Taiwan problem is at the top of the list of China's priorities in the negotiation. It needs great skill to put an end to Vatican–Taiwan diplomatic relations without putting the local church in Taiwan in a difficult

---

[16] *Jesus* (April 1986): 86.

position, and at the same time causing the least possible offence and embarrassment to the Taiwan government. In undertaking these considerations the Vatican is not acting as an inward-looking self-sufficient body but as a living Church with a universal character.

A spectrum of suggestions with different emphases have been made by some scholars, clergy and theologians. Some of these are accommodating enough to meet the demands of China while the other aims at preserving the orthodox Catholic teaching at all costs. Then there are some lying between these two extremes. These suggestions are as follows:

The Anglican inspired model

The discussion of this model on the Chinese church first started in the Bastad Meeting, Sweden, and Louvain Meeting, Belgium, in 1974.[17] Since then continuous discussion of this model by some very liberal Catholic theologians has been taking place. This Anglican inspired model suggests that the communion with the Bishop of Rome does not imply submission to an authority which stifles the distinctive features of the local churches.[18] That directly leave much more room for the autonomy of the local church which has the Chinese Government at the back to demand independence of church affairs. Originally this model has been discussed by some Catholic and Anglican theologians on the reunion of the Anglican and Catholic churches. This model could not integrate so directly and closely with the Holy See and the Eastern Rite of the Catholic church. Direct communion with the Holy See on the lines of a father–son relationship would be too stifling, it will be an uncle–nephew relationship. This means a greater degree of autonomy in dealing with internal church affairs but at the same time keeps a certain degree of necessary communion of a non-stifling nature with the See of Rome.

The uncompromised model

Those who entertain this trend of thought, put great emphasis on the orthodoxy of Catholic doctrine, especially the communion with the Pope. This model aims at denouncing the CPA which has been taken at its face value and its demands of independence from the

---

[17] The discussion papers of these meetings were compiled and published, see *Christianity and The New China* (the USA National Committee for the Lutheran World Federation, 1976).
[18] For this Anglican inspired model, see *The Final Report. Anglican-Roman Catholic International Commission* (London: Catholic Truth Society and SPCK, 1982).

Holy See. The advocators of this model believe that Catholic faith cannot be compromised with the demands of the CCP nor concealed. One cannot renounce an individual article of faith, for the sake of adapting to government requirements. The priests at work now, have all been educated in the theology of acknowledging the Pope to be the head of the Church. They are able to keep this faith in their hearts. But the priests of the future will not have this faith in their hearts. This principle of the CPA absolutely cannot be accepted. As regards the faith, one can only believe or not believe; there cannot be a proportional belief or a half-belief. This is the clear cut attitude that these uncompromised hardliners take. Consequently, they take the unofficial sector of the Catholic church in China as the orthodox believers. They are honoured as martyrs who have maintained their fidelity to this matter of faith. Resistence will be given to governmental interference in order to keep the orthodox Catholic faith.

The 'Chinese Rite' Catholic Church Model
Wherever there is a Catholic church community headed by a local bishop it is a local Church in its own right. Among all the bishops, the bishop of Rome enjoys the status of president ex-officio or the 'first among equals'. Within the Latin Rite of the Roman Catholic church, the position of the Bishop of Rome, the Pope, has been considered higher than that of other bishops and invested with the authority to nominate or oversee the appointment of a local bishop and recall the facilities of the same. Within the Eastern Rite of the Catholic church there is a communion with the Roman church in all the essentials of Christian belief, morality and worship. It recognises the Pope, the Patriarch of the West, as the supreme head of the Church, but it differs from the Roman church in its liturgy and rites, laws and customs.[19] Although it acknowledges the primacy of the Pope and has communion with See of Rome, the eastern church not only has full autonomy to run its own affairs, but also the eastern Patriarch has full authority to appoint bishops. The Pope only recognises the appointments but has no right to veto or nullify them.

Actually this eastern Catholic church model was suggested by Cardinal Casaroli in 1982 as one of the possible ways to solve the problem. He mentioned the possibility of a 'special Chinese Rite'

[19] *Catholic Almanac 1970* (Paterson, New Jersey: St. Antony's Guild, 1970), p. 345.

after the style of the Eastern Rite.[20] Reunion under this model would not basically affect the Pope's authority which rests in two circumstances: 1. the ecumenical council and 2. the person of the supreme Pontiff himself. In the days to come the Ecumenical Council will carry much greater church authority than the person of the Pope, or the machinery of the Vatican. That will directly leave much more room for autonomy of the local churches. In actual practice, the Chinese Bishops' Conference could take care of the internal religious affairs. To oblige the Chinese government, the Chinese Bishops' Conference could nominate their own bishops and the Holy See gives its recognition.

The pastoral model

Those Catholic leaders who do not believe that diplomatic means are the only means to build up the Chinese Catholic church, switch their hope to the pastoral approach. For them, no attention is paid to the question of compromise or independence from Rome. They have respect and good faith in the Chinese Catholics who can solve their own problems of church and state relations in their own time with support from outside. That is why they render assistance to the Chinese Catholics in order to strengthen the pastoral capacity of the Chinese church, believing that the Chinese Catholics have their own way to practise their genuine Catholic faith. Overseas Catholics sending religious literature and financial aid to Chinese Catholics making friendly relations with both CPA and non-CPA Catholics, sending teachers of philosophy and theology on a short term basis to Chinese Catholic seminaries, believe that with these aids to strengthen doctrinal formation, the Chinese Catholics will know what to do in religious matters.

A suggestion coming from Taiwan

All the above mentioned models and suggestions do not have much to say about Vatican–Taiwan relations. However, Archbishop Lokuang, a senior Catholic leader in the Taiwan church, explicitly expressed for the first time in public his views regarding the Church in China in *Christian Life Weekly* 11 May 1989 issue. In his article, Lokuang articulated the question of Vatican–Taiwan relations. Lokuang argued that 'the Apostolic Delegate [Archbishop A.

---

[20] Michael Parks, 'Feud among Chinese Catholics sours hopes for Vatican ties', *Los Angelos Times*, 24 April 1982.

Riberi, the Apostolic Internuncio] was expelled by the communists. It was the Communists who chose to break relationship with the Holy See . . . What right do they have to ask the Holy See to break relationship with the Republic of China in Taiwan?'[21] Lokuang also expressed his view on the procedure of negotiation and advocated that the bishops on the mainland should distance themselves from the political problems between the Church and CCP. He said:

With other countries, Communist China has also negotiated first and then when both sides agree, they ask the other country to break relationships with the Republic of China. Communist China states that the Holy See does not recognise its political authority but it does not negotiate with the Holy See. Also, it does not recognise the Pope's authority to govern the Church. How can the Holy See negotiate with it? The bishops of the Patriotic Association should understand this problem. They should not put this problem on their shoulders. Even if the Holy See gives in to all the demands of the Communists, they will not gain any benefit from it. They should not speak about this [political] problem.[22]

The Vatican has reiterated that the communion with the universal Church should be through the communion with the Holy See who is the supreme head of the Church. These suggestions and models can offer a range of selections depending on how tolerant and flexible Rome will become vis-a-vis questions of communion with the Holy See and the appointment of bishops.

Furthermore, the Vatican has several times claimed that the Holy See has spiritual authority over the Chinese Catholics in religious matters, and that the Catholics in China should have religious ties to the Pope. Before any agreement can be reached, the question as to what are "religious" or "spiritual" matters has to be defined and agreed by both sides.

The appointment of bishops: the practical problems
In fact when one looks at church history one finds that the papal claim to appoint all bishops only entered the general Catholic Canon Law in 1917. The statement is in Canon no. 329, paragraph 2. In all the eastern churches, the ancient custom remains that they elect their bishops and merely inform Rome. (The Vatican theorists may, of course, have argued that the power of eastern bishops only

---

[21] Lokuang, 'My Views Regarding the Church in China', *Christian Life Weekly*, 11 May 1989.
[22] Ibid.

becomes lawful once Rome has 'approved' the reported election.) In much of the west, bishops were elected and appointed by many means, especially by kings. Due to the oppression of local churches by tyrannous kings, papal interventions began mainly in the tenth to eleventh centuries and grew gradually. At the First Vatican Council (1870), it was stated that bishops hold their authority 'under' the Pope. During the nineteenth century, the idea of a Catholic church modelled on a centralised monarchical empire came to dominate the papalist canonists, but it was only the widespread collapse of Catholic monarchies which made it possible for the papal claim to be inserted in the new and (first ever) general Code of Canon Law in 1917.[23] The Chinese government has mentioned the 'concordat' in its 'Open Letter to the Clergy and Laity'.[24] This implies that the concordat practice in the appointment of bishops should be acceptable to the Chinese political leaders. The Vatican should be willing to formulate a concordat with China to settle religious affairs, including the appointment of bishops, in exchange for other concessions from China, e.g. prior notice could be given to China before an appointment was announced, so that objections could be made.

At the present stage, the Vatican still frowns on certain practices since the Chinese Bishops' Conference has not as yet laid down the terms of the appointment of bishops. In fact, these rules and conditions are important in the tradition of the Latin Rite, e.g. that the candidate must be a celibate. Thus it is difficult to convince the Vatican that the CPA is sincere in observing the law of the church, when there are quite a number of bishop candidates who are married and their marriages are both illegal and invalid. In spite of the fact that the selection of bishop candidates rests mostly with the government, the silence of the Chinese Bishops' Conference on this issue could not convince the Vatican that this church institution is mature enough to act according to given rules and regulations. It is interesting to note that the CPA has laid down conditions for recruiting candidates for their seminaries, and celibacy is one of the indispensable conditions. But the same celibacy does not apply to a

[23] The whole problem has been discussed intensively in a book written by the members of the Catholic Theological Faculty of Tubingen, Germany in the late 1960s. See G. Biemer *et al.*, (eds.) and trans. by L. and A. Swidler, *Bishops and People* (Philadelphia: Westminster Press, 1970), chapter 3, pp. 38–53.

[24] Appendix III, 'An open letter to the clergy and laity'.

bishop who occupies a more prominent position than a seminarian. Yet, as one looks at this problem more closely and from a different historical perspective, one might understand how much untold difficulty the church leaders in the Chinese Bishops' Conference and the CPA are facing. First of all, many clergy were compelled to marry at the time of the Cultural Revolution and Gang of Four. During political purges, some of them had rightly or wrongly made accusations against their fellow clergy and laity. At the present stage, quite a number of married bishops are in key posts. Out of a feeling of guilt the CPA church leaders and Chinese bishops tried to avoid questions of church discipline, since they themselves are defective in this regard. At the same time they are wary of attacking one another on this aspect of church order. This explains why the church leaders let bygones be bygones and insist that the observance of this church role comes into force only with the next generation. For future dialogue, if the Chinese Bishops' Conference could list out the conditions for the selection of bishops in clear and candid terms, the Vatican then would have no reason to oppose this type of self-selection and self-consecration of bishops, but could give its approval on agreed principles.

CPA or non-CPA status: free choice for Chinese Catholics
In the course of dialogue it must come about that the Vatican will have to acknowledge the legal status of the CPA which has the support of the Chinese government, but at the same time the Holy See cannot abandon the non-CPA Catholics. The Vatican has always upheld the legal status of the non-CPA Catholics, who are mostly underground. Even with the support of the Chinese government it seems the status of the CPA is going down and becoming meaningless in itself. First of all there are many CPA bishops who are loyal to Rome and have their men leading the provincial CPAs in their dioceses. Secondly, recently, the CPA was degraded by the Chinese bishops who, in a meeting of the Bishops' Conference in April 1989, demanded that the Bishops' Conference not the CPA should be the first to make decisions regarding the affairs of the church. The bishops are the primary administrators of the diocese. Thus, the CPA must be at the service of the Bishops' Conference, not otherwise they said. Under these circumstances, would the Chinese government continue to give its support to an association whose function is eclipsed by the Chinese Bishops' Conference and whose

status is declining? At this juncture, the eight points on religious freedom advanced by the bishop of Hong Kong to safeguard the Catholics there after 1997, could be a blueprint for negotiations on religious matters in China.[25] If after careful thought and skilful negotiation these eight points could be accepted by the Chinese government and the Hong Kong bishop, even with some modifications in the light of the Chinese Constitution, these same modified eight points could eventually be applied also to the non-CPA Catholics.

Through conversations with visitors to China, some Chinese Catholic leaders have even suggested that the Chinese government could be asked by the Vatican to give free choice to the Chinese Catholics whether they be CPA or otherwise.[26] This would entail the recognition by both sides of two groups of Catholics in China, one directly linked with Rome with a father-son relationship under a modification of a concordat. A further plan could be mapped out to foster the union of these two groups later. This type of 're-union' should not harm the religious sentiments of the adherents of either group, and at the same time would enable the government and the church to buy time for further possible moves in its implementation and modification.

The Taiwan question

As far as the Taiwan problem is concerned, one has reason to believe that it need not be an obstacle to the Sino-Vatican rapprochement, since the Vatican has been contemplating following the US model by recalling its Chargé-d'affaires from Taibei and sending a papal delegate of non-diplomatic status instead. But the procedure to be followed in working out this plan is extremely important and it has to be performed with utmost prudence and care. A possibility is that China could smooth over the whole thing by inviting back the Papal Chargé-d'affaires, who is now located in Taibei, to Beijing. Beijing has good reason to do so, since it is public knowledge that forty years ago the Papal representative went to Taibei because he was expelled by the PRC in the early 1950s.

---

[25] Bishop John Wu, 'Declarations on the future of Hong Kong' (Hong Kong: Catholic Information Service, 23 August 1984), art. 6.
[26] This was reported by a Chinese priest who resides abroad. When he visited Anhui Province in 1985 and 1986 he discussed this issue with the Catholics there.

Studies by an Ad Hoc committee

An Ad Hoc committee consists of specialists who study and analyse the data collected from all sources. So far the Vatican has not yet set up an Ad Hoc committee to prepare negotiations, but since the meeting between Zhao and Cardinal Sin the summoning of such a committee may not be far off. For such a committee to function properly, the top leaders have to guide it as to what can be compromised and what cannot, how far compromise can go, where the bottom line must be drawn and so forth. All these decisions have to be made by the top leaders, while the specialists on the Ad Hoc committee can only work out the minute details by sorting out the suggestions and presenting a package for the leaders.

It will be a very difficult process to integrate different suggestions, sometimes contradictory, into a whole package. No doubt visits are very convenient for the collection of data, but divergent suggestions collected from various visits will complicate the process of study.

When the ground is prepared and the principles of negotiation have been laid down, the leaders keep in close contact with the Ad Hoc committee for constant advice before each step of the negotiations can take place, because each step has great implications not only for the issues involved but also for the further progress of the talks. A sound agreement cannot be reached unless it is approached step by step. Each step has to be designed by the specialists on the committee and approved by the authority or leaders concerned.

Interim visit of dignitaries

Interim visits by high-ranking officials to each other's governments for brief discussions are essential when differences are too big to overcome and the negotiators cannot proceed further without authorisation to concede or to compromise on a given point. Further compromise cannot be made unless discussion and clarifications are undertaken by senior officials. Such meetings are almost the final opportunity to identify once more the area of difference in some thorny questions.

In the process of discussion it is advisable to draw up some directives to deal with those difficult problems on which neither side can cede too much, because of basic principles and beliefs, such as on the family planning issue. To be successful, this should be done in the spirit of respect and understanding for the other party's standpoint. Directives are valuable because they do not carry the force of law, especially since there are many forms of birth control, and abortion is only one of them. In the long run, it would be more humane to offer more leeway to the Chinese Catholics, who are sandwiched between the law of the church and the law of the state.

In view of the complexity of the issue, the very special nature of the Vatican and the Catholic church and the internal problems facing China at this stage of modernisation, it would be unrealistic to think it would be possible to follow the conventional manner of negotiations, through the rather simple exercise of dialogue between the negotiating teams and with a package of agreements emerging in a relatively short period of time, like the Sino-British negotiation on the future of Hong Kong. In other words, the negotiations between China and the Vatican will be very difficult mainly because of their complexity and the delicacy of the procedure. Its advisers will have reason to suggest to the Chinese government that each aspect of the problem should be carefully considered before any agreement can be reached, because the repercussions will be tremendous and far-reaching. Basically, the Vatican claims some rights over the citizens of the PRC which by cultural tradition and by atheist belief the government of China is unwilling to share with any foreigner, much less a foreign religious leader. Furthermore, an agreement could enable the Vatican not only to have some rights over the Chinese Catholic population of this generation, but also over those Chinese who will join the Catholic church in generations to come. However, the continuum in state-to-state relations stretches from close friendship to hostility. There is no need for negotiation if the relationship between the two states is good but it is impossible to negotiate if both are hostile to each other. With common objectives and positive signals, when two states have some common ground to work on, negotiation is possible. Rome took the initiative publicly long ago, after the death of Pius XII in the early 1960s, and China should cease being hostile to the non-CPA Catholics while negotiations are being carried out.

CHAPTER 9

Conclusions

The clash of authority between the head of the Roman Catholic church and secular state leaders has been going on through every stage of European history. In the Middle Ages when the Catholic church possessed tremendous wealth and power it could easily overshadow the might of kings and emperors. The Holy Roman Emperor standing three days in sack clothes in the cold winter of 1077 A.D. at the door of Canossa castle in northern Italy to ask forgiveness of Pope Gregory VII was the most vivid example of the victory of church over state. For many centuries these conflicts took place in a social milieu imbued with Christian cultural heritage. Since the dawn of the modern age, the Catholic church has been greatly challenged by the ever-growing secular power, to the extent that the vast Papal state has been drastically reduced in its territories to the present day Vatican of less than a half square mile, and Popes have had to formulate several concordats with heads of modern states after a series of conflicts with the political leaders of for example France, Italy and Austria to name a few.

The form of the church-state conflict in western Europe was not the same as that with the Communist states which gradually developed after the Bolshevik Revolution in 1917. The political conflicts between the Roman Pontiff and the Communist state leaders was very much aggravated by incompatible ideological differences – Catholicism versus atheist Marxism–Leninism. The clash of the Vatican with Communism is a new product of this century. After more than half-century of confrontation with the Soviet Union and the east European bloc, the Vatican began to switch to co-existence through the use of diplomacy instead of condemnation and confrontation. However, the Vatican's Ostpolitik needed some modifications before it could be applied to China after 1949, because the post-1949 Sino-Vatican conflict has been aggravated by the cultural clash between Confucianism and Catholicism, and the clash between patriotism and imperialism in the persons of Chinese intellectuals and foreign missionaries in the late nineteenth century.

The clash of political authority between the Holy See and the Chinese Emperor was crystallised in the controversy of the Chinese rites, which was the result of the cultural clash between Confucianism and Christianity. The nineteenth-century clash of authority exemplified by foreign missionaries and the literati-gentry class was the personification of the same old cultural conflict between Christianity and Confucianism. The cultural clash between Confucianism and Christianity would have been reduced in scale if the Jesuits' policy of accommodation, i.e. of integrating the incompatible *modus vivendi* and conducting dialogue with the Chinese in terms that were relevant to their own culture as suggested by Francis Xavier and practised by Matteo Ricci, were followed by the foreign missionaries who came to China after Ricci. The Papal Bull 'Ex Illa Die' of 1721 unilaterally pronounced a prohibition against honouring Confucius under the pain of excommunication for Chinese Catholics, a step by Rome which deprived the Chinese Emperor of his right to make the final decision. The banning of Catholicism in China was the outcome of the clash of authority between the Pope and the Kangxi Emperor. Actually the struggle for political authority was disguised as a struggle over moral authority by Kangxi when he claimed that he would not allow the heterodox Western teaching to eclipse the orthodox teaching of Confucianism.

The weak political power of the Qing Court was unable to pick up the gauntlet thrown by the imperialist western powers who backed up missionary work. This explains why the Tongzhi and Daoguang Emperors did not dare ban Christianity and expel foreign missionaries as their forefathers had done. It also illustrates that, in the struggle between church and state, when the state is strong and powerful enough it can dictate the terms of the church's existence within its domain. However, if a state is weak, a foreign religion backed by a foreign political power can dictate terms to the host country. The Holy Roman Emperor going to Canossa as demanded by Pope Gregory VII and the banning of Catholicism by Kangxi speak for themselves on those points. Therefore, once the PRC was established, it immediately exercised its authority to dictate terms to foreign religions.

Looking at the historical background, one can see that there have been three dimensions to the clash between the CCP and the Vatican since 1949. First of all, out of a superiority complex about Chinese culture (as manifested in Han Yu's famous treatise in the Tang Dynasty), the CCP like most Chinese had no liking for Catholicism, a form of foreign belief which it regarded as heterodoxy. Secondly, because of patriotism, the CCP in the 1950s conducted all sorts of campaigns to rid China of the influence of the imperialist powers. The Catholic church in China was hit because it was linked with the west, and the Vatican was regarded as one of the imperialist powers. Even the good work done by the missionaries in health care and education since the nineteenth century was perceived by the CCP as part of the imperialist culture. Anti-imperialism in China reached its peak when China joined in the Korean War, and the Catholic church was suppressed most severely at that time. That was why the CPA was created and Chinese Catholics were ordered by the CCP to express their patriotism by renouncing the Pope and the Vatican. The third dimension of the clash of authority has been the ideological clash between Communism and Catholicism as represented by the CCP and the Vatican. Ideologically, atheist Communism and Catholicism have very little in common and their adherents are not very sympathetic towards one another. The ideological clash of authority between Communist China and Catholicism is a deep-seated problem. As atheists, the Chinese Communists find it difficult to tolerate religious belief, including Christianity. However, since the CCP adheres to Marxist historical materialism it holds that religion is a product of a presocialist stage of development and that it will inevitably disappear with the advent of the Communist stage of social development. Thus in periods when leftist ideology prevailed and the advent of the Communist stage was proclaimed to be nearer there was less tolerance for religion and intellectual diversity. But in periods such as since 1978 when socialism is seen as in its early stages, there has been greater tolerance. In such a period of more tolerance the CCP is prone to experience conflict between more orthodox centralists, and reformers who are more inclined to accommodate heterodoxy including religion.

When the Catholic church first encountered the PRC in the 1950s no accommodation was made; both sides were not only unwilling to compromise but they also kept emphasising their own traditions and practices at the Chinese Catholics' expense. For political reasons, the CCP could not accept that the Chinese Catholics, no matter how small in number they were, should have their loyalty diverted to the Pope, the head of another sovereign state. For religious reasons the Chinese Catholics could not break away from Rome as demanded by their government. Thirty years have passed and ensuing deadlock in church and state relations has continued and benefited no one.

The attempt at normalising Sino-Vatican relations would not have been possible had both sides not become more accommodating. On the Vatican side, relations with Marxism–Leninism and Communist parties have altered drastically since the Second Vatican Council (1963–5). This Council has also changed the relationship between local churches and the Holy See, and offered more room for national cultures to be expressed, both liturgically and institutionally, as well as allowing ideological pluralism within the church. Following the Vatican's Ostpolitik, the Pope's policy towards China has become increasingly conciliatory in a very public way since 1970. Thus the ideological conflict between the Holy See and China has been reduced by liberalisations in the last ten years, both within the Catholic church and within the CCP since the death of Mao.

The modernisation in China has been one of the reasons for the CCP to be more tolerant towards its ideologically non-conforming subjects including the religious believers. Another related reason is China's attempt to improve its image in the international arena so as to enhance its new open door policy. Relaxation of ideological controls has given a greater role to the educated and professional groups in working for modernisation. In view of the United Front policy, Deng Xiaoping's repeated remark that the intellectuals belong to the working class is a clear reflection of the intention of the Chinese government in this matter. On the other hand, the loosening of the ideological grip also deliberately allowed the revival of religious activities, in the hope of attracting financial aid and technological assistance from overseas, including overseas Catholics. Yet in the modernisation period, the clash really still exists.

On the one hand, in the post-Mao era, personal freedom seems much more widely extended; politically, academically, culturally and even sexually.[1] In religious matters, to be a believer has ceased to mean the risk of jail or other form of punishment solely on the grounds of going to church. Yet, on the other hand, Catholics are still being punished for their beliefs. This is a contradiction. Although greater freedom has been granted to religious activities, little proof has been given that the CCP can afford to let religious doctrine flourish, that the religious hierarchy exercises its authority freely. The special nature of the Catholic church which requires its adherents to accept the Pope in the Vatican as their supreme religious leader poses a threat to the Chinese Communist leaders, who for cultural and political reasons do not like to share this leadership with the head of a foreign religion. Pope John Paul II in his Manila speech touched upon this sensitive issue when he stated that he was convinced that 'a genuine and faithful Christian is also a genuine and good citizen'. His argument is based on the Gospel message of giving to Caesar that which belongs to Caesar, and to God that which belongs to God. In the previous dealings between church and state in China, it seemed that the two parties came to the point of clashing whenever they sought the right to make the final decision on what was God's business and what was Caesar's. The appointment of the archbishop of Guangzhou is a typical example of this nature, and it was a great set-back in the normalisation of Sino-Vatican relations. Above all, the controversy over the appointment was not the first case of the kind and would not be the last; other social issues could lead to a clash of authority in the future.

China's response to the Vatican's overture

Indeed, China did not respond enthusiastically to the Pope's speech in Manilla or to Casaroli's invitations to talk, nor did China reject the Vatican altogether. It might be that China was still suspicious of the Vatican, and found it more prudent to deal with the Vatican on the complicated church affairs with care. This is suggested by the fact that the leading CPA bishop, the Bishop of Beijing, was asked to pass on the wish to the Vatican that Vatican–Taiwan relations

[1] Ji Wen, 'Liu Binyan Jiangdi Sige Gushi [The four stories told by Liu Binyan]', *The Nineties*, 203 (December 1986): 85. Liu is reputed to paint a true picture of socialist China. At the International Congress of Writers held in Shanghai, November 1986, Liu remarked that there were many social, political, economical and sexual themes waiting for writers to explore.

should be severed to demonstrate goodwill towards the PRC. The release of Bishop Dominic Deng, and the permission given to him to go to Rome, were gestures speaking for the CCP's positive attitude towards rapprochement. China was furious with the appointment of the Archbishop of Guangzhou, not only because it regarded this as interference by the Vatican in its internal affairs, but also because this was the last thing it expected the Vatican to do at a time when it was awaiting some 'good' deeds from Rome as a demonstration of the latter's sincerity after the Pope's moving and conciliatory speech at Manila. After the blunder of the appointment, China could have closed the door on the Vatican altogether, by putting a tighter grip on the non-CPA Catholics as well as by refusing any kind of contact with outside Catholics and by rejecting the material and financial aid they offered. China's permission for the interactions between Chinese Catholics and outside pro-Vatican Catholics after the setback of the appointment speaks for Beijing's willingness for dialogue in its own good time.

The Vatican's stance in Sino-Vatican relations

More than once, the Vatican has made it clear that the Chinese Catholic church should have communion with the universal church through communion with the Pope; for the Holy See should have spiritual leadership over the whole Catholic church including the Chinese Catholics. That is the basic doctrine of the Catholic faith which should be observed in full, as claimed by the Vatican. The rest of the quarrel over religious practice can be negotiated. Learning from its experience in dealing with the Pax Association in eastern Europe, the Vatican was able to deal equitably with the CPA. At this stage, in fact, the Vatican indirectly dealt with all the Catholics, both the CPA and non-CPA, with pastoral concern. In principle, its officials tried to instruct those going to China that they should show a great amount of kindness, understanding, sympathy, prudence and pass no moral judgement on the CPA's independence from the Holy See. But the Vatican does not accept the CPA Catholics as the only members of the Catholic church in China, since it is closely associated with the non-CPA Catholics. However, no 'communicatio in sacris' is the only reservation the Vatican has been making until a feasible way is found to settle the question of the status of the CPA clergy.

The Chinese version of the Vatican's Ostpolitik

The architect of the Vatican's Ostpolitik, Cardinal Casaroli, Secretary of State to the Vatican, began to implement the conciliatory policy of Ostpolitik towards China in the latter part of the 70s, with modifications according to the situation existing there. It must be noted that the Ostpolitik was applied quite differently in different countries and reaped various results. In Poland, for example, where the Polish Catholic church is almost totally identified with Polish nationalism and culture, the Ostpolitik adopted a different approach with different results from what transpired in Hungary, Yugoslavia and Czechoslovakia. If there are shades of difference in its implementation in various parts of eastern Europe, much greater difference must be applied to China where the Catholic church is unique in terms of its background and in terms of church and state relations. At first the seeking of informal contact with China in order to initiate a dialogue was the main strategy that the Vatican employed. The contacts were not confined to meetings with top officials but were extended to all levels of Chinese life. Visits by cardinals, priests, bishops and laity, whether on guided tours or on private trips to their families in their home towns, all served the purpose of friendly interactions which could banish unnecessary fear and misunderstanding between the Chinese Catholics and to some extent Chinese officials and Catholics in the outside world.

The Vatican has made many friendly gestures, such as the Pope's speech in Manila, and Cardinal Casaroli's proposals to solve the problems of Taiwan and the CPA. The CPA's reactions to all these was negative. One has reason to believe that the CPA is being supported by the Chinese Communist party, but the CPA itself has failed to move forward with the times or keep pace with the CCP, because the CPA still talks the language of the 1950s as if Mao were still alive and the Chinese volunteers were still fighting in Korea. Due to a feeling of guilt the CPA demonstrates a certain degree of fear of facing church discipline, which they think might be inflicted on them after a possible rapprochement. Secondly, there is strong evidence to prove that the Chinese political leaders resent any gestures towards the country's Catholics from the Vatican, even if they involve only prayers. The CCP in answering the query of the Malaysian government on its retaining contacts with the underground organisation – the Malayan Communist Party – while trying to establish a diplomatic relationship with Malaysian Government, the Chinese leaders drew parallels saying its contacts are permissable just as international contacts are maintained by religious organisations.[2] Hence resentment at the Vatican is a second strand in the situation.

Because of the nature of the Pope as head of a sovereign state, when he exercises his religious authority to appoint local bishops, this causes some negative impact on 'low' politics in China, even though it does not affect 'high' politics. The appointment of Bishop Dominic Deng Yiming as the Archbishop of Guangzhou was a typical case of this kind. The controversy represented a major clash of authority between the Vatican and China. Traditionally it was the supreme head of state, the Emperor of China, who appointed officials to lead the people, but the right of appointment of bishops has been jealously guarded by the Vatican. Thus the appointment of bishops, the ones who teach the congregations, was a thorny question which crystallised the conflict. It made the Sino-Vatican clash, which started off as one over ideological differences change into a political and social issue over the question of leadership. Whom should the Chinese Catholics follow, the cadres in the communes or the bishops and priests in the church, especially over controversial issues like family planning, civil marriage and other social problems?

The autonomy of the Chinese Catholic church

Of the few mentioned suggestions for the possible solution for the Chinese Catholic church, the Anglican church would be more acceptable to China since it offers greater autonomy than that of the eastern Catholic church. This Anglican model would no doubt be fraught with dangers to the Vatican, running the risk of further decentralisation of this centralised and in practice rather feudal religious institution – although decentralisation has been demanded by all the local churches in recent years. In fact the autonomization of the Chinese church would be a step to further reduce the important role and power of the Roman Curia, which is something like the headquarters of a transnational institution. Yet this is a step towards the renewal of the church, because it enables it to rethink its

---

[2] *Xinhua News*, 28 February 1984.

role in the modern world according to the local situations and respond to them accordingly. Paradoxically autonomy would be a catalyst for the indigenisation of the Chinese Catholic church, making it a more truly Chinese church both politically and culturally.

The Vatican is waiting

The Vatican has never given up hope in its dealings with China. In fact, through third parties, contacts with China have never been halted. The ability of the Vatican to deal with a Communist state in mutually beneficial ways is indeed put to the test when it faces China. Future dealings with other Communist states will rest on its success in promoting this bilateral relationship. The quiet and intrinsic benefits to be gained from improving it would not be inconsiderable. More and more the local church in Vietnam is calling for the attention of the Vatican, since political oppression there is gathering momentum, and church and state relations are getting more tense than ever. The Ostpolitik has not been carried out as successfully as it was hoped in the east European bloc. It would be natural for the Vatican to wish that it could work well in China. Yet the chance to initiate a church and state dialogue in the Soviet Union might not be impossible under Gorbachev's 'glasnost' policy. The opportunity for openness in Soviet foreign affairs might not last long and the grand celebration of the millennium of Christianity in the Soviet Union could be a once-in-a-blue-moon opportunity for the Vatican to improve its contacts with the USSR. The Vatican should not miss the chance to have some form of dialogue with Gorbachev's government, and success in dealing with the Soviet Union would have a positive bearing on the Vatican's dealings with China.

In principle the Vatican should reserve the right to work towards the well-being of the Catholic religion, in exchange for the sharing of administrative authority. But neither side can afford to press too hard. In fact for the time being the informal contacts through visits and occasional discussions are sufficient because they are bringing more accurate understanding to both sides: to the Vatican on the religious situation in China, and to the PRC on the situation of various local churches round the world. In fact their past unpleasant memories of the Christian church would not be so easily forgotten by the Chinese, if it were not for the church's concrete contribution to the well-being of the Chinese people in the modernisation programme. The image of the Catholic church might gradually change, and the new policy of the Vatican, under Pope John Paul II, of working for the well-being of all mankind, should bear long-lasting fruits for the Chinese people, who also yearn for democracy, respect for human rights and freedom of conscience.

Sino-Vatican informal contacts

The indirect contacts, starting from the death of Mao and up to 1986, have gone through two stages. The controversy over the appointment of the archbishop was the watershed dividing them. Before the appointment, Cardinal Casaroli showed much initiative in contacting the Chinese officials with the hope of normalising Sino-Vatican diplomatic relations as his prior aim. He hoped that the establishment of diplomatic relations with China would follow. The internal questions of the CPA and non-CPA Catholics and other related problems could be considered and solved at a later stage. One recognises that this was the typical approach of the Ostpolitik as applied to eastern Europe by the Vatican. The Chinese also displayed goodwill by allowing Bishop Dominic Deng to leave Chinese sovereign territories. Presumably they too sought closer understanding, even before progress on the Taiwan issue. The blunder over the appointment obliged the Vatican to turn from direct official contacts to informal church contacts, since Chinese officials did not directly respond to its overtures. On top of this, in 1985, Pope John Paul II expressed the opinion that he was not too anxious to normalise Sino-Vatican relations if he could not have contact with the Catholic Church in China. This meant that the Vatican would not be satisfied only with summit diplomacy, which it regarded as a means to its end.

Delay in Sino-Vatican dialogue

The optimistic assessment that the CPA is moving towards Rome in its own way does not mean that it could yet invite the Chinese government to the negotiating table to have a meaningful talk with the Vatican. The reason for the delay in turning informal contacts into direct dialogue must be China's view of the Vatican as a sovereign state, a transnational actor whose head wishes to exercise his religious authority over the Chinese Catholics. One sees that the cultural conflict in the last century created many problems for the Catholic church in China. The PRC leaders attach a considerable amount of political importance to this question, which is trivial in size, but very complex when looked at from the perspective of China's foreign affairs. Although it would be imprudent and unrealistic to seek a hasty solution to this extremely complicated church and state problem in China's 'low' politics, it would be equally imprudent and unrealistic to have the solution of the problem indefinitely delayed, since an accommodation of these issues would have emerged more easily through Sino-Vatican negotiations before the Hong Kong Agreement was signed, and before China launched the anti-liberalism movement.

On the world stage, religious leaders like the Archbishop of Canterbury and the Pontiff of the Vatican are not the only ones to challenge authoritarian rulers over their violation of human rights. The abrasive and uncompromising speeches that the British Prime Minister, Mrs Margaret Thatcher, made on human rights in the Kremlin on her recent visit in March 1987 reflected well the attitude of the west.[3] Even at the Third Summit Meeting in Washington in December 1987, in the course of discussing disarmament between the two superpowers, President Reagan also raised the same human rights question with Gorbachev.[4] The western democracies now are to challenge the Soviet Union on this delicate human rights question, which most Communist party states jealously guard as an internal affair, immune from external interference. In spite of the fact that China has not put its signature to the 1974 Helsinki Agreement as the Soviet Union did, some British politicians challenged China over human rights and there are others who would 'interfere in China's internal affairs' over this issue. It was reported that when Chancellor Kohl of West Germany and the Irish Prime Minister, Fitzgerald, visited China in 1986 they both asked the Chinese leaders about the Chinese religious dissenters. Would China regard the British MPs and its German and Irish guests as interfering in its internal affairs? In 1983 Michael Yahuda, an expert on China's foreign affairs, remarked that China was still far from sharing the patterns of interdependency with other countries that

3 *The Guardian*, 30 March 1987, 31 March 1987.
4 *BBC 1 TV News*, 3 December 1987; *The Guardian*, 9 December 1987.

characterise the international relationships of most states in the world.[5] Yet, if China decides to move towards greater involvement and interchange with the outside world, it has no other course open to it but to observe the rule of interdependency, and it cannot turn a deaf ear to the request of the Vatican for a dialogue. In fact China's skill in dealing with this vexing and for Beijing less than vital matter of the Vatican will be a test of the sophistication of its diplomacy.

With diplomatic negotiations accompanied by concessions, compromise, good timing and skill, the very difficult problem of the struggle for authority, as in the Sino-Vatican conflict, can be managed in a feasible manner. It is never easy when the atheist and the religious believer try to come to terms in an environment where state control is prominent and religion has penetrated from outside the borders. The settlement, if there is any, can, however, be made in such a way as to give neither side a feeling of loss in legitimacy or authority. For example the agreement would not jeopardise China's upholding of its four cardinal principles – to uphold Marxism–Leninism and Mao Zedong Thought, the Chinese Communist party leadership, the proletariat dictatorship, and Socialism – while the Vatican would find that its orthodox Catholic doctrine would suffer no set-back because of its concessions made to China.

It is true that this kind of agreement is of secondary importance to China's politics, as compared with those high political issues involving national security and the economy, yet its uniqueness is still significant. This is partly because China has complicated historical experiences in encountering foreigners but mainly because of the difficulties arising from the nature of the Vatican – a sovereign state in every sense of the word – and of the Roman Catholic church – a universal religion of transnational character. Therefore the difficulties involve: (1) organisational questions of a state, (2) organisational problems of a universal religion and (3) human rights of some Chinese individuals who are believers in Catholicism.

As we have seen, several factors combine to make the CCP's handling of all religious issues problematic, but it is the sovereignty of the Vatican that makes the independent administration of the Catholic church especially difficult. Paradoxically it is because of the particular nature of the Catholic church, with a sovereign state behind it, that it can avoid manipulation by any power but, at the

[5] Michael Yahuda, *Towards the end of Isolationalism: China's Foreign Policy After Mao* (London: Macmillan, 1983), p. xii.

same time, it is liable to come into conflict with other sovereign states. The nature of the Vatican makes the Catholic church reach out across the Chinese boundaries (or put in other terms the Catholic church invites the Vatican's influence to be present within the Chinese borders), asking China to share some of the authority which for centuries has been jealously guarded by Chinese political leaders.

Therefore a Sino-Vatican Agreement could not be taken as a full solution to the church-state conflict. First of all we must admit that it is unrealistic to expect that once an agreement is signed the Sino-Vatican dispute would be over once and for all. One can only say that such an agreement would become the instrument to handle the problem for the first time in Chinese history, making previous deadlocked questions soluble. The foundation of any agreement could only be built on a relaxation of principles by both sides that would provide an environment to allow further rapprochement. Problems could arise, for example, for reasons not necessarily connected with Sino-Vatican relations, if the Pope, for example, should decide to tighten up church discipline owing to some unforeseen factors, or if future Chinese leaders should decide to switch back to the 'leftist' line. In either case the agreement would not be honoured as originally envisaged. Thus the successful implementation of any agreement would be contingent on nurturing the original basic environment in which it was concluded.

Even without any reverting to strains in social, political and religious environment, the implementation of the agreement at grassroot levels and the interpretation of the meaning of details in the agreement could also invite a host of unforeseen problems. Judging from the experience of how many difficulties the low- and middle-rank cadres have encountered or created in implementing the directives of Beijing in various aspects of reform in Chinese society, it is possible to anticipate regional and local divergences in the practical implementation of such an agreement. It is of course far too early to consider how the resultant problems might be solved. Another series of problems will arise from the Catholic groupings themselves. If we can find disagreements among religious believers regarding changes and reforms in religious matters, especially after the Vatican II period, we can envisage some amount of disagreement between the CPA and non-CPA Catholics. When the central body of the CCP decides something it does not always mean that the policy will be followed all the way through. It will be even more difficult for CPA and non-CPA Catholics and cadres to be reconciled by an agreement at the top. They have a long history of mutual suspicion, feelings of betrayal that may override their feelings of mutual compassion – especially as those sentiments may be complicated by differential treatment by local CCP cadres.

Although it may be said that these church-state relations look likely to be built on shifting sands and will not give the assurance so desperately desired by the Chinese, it is the best that both China and the Vatican can offer. The application of a church and state agreement that depends on so many factors, may reach a point where it might not work out as satisfactorily as hoped by all sides.

However, such an agreement would be the point of departure for continued negotiations but with the inevitable problems that will arise in church and state relations because of the tensions caused by the special nature of the Vatican and by the historical as well as the political background of China. Such an agreement itself would have the special characteristics of an international agreement that would be applied to the domestic scene in China. How can one be so sure that everyone involved will implement the letter of the agreement correctly and have the words carried into proper action by everyone in the church? Even with an agreement, religious affairs could get out of hand. The main function of such an agreement would be to set up a framework to handle these most complicated problems in a manageable way. Perhaps as with the Sino-British Agreement on Hong Kong, a Sino-Vatican Agreement would also be a declaration of good faith by all sides to carry out the main objectives in a future that will be inevitably difficult.

Postscript

INTRODUCTION

Since completing this research, some major events concerning the development of Sino-Vatican relations have occurred and they demand our attention. Although the meeting of Cardinal Sin and Zhao Ziyang in November 1987 was a sign of breakthrough which could have heralded a rapprochement, a closer look at more recent events suggests that church-state reconciliation was not so easy as expected. Even before the 4 June massacre at Tiananmen, insoluble problems arose from the market-based Chinese economy which led Premier Li Peng to switch back a little to a planned economy. This change generated a degree of uncertainty about China's political orientation. Major social and political developments in China (1987–9), such as the crackdown of the riot in Tibet and the pro-democracy demonstration in Beijing, immediately following the death of Hu Yaobang, highlighted the ever-increasing demands of the people on the one hand and the ruthlessness of the party towards the dissidents on the other. After the crackdown on the pro-democratic movement, the Chinese authorities arrested thousands of dissidents, tightened regulations for students wishing to go abroad, cracked down on the unofficial Catholic and Protestant leaders, and revived Maoist practices of indoctrinating the youth, workers and the enlisted men. But the most important step was to place old people once more at the pinnacle of power. All this not only shocked the whole world but also turned a new page in China's internal rule, the CCP's legitimacy and its international relations with the west.

However, the development of Sino-Vatican rapprochement, which largely depends on the tolerance of the party, has been affected immensely. Even without the pro-democratic demonstration, China's religious policy in general, and towards the Catholic church in particular, may not have been relaxed further as many expected, because of political considerations. After the crackdown on the dissident movement, there was no visible progress in the development of Sino-Vatican relations *vis-à-vis* the government's switch back to more political and ideological control as announced in the 4th Plenary Session of the 13th Central Committee of the Chinese Communist party meeting at the end of June 1989.[1]

Not long after the tragic failure of the liberal students at Tiananmen Square, one witnessed the abandonment of Marxist–Leninist orthodoxy throughout eastern Europe and the emergence of political pluralism in the Soviet Union whose political leaders learned from China and allowed political reforms, thus hoping to achieve economic revival. The collapse of traditional Leninist regimes in Europe has complicated and intensified China's internal political crisis, while further weakening its already damaged international position.

During this period, one could witness the continuous growth and the surfacing of activities of the unofficial sector of the Chinese Catholic church. Overseas Catholics for the first time, through correspondence and personal contacts, have been able to see more clearly the unofficial Catholic church and its dispute with the CPA Catholics. In other words, the Chinese Catholic church is now entering into a new phase of development. More religious believers are practising and working for their religious faith than a few years back due to greater tolerance from the government in every aspect of life. It is a big change from the time of all-out persecution during the Cultural Revolution.

The characteristics of this kind of religious tolerance are twofold: first the degree of religious freedom is much less than the social and economic freedom for the same period in China, and also much less than religious freedom in the west. Secondly, religious tolerance fluctuates with the state's tolerance towards non-conformists. For example, after the 4 June massacre when the government was hunting non-conformist students and intellectuals, surveillance on religious groups was intensified although it was clear that no religious group was involved in the pro-democratic movement.

It is worthwhile to note that even before the Tiananmen massacre which brought China back to ideological conformity and orthodox

[1] *China Daily*, 26 June 1989.

19 Bishop Louis Jin Luxian, Bishop of Shanghai. *Source: Kung Kao Po* (The Chinese
Catholic Weekly).

Marxism–Leninism, in religious matters China had reverted to a
tightened road by demanding non-interference by the Vatican in
China's internal affairs, even in religious matters. By issuing a
'Document 3', Beijing explicitly demanded Chinese Catholics follow
the party line and not accept financial aid from foreign religious
bodies. Nevertheless, an abundance of foreign assistance streamed in
to Chinese Catholics who claimed that it came from private donations or from foreign organisations and Catholic funding agencies
without any obligations or pre-conditions. Yet China knew too well
that many of these 'gifts' were given with the Vatican's encouragement behind the scenes. In fact, Wu Xueqian, the Chinese Vice

Premier and former Minister of Foreign Affairs, specifically called upon the Vatican in November 1988 to stop interfering in China's religious affairs.[2] This reflected the displeasure of the Chinese government with the ever-growing activities of the unofficial section of the church, who are as a whole loyal to the Vatican, and with the support from outside Catholics.

At this early stage of exchange of opinions as well as of negotiation by low rank officials from both sides, apparently there were still a couple of the old obstacles between China and the Vatican on the road to rapprochement. The one leaked out to the public was the disagreement on both sides on the accessibility of the future papal representative to the Chinese Bishops.

The arrival of the informal papal representative, with the rank of Chargé-d'affair to China, in Hong Kong at the end of April 1989 (Beijing was informed), turned a new page in Sino-Vatican relations as well as striking a new but unusual note in the progress of the developments within the Chinese church and in its relations with Hong Kong.

The riots of Xinjiang Muslims in April 1990 and the awarding of the Nobel Peace Prize to the Dalai Lama, the Chinese religious dissenter, in October 1989, the formation of the Chinese Bishops conference of the unofficial sector in November 1989, and the involvement of the US-based Taiwan Buddhist leader in the quasi-defect of the ex-director of the Xinhua News Agency, Hong Kong Branch, in May 1990, complicated the already sensitive religious matters in China.

In Hong Kong, the bridge church, the exodus of professionals, and the poor response to the second draft of the Basic Law revealed that the nearer the colony gets to 1997 the more of its people lose their confidence in the in-coming Chinese government. The week after the 4 June incident, the number of applicants for immigration to Canada, Australia and the US rose suddenly, and the Hong Kong people demanded from the UK the Right of Abode. From the date of the signing of the Sino-British Agreement, the Catholic church in Hong Kong pronounced that it would stay behind to face the change and to be the source of confidence and hope to the territory. This bridge church between Hong Kong and China becomes increasingly active partly because of its close interaction with China, but also

[2] *Asia Focus*, 10 December 1988.

because it has to prepare its Catholics for the political transition with a 'Ten Years plan' based on pastoral orientations. The elevation of its bishop to the rank of a Prince of the Church by conferring on him a cardinal's red hat cast a long shadow over the yet unresolved Sino-Vatican relations, especially when it arouses the suspicion of the Chinese government.[3]

This chapter attempts (1) to discuss the special features generating from the rapid growth of the Chinese Catholic church, and its impact in the context of church–state interactions, (2) to assess the development of negotiations between China and the Vatican, and (3) to evaluate the research findings: problems related to teaching authority, 'the magisterum' between the state and church as a response to the hypothesis set at the beginning of this book.

CHINESE POLITICAL AND SOCIAL LIFE BETWEEN 1987 AND 1990

During these three years (before the 4 June 1989 massacre) there was tremendous decentralisation of authority within the socio-economic system. There was much less use of ideological mobilisation and coercion, much greater use of persuasion and of tolerance for greater adaptation of policy at local levels. No major political disasters were seen when the attention of the government was drawn to the concerns of rising prices and overheated economic growth, and other related problems. The two annual meetings of the National People's Congress (NPC) and the Chinese People's Political Consultative Congress (both held in March 1989 with their inconclusive results) left an uncomfortable degree of uncertainty concerning China's political future. The work report of Li Peng, the Prime Minister, presented at the 2nd Session of 7th NPC, offered little solution to the chronic economic crisis, except to intensify the country's programme of austerity and decentralisation, as announced in September 1988, to cure social and economic evils generated from market-based reform espoused by Zhao Ziyang as premier in recent years.[4]

---

3 In an interview with Shanghai Bishop Jin Luxian by the writer, in June 1988 soon after the announcement of Wu's elevation to the cardinalate, Jin reflected the suspicious attitude of Beijing leaders who held the opinion that the Vatican wanted the pro-Rome Bishop Wu of Hong Kong to be the head of all Chinese bishops, including those Chinese on the mainland, and therefore gave him the Cardinal's hat before returning Hong Kong to Chinese sovereignty. Jin remarked that this did not coincide with the spirit of mutual respect and non-interference in the Sino-British Agreement 1984.
4 *China Daily*, 21 March 1989.

Until the military suppression of 4 June 1989, it seemed that Chinese leaders were battling, in a rather relaxed social atmosphere, against new problems arising from pluralism in ideology. The Politburo found it very difficult to deal with a nation like China in the absence of an agreement as to what kind of social norms should govern society and because of the lack of principles governing behaviour.[5]

In March 1989, Tibetans staged a riot against the brutal treatment they received from the local Han officials. The riot in Tibet was crushed with an iron hand by declaring martial law in Lhasa for the first time in the PRC.[6] The apparent return of order in this part of China through suppression hinted at the underlying socio-political crisis, exemplified by religious problems existing since the 1950s, and which could erupt at some time in the future if political leaders in Beijing failed to handle the situation with greater tolerance. In the midst of political and economic uncertainty, were the student demonstrations in Beijing and other major cities, triggered off by the funeral of the former disgraced Party Secretary General, Hu Yaobang, on 22 April 1989. Later on the student movement escalated to a mass pro-democratic movement asking for more freedom and democracy. It was a signal indicating that people were unable to tolerate bureaucracy, corruption, and high inflation which had been prevailing in Chinese society. At first they asked for a cleaner and better government because they had been allowed to see how human rights had been honoured and how democracy had been gaining an upper hand in the neighbouring territories, such as the Philippines, Korea and Taiwan.

The brutal slaughter of pro-democratic students and civilians in Beijing was ordered by Deng himself, with squadrons of tanks crushing civilians and tents occupied by students at Tiananmen Square. Soldiers fired machine guns and rifles intermittently for several days and nights on the streets of the capital. The single night of terror from 3 to 4 June transformed the world's admiration for Deng's achievements over the past decade into revulsion, normally reserved for pariah states such as South Africa under Botha and

[5] The lack of social norms have been felt for some time at the grass root level, but it was brought up by Professor Kenneth Lieberthal in *The first Electronic Seminoar on US-PRC Relations*, 18 October 1988, United States Consulate General, Hong Kong, p. 33.

[6] *South China Morning Post*, 8 March 1989; *The Hong Kong Standard* 8 March 1989; *Ming Pao* 8 March 1989, 10 March 1989.

Libya under Gadarfi. The bloody suppression followed by a countrywide hunt for student and intellectual leaders accused of 'inciting organised counter-revolutionary activities' put the party as well as the government directly in the opposite camp to the mass of people. No one knows the exact number of dead, but an estimation reaches up to 7,000 and the number arrested up to 10,000.

China stubbornly rejects the changes that are sweeping the communist world. After the turmoil, it seemed that Deng was still holding the grip of the whole nation, yet the government lost much of its authority and legitimacy, leaving itself isolated and condemned at home as well as abroad. There are even fears that Chinese Communism may become a discredited tool after the tide of change which has been sweeping across eastern Europe and the Soviet Union. The consequences of the crackdown were the destruction of everything that Deng's interregnum had achieved: the restoration of order and minimal norms of civil government after the Cultural Revolution.

The resistance by students and intellectuals will be long-lasting and the consequences far-reaching. They were forced to go underground to escape from the police, while a handful of them were smuggled abroad.[7] It seems that China was determined to stage a campaign of 'Anti-bourgeois liberalism' which was taken as the main cause of the recent 'riots' by the hardliners in the new Politburo.

It is not so easy to calculate China's total economic loss in terms of cancellations by foreign tourists, withdrawal of foreign investment and suspension of foreign aided projects. The problems affecting China's economy were aggrevated by Beijing's crackdown on the dissidents. A high rate of inflation, a shortage of foreign exchange, persistent problems in obtaining raw materials and postponement of new international loans in the aftermath of the crackdown were the main problems facing China. It was reported that after 1988 Chinese officials had to give promissory notes to buy grain from farmers, and during the years 1989 and 1990 the situation was expected to worsen.[8] Difficulties in the rural economy alone caused immense headaches to China. Another cause of nationwide discontent has been the laying-off of hundreds of thousands of farmers who worked in the construction industry, when the government slowed down

[7] *South China Morning Post*, 29 June 1989; *Hong Kong Standard*, 29 June 1989.
[8] *International Herald Tribune*, 29 June 1989.

public construction. Also the sudden drop in tourism and the decision by the west to limit or postpone loans are the main causes of the enormous shortage of income. Take China's hotel industry for example: hotel and real-estate deals – mostly loans – totalled US$5.5 billion and accounted for 35 per cent of total foreign investment in China over the past decade. The international boycott of China and the slump in tourism, caused by the Beijing massacre, put most hotel loans in trouble. Most foreign bankers want their loans re-scheduled. With the sudden drop in income from tourism in 1989 to US$1.81 billion, 20 per cent less than in 1988, a few hotels will eventually go bankrupt, as viewed by some analysts.[9] This is one of many examples of China's economic crisis. But what worried Beijing was Washington's consideration of the question of whether to renew China's most favoured-nation (MFN) status. President Bush announced that the extension of one more year to China of the MFN status was not because China had improved its record in respecting human rights in the year since the 4 June massacre, but because he did not want to hit Hong Kong's economy which was closely linked with that of China. From a strategical point of view, it was in the US interest to have a peaceful atmosphere in the Far East, when much of its attention has to be given to Europe which is now undergoing a great change both politically and economically. Consequently, the betterment of China's economic life could stabilise the Pacific area.[10]

Shortly before the MFN status was discussed in Washington, the curfew of Lhasa was called off and some 4 June detainees of a secondary nature were released, and Chinese political leaders admitted that not only the students should be blamed but that they should take some of the responsibility for the massacre.[11] Could all these actions be taken as signs of contrition? It was too early to prove that this was so. However, one thing was true – this was a message to Washington for more favourable consideration when extending economic privileges to China. Are the officials in Beijing really repentant of their notorious record for lack of respect for human rights, which include religious freedom? The Muslim revolt in Kashgar of Xinjiang Province, and the arrest of pro-Vatican Catho-

9 Elizabeth Cheung, 'Ill-Starred Ventures', *Far Eastern Economic Review* (26 April 1990): 54.
10 *South China Morning Post*, 25 May 1990, *Hong Kong Standard*, 25 May 1990. *Far Eastern Economic Review* (3 May 1990): 42–3.
11 *Ming Pao*, 23 May 1990, 29 May 1990.

lic bishops who wanted to form their own episcopal conference, speak for themselves.

The riot of the Xinjiang Muslims was suppressed by armed force. The riot in Akto county, part of the Kizilsu Kirghiz Autonomous prefecture near the city of Kashgar, on 5–6 April 1990, was intended to establish a separatist Islamic republic and to proclaim a 'Holy War' against the 'heathens' from Xinjiang, who are mostly Han Chinese officials.[12] It was reported that the immediate cause of the riot was the dispute between the Muslims and the Han officials who had announced the regional policy of curbing the number of schools for Muslim studies and also of the building of Mosques. The growth of religious zeal was also influenced by the Xinjiang Muslim's counterparts in Central Asia who, under Gorbachev's Perrestrokia, could revitalise their religious activities because control from Moscow had been greatly reduced.[13]

In spite of surveillance the revitalisation of Catholic activities with a considerable amount of assistance from abroad was moving ahead with leaps and bounds, so much so that it attracted the state's interference.

THE RAPID DEVELOPMENT OF THE CHINESE CATHOLIC CHURCH

In the year 1988, one witnessed the rapid revival of the Chinese Catholic church. According to the information given by Bishop Zong Huaide, president of the CPA, in China there are 112 Catholic dioceses with a Catholic population of 3.4 million, with fifty-seven bishops heading about 1,000 priests and administering religious duties in more than 1,000 churches and 2,300 chapels. Recently, religious sisters have been mobilised rapidly to assist with pastoral work in parishes. There are more than 1,500 religious sisters and there are over twenty sisters' novitiates in which there are more than 300 young women undergoing formation for religious life. There are seven national and five diocesan seminaries for priestly formation and there are about 630 seminarians.

Some of these place of worship are newly built, repaired, or reconstructed. Nevertheless these churches are packed with the

[12] *Far Eastern Economic Review* (3 May 1990): 10–11.
[13] *Far Eastern Economic Review* (3 May 1990): 10–11, (24 May 1990): 32–4; *Ming Pao*, 13 April 1990, 19 April 1990, 17 May 1990.

faithful and there are annual baptisms of about 40,000. In Tianjin, in the summer of 1988, there was a course on Catholic doctrine open to non-Catholics who were interested in the Catholic doctrine. It was reported that there were more than 300 participants and many of them were young intellectuals.[14] Social norms are now absent in Chinese society and the party fails to generate moral principles as it did before. Thus, it is comparatively easy for religion to attract young people. In the midst of the rapid development of the Catholic church in China there are a couple of issues which deserve our attention.

Catholic assistance in modernisation: a new model of mission

The lack of governmental funding, caused Chinese tertiary educational institutes and some social service institutes to turn to overseas assistance for teachers and for funding for social services. In this context, professionally qualified Catholics from overseas, with the intention of assisting the Chinese people as well as the Chinese Catholic church, rendered their services. In fact, it can be taken as a new model of mission service. In Hong Kong, for example, in 1987, a pioneer group of Catholic intellectuals both clergy and laity formed an organisation, the Association for International Technological, Economic and Cultural Exchange (AITECE), to facilitate the modernisation of China.[15] These intellectuals work with government and church-related bodies in China in such areas as recruiting language teachers and academic experts, and in facilitating health, educational and social welfare projects sponsored by groups or individuals, since no international religious congregation is allowed to operate in China in the traditional sense of mission work. There are increasingly more overseas Catholic religious and laity groups sent to serve in China through the recruitment of AITECE. Apart from assisting in tertiary education, this organisation also seeks to assist small business enterprises run by church groups in various parts of China. Such enterprises, which have been gaining popularity in recent years, not only earn money for the church, but also help the Chinese government to solve employment problems and to promote the country's prosperity. It would be too naive to think that Beijing does not know the motivations of these Catholic organisa-

[14] *Tianjin Ribao*, 28 February 1989.
[15] *Sunday Examiner*, 26 August 1988.

tions including Caritas Hong Kong, Missio and Miserior of Germany, as well as the Catholic Relief Service in New York. They have been financing social projects in various parts of China with the sole purpose benefiting the Chinese Catholic church.

The desperate need of social development, especially in the interior provinces with less opportunities to receive overseas aid, urges the local provincial government to be more tolerant towards these Catholic projects whose donors are Catholics but whose benefits are extended to the common folk regardless of their religious belief. Skilfully, foreign donors entrusted these projects, such as establishing medical clinics and nurseries, into the hands of local church leaders to enhance their local reputation and social influence.[16] More and more rural and urban Catholic social projects have been mushrooming together with Catholic activities. Take Hong Kong Caritas for example; as recorded there were more than twenty projects offered by Caritas in 1988 on child care, rehabilitation, special education for the retarded, and formation of nursing and educational personnel. These projects included building a boarding school for 130 retarded children in Guangzhou, with financial assistance from Germany, and offering training courses in child care and occupational therapy at Normal University in Guangzhou. There was also technical advice on establishing a printing press in Shanghai and donating equipment to social centres for children in Beijing. The German Miserior and Swiss Caritas are the chief contributors of funds for these social projects.

Though Caritas Hong Kong declined to state the exact amount of expenditure for China, Miserior in 1986 gave Caritas in Hong Kong a China Discretionary Fund to enable Caritas to process small projects directly. The Caritas' donation, more than US$100,000 for relief work for the victims of the earthquake in Yunnan Province in 1988, is only the tip of the iceberg of the huge amount spent on these Catholic projects.

In spite of receiving financial and professional assistance, local authorities made it clear that all these will be given on a private basis, incurring no obligation. Local religious cadres have been instructed more than once by Beijing that all donations and gifts should be given in the name of an individual or an organisation but

---

[16] According to the regulations of German Missio and Miserior, their social projects cannot be financed unless the local Catholic bishops are involved as the supervisors of those projects.

not by a foreign church.[17] This reiterated instruction apparently intends to exclude any influence coming from Rome. It is too early to say whether it can keep the Chinese church from staying outside the sphere of influence of the Vatican when the church continuously receives assistance from those foreign organisations which have a close relationship with the Vatican. Once a financial relationship is established, even with church-related agencies, a local church can hardly uphold its financial independence in the future. In the long run, if foreign aid continuously flows in as it did before 1949, it will be more difficult for the Chinese church to maintain the principle of the three selfs – self supporting, self administering and self-propagating – on which the government has been insisting since 1957. In the spring of 1990 a verbal message was sent from the interior, to a local Chinese CPA bishop of Sichuen Province telling him that in the future he should not receive donations from abroad, even on a private basis.[18]

Formation programme for priests and sisters

The rapid growth in the numbers entering the vocation is a very promising sign as both priests and religious sisters who survived the Cultural Revolution are old and the training of their successors is the first priority in church administration. However, the lack of qualified teachers and textbooks poses serious problems to the formation programme. Also of interest to church authorities is what motivates men and women to enter the vocation. The transfer of the candidate's residential registration (Hukou) from the remote countryside to the seminary located in a big city, attracts Catholic young boys and girls from rural areas, not to mention other attractions such as foreign connections which might eventually open the chance for them to go abroad.

As far as quantity of candidates is concerned, a good number of seminarians (630 as quoted by Bishop Zong Huaide) can offer great hope that in the near future a considerable number of priests could be ordained. But qualitatively speaking, one has reasons to be worried, because these seminaries operate under varied circumstances and generally under precarious academic environments when qualified teachers and good teaching materials are lacking. As

[17] This was revealed by a leader of the CPA of an interior province in March 1989.
[18] This oral message came to the writer through private communication in November 1989.

a matter of fact, they need books in Chinese on biblical studies, theology, and philosophy for study for the priesthood. Since many seminary library collections were ruined during the Cultural Revolution, updated books and documents have been sent by Catholics outside China or brought from Shanghai where the only Catholic printing house has been set up for the first time since 1949.

Special permission has been obtained from the government for the Shanghai regional seminary to invite overseas priests and sisters to give short courses in the seminaries and to have some gifted seminarians and newly ordained priests sent to Hong Kong and abroad for training, with the aim of their becoming part of the seminary staff. Bishop Jin Luxian of Shanghai revealed that about fifteen scholarships from overseas colleges are available for his seminarians to study abroad. It was reported that he is training them in language skills. In choosing the right candidates, he said, he must make sure that the students will return and become priests.[19]

In other provinces, where international missionary societies still have their Chinese members, after surviving the storms of the past few decades, candidates are attracted to join that particular missionary order while devoting their energies to church service in China. With the consent of the local bishop, formation of these young men and women has been carried out under the auspices of these missionary societies with the particular intention of their serving the Chinese local church. These young priests and nuns belong to international missionary societies like that of the Jesuits and Franciscans, while juridically under the local bishop and working for the Chinese church. What would be the reaction of the government to this kind of formation which does not go along with its principles?

Instead of training patriotic religious workers who will carry out the state policy on religion as expected by the party, in practice, eventually it aims at training priests in the Catholic tradition.[20] The more seminarians who are sent for the orthodox training for the Catholic priesthood, the greater is the chance of preserving the true spirit of Catholicism which demands its faithful to have communion with the Holy See. It seems that even the Chinese leaders are not willing to allow the Catholic church in China to take its natural course, and they keep on insisting that ties with the Holy See are cut. But right now there are too many irons in the fire especially after the

[19] *Sunday Examiner*, 24 May 1989.
[20] Appendix I, 'Document 19'.

crackdown on the pro-democratic movement since when most of the government's attention has been drawn to other more important political and economic matters, leaving little energy for relatively unimportant Catholic affairs. The bishop of Shanghai has exercised great influence on the government by enhancing the international connections of the official sector of Chinese church. It is difficult to find other good reasons to explain why the government allows the Chinese church to accept Catholic scholarships for theological and other church-related studies at this particular seminary which receives 'cream' candidates from practically all over China.

Moving towards the Holy See

There are quite a number of Catholic clergy and bishops who openly express their 'Catholic' view. Take the first China-appointed Bishop Dong Guangqing for example. He openly told a group of Catholic reporters in the winter of 1988 that prayers for the Pope are offered after masses in his diocese. He openly revealed that he accepts the primacy of the Holy See in the Catholic church in Faith, and two other China-appointed prelates, ordained in recent years, of Xian, Shanxi Province, and Yibin of Sichuen Province, share Dong's conviction, speaking to the same group of international Catholic journalists.[21] This acknowledgement has caught the attentions of dignatories of the Vatican. Cardinal Sin writing to Cardinal Tomko also spoke for these China-appointed bishops: 'I am convinced that the great majority of (Chinese Catholics), not only in the underground [unofficial] church[22] but also in the so-called 'official' church, live in their hearts and want to live ever more openly in communion with the Holy Father.'

A price has to be paid for those who are loyal to Rome while still in the CPA. One bishop in south China told a Catholic reporter that he is under close surveillance by the CPA, because the CPA suspects

[21] *Asia Focus*, 28 January 1989.
[22] The writer would very much prefer church activities conducted outside the periphery of the official sponsorship of the Catholic Patriotic Association to be called 'unofficial church activities' instead of 'underground church activities' as called by many. Since many of their activities become more and more open especially in rural areas when the whole population of those villages embrace the orthodox Catholic faith. At this stage of relaxation it is unfair to call them an 'underground church' suggesting that their activities are illegal.

him of being a member of the 'gang of the Pope' as he claimed that he has never hidden his fidelity.[23]

Disputes between CPA Catholics and non-CPA Catholics

The dispute between these two sectors of Catholics is the last thing that anyone who is concerned for the well-being of the Chinese church would like to see. Unfortunately it is the first unwanted fruit reaped from this relaxed period. From the beginning of its establishment, the CPA has been suffering from the government's attempts to select married priests and bishops to discredit the church. The government is now caught in its own trap and has had to reverse its policy since such a move has long since been rejected by Catholics.[24]

In northern China, with non-CPA Catholics clustered in certain rural areas, their once clandestine religious activities can be performed in public now that the government has relaxed its control. It is very easy for them to have open dispute with these CPA Catholics, when the former take the CPA as renegades and they themselves as heroes who survived the persecution. It was reported that these two groups fought even in the church. Accusations have been made by the CPA that the non-CPA Catholics receive aid in the form of religious literature and money from abroad. This draws the attention of the police of the Security Bureaux to the unofficial Catholics and subsequently to the raiding of the latter, and the arrest of unofficial clergy has taken place. The most recent incident took place in Youtong, a Catholic village near Shijiachuang in Hebei Province, where thirty Catholics, including the clandestine bishop, were arrested, 350 were wounded and two died.[25] This affected the attitudes of a few of the non-CPA Catholics who became harsher towards the CPA Catholics. Verbal attacks were launched at the CPA Catholics, highlighting the latter's failures in not being loyal to Rome and in not keeping priestly celibacy, while CPA clergy accused the non-conformist sector of ordaining priests without adequate preparation in theological and secular studies.[26] The unequal distribution of foreign assistance aggravated the feud

[23] *Asia Focus*, 11 March 1989.
[24] Ibid.
[25] Ibid., 29 April 1989.
[26] Shanghai Jin Juxian repeatedly made this remark on the clandestine ordination made by the non-official Catholic church on many occasions. He repeated the same accusation when he was interviewed by the writer in June 1988, Hong Kong.

between these two groups of religious believers. Their feud has reached such an impasse it is as if they have forgotten the essential Christian teaching – love one another as Christ loves us.

When external pressure on religious practices had been relaxed considerably, some CPA leaders even made public statements to denounce the CPA. Take Bishop Ma Ji of Pingliang, for example; he is a China-appointed bishop in Gansu Province in north-west China, and he has openly renounced the CPA as well as resigning from all CPA posts at both national and provincial levels. In his open letter he described the three national church organisations – the Catholic Patriotic Association, Catholic Church Administrative Commission and the Chinese Bishops' Conference – as 'collapsing, isolated and unpopular'.[27] It was reported that the renunciation was first announced in July at an assembly of provincial cadres and that copies of the declaration were passed on to the CPA, its provincial chapter, and related government bodies in August 1988.

Bishop Ma in the statement explained his move by making five allegations about certain senior leaders of the three state-sponsored Catholic organisations: they have broken their vows of celibacy, have defied the Pope's primacy, are incapable of bridging the gap between the church and the government, they lag behind China's open policy but maintain the ultra-leftist ideas of the 1950s, and are corrupt in the way they handle church property.[28] It was reported that Bishop Li of Tianjin, Bishop Zhang of Taiyuan, (Shanxi), Bishop Zhao of Tianshui (Gansu) signed Ma's statement endorsing his declaration.

In view of the CPA's background, gradually many Catholics in China have become more and more indifferent to the CPA, and its role has been greatly eroded by the surfacing of unofficial Catholic activities, and many persons in charge of mainland dioceses, especially in north-west China, have already abandoned their respective CPA Units.[29]

It was reported that, after the crackdown of Tiananmen, the CPA, the Chinese Bishops Conference and the Catholic Administrative Committee, like many governmental and civil organisations, expressed their support of the civil authorities as demanded by the

---

[27] Bishop Ma Ji's letter appeared in *Shantao Weekly* (Taiwan), 4 December 1988; and the news was brought to the English speaking world by *Sunday Examiner*, 6 January 1989.
[28] Ibid.
[29] *Sunday Examiner*, 6 January 1989.

nervous Chinese government.[30] Governmental pressure can be the only reason to explain why the Chinese church acted against Christian principles in supporting such a government whose hands are stained with the blood of its own people. From the viewpoint of Li Peng, Deng Xiaoping and Yang Shangkun, the church should give its support to the government since the Holy Father once remarked that a good Christian should be a good citizen.[31] Therefore, it is right and just for this group of religious citizens, together with many organisations, to support the government which desperately needs it, if the government is to do right by its people. The alliance with a government which has committed a crime against humanity will add to the unpopularity of the CPA both at home and abroad. Indirectly it gives more chance for the non-CPA Catholics to win their confrontation with the CPA. As a matter of fact, the Shanghai Bishop, Jin Luxian, in one of his talks at the Study Meeting of the Working Staff of the Shanghai CPA, revealed the spreading influence of the non-CPA Catholics. He remarked:

Actually within the country, there are in some regions underground forces running wild. Within the whole country, in the province of Hebei, there are close to one million Catholics. However, the number of Catholics controlled by the underground is superior to the one above ground. There are underground activities also in Tianjin, the north-east, Shanxi, Shaanxi, Gansu, etc. Moreover, these are presently progressing towards the south . . . On the surface, the Shanghai diocese is peaceful; in reality the underground is making preparatory work. Those who have come out of the camps of reform through labour do not come back to the diocese. These people are very united in their work. Some who are close to eighty years old are working strenuously despite the hardship. We should not feel the day is peaceful. The Vatican is using these forces to oppose us.[32]

The overtones of Bishop Jin's talk and the public statement of Bishpo Ma Ji all reveal the antagonistic attitudes of these two sections of Catholics towards each other.[33] The government at this juncture could easily make use of the 'divide and rule' strategy, and let them fight among themselves leaving no time or energy to

30 *Catholic Church in China* (3 Sept. 1989): 18–19.
31 Refer to the Pope's speech in Manila to the Chinese on 29 February 1981. *Sunday Examiner*, 6 June 1981.
32 *Church Bulletin*, (7 December 1988): 5–11.
33 There are more public statements circulating in Hebei province pointing their accusing fingers at church leaders in Beijing and other places in Hebei without any proof. Some prominent figures in Beijing Nantong and the Seminary were even named as Communist party members.

propagate the Catholic faith. The dispute is a real test for the Catholic church. The Pope often preaches reconciliation which is the main theme of those who work for the mission in China. Indeed, CPA and non-CPA Catholics have so many problems in common that they could work together in a joint effort to find solutions. These problems are those of reclaiming church property and formation of seminarians, religious sisters and catechists. Since bridge churches have been playing the role of closing the gap between CPA and non-CPA Catholics, it is hoped that they can work along these lines.

Non-CPA Catholics form their own Episcopal Conference

Some Catholic bishops recognised by Rome but not by the government, on 21 November 1989 gathered themselves together in Zhangerce Village, Sanyuan District near Xian, the provincial capital of Shaanxi Province of north-west China. This meeting was the first of their own episcopal conferences, and was called to establish links between all of China's Vatican appointed bishops and to offer a visible and unified leadership for the whole Catholic community in China. The Zhangerce participants chose three prominent non-CPA bishops who were not at the meeting as leaders. Bishop Fan Xueyan of Baoding was chosen as the president, Archbishop Deng Yiming of Guangzhou and Bishop Gong Pinmei of Shanghai now living in the United States were chosen as vice presidents.[34] It was the intention of this conference to eventually incorporate the whole Chinese church. It was reported that the Vatican did not know of the setting up of this conference beforehand and was not happy with the decision taken at Zhangerce to establish a new Bishops' Conference. Another source reported that the Vatican not only disfavoured such an initiative but had also urged those involved to be prudent and not to take such action. The conference did not give any consideration to the government sanctioned Chinese Bishops' Conference.[35]

The setting up of this new episcopal conference posed a thorny question for the Vatican. It was this group of church leaders who had suffered for the past four decades because of their loyalty to the Holy See, and who came to know about the possible rapprochement between the CCP and the Vatican. For fear the Vatican would compromise too much with the Chinese government at their

[34] *Asia Focus*, 17 March 1990.
[35] Ibid., 17 March 1990, 31 March 1990.

expense, the non-CPA leaders just set up their hierarchy to strengthen their own muscles. The existence of two Chinese Bishops
Conferences added one more headache to the already complicated
programme of Sino-Vatican negotiation.

The participants ignored the legitimacy of the Beijing-based
Chinese Bishops Conference founded in 1981, by calling on themselves 'to continue the Shanghai Episcopal Synod of 1924'. It was
quoted from their document which stated: 'Today, we the bishops of
China have gathered together; a period without a unified leadership
of the Chinese church has come to an end. We feel it is our duty,
under present circumstances, that we unify our leadership and
establish a link among ourselves . . .'[36]

This attitude antagonised the Chinese government who from the
beginning refused to recognise the legitimacy of these non-CPA
bishops. Subsequently, arrests took place. All of the Zhangerce
meeting participants, including several bishops, at least four priests
and some lay leaders were detained by China's security officers.
They are among the more than thirty Catholics reportedly apprehended by authorities since late November 1989. Ren Wuzhi,
director of the State council's Religious Affairs Bureau in China
denied that any Catholic bishops and priests had been detained
when he was questioned by reporters during his visit to Hong Kong
in March 1990.[37] As usual the Chinese authorities have not
respected the Catholic position that once a bishop is ordained he is a
legitimate bishop whether he is recognised by the state or not. Also it
was not the first time in Deng's modernisation era that China, after
the arrest of non-CPA bishops, denied the arrest. This stems from the
root of the problem, the clash of authority.

The hard-won channel for Sino-Vatican dialogue had been
interrupted once on the issue of 'The appointment of Deng Yiming'
(1981). After several years of hard work by various bridge churches,
it was only in 1987 that the CCP consented to resume formal
dialogue, but there is a long way to go before any results will be seen.
When the Liberal party leader Zhao Ziyang was disgraced, hard-
liners in China would not favour dialogue with an international
religious organisation, after the June 4 incident, even if it did revert
to conformity in ideology. The untimely pursuit by this group of
church leaders would dampen the chance of smooth Sino-Vatican

[36] *Asia Focus*, 17 March 1990.
[37] Ibid.

dialogue. The Vatican was really caught up in this incident. The Holy Father could not openly say 'yes' or 'no' to this new Chinese Bishops' Conference. According to the Canon Law, this group of Chinese bishops who were recognised by the Pope are legitimate in every sense of the word. The Vatican could only express its disapproval of the untimely set up of this bishops conference through indirect channels. Fr. Paul Pang, the head of the Overseas Chinese Apostolate of the Sacred Congregation for the Evangelisation of Peoples (SCEP) told the Washington based Catholic News Service that the SCEP had asked the Zhangyi meeting organisers not to form a conference.[38] On the other hand, Cardinal Wu of Hong Kong publicly asked for an explanation of the reasons for the arrests when he spoke at a dinner honouring the eight religious delegates headed by Ren Wuzhi, the director of Religious Affairs Bureau, when they visited Hong Kong in March 1990.[39]

SINO-VATICAN RELATIONS

Directives from the Vatican on dealing with China[40]

An eight-point directive revealing the Vatican's position on how to deal with China appeared in September 1988 and has been circulating among Catholics as a set of guidelines, especially for those who through their work act as a bridge between the universal church and the Chinese church. The text grew out of a consultation in March 1986, arranged by Cardinal Josef Tomko, prefect of the Congregation for the Evangelisation of Peoples, with certain Catholics who keep in touch with developments in the church in China, especially on the growing contacts it has with the universal church. Although the text is not weighty as doctrine nor binding as law, it displays the Roman Curia's position on sensitive questions such as papal supremacy and the relations between the CPA and the non-CPA Catholics. Citing the Dogmatic Constitution on the church (Lumen Gentium), it declares:

[Since] the lasting and visible source and foundation of the unity both of faith and of communion [L.G. n. 18] in the Catholic church is the Roman

---

[38] *Asia Focus*, 31 March 1990.
[39] Ibid., 24 March 1990.
[40] The whole text is in Appendix IV.

Pontiff, those who do not profess and do not maintain communion with the Pope cannot be considered Catholics.[41]

At this stage of the Sino-Vatican negotiations, when compromises can be expected by both sides, the text asserts: 'Communion with the Pope is not only a question of discipline, but above all of Catholic faith.' This implies that the Vatican will compromise on matters of secondary importance but will not accept the view that the Chinese Catholic church is independent from the Holy See.

The Vatican sees fear and uncertainty arising among Chinese Catholics who paid heavily for refusing to cut themselves off from the Pope and who may feel victimised by any Sino-Vatican rapprochement. Therefore the text praises those loyal faithful.

Though Rome refrained from condemning those who joined the CPA, it does not appear ready to cede to the wishes of the Chinese government and recognise the CPA's sole legitimacy by excluding unofficial Catholics whose activities were conducted mainly outside the CPA. Albeit reluctantly at this stage, Rome explained its position on the CPA by pointing out the nature of the CPA and giving its guidance to Catholics on how to relate to it. It referred to the Constitution of the Chinese Catholic Patriotic Association of 1957, which declared the intention of renouncing the fundamental ties with the Supreme Pontiff and with the Holy See, and of submitting the community of Catholic faithful to the direct control of the civil authorities. The second point of the directive states that

No Catholic in conscience can accept the principles of an association which demands the rejection of a fundamental element of his or her faith, such as the indispensable communion with the Roman Pontiff, the visible head of the church and of the college of the Catholic bishops of the world, which cannot exist without him as head.[42]

While acknowledging that:

certain more recent positions adopted by some representatives of the CPA would seem to indicate a certain change of attitude and a tendency on the part of the same CPA to assume a more political than religious role as a means of communication between the church and the government.[43]

The text adds that the CPA is seeking even now 'to control the choice and ordination of the bishops in each diocese and the

---

[41] Appendix IV, 'The Vatican's Eight-Point Directive on dealing with China' (private circulating material).
[42] Ibid.
[43] Ibid.

activities of the various diocesan communities ... from 1958 on, by reason of an initiative of the CPA numerous episcopal ordinations took place in mainland China without the necessary consent (apostolic mandate) of the Roman Pontiff.' This implies that one-sided episcopal appointments are unacceptable by either side, so a feasible solution agreeable to both church and state should be sought through negotiation.

As interaction between the Chinese Catholic church and the universal church has been increasing, even Catholic bishops and clergy outside the mainland seem to seldom question the legitimacy of CPA-elected Chinese bishops. The latter are often regarded as the sole legitimate religious leaders of the Chinese Catholic church and indirectly as leaders of the unofficial church which is so active in areas beyond governmental control, mainly in the countryside, even if they have been undermined to a certain degree.

As far as the CPA bishops are concerned, the Vatican has its own assessment:

According to the doctrine of the church and its canonical discipline, such ordinations are to be considered gravely illicit; both the one who receives the ordination and the one who confers it incur a 'latae sententiae' excommunication reserved to the Apostolic See.[44]

Based on what it understands to be the manner of such consecrations and on other information, the Vatican text suggests that such consecrations may not be invalid, but adds: 'Naturally, in such a situation, a definite judgement is possible only after each case has been attentively and duly examined under every aspect.' It may at first seem harsh to quote Canon Law and refer to doctrine, but to read between the lines one could conclude that mentioning 'latae sententiae' excommunication reserved to the Apostolic See by the Apostolic See itself is an indirect reminder to the CPA bishops that there is a possibility of avoiding the 'latae sententiae' excommunication, if one wishes to do so.

Regarding sacraments administered by priests ordained by bishops who are not recognised by the Roman Pontiff, the Vatican texts states the view that 'the presumption remains for the validity of their ordination and therefore also for that of the sacraments

---

[44] Cf. Decree of the Holy Office dated 9 April 1951 and Canon 1382 of the Code of Canon Law.

administered by them'. How many of these CPA clergy are actually unrecognised by Rome is still a big question. Probably not all of them fall into this category, but only those who have deliberately and publicly refused to have communion with Rome. Since this kind of 'recognition' cannot be openly noted, ordinary Catholic visitors to China just receive the sacraments in good faith and find that the following recommendations are not very appropriate to the actual situation in China, though the content is superb from a doctrinal point of view. Thus point 4 of the directive recommends:

With regard to the necessity of assistance at Mass and of the reception of the sacraments, Catholics are to look for priests who have remained faithful, that is those in communion with the Pope. Nevertheless, in order to meet the requirements of their spiritual welfare, Catholics can have recourse to other priests also, on condition that they avoid the occasion of scandal and the danger that such actions might harm the complete content of the Catholic faith which as has already been noted, requires full communion with the Roman Pontiff.[45]

In point 5, the Vatican text asserts that 'communion in sacris' should be avoided – an instruction which is like one given previously to clergy visiting China and which is understandable and practical to follow. It states that 'on the occasion of visits outside mainland China, such persons may not be invited or allowed to celebrate liturgical acts in churches or Catholic institutions'. But one wonders whether such actions by bishops and ecclesiastics who visit the mainland can positively foster reunion or will drive a wedge between the universal church and the Chinese church. Unofficial Catholics are not fools. They can tell who are legitimate bishops and who are not. For example, they flocked to see Cardinal Jaime Sin of Manila, to kiss his ring and kneel down for his blessing while ignoring Chinese church dignitaries who accompanied the cardinal on his first visit to the cathedral in Beijing. Moreover, it is beneficial to have pro-Rome church leaders from outside China appear even in open churches run by the CPA, because loyal Catholics are reminded that they are not forgotten. Putting the jurisdiction questions aside, orthodox Catholicity is still flourishing in China, and the appearance of orthodox clergy is a sign of communion with those who embrace the same faithful intact.

In Point 6 the Vatican offers a prudent suggestion to tackle

---

[45] Appendix iv, 'The Vatican's Eight-Point Directive on dealing with China'.

problems arising from the insufficiency of textbooks and teaching personnel among the unofficial Catholics:

The Church has the right and duty, in China as well as elsewhere, to have its own seminaries where its clergy are formed. If, however, that were to be prevented and if it were not possible to adequately form the candidates for the priesthood in another way, even privately, then such candidates could be sent to the seminaries opened under the control of the Patriotic Association, but only on condition that the general orientation and formation imparted there follow the teaching and directives of the Church. Such a possibility should be evaluated according to local circumstances, keeping in mind also the persons who direct such centres of formation.[46]

Also textbooks and literature should faithfully communicate the doctrine of the church.

However, the last point of the Vatican's directive deals with aids from outside. The text says: 'Any assistance is to be directed to initiatives which serve to maintain the correct doctrine and spirit of faith of the Catholic church.' Overseas Catholics are not so naive as to put up with the great difficulties of recruiting all manner of assistance, including money and personnel, to help China and then of the Catholic church not to receive the benefit. Therefore before Catholic projects in China are undertaken by overseas Catholic organisations, a legitimate bishop's approval is required. As a matter of fact, some projects at first appear to have no direct link with the Catholic church, but they can do more good in the long run than people expect. A Jesuit project provides all sorts of material assistance to help young Chinese post-graduate students in California, United States, mainly to solve their temporal needs. Such timely help can change the ideas that these young intellectuals, who will become leaders in the future, have about the Catholic church in Hong Kong, the threshold to mainland China, as well as in the neighbouring countries to China. Recently many Catholics are busy sending religious literature to China, as well as giving financial subsidies to the unofficial Catholics when the latter are more free to organise themselves in carrying out religious activities. How to aid the development of those loyal Catholics, but at the same time not antagonising the official CPA by challenging the CPA's legitimacy, is the first problem the Vatican has to tackle before working further for reconciliation between the CPA and the non-CPA Catholics.

[46] Ibid.

Response from China to the directives

Though the directives were meant for private circulation among Catholics outside the mainland, one must expect that China had access to this document. It is reported that the directives anger Chinese officials as well as church leaders, even the more moderate ones, and set things back to such a great extent that several government officials confided to one of the bridge-church's personnel that their original expectation for the resolution of Sino-Vatican relations during their term of office might not now happen in their lifetime.[47] Then the Chinese Vice Premier and Foreign Minister Wu Xueqian, speaking at a Chinese Catholic church's celebration of its 30th anniversary of self-election and self-ordination of bishops in mainland China, told the Vatican to stop interfering in the internal affairs of the People's Republic of China, especially in the field of religious affairs. Wu's statement refers to the Vatican's Eight-Point Directive, as well as to the Vatican's approval of the secret ordination of bishops and priests. Wu's speech went like this:

Religious organisations or individuals should not accept instructions and monetary subsidies from foreign religious forces to carry out organized activities in China ... The improvement of China-Vatican relations can be possible only if the Vatican cuts its so-called diplomatic ties with Taiwan and regards the mainland Chinese government as the only legal government of China and stops interfering with China's internal matters, including religious affairs.[48]

Wu's speech reflected the party's attitude to the Catholic church at this stage ten years after the open door policy when foreign interactions with the Chinese Catholics caught the attention of the Government and who feels that it is time to reiterate its stance on Catholic matters. That was why not only verbally he laid down the bottomline on the Chinese side in Catholic matters but systematically makes it a documentation – 'Document 3'.

China's policy on the Catholic Church: 'Document no. 3' 1989

In February 1989, the party's Central Office and the State Council ordered the Central Committee's United Front Department and the Religious Bureau of the State Council to issue a document, no. 3,

[47] Fr. Anthony Chang, 'A view of recent Sino-Vatican matters', *Asia Focus*, 29 April 1989. Chang is the editorial consultant of *Yi-China Message*.
[48] *Asia Focus*, 10 December 1988.

on 'Report on Strengthening the work concerning the Catholic Church under the New Situation'.[49] This report provides a serious analysis and outline on the guiding principles and concrete policies on the work concerning the Catholic church. It is based on the criteria laid down by the Party Central and the State Council on how to handle Sino-Vatican relations in connection with the present situation of the Catholic church in China. The essence and the main points of the document are summarised as follows:

1 The direction of an independent, self-ruling, self-administering Catholic church must be firmly implemented and indoctrination of clergy and faithful must be strengthened. The basic principles of the Sino-Vatican relations are:

  (a) The Vatican must sever the so-called 'diplomatic relations' with Taiwan and accept that the People's Republic of China is the sole legitimate government of China.
  (b) The Vatican should not interfere in the internal affairs of our country, including non-interference in the religious affairs of our country.

2 The policy must be continuously and firmly implemented that the Catholic church should be helped to solve the problem of self-support.

3 To solve the question of the underground force of the Catholic church.

4 Strengthen the guidance of the Catholic church.[50]

Unlike other documents on religious matters which are meant for world religions such as Buddhism, Islam, and Christianity, including Catholicism, this Document 3 is aimed at nobody but the Catholic church. The Chinese government in the first part of the Document laid down its principles on Sino-Vatican relations by reiterating that the Catholic church in China should move against its own foundations and be independent from the Holy See. It is not new that China is interested in reaping the political fruit of isolating Taiwan from the international community in Sino-Vatican relations.

It is possible that the foreign aid from outside Catholics and the results of the attempts to cement the broken relations between the Chinese Catholic church and the universal church generate a negative impact on the religious policy of the state. Foreign aid

[49] The English translation of the summary of 'Document 3, 1989' (hereafter it will be called 'Document 3') is in Appendix V.
[50] See Appendix V.

causes considerable alarm to the government which calls upon local authorities to solve the problem of self-support by giving back church properties and granting necessary fund for religious activities. It aims to take away any chance of the Chinese Catholic church reverting to Rome through financial contacts.

While the Vatican is contemplating on how to legitimise the unofficial Chinese Catholics, it seems that the Chinese government is thinking the other way, by cracking-down the same so-called 'underground force' of the Catholic church. At the same time tighter control is placed on the official sector of the Catholic church in China making it follow more closely the party line under the united leadership of the party committee and the government.

It was reported that in April all Chinese bishops and chairmen of all provincial CPA were summoned by the government for a meeting in Beijing to discuss how to implement Document 3 at the grassroot level.[51] After that, many Chinese Catholic dioceses became more cautious in accepting foreign aid. Since the crackdown on the pro-democratic movement in Beijing, the security police are too busy with more important matters, such as hunting student and liberal leaders rather than keeping an eye on small-scale Catholic affairs which become of secondary importance. Therefore, there is no news of repression in the unofficial sector of the Catholic community.

Apparently, the local authorities are in financial difficulties since the 4 June massacre, and it is impossible for them to grant financial help to local Catholics as requested by the central government. Many foreign projects are suspended and foreign aid has dropped; foreign Catholic aid, however, is still available. Naturally, it will be too difficult for the Chinese religious and civil authorities to resist the temptation not to accept financial aid from the universal church when not a single cent can be obtained from the local government for the time being. Up till 1989, foreign Catholic funding agencies continue to sponsor Chinese church projects in rural areas. In the process of transmitting the funds, both the donors and the recipients agree that the donations come from individual Catholics but not in the name of the Catholic church. The central government ordered that no financial aid from the universal church could be received but it has not stated that individual donations should also be rejected.

[51] *Kung Kao Po*, 4 August 1989.

Negotiations: different voices from different corners

From the issuing of the Eight-Point Directive from the Vatican and the response from the Chinese government one may realise that the present stage of the Sino-Vatican relations are far from being near to rapprochement. It was confirmed by a reliable source that there is a long way to go before the Vatican and China can have their relations normalised. At the first stage of direct contact, there are a couple of matters on which both of them can not arrive at a common understanding. The first regards the access of Chinese bishops to the future Papal representative in Beijing. No Chinese citizen, including Catholic bishops, is supposed to communicate with a foreign government's representative directly, i.e. without going through the Chinese government. But it is a very normal practice as well as the intention of the Pope that he should be allowed to get in touch with local bishops through the Papal Nuncio directly and freely. The second is that it seems that both sides cannot reach an agreement on the legitimacy of the CPA and non-CPA Catholics. While China claims that the sole legitimacy rests with the CPA, the Vatican insists that the non-CPA Catholics should be legitimised as well. This explains why China begins to protest when the amount of backing from the Vatican for the unofficial church goes beyond the limit of its tolerance. The attempt to set up the episcopal conference of the non-CPA bishops added more complications to this thorny question.

At this stage one could argue that Sino-Vatican negotiations are at the first stage, that of exchanging opinions on key issues. Needless to say there are many things preventing the reaching of a common understanding and compromise on both sides. It seems that both parties are not as tolerant as they should be, and they have not yet reached a state of dialogue. The issuing of the Vatican's 'Eight Directives' and the Chinese government's 'Document 3', reflected that both are insisting on their orthodox stand points without any spirit of tolerance and openness. One could suggest that the issuing of 'Document 3' was a retaliation to the Vatican's 'Eight Directives'. The arrest of non-CPA Chinese Catholic leaders also reflected that China's relations with the Vatican were not that warm, although China was desperately trying to improve foreign relations since she had been boycotted by the west after China's crime against humanity in gunning down the innocent and patriotic students. The papal reception given to the Tibetan exile leader, the Dalai Lama, when he was on his way to receive the Nobel Peace Prize in Autumn 1989 reflected that there was no progress in Sino-Vatican dialogue, otherwise the Pope would not have sacrificed the hard-won chance for dialogue by the Dalai Lama's Papal audience.

There are many reasons for this development of the Sino-Vatican dialogue; one of the main reasons lies in the bureaucracies which are entrusted to handle the negotiation. Although China and the Vatican have not officially announced which of their offices are responsible for the contact and the negotiation, yet from the issuing of the Eight-Point Vatican Directive from Cardinal Josef Tomko, Prefect of the Congregation for the Evangelization of People, one may realise that this office of the Roman Curia is handling the case and consequently it is natural for this office to give emphasis to doctrinal and disciplinary matters which are the areas of its concern. Then with the absence of the more tolerant Prefect of the Secretary of State, the architect of Ostpolitik, Cardinal Casaroli, from the scene, not only will diplomacy be undermined but tolerance in principle will be difficult to achieve. That is why the Vatican takes a religious orientation in the negotiations, putting more emphasis on doctrinal problems and church discipline, hoping to solve the intricacies of religious questions in China through negotiations.

In China, the statement of Wu Xueqian accusing the Vatican of interfering in its internal affairs, including interference in religious affairs, and the silence of the other leaders such as Yan Mingfu, a Central Committee member of the CCP and head of the United Front Department, who also attended the celebration of the 30th anniversary of the self-election and self-ordination of Chinese bishops, indicates that it is not the more tolerant United Front Department which has taken over the talks with the Vatican, but the less flexible Vice Premier and former Foreign Affairs Minister Wu Xueqian. It is not unusual for Wu Xueqian to view this case as a political issue arising between two states and not as a religious matter, between a state and a religion.

Since the suppression of the pro-democratic movement, more intolerance is the underlying tone of the party. The moderate party boss, Zhao Ziyang was sacked by the paramount leader Deng because Zhao was accused of being too lenient with the protesters in Tiananmen. He was replaced by Deng's hand-picked Jiang Zimin who appears to be ready to do the will of the conservative octagenarians in the Politburo. In this political climate, it is widely believed that the policy of opening to the outside world is problematic, particularly if cultural and economic contacts with the west become identified as a source of the 'bourgeois' influence, underlying the student demonstration. The budding of the Sino-Vatican rapprochement, which was possible in Zhao Ziyang's time, will suffer a set back in this political climate when pluralism of ideologies is not honoured. Moreover, at this stage of development, the Chinese leaders in Zhongnanhai are preoccupied with so many major problems, little attention is given to the small-scale Sino-Vatican negotiations which are regarded by China as minor issues.

Because of the bloody suppression, people's anger smouldered towards the army and the party can further drift apart from the government and its ideology. Their total despair of the party and the government provides a bigger ideological vacuum for them to turn to the Gospel if it can be properly translated into deeds in providing for the poverty-ridden Chinese people through humanitarian assistance based on love, fraternity and respect of human dignity. In the 1980s there have been a handful of missionaries from outside entering China, who serve silently as experts on a short-term basis. They are doing what Matteo Ricci did some 400 years ago. However, the hostile situation in China, because of material backwardness, governmental suspicion and cultural isolation, limited the number of these missionaries. This kind of meaningful service is always welcomed by the people and consequently it can do much to strengthen the Catholic church. Evidence reveals that old Catholics in remote areas of interior China still remember the foreign missionaries of forty years ago just because the latter did good things for the rural communities.[52]

Since the massacre, no one can foresee how stable the Chinese society will become in the near future. Many foreign governments, during the turmoil in the six month period after the massacre, advised their subjects to leave China. Even since peace has been restored, apparently they do not view China as a safe environment for their own citizens to work in for the foreseeable future. Thus, up to the last quarter of 1989, many foreign embassies and consulates gave no guarantee to their subjects, including those missionary

---

[52] Recently Hong Kong Catholics received letters from some Catholics in remote areas of China enquiring the whereabouts of some foreign missionaries who were expelled in the 1950s. These missionaries were highly praised and remembered by these Catholics.

experts, for their safety when the latter express their wish to go back to China to work.

In spite of the fact that economic sanctions have been imposed on China by various western governments, sending a clear message to Beijing that 'the loss of private capital, skills and technological know-how is the price it must pay for the disregard of human life' as remarked by an American politician.[53] Yet Catholic aid of a humanitarian nature continues to be given, if not to be increased, in rural districts to lessen the hardships, even if on a very small scale, caused by economic difficulties. Even sincere Catholics are not prepared to formulate a warm relationship with this government on a diplomatic level.

Divergent voices among the Cardinals in the Vatican about the eight-point directive add further complexity to the issue. In October 1988, Cardinal Jaime Sin wrote to Cardinal Tomko with an accompanying canon law study in response to his views on the eight-point directive. He presented two major points of disagreement on the Vatican's views on bishops of the official church and their ordination without papal consent.[54] He argued:

In dealing with the bishops of the official church, I take always good care of reminding them of the need for communion with the Holy Father, as pertaining to the essentials of our Catholic faith. At the same time, they also deserve a word of appreciation for the monumental work they have done in a few years to recuperate the church's properties, to build or rebuild about 1,000 churches, to open 15 seminaries, to begin novitiates for local sisters, etc. In addition we must not ignore the fact that a number of non-official semi-underground Catholic communities, now flourishing in many regions, are able to operate more freely because of the silent approval and benevolent regard of the so-called 'official' Catholic authorities.

We may commit a grave injustice if we give the impression that all the bishops ordained in China 'sine mandato apostolico' are *de facto* schismatic or excommunicated. Canon 1382 must be interpreted in the light of Canon 1321: 'Nemo punitur, nisi externa legis vel praecepti violatio, ab eo commissa, sit graviter imputabilis ex dolo vel ex culpa'; and in the light of Canon 1324 which in parag. I lists a number of causes which excuse from *latae sententiae* penalties because they diminish or remove the conditions required to make such violation of the law 'graviter imputabilis'. Some of these causes were clearly present in the extreme situations in which these Chinese bishops have had to live since 1949. (Please consult the enclosed study on the Chinese Bishops ordained 'sine mandato apostolico').

53 *International Herald Tribune*, 30 June, 1989.
54 See the whole text of Cardinal Sin's letter in *Yi-China Message*, 8: 1 (Feb 1989): 8–11.

My personal opinion is that in this matter of the excommunication discreet silence is in order and no reference should be made to Canon 1382 without referring also to the others.

In the present context of the church in China, there are two dangers that all of us must avoid with equal zeal and determination. One is wounding the sensibility of those Catholics who have suffered much for their fidelity to the Holy Father. The other danger is to alienate even further those in the 'official' church who, though influenced by the political evolution of China, are actually seeking communion with the Holy See.'[55]

Apparently Cardinal Sin's view on the complexity of the situation in the Chinese church gains the support of pro-China Catholics and they regard his view as more oriented to the future and to resolving the problem.[56] Will Cardinal Sin's tolerance be the substitute for Cardinal Casaroli's flexibility when dealing with communist states? This is what many are waiting to see. It is suggested that it would be prudent and beneficial to give at least as much attention and consideration to Cardinal Sin's response as to Cardinal Tomko's directive.[57]

China is not yet ready

The Sino-Vatican rapprochement has now entered a new phase, but many obstacles lie ahead. Problems encountered by both sides are difficult, so much so that no common understanding has been developed on key questions of legitimacy and authority. One may say that China is not yet ready for the rapprochement, because there are still Catholic dissidents in jail. The very influential Bishop Fan Xueyen of Baoding, Hebei Province, is still under house arrest because he was nominated as the possible president of the non-CPA Chinese Bishops' Conference, and there is no signal that he will be set free. The raiding of Catholic villages and the arrest of Catholic leaders are still taking place from time to time. China and the Vatican are not dancing with the same tune when Vatican appointed bishops were not recognised by the Chinese Government. Even though Bishop Gong Pinmei was released and was allowed to stay in the US for medical treatment, the charge against him, of opposing land reform and for being anti-revolution, has not been withdrawn.

55 Ibid.
56 Father Anthony Chang, 'A view of recent Sino-Vatican matters', *Asia Focus*, 29 April 1989.
57 Ibid.

In the early 1970s when Sino-US rapprochement was developing through certain stages of negotiation and bargaining, both the US and the Chinese government were ready to work further towards rapprochement. Bishop Walsh, an American missionary to China was released from Shanghai, upon the request of the US, as a signal of the goodwill of China. At this stage one is waiting to see the sign of goodwill from the Chinese government, before one can optimistically expect any progress in negotiations.

The second piece of evidence one needs to ensure rapprochement lies in the return of expropriated church property and land by the Chinese government. In fact this land and property was erroneously perceived as belonging to the Vatican but they originally belonged to Roman Catholic missionary orders. As reported, except for a very few, most expropriated church properties have not yet been returned. The government simply allows factories, institutes and individual families to occupy these sites, or retains the compensation money. In Shanghai, the properties of the Paris Foreign Mission (Société des Missions Etrangères de Paris) were confiscated in the 1950s and compensation for this was calculated by the government at RMB$40 million. The Paris Foreign Mission would like this huge amount to be distributed for religious purposes among fourteen dioceses which were formerly under the care of that mission order. In spite of the fact that these fourteen dioceses have been in need of financial aid for various projects, it seems that the government is not yet prepared to release the whole amount or even part of it. At the present high inflation rate of 50% looming in China, even if the full amount were obtained now, half of its buying value would be gone.

At a diplomatic level, it is not surprising that both China and the Vatican will have to take a new look at their relations, for ideological and political reasons. Amidst worldwide condemnation, China may be anxiously looking for the friendship of the Vatican at this time of isolation. However, many Catholics have expressed that they do not want to see any Vatican official shake the blood-stained hands of Li Peng or Deng Xiaoping. Since the Vatican has expressed more than once that its diplomacy is motivated by moral causes and not politics, Catholics demand that the Vatican should stick to its principles.

In general, the Chinese are not positively inclined towards religion, because some religious sects have been involved in some incidents which have caused embarrassment to the Chinese government. The relaxed atmosphere enjoyed by the Muslims in Central Asia has become the main source of inspiration when asking for more freedom and independence for the Muslim minorities in Xinjiang. The award to the Dalai Lama of the Nobel Peace Prize strengthens his bargaining power on the question of Tibet. The quasi defection of Xu Jaituen the newly retired director of Xinhua News Agency, the quasi Chinese embassy in Hong Kong, to USA in May 1990 was through the assistance of a popular Buddhist monk Master Xinyuen of Taiwan. To the people in the west, since Xu was the high-ranking official defecting from China, his going to US for 'a rest and for sightseeing' shocked the colony already lacking in confidence – Hong Kong at its later stage of transition.

The Catholic church is better prepared

Although there is no unanimous voice from the Vatican as well as from the various bridge-churches' personnel on the way to deal with China, one is delighted to see the breakthrough that came from a meeting of various bridge-churches. Leaders of major Catholic 'China bridge' institutes met in Hong Kong on 2 to 3 March 1989 for the first time to share information about the development of their projects as well as to study the current situation of the Chinese Catholic church in mainland China. It indicates that relationships between these bridges have become much warmer than before. Though at this stage they are not prepared to co-operate on any joint project for China, the ice has been broken and it is not impossible that in the future they will gradually achieve unity among themselves.

Although many are encouraged by the fact that the majority of China-appointed bishops express their loyalty to the Holy See, the abortive meeting of the prominent but mysterious figure, Bishop Jin Luxian of Shanghai, with the Pope is the tip of the iceberg of this complicated picture as well as a snub by China.[58] The Vatican, as usual, is more eager than its counterpart to formulate a concordat and to renew its ties with China, but a China which not only recognises the moral leadership of the Pope but also realises that the Vatican cannot help to solve the problem of Taiwan.

The Pope, when referring to the massacre at Tiananmen Square,

[58] 'Congress Record – Senate', US Government, Washington, S3350, 10 April 1989.

expressed his 'horror' and 'pain' that so many lives were cut short, presenting the victims as 'martyrs'. He hoped that 'all contradictions and sufferings can eventually bring about a new human and Christian advent'. His message was diplomatic enough not to close the door forever on Sino-Vatican rapprochement, and he skilfully concentrated the gravity of his speech on the students at Tiananmen Square by eulogising them as martyrs.[59] It is expected that the Vatican will simply watch the changing political scene in China, while keeping the door open to make further contact possible. Every interaction at this time should be at a halt under the new Li Peng government which is less tolerant. Sending more missionaries/ experts to serve in China, and to sponsor more projects for social development could be a feasible way to preach the Gospel by deeds, and these can be emphasised more by the Vatican at this stage.

The arrival of the informal Papal envoy, Monsignor J. P. Gobel, with the official title of 'The First Secretary in China Affairs of the Papal Nunciature in Manila' in Hong Kong in May 1989 with the consent of China, marks a turning point in the Sino-Vatican relations. The sending of Monsignor J. P. Gobel to China (stationed in Hong Kong) does not mean that reciprocally China is ready to send its representative to the Vatican. His staying in Hong Kong indicates that Beijing is not yet ready for a Papal representative. China consented to this appointment because it provides someone through which to pass on complaints about any undesirable and incompatable activities by Catholics. The blooming of Catholic activities for China as well as in China needs a co-ordinator, and the Vatican also requires its official to be near China for consultation and information.

The scheduled Papal visit to Hong Kong and Macau in October 1989 might be the last time these territories could offer such a welcome to the Supreme Pontiff, the highest leader of the Catholic church, before they revert to a government who embraces atheist Marxism-Leninism as its ideology. This Papal visit could have offered an excellent opportunity for higher officials to meet and to clarify some difficult and thorny points. As usual, the Papal gesture of open arms and his speech would have given a boost to the Catholics in a territory which is threatened by the Communist takeover. Unfortunately, the Vatican unilaterally announced that

---

[59] *UCAN News Dispatch*, no. 511, 21 June 1989.

the proposed visit will be cancelled due to the recent crackdown on the pro-democratic movement in China.[60] The Vatican regards this visit as inappropriate in view of the massacre.[61] The cancellation of the Papal visit is a gesture by the Vatican indicating that the Holy father does not approve of China's savageries against thousands of its young people. Thus, the Holy See decides to keep a distance. In order to be true to its principles – for religious purposes and to serve peace and morality – the Pope has made the prudent choice to protest against China's brutality by paying a high price in freezing Sino-Vatican relations for the time being. The cancellation of the visit also entails cancelling the meetings which are scheduled for the Chinese and the Vatican officials for further discussions to clarify and identify some thorny questions on the Sino-Vatican rapprochement. At this stage of political developments in China, when pluralistic ideologies are not encouraged as a whole, and less tolerance is given to oppositions, no one will believe that Li Peng's officials can make much progress in the Sino-Vatican discussions whose success largely depends on tolerance and a willingness to compromise.

HONG KONG THE BRIDGE-CHURCH AFTER THE MASSACRE IN BEIJING

The Chinese army's slaughtering of civilians in Beijing shattered the already declining trust in Hong Kong that the Chinese government will respect the guarantees of human rights and civil liberties outlined in the Sino-British Agreement of 1984. The Catholic leaders in Hong Kong not only have to face the problem of how to render pastoral service to those frustrated Hong Kong people who for various reasons are unable to migrate like many of the rich and professional. In the course of the transition period to 1997, the Catholic church in Hong Kong is facing a big dilemma in its relations with the incoming Chinese government which has a recent record of killing its own children.

The Hong Kong Catholic diocese has sent its representatives to join the Hong Kong Alliance in Supporting Chinese Pro-Democratic Movement. This Alliance under the well-known leadership of Martin Lee and Szeto Wah has not only stirred up support for the Beijing students but has also sent material aid to Tiananmen, so

[60] *Ming Pao*, 9 July 1989.
[61] Ibid.

much so that one of their men, Lee Chuk Yan, was detained in Beijing. Lee was released only through the interventions of London and the Governor of Hong Kong. While condemning students and their supporters as anti-revolutionaries, the Hong Kong Alliance, including its representative from the Catholic church, has also been defined as anti-revolutionary by China. More than once China complained of interference in its internal affairs by outsiders, implicitly implying that the Hong Kong Alliance was one of them. In the eyes of the Chinese leaders, the Hong Kong church is stepping out of line and meddling with China's politics. This involvement might influence China when considering its relations with the Vatican.

Because it is a bridge church, the Hong Kong Catholic church has to be very sensitive to the triangular relationship which exists between China, the Vatican and Hong Kong. This poses a difficult task for the Hong Kong Catholics who have to strike a balance between being a good citizen in the eyes of the Chinese government and a good Christian in the eyes of the church, especially since the Holy Father in his Manila trip of 1980 had defined that a good Christian should be a good Chinese citizen.[62]

CONCLUSIONS

Many Catholics in China long for the normalisation of Sino-Vatican relations, which might provide the right conditions for the growth of the church after a long winter of more than thirty years.[63] With twists and turns, both China and the Vatican have been working conscientiously for such an end. Recent developments on both sides have greatly affected both the content and the manner of the negotiations. The abortive Papal visit deprived the high officials of China and the Vatican of the opportunity to meet to clarify some thorny points and to exchange views on some unsettled matters. When the Holy Father decides to play the role of a moral leader of the world, he cannot afford to turn a blind eye to China's massacre. His refusal to visit Hong Kong and Macau may bring the slow development of Sino-Vatican negotiations to a complete halt. On the other hand, the Vatican will defeat its purpose by hastening the

[62] *Sunday Examiner*, 5 March 1981.
[63] *Asia Focus*, 11 March 1989. 'Life of the church in China', *Correspondence* 32 (October 1988): 5–10.

formulation of the diplomatic Sino-Vatican relations with Li Peng's government.

The Sino-Vatican rapprochement only promises a breathing space for the Chinese Catholic church. The manner of survival in terms of coping with China's needs is a great test for the Chinese Catholics. The present gestation period, in the development of the Chinese church, with foreign assistance, might cast the mould on future development. It is very important that the leaders of the Chinese Catholic church learn from the history of the church in China and are careful to accept foreign aid in such a manner that its own Chinese identity can be nurtured and its communion with the Holy See maintained.

It is unrealistic to expect Chinese Catholics to contribute directly on a substantial scale to the entire modernisation programme, yet this does not mean that Chinese Catholics can be exempted from the responsibility of restructuring society in the spirit of patriotism. They should offer their share accordingly. Also overseas Catholics in the capacity as experts in foreign languages, science and managerial skill can contribute their share to demonstrate their sincerity in translating their mission spirit of charity into action through selfless service. Is it a new kind of mission to spread the message of Christ by practice more than by preaching.

At this stage of development, China's economic reform has been greatly tarnished by corruption and all sorts of economic crimes. The military crackdown of pro-democratic protestors adds fuel to the fire. Scholars are of the opinion that corruption has been so widespread that the social norms that should govern the nation are lacking. Principles for guiding human behaviour are missing. It seems that no one can tell what is right to do and what is honourable to do, and what is not so right and what is not so honourable.[64] Maybe it is one of the reasons why corruption and bribery have been so widespread in China when moral values have not been honoured and social norms are absent. Can Christian values as preached and practiced by Chinese Christians take the lead in restoring social norms and moral values? There can be no greater help than for the Chinese Catholics to contribute in the area of moral reconstruction as a means to facilitate China's modernisation. At the same time, can

[64] This was how Professor Kenneth Lieberthal of University of Michigan felt when he spoke on 'The first electronic seminar on US–PRC relations', 18 October 1988, United States Consulates General, Hong Kong.

the Church work with the consent of the government for the good of the people, particularly at this difficult moment of suffering from international isolation?

Since the present government is not the ideal partner to negotiate with on the Sino-Vatican rapprochement, the Holy See can do nothing but wait for the appropriate time for diplomatic interaction. The papal reception given to the Dalai Lama was a sign that Sino-Vatican relations were frozen. In fact, the Vatican has no reason to hasten the development of this relationship by sacrificing its principles. At present, the Chinese church is not in danger of becoming schismatic, because religious life there has been resuming to such a degree that its survival is not a problem. The normalisation of Sino-Vatican relations would only provide grounds for its further growth. Nevertheless, this growth will not only depend on the diplomatic skill of the Vatican but on the spiritual strength of the Catholic church itself.

When more exciting things have been happening in Taiwan, which appears far more flexible and active in its foreign relations, Beijing definitely finds that it will be far more insufficient to isolate Taiwan by just terminating the Vatican–Taiwan diplomatic relations. The 'One China Two Governments' model as advocated by Taibei poses many more difficulties to Beijing than it used to, when this island has been very flexible in foreign interactions and its economy is growing by leaps and bounds. The Vatican can offer less and less in solving the problems between Beijing and Taibei, and the possible alternative left for the Vatican will be helping the party in dealing with moral problems. This is a really big challenge to the Catholic church in general and the Chinese Catholic church in particular. How can the Chinese Catholic church revitalise its spiritual strength to accept this challenge is an important topic that deserves further research and study in its own right.

Clashing of the teaching authority, the 'Magisterium'

After surveying religious problems in China over the last forty years, one may feel that it is the Magisterium (the authority to teach) that has been the main reason for church-state conflict in PRC. In other words, the magisterium of world religions such as Buddhism, Islam and Christianity has been posing challenges to the teaching authority of the CCP. Thus, it explains why, ever since its establishment in 1949, the state constantly has problems with religions. In the 1950s and 1960s, the riots in Xinjiang province and other north-west territories by minorities who were mostly adherents of Islam, and the armed uprising in Tibet leading to the exile of the Dalai Lama were the latest attempts by these minorities in their fight for religious freedom, without interference from the atheist party; especially when Islam and Buddhism have become important parts of their own cultural heritage as Christianity has to Greco-Roman culture. The launching of the Three-Selfs movements among Christians and the establishment of Chinese Catholic Patriotic Association were concrete measures by the political leaders in Beijing to curb the magisterium of Christianity.

Since religious leaders together with non-conformist intellectuals were purged in major political movements, such as Anti-Rightist and the Cultural Revolution, it confirms that the CCP did not allow the existence of those whose teachings did not rest with the party.

On the other hand, for political reasons especially in the light of the United Front strategy, the party has a tradition, handed down from the teachings of Mao, to treat religion with great caution and mobilise religious adherents to attain the goal set up by the party. So in such a political climate the United Front could have more room to exercise its tactics in an atmosphere where more tolerance of pluralism is found in socio-economic life. Thus, in this context, a very limited degree of freedom was given to religion as a symbolic action to encourage the participation of non-conformist intellectuals in the modernisation programme. Also it was hoped to give a better impression to foreigners by announcing that religious freedom prevailed in China so as to encourage foreign aid in technology, finance and managerial skills which are so essential to economic development at this stage of modernisation.

In the light of Deng's open door policy, when Beijing lifted its controls on the nation's socio-economic life, comparatively speaking China still did not enjoy as much religious freedom as it should. Much of the party's grip was still with religion in general and Catholicism in particular. The central government did not interfere with local economic activities, especially in those regions which were involved in foreign trade and foreign investment to any great extent; but the same central government refused to allow the same degree of freedom to world religions, including Christianity.[65] Nevertheless, a certain degree of freedom in religious activities, which the CCP regards as cultural practices (especially those religious practices among Buddhists in Tibet and Muslims in the northwest), were allowed, while religious literature, which is one of the major channels of inflow of religious teaching, were not allowed into China by mail. Again this religious policy stems from the principle of resisting the teaching authority of religion. To insist on the state appointment of Catholic bishops and to refuse the spiritual leadership of the Pope, when there is clear knowledge that the local church in the post-Vatican II era has enhanced much of its autonomy and there is ample room for the influence of local culture in theology and liturgy, are because the Catholic church with the Pope as the head has been posing and will be posing too big a challenge to the teaching authority of the Communist party and Marxist-Leninism which is declining very rapidly in the Communist world.

The wind of reform swept over the eastern Europe and consequently inspired the USSR headed by Gorbachev to march into perestroika and the market economy. The Soviet Union loosens its grip on ideology and Gorbachev's meeting with the Pope was hailed by the west as the beginning of the normalisation of Soviet–Vatican relations. At long last the Pope's desire to visit the Soviet Union was granted. But even before preparations for this important event were begun, the Pope was invited to visit Czechoslovakia. On this his first visit to eastern Europe other than Poland, the Pope candidly remarked that Communism had no future. The only question which remains is how and when will communism collapse. The Pope in the same speech remarked that the livelihood of central and eastern Europe has been ruined by authoritarianism and materialism.[66] What will China think of Pope John Paul II when it claims adherence to the Four Principles and to orthodox Communism, and refuses to grant more ideological freedom. China knows very well that reform swept over eastern Europe and the Soviet Union and that the massacre at Tiananmen on 3–4 June 1989 has aroused many negative reactions throughout the whole world. Only Communism can provide the political platform to give legitimacy and authority to the aged leaders in Beijing. Therefore the comments on

[65] For the party's control on world religion please see 'Document 19'.
[66] *South China Morning Post, Hong Kong Standard, Ming Pao* (22 April 1990).

Communism by the Holy Father will be seen as very irritating and unfriendly in Beijing.

For Catholics, even before the 4 June massacre, the appearance of 'Document 3' had put the Catholic church back in the small cubicle of confinement, as if matters had returned to the repressive times of Mao's era. It appeared as though the wheel had come full circle even before the massacre of Tiananmen. Thus, one has reason to believe that the CCP has decided to control everything within its boundaries, including religion, and exercise its magisterium even on divine matters. Some China observers have remarked that China's open door policy is being carried on but with two steps forwards and one step backwards. If this is true in socio-economic life how much more it is true in religious policy.

The wave of reform and liberation is sweeping across the Soviet Union's Central Asia, whose people have a shared culture and religion with Iran and Xinjiang rather than with the Russians. The restoration of Islamic practices, inspired by their counterparts in Central Asia, without the permission of Beijing was the major cause of church-state tension of the Xinjiang Muslim minorities which resulted in bloodshed.[67] The riot in Lhasa, the capital of Tibet, was caused by discontent among Tibetans, especially among Buddhist monks and nuns, and is the result of the struggle between Beijing and the Dalai Lama for teaching authority over Tibetans.

Over the past decade, Beijing has granted a limited amount of freedom in religious activities, during which period the state's image and its foreign relations have been improved, but the party from the beginning has never been prepared to allow the doctrinal and administrative control of religion to slip from its grip. The detention of Catholic leaders, the ruthless crushing of riots in Tibet and Xinjiang repeatedly happened in the 1950s as well as in the 1980s for the same reasons: some Chinese Catholics and some Xinjiang Muslims as well as Tibetan Buddhists want freedom of religious expression which is not allowed by the party. All this reveals that China is determined to guard the teaching authority even in matters relating to the Supreme Divinity with whom the party claims that it has little association and in whom the Communists proclaim they have no belief.

In Chinese history, the emperor of each dynasty called himself the 'son of heaven' and represented the Supreme Divine Being to

[67] 'Piety and patriotism', *Far Eastern Economic Review*, 24 May 1990: 32. SWB FE/0752 B2/6, SWB FE/0751 B2/4 B2/3, SWB FE/0760 B2/1.

command every aspect of life of the subjects in his domain. And 'religion' in Chinese is translated as teaching (jiao); Buddhism is translated as Fao Jiao (the teaching of Buddha), Catholicism is Tian Zhu Jiao (the teaching of the Master of Heaven). If these religious teachings did not pose any socio-political or cultural threat to the regime and could be circumscribed by orthodox Confucianism then the emperor would not ban them as such. That was why Buddhism as practised in China had evolved to become quite different from that in India, its place of origin. Catholicism has a long history in Europe of converting pagans. Magisterium has been an important part of this largest branch of Christianity. The Pope has long been called as the 'Vicar of Christ'. The clash of teaching authority was inevitable between the son of heaven and the vicar of Christ if they claimed for themselves absolute power to teach their subjects their own ideologies. If the clash were not over the issue of Chinese rites it would have been over other issues. In the late Qing period, the clash of teaching authority was at a lower level of society between the missionaries and local intellectuals who represented the hierarchy and were sent to teach the mass of the people.

In the KMT period, the incident of the Anti-Christian Movement in the 1920s was the continuity of anti-imperialism and the anti-foreign mood of late Qing. The Movement to Restore Educational Rights 1924–8 was the transfer of the right to educate students from the hands of Christian missionaries into the hands of the government. Though the KMT government itself did not take the initiative, it was radicals, prompted by Chinese nationalism, who encouraged this movement towards civic education and the elimination of foreign educational institutes.[68] The purpose of the movement is very clear; it was an attempt by the Chinese government and its intellectuals to get Christians to surrender the right to teach their juveniles.

In the People's Republic of China one cannot expect that religion will be treated kindly. Both Mao Zedong and Deng Xiaoping are Marxist as well as Chinese and patriots. Christianity being contradictory to atheism is distasteful to Marxists. The Chinese, who should embrace patriotism, should not have a liking for any foreign religion. As those who are at the highest pinnacle of power to command the whole nation, and entrusted the dictatorship to the

---

[68] For the detail of the Movement of Restoring Educational Rights see Jessie Gregory Lutz' *Chinese Politics and Christian Missions* (Indiana: Cross Cultural, 1988), pp. 91–129.

ruling party – the CCP – there is no way that Chinese political leaders can share part of the teaching authority with Catholics. In Mao's era, the long winter which all world religions such as Buddhism, Islam and Christianity experienced, can speak for itself. Even in the modernisation period, Deng desperately needs means to promote both internally and externally the modernisation programme, thus a limited degree of freedom has been granted to religions including Catholicism. 'Document 19' can be seen as the boundary of that freedom or the bottom-line drawn by the state on its religious toleration.

Then the specially tailored 'Document 3' issued in February 1989 was the second warning from the state that Chinese Catholics have gone too far, as judged by party standards. Therefore discipline had to be tightened up but in a relaxed socio-economic context until the crackdown of the 4 June pro-democratic movement.

Before the crackdown of the non-conformist students, the nonconformist Catholic leaders were asked to toe the party line, to be docile to the teaching authority of the party. Unfortunately the nonconformist Catholic leaders insisted on being obedient to the teaching authority of the church, which was why the participants of the Zhangerce meeting and related persons were arrested. So long as the PRC carries on with Communist party dictatorship as its political orientation, the clash between the teaching authority of religion and state will continue if it does not accelerate. Since the end of the Second World War, whether in Capitalist regimes or under communist rule, the Christian church has been the supporter of big mass movements, while Islam can inspire its adherents to die for the 'Holy War'. These two forces together with the Buddhist Tibetans who have continuously challenged the teaching authority of Communism will continue to pose the same threat to the CCP's teaching authority in days to come. Thus, the clash between the teaching authority of the church and state will be repeated again and again. The normalisation of Sino-Vatican relations can only ease the pain of the people torn apart by this clash of authority.

15 AUGUST, 1990   BEATRICE LEUNG

Letter from a Catholic in Qinghai

Dear Brother & Sister of Radio Veritas,

First, I would like to thank the Lord for having protected us in all our difficulties and trials. For a long time I did not write to you but we were always together through the airwaves and your voice. Through the good evangelical news, I was consoled in my sorrow and was shown the way during the time I got lost. I sincerely thank the Lord for His continuous providing.

I did not write during the past months because my schedule was quite tight. I was very busy. But during the Chinese New Year, I took the opportunity for a few days vacation. I went to a far-flung village to visit other Christians. They were so eager to see a pastor. I saw how strongly they are perserving in their faith, keeping their Christian principles in life. When I saw them like sheep without a shepherd, I felt so ashamed – I could not fulfil the duty of a pastor to them because of my other assignment. Besides, often, after leaving the places I visited, the government people would start to investigate why I was there, what I did or talked about, and cause some troubles for the people.

In Qinghai Province, because it is so far away and relatively more backward than other provinces, the directives concerning freedom of religion are not yet implemented (this is not the case in other places). Since I am a cadre, and have a diploma, I was not very much bothered; but I could not do as much pastoral work as I would want to.

There are two old nuns who are very faithful to the Church. They firmly refuse to join the CPA. But there are two other nuns who joined the CPA and they even tried to convince me and the two old nuns to join them. But we refused. A certain Fr. Yang was sentenced to four years imprisonment because he refused them.

Dear brothers and sisters, many of us now belong to the Silenced Church, as mentioned in your broadcast. But we are determined to keep our faith, to be faithful to the Pope and our Mother Church. We may shed our blood and die, but that will not change our resolution. I am always ready if that day should come. For the unity of our Church and for Jesus Christ, I am always ready to sacrifice everything. Jesus, as in the boat, is not sleeping; but testing our faith. I have full confidence in Him. I will not retreat. I will not despair or give up hope. I will fight until the end. For thirty years, God has taken care of me especially when there were dangers and I came out unharmed. He loves me. I should be a witness to His truth. I have no reason to betray Him, to harm Him.

Brothers, to tell you the truth, I am lonely. You are my best friends. To listen to your broadcasts of the holy words of God is a must for me, an essential part of my daily life. Through you, God showed me the way, gave me the strength. I want to walk on the road of virtue, but I am so weak and so sinful. I know very little Catholic doctrine. I need your help and your prayers in asking God to give me His grace in order to follow Him. I hope that at the end of my earthly life, I can say the same thing as St. Paul said: 'I have fought a good fight, I have won the race, I have kept my faith . . .' The road ahead is rough. Our work is heavy and full of difficulties. I am so small and weak but I am not frightened. With God's help, all this can be overcome. I am a tool in God's hand. Any way He wants to use me. He may. My only request: that He does not leave me.

Name Withheld

P.S. Please greet in my name the brothers and sisters of the Chinese Programme of Radio Vatican.

The English translation of 'Document 19' issued by the CCP Central Committee in 1982 (classified)

The Chinese Communist Central Committee on Printing and Distributing the Circular concerning:

'THE BASIC POLICY AND STANDPOINT OUR COUNTRY SHOULD HAVE ON THE RELIGIOUS QUESTION DURING THIS PERIOD OF SOCIALISM.'

To:

All provincial party committees;
All city party committees;
All party committees of the autonomous regions;
The party committees in the large military areas;
The party committees in the provincial military areas;
The party committees with the field armies;
The party committees with the central departments under the Party's Central Committee and State Council;
All leading Party groups within the ministries and commissions of the State organs;
All central headquarters of the Military Commission of the Communist Party's Central Committee;
All party committees within the military;
All party committees within civil organizations:

The Secretariat has made a recent study of the religious question, and has drawn up a document entitled:

'THE BASIC POLICY AND STANDPOINT OUR COUNTRY SHOULD HAVE ON THE RELIGIOUS QUESTION DURING THIS PERIOD OF SOCIALISM.'

This document sums up in a more systematic way our party's historical experience, both positive and negative aspects, of the religious question since the founding of the People's Republic. It clarifies the basic standpoint and policy our Party has taken towards this religious question.

After each provincial, urban and autonomous regional committee, as well as each party committee within the Central departments under the Central Committee and State Council, along with each party group within the ministries and commissions of the State organs has received this document, they must carry out a serious investigative study and discussion, as well as supervise and check up in good time on the implementation of each item of this religious policy.

The Central Committee considers that such a summing up of the religious question can make us more aware at this time of the actual situation. The party also needs to make further progress in this systematic summing up of experiences in all other aspects of its work as well as in other areas and departments. Since the smashing of the 'gang of four', and especially since the third plenary session of the eleventh Central Committee, our party has gained very important results from its summing up of its own historical experiences. We have a concentrated expression of this in the sixth session of the eleventh Central Committee when they passed the 'Resolution On The Several Historical Questions Facing Our Party Since The Foundation Of The People's Republic'. This marked the fact that our party in its ideological leadership, had already completed its historical task of restoring social order. But from another aspect, i.e. viewing our party's work on all fronts, and in all areas and departments, we must say that this work of summing up our experiences is yet insufficient.

Therefore, the Central Secretariat hopes that party committees on each level, mainly, the Central Committees on the provincial, urban and autonomous regional levels, as well as the ministries and commissions of the State organs – along with party committees and party organizations, – concentrate their principal efforts within the coming 2 to 3 years on completing the prerequisites for doing well the task at hand. They should make further efforts in seriously carrying out an investigative study on those areas and departments for which they are responsible, systematically summing up the positive and negative aspects of their historical experiences, forming a series of viewpoints and methods which are suitable to the conditions within their areas and departments, and which intimately tie in theory and practise. The Central Secretariat believes that only by conscientiously grasping hold of this key link, and expending painstaking efforts, can one definitely come out with new results, and very effectively raise the ideological and theoretical level of all party members. Thus they will gain accurate and effective methods of work and open up a brand new era as our country, facing the remaining 20 years of this century, goes about the great task of building up socialism.

The Central Committee of the Chinese Communist Party

March 31, 1982

'THE BASIC POLICY AND STANDPOINT OUR COUNTRY
SHOULD HAVE ON THE RELIGIOUS QUESTION DURING THIS
PERIOD OF SOCIALISM'. (March 1982)

I

Religion is an historical phenomenon pertaining to a definite period of
human development. It has its own cycle of emergence, development and
demise. Religious faith, religious sentiment and religious ceremonies as well
as religious organizations which fit in with this faith and sentiment, are all
products of the history of society. The earliest emergence of the religious
mentality reflected conditions during which the forces of production were
at a very low level. It expressed the sense of awe of primitive man as he
faced natural phenomena. After evolution towards a class society, the
clearest reason for the existence and development of religion lay in the fact
that men were controlled by certain blind forces in society alienating them,
and from which they were unable to escape. Another reason was the fear
and despair of the working classes as they faced the immense misery created
by the oppressive social system. A third reason was that the oppressing class
needed to use religion as an opiate and as an important and vital means of
controlling the masses. Now in a socialist society, with the extermination of
the oppressive system and the oppressing class, the class origin behind the
existence of religion already has been cut off at its roots. But owing to the
fact that the development of people's awareness always falls behind the
actual social situation, old ideas and old customs cannot be completely
wiped out within a short period of time. Rather a long process of struggle is
needed in order to give maximum development to the social forces of
production, to insure the maximum amount of material riches and to
establish social democracy in the highest degree, as well as to develop
education, culture, science and the arts to their furthest limits. Because we
cannot free ourselves within a short period of time from various hardships
brought on by large-scale natural and man-made calamities and because
class struggle still exists within certain limits and given the complex
international situation, religion will, therefore, still have influence over a
part of the people in a socialist society. So it will necessarily continue to exist
for a long period. Eventually, as human history will show, religion will
disappear. But this will happen only after all objective conditions have been
met, having passed through the period of socialism and a long development
of communism. All party members must have a clearheaded awareness of
the protracted existence of religion under socialist conditions. Those who
think that, following upon the establishment of the socialist system and with
a certain degree of economic and cultural progress, religion will die out
within a short period, are not being realistic. Those who think they can rely
upon administrative decrees or other coercive measures to wipe out
religious thinking and practices with one blow, are even further from the

basic standpoint Marxism takes towards the religious question. They are entirely wrong and will do no small harm.

I I

Our country has many kinds of religion. Buddhism already has a history of around 2,000 years. The Daoists' history is over 3,700 years. Islamism has been in our country over 1,300 years. Catholicism and Protestantism mostly developed after the Opium Wars. As for the number of religious adherents, we have at the time of the liberation about 8,000,000 Muslims. At present there are about 10,000,000 believers. (The chief reason for this increment is owing to the increase in population of the 10 minority ethnic groups believing in Islamism.) At the liberation the Catholic Church had about 2,700,000 adherents; now they have more than 3,000,000. Protestants at the time of the liberation had about 700,000 adherents; now they have about 3,000,000. Buddhism (including Lamaism) has almost the entire population among the ethnic minorities of Tibet, Mongolia and Liao Ning are religious believers. Among the Han race, Buddhism and Daoism still have a considerable influence at present. Naturally, out of the total population of our country, especially among the Han race which has for the largest number of people, those who believe in supernatural beings are a considerable number. But the proportion of those who actually adhere to religion is not very great. If we compare this number at the time of the liberation with the present overall number of religious believers, we will see that it has increased somewhat, but if we compare it with the absolute growth proportion of the total population, then there has been a decline. We must fully reckon with the fact that the religious question has a definite complexity. To sum up we can say that in the old China during the long feudal period, as well as the last 100 years or more of a half feudal and a half colonial society, all the religions in our country had been controlled and used by the ruling classes. This resulted in producing significantly negative results. Within our country, the class of feudal land owners, feudal lords, and the reactionary war lords along with the bureaucratic capitalist class, mainly controlled the leadership of the Buddhists, Daoists and Muslims. Afterwards foreign colonial and imperialist forces mainly controlled the Catholic and Protestant churches. After liberation there was a thorough transformation of the social-economic system and a major reform was made of the religious system, and so the state of religion within our country has already undergone a radical change. The contradictions which we find in religion now mainly belong to the category of contradictions contained within the people. Nonetheless this religious question will continue to exist for a long period of time within certain limits. It has a definite mass character, and in several areas is interwoven with the question of ethnic nationalities. It is also influenced by some class struggles and complex international elements. Therefore, this religious question will continue to have an important meaning which we cannot underestimate. The question is: can we handle this religious question properly as we work towards national stability and ethnic unity; as we develop our international relations while resisting the intrusion of hostile forces from abroad; and as we go on constructing a socialist civilization which has both material and spiritual values? This, then, demands that the party committees on each level, as they face up to the religious question must adopt an attitude which is in accord with what Lenin said: 'to be especially alert', 'to be very strict', and 'to thoroughly think things out'. To over-exaggerate the seriousness and complexity of the question, and so panic would be wrong; to ignore the existence and complexity of the actual question, and so lower ones guard and let matters drift, would also be wrong.

III

Since the founding of the People's Republic, our party has walked a winding road in its dealings with the religious question. In summary we can say that during the 17 years following the establishment of the new China up until the 'Great Cultural Revolution', our party, under the direction of the Central Committee correct policy, both general and specific, towards religion, had achieved important results, though there were also some important faults as well. We did away with imperialist influences within the churches, and promoted the independent, self-governing autonomy of the churches as well as the 'Three Selfs Movement' (self-propagation, self-government and self-support). We made Catholics and Protestants cease being tools of imperialist aggression and become an independent, self-governing, autonomous religious enterprise for Chinese believers. We abolished the special rights and the oppressive, exploitative system of a feudal religion. We exposed and attacked those reactionaries and bad elements who hid under the cloak of religion. We made Buddhists, Daoists and Muslims break away from the control and manipulation of the reactionary classes. We proclaimed and carried out a policy of freedom of religious belief, enabling the broad masses of religious believers not only to achieve a complete political and economic emancipation along side with each of the national ethnic groups, but also enabled them to begin to enjoy the right of freedom of religious belief. We carried out a policy of winning over, uniting and educating religious personages, and thus united together the broad masses of patriotic religious personages. We also assisted and supported religious people to launch friendly movements on the international front. These have brought about good, positive effects. But, since 1957 'leftist' errors in this religious area gradually developed, and in the mid-sixties progressed even further. Especially during the 'Great Cultural Revolution' Lin Biao, Jiang Qing and others in the anti-revolutionary gang with ulterior motives made use of these 'leftist' errors, and wantonly trampled upon Marxist–Leninist–Maoist thought concerning the scientific theory on the religious question. They totally repudiated the party's correct policy towards religion which it had adopted since the founding of our People's Republic. They radically did away with the work the party had done on the religious question. They forcibly forbade legitimate religious activities of the mass of religious believers. They treated patriotic religious personages, as well as the ordinary mass of religious believers, as 'targets for dictatorship', and fabricated a host of wrongs and injustices and pinned these upon religious personages. They even misinterpreted some customs and practices of the ethnic minorities as religious superstition, which they then forcibly forbade. In some particular places they even repressed the mass of religious believers, and destroyed national unity. They used violent measures against religion with the result that this enabled religious movements to go underground and owing to the disorganized state of affairs to make some headway. A minority of anti-revolutionaries and bad elements made use of this situation, and under the cover of religious activities boldly carried out illegal criminal activities as well as destructive anti-revolutionary movements.

After the smashing of Jiang Qing's anti-revolutionary clique, and especially after our party held its third Plenary session of the 11th Central Committee, its correct aim and policy towards the religious question was progressively restored. In implementing and carrying out our religious policy, we have opened both Buddhist and Daoist temples, as well as churches and places for religious activities. We have restored the organizations and activities of the religious patriotic societies. We have won over, unified and educated religious personages. We have strengthened the unity between believers and non-believers in each ethnic group of people. We have righted wrongs and have launched a movement for friendly international relations between religious believers as well as resisted the intrusions and such like things of hostile religious forces from abroad. In all this, we have undertaken a large number of tasks, obtaining remarkable results. In this new historical period, the party's and the government's basic task in its religious work will be to firmly implement and carry out its policy on the freedom of religious belief; to consolidate and expand the Patriotic political alliance in each religious ethnic group; to strengthen their education on patriotism and socialism, and to bring into play the positive elements among them in order to build a modern and powerful socialist state, and to complete the great task of unifying the country as well as to oppose hegemonism and to strive together to protect and preserve world peace. Now in order to implement and carry out the party's religious policy totally and correctly, the main thing at hand to do is to oppose 'leftist' erroneous tendencies. And at the same time we must be on our guard to forestall and put down erroneous tendencies which would just let things slide along. All Party members, Party committees on all levels, and especially those departments on all levels which are responsible for religious work, must conscientiously sum up and assimilate the historical experience the party has had since the founding of the People's Republic in the work on the religious question. They must consider this question from both its positive and negative aspects. They must make further progress in knowing well and even mastering the objective law governing the emergence, development and demise of religion. They should overcome every obstacle and difficulty and resolutely see to it that the religious policy of the party stays on the course laid out for it by the scientific doctrine of Marx, Lenin and Mao.

IV

The basic policy the party has adopted towards the religious question is to respect and to protect the freedom of religious belief. This is a long-term policy; it is a policy that we must continually carry out and implement up until that future time when religion will of itself disappear. What do we mean when we say: the Freedom of Religious Belief? We mean that since every citizen has the freedom to believe in religion, he also has the freedom not to believe in religion. He has the freedom to believe in this particular religion as well as the freedom to believe in that particular religion. And within one religion itself he has the freedom to believe in this particular sect as well as the freedom to believe in that particular sect. He who in the past believed in no religion has now the freedom to believe in religion. Likewise he who in the past believed in religion has now the freedom not to believe in religion. We Communists are atheists. We must be unremitting in propagating atheism. Yet at the same time we must understand that to simply make use of coercive measures to deal with people's ideological questions, and those belonging to the spiritual world – and this includes the question of religious belief – will not only produce no results, but will be extremely harmful. We must understand furthermore that in the present stage of affairs, the difference that exists between the mass of believers and non-believers is purely secondary. So if we one-sidedly emphasize this difference, even to the point of giving to it prime importance – for example, by discriminating against and attacking the mass of religious believers, while neglecting and denying the fact that the basic political and economic welfare of the mass of both religious believers and non-believers is the same – then we forget that the party's basic task is to unite all the people (and this includes the broad masses of believers and non-believers alike) in order that all strive to construct a modern, powerful, socialist state. To act otherwise would only increase the estrangement between the mass of believers and non-believers as well as incite and aggravate religious fanaticism. This would result in serious consequences for our socialist enterprise. Therefore, our party bases its policy of the freedom of religious belief on the theory constructed by Marxist-Leninism. It is the only correct religious policy that genuinely conforms to the people's welfare.

Naturally, as we go about the process of implementing and carrying out this policy which emphasizes the guarantee of freedom which people have to believe in religion, we also must, at the same time, emphasize the guarantee of freedom that people have not to believe in religion. These are but two indispensable aspects of the same question. Any action which forces a non-believer to believe in religion, just as any action which forces a believer not to believe in religion are both infringements upon others freedom to religious belief and, as such, are both grave errors and not to be tolerated at all. Guaranteeing freedom of religion not only should not hinder, but should also strengthen the party's efforts to disseminate a scientific education as well as strengthen its propaganda against super-stition. Furthermore, it must emphasize and point out that the central point at issue in the policy on the freedom of religious belief is precisely to see to it that this question on the freedom of religious belief becomes a question of each citizen's personal freedom to choose as he likes, his own private affair. Now the political power in a socialist state can in no way be used to promote any one religion, nor can it in any way be used to forbid any one religion, as long as there is question only of legitimate religious beliefs and practices. At the same time religion will not at all be permitted to meddle in the administrative and juridical affairs of state, nor intervene in the schools or public education. It will be absolutely forbidden to force anyone to become a member of a church, to become a monk or nun, or go to the temples and monasteries to study scripture, especially if they are youths under 18 years of age. In no way will religion be permitted to recover its special feudal rights which have been abolished or to return to that system where religion exploited and oppressed others. Nor will religion be permit-ted in any way to make use of religious pretexts to oppose the party's leadership and the socialist system, to wreck national unity or the unity binding together ethnic groups within the country.

To sum up, our basic starting point and the firm foundation for the way we handle the religious question and implement and carry out our policy of the freedom of religious belief lies in the fact that we wish to unite the mass of believers and non-believers, and enable them to centre all their will and strength on this goal common to all: to build a modern, powerful socialist state. Any action or speech that deviates in the least from this basic line is completely erroneous, and must be firmly resisted and opposed by both the party and the people.

V

To win over, unite and educate persons in religious circles is primarily the task belonging to those professional religious personnel. It is also the essence of the party's work on religion and a most important condition and prerequisite for the party to implement and carry out its religious policy. At present throughout the country, there are about 59,000 of these professional religious personnel in all. Of this total number about 27,000 are Buddhist monks and nuns, including lamas. More than 2,600 are Daoist priests and nuns. Professional religious personnel among the Muslims number about 20,000. There are about 3,400 Catholic professional religious personnel, while there are about 5,900 Protestant professional religious personnel. Owing to the natural attrition of many years the present number of professional religious personnel as compared to the first years after liberation has greatly decreased. The political situation behind their class origin, experience, beliefs and ideology is quite diverse. But we can say in brief, that by far the great majority of them are patriotic, keep the law and support the socialist system. It is only a very small minority that oppose the constitution and socialism even to the extent of colluding with foreign anti-revolutionaries and other bad elements. Many of these professional religious personnel not only maintain intimate spiritual ties with the mass of religious believers, but they also have an important influence over the spiritual life of the masses which should not be underestimated. Moreover as they carry out their more formal religious duties, they also perform work which serves labour in many ways and benefits society. For example, they safeguard Buddhist and Daoist temples and churches as well as protect historical religious relics. They engage in agriculture and afforestation. They carry out the study of religion, etc. Therefore, we definitely must pay sufficient attention to all these persons in religious circles, and primarily to all professional religious personnel, unite them and help them make progress. We must unrelentingly yet patiently push forward their patriotism and law-abiding spirit, their support of socialism as well as their support of and education in national and ethnic unity. In the case of Catholics and Protestants we must still strengthen their education in the independent self-governing autonomy of their churches.

We must make appropriate arrangements for the livelihood of these professional religious personnel, and conscientiously carry out what pertains to our policy. This is especially true regarding well-known public figures and the intellectuals. Here we must speedily implement our policy of supplying them with an appropriate remuneration. We must pay very close attention to and re-examine those injustices perpetrated against persons in religious circles as well as the mass of unbelievers which have not yet been redressed. We must redress them in accordance with the facts, especially those more serious injustices which can have grave consequences. These we must give special attention and resolve them within a definite period of time. We must foster in each religion a large number of fervent patriots who will accept the leadership of the party and the government, walk firmly on the road of socialism, and safeguard national and ethnic unity. They should be learned in religious matters and capable of keeping close links with the representatives of the religious masses. Furthermore we must organize respective persons in religious circles according to their different situations and capabilities to take part in productive labour, in serving society, and in the study of religious science. They should also take part in patriotic political movements and friendly international exchanges. All this is done in order to mobilize the positive elements among these religious circles to serve the socialist modernization enterprise.

In addition, with regard to those older religious professionals whose term of imprisonment has been completed or whose term at labour reform has ended, as well as those who have not yet been approved by religious organizations to engage in professional religious activities, each case must be dealt with as actual conditions show. Those who prove to be politically reliable, arc patriotic and law abiding, and are versed in religious matters can, upon examination and approval by the patriotic religious organizations, be allowed to perform religious duties: as for the rest, they should be provided with the means to earn a living.

From a world outlook, Marxism is incompatible with any system professing belief in God. But from the outlook of political action, Marxists and patriotic religious believers can, indeed must fully unite together in common effort to form a united front to build up a modern socialist structure. This United Front must become an important constitutive element of the party as she, during this period of socialism, guides the patriotic united front in all its vast extension.

VI

To make equitable arrangements for places of religious activities is to implement the party's policy on religion, and is an important material condition for enabling these religious activities to become normalized. At the beginning of the liberation there were about 100,000 places for religious activities in all. At present there are about 30,000. Included in this figure are Buddhist and Daoist Temples, churches, meeting places of simple construction, as well as those places voluntarily built by religious believers themselves. The question now at hand is that we must take effective measures, according to various circumstances, to make equitable arrangements for these places of religious activities. We must restore step by step and in a planned way a number of Buddhist and Daoist temples and churches in some large- and some medium-sized cities, in those religious places which are historically famous, and in those areas where religious believers reside in compact communities, especially where ethnic minorities live. Those famous Buddhist and Daoist temples and churches which enjoy both national and international prestige as well as possess cultural and historical value, must, depending upon conditions, be progressively res- tored as far as is possible. But where believers are few in number, with little influence and in those places where Buddhist and Daoist temples have already been demolished, then we must work out measures to suit the actual conditions and do things simply and thriftly. The principle that we follow is whatever will be a help to production and the livelihood of the masses. After consultation with the mass of religious believers and import- ant persons in religious circles, and based on the willingness of believers to cooperate, we should set aside several places for religious activities which can be simply constructed. In the process of restoring places for religious activities, outside of getting government approval and an appropriation, we must not make use of the financial resources of either country or collectively to build or repair these temples and churches. And we must take particular care against the indiscriminate building and repairing of temples in rural villages.

We should also direct the voluntary contributions offered by the mass of religious believers for reconstruction work, so as to build as little as possible. Much less should we go in for large-scale construction work lest we consume large sums of money and material goods as well as manpower and thus obstruct the building up of the socialist material and spiritual civilization. Of course we should not demolish existing structures. Concerning these older structures we should fully consult with the mass of religious believers and important persons in religious circles to reach a satisfactory solution based on the actual situation.

All those normal religious activities which are held in places designated for religious services as well as those that, according to religious custom, take place in the homes of the believers themselves – such services as worshipping Buddha, chanting scriptures, burning incense, praying, explaining scripture, preaching, saying Mass, baptizing, initiating into monkhood or nunhood, fasting, celebrating religious festivals, annointing the sick and dying with oil, holding requiem services, etc. – are all to be conducted by religious organizations and religious believers themselves. They enjoy the protection of law and no one at all should interfere with these activities. With the approval of the responsible government department, Buddhist and Daoist temples and churches can sell a certain quantity of religious reading matter, religious articles and religious works of art. As for Protestants meeting to hold religious services in their homes, this in principle should not be allowed, yet this prohibition should not be too rigidly enforced. Rather persons in the patriotic religious organizations should make special efforts to persuade the mass of religious believers to make more appropriate arrangements.

All places for religious services are under the administrative control of the bureau of religious affairs, but the religious organizations and the professional religious personnel themselves are responsible for their management. Religious organizations should see to the arranging of the time for religious services, their scope and their frequency. They should avoid interfering with the social order, and the times set aside for production and labour. No one should go to places for religious services to carry out atheistic propaganda, nor to incite arguments among the mass of religious believers as to whether God exists or not. In like manner, no religious organization or believer should propagate or preach religion outside of those places designated for religious services; nor make propaganda for religion nor hand out religious tracts or other religious reading matter which has not obtained approval for publication from the responsible government department.

In order to insure further normalization of religious activities, the government should hereafter, in accordance with due process of law, consult fully with representatives from religious circles in order to draw up feasable religions legislation that can be carried out in practise.

Important Buddhist and Daoist temples and churches which are famous for their scenic beauty, are not only places for religious activities, but are also cultural institutions possessing important historical value. So with regard to these temples and churches, responsible religious organizations and professional religious persons should be charged with making painstaking efforts to safeguard them by seeing that these monuments receive good care, that the buildings are kept in good repair, and that the environment is fully protected so that the surroundings are clean, peaceful and quiet, suitable for tourism. The income derived from alms and donations which these temples and churches receive can, under the direction of the responsible government department and the religious organizations, be used mainly for the upkeep. A part of this income can even be used as a stimulus and reward for those professional religious people in charge who have been outstanding in this regard.

VII

To give full play to the function which the patriotic religious organizations play is to implement the party's religious policy and is an important organizational guarantee for the normalization of religious activities. Altogether there are eight national patriotic religious organizations: there is the Chinese Buddhist Association, the Chinese Daoist Association, the Chinese Islamic Association, the Chinese Catholic Patriotic Association, The Chinese Catholic Religious Affairs Committee, the Chinese Catholic Bishops Conference, the Chinese Protestant 'Three Selfs' Patriotic Movement, and the Chinese Protestant Association. Besides these there are a number of social groups and local organizations having a religious character. The basic task of these patriotic religious associations is to assist the party and the government carry out and implement its religious policy on the freedom of religious belief, to help the broad mass of religious believers and personages in religious circles to continually raise their awareness of patriotism and socialism, to represent the lawful rights and interests of religious circles, to organize normal religious activities and to manage well religious affairs. All patriotic religious organizations must follow the party's and the government's leadership. Party and government cadres in turn must become adept in supporting and helping religious organizations to solve their own problems. They should not monopolize and do things these organizations should do themselves. Only in this way, can we fully develop their positive characteristics and allow these patriotic organizations to play their proper role, and enable them, within constitutional and lawful limits, voluntarily to perform useful work. Thus they become in reality a religious group having positive influence, and can act as a bridge between themselves and the party and government as it carries out its task of winning over, uniting and educating personages in religious circles.

Furthermore, in order to enable each religion to meet in a satisfactory way its expenses needed in carrying out its program of self-support and self-management, we must conscientiously carry out the stipulated policy governing income from house property and rentals. As for the contribution and donations made by believers, there will be no need to interfere as long as they are freely offered and are small in quantity. But we should convince professional religious personnel that private possession of religious income from temples and churches is not allowed, and that any action that forces contributions to be made is forbidden.

VIII

To plan the training and education of the younger generation of patriotic religious personnel will have decisive meaning for the future image of our country's religious organizations. We should not only continue to win over, unite and educate the present generation of persons in religious circles, but we should also help each religious organization set up religious seminaries, to train well new professional religious personnel. The task of these seminaries is to create a contingent of young patriotic religious personnel who, from the political aspect, fervently love their motherland and support the party's leadership and the socialist system, and possess furthermore sufficient religious knowledge. These seminaries should hold entrance examinations and admit students from those youths who are patriotic, who wish to devote themselves seriously to this religious profession and who have reached a certain level of cultural development. They should not forcibly enrol those persons who are unwilling to undertake this profession or who lack the necessary cultural foundation. Those young professional religious personnel who prove unfitted for this profession should be transferred elsewhere.

All of these young professional religious personnel should continually heighten their awareness of patriotism and socialism, and make efforts to improve their cultural level and their religious knowledge. They should loyally implement the party's religious policy. They should show respect to all those upright patriotic professional religious personnel of the older generation, and conscientiously learn and imitate their good qualities. These older and upright patriotic professional religious personnel should in their turn cherish these younger patriotic professional religious personnel. In this way these young patriotic religious peronnel will become integrated into the patriotic progressive elements of the religious world, and both become, under the leadership of our party, the mainstay which will insure that religious organizations go in the correct direction.

IX

Our party proclaims and implements a policy of freedom of religious belief. But of course this does not mean that Communist party members can freely believe in religion. The policy of freedom of religious belief is directed towards the citizens of our country; it is not applicable to party members. The difference between a Communist party member and the average citizen lies in the fact that he is a member of a Marxist political party. There can be no doubt at all that this party must be an atheistic party, and not a theistic one. Our party has on many previous occasions clearly stated: a Communist cannot be a believer in religion; he cannot take part in religious activities. Any member who persists for a long time in going against this prescription should be told to leave the party. This prescription is altogether correct, and as far as the party is concerned, it will continue in the future to insist on it being carried out and implemented. The present question is: the implementing of this prescription among those ethnic minorities whose people are basically all religious believers, must meet the actual situation, and so make use of the proper measures and not over simplify matters.

We must realize that although a considerable number of communist praty members among these ethnic minorities loyally implement the party line, do positive work for the party, and obey its discipline, yet they cannot completely shake off all religious influence. Towards these party members, party organizations should in no way proceed to cast them aside, but, while taking measures to develop more fully their positive political activities, should at the same time patiently and meticulously carry out ideological work, helping them gradually to acquire a dialectical and historical materialistic world view, and gradually shake off the restraints of a religious ideology. Obviously as we go about expanding our membership we must take great care not to be rushed into recruiting those who are devout religious believers having strong religious sentiments. As for that very small number of party members who have shown an extreme perversity in that they not only believe in religion, but have also joined with those who have stirred up religious fanaticism, even to the point of using this religious fanaticism to oppose the four basic principles, to attack the party line, its aim and policy, and wreck national integrity and ethnic unity, persons as these have already completely departed from the standpoint fundamental to party members. If after having undergone education and criticism, they continue to persist in their erroneous position, or feign compliance, then we must resolutely remove them from the party. If they have committed any unlawful criminal acts, then these must be investigated to fix responsibility before the law.

Even though those party members, who live at the grass roots level among those ethnic minorities whose people basically all believe in religion, have already freed themselves from all religious belief, yet if they were to refuse to take part in any of those traditional marriage or funeral ceremonies or mass festivals which contain some religious significance, then they would find themselves cut off and isolated from the masses. Therefore, those prescriptions which forbid party members who live among these ethnic minorities from joining in religious activities, must be dealt with according to the concrete circumstances in order to let party members continue to maintain close links with the masses. Although many of these traditional marriage and funeral ceremonies as well as mass festivals among these ethnic minorities still contain some religious significance, and have religious tradition as source, yet they have already essentially become part of the make-up of ethnic tradition and customs. So as long as our comrades, especially those living at the grass roots level, note clearly on the ideological level the line marking off religious belief, then they can in their daily lives show appropriate respect to and go along with these ethnic customs and traditions. Of course this does not mean that those customs and traditions which prove harmful to the physical and mental health of the masses should not be subjected to an appropriate reform in accord with the desire of the majority of the people. But to lump together these ethnic customs and traditions without any further distinctions, is not right and will be harmful to ethnic unity and the correct handling of the religious question.

All our party comrades must profoundly realize that our country is a socialist state made up of many ethnic minorities. In this question on the relationship between religion and the ethnic minorities, each minority and each religion is differently situated. Some ethnic minorities basically have all the people believing in one particular religion, for example, Islamism and Lamaism. Among these peoples the question of religion and ethnicity is intermingled. But among the Han race, Buddhism, Daoism, Catholicism and Protestantism have basically no relationship with ethnic background. Therefore, we must become adept in distinguishing very concretely the particular situation of each ethnic race and of each religion. Likewise we must become adept in objectively sizing up the differences and relationships between the ethnic question and that of religion, and so correctly proceed in handling them. Certainly we must be vigilant and oppose any use of religious fanaticism which divides our people, as well as any words or deeds which damage unity among our ethnic races. If in the present great struggle in which we strive to lead such a great nation as ours with so many ethnic races onward to become a modern socialist state, our party cannot with a clear mind and a firm step master this particular question, then we shall not be able with any success to unite our peoples to advance together towards this goal.

X

We are determined to safeguard all normal religious activities. At the same time we also mean to resolutely crack down on all those illegal criminal activities as well as those destructive anti-revolutionary ones which hide behind the facade of religion. Included in this crack down are all those superstitious practices which fall outside the scope of religion and are injurious to the national welfare as well as to the life and property of the people. We will severely punish according to law those anti-revolutionary elements as well as other criminal offenders who hide behind the facade of religion. If those former religious professionals, once their term of imprisonment is up and have been released, go back once again to engage in these criminal activities, then they will be punished again in accordance with the law. All those reactionary secret societies, sorcerers and witches, who had been banned, without exception will not be permitted to resume their activities. All those who spread fallacies to deceive people and all those who hoodwink people out of their money will, without exception, be severely punished in accordance with the law. Party cadres who profit by these unlawful activities to accumulate wealth, will be dealt with all the more severely. Finally all those who make their living by phenology, fortune telling and geomancy should be educated, warned and helped to earn their living through their own labour, and not engage again in these superstitious practises which only deceive people. Should they not obey, then they should be dealt with in accordance with the law.

As party committees on each level and pertinent government departments deal in law with all these active anti-revolutionary elements and other criminals who lurk within religious ranks, they must pay very close attention to the proper use of public opinion. They should make use of irrefutable facts to fully expose how these bad elements used religion to further their anti-revolutionary activities. In this way they should clearly delineate the line dividing normal religious activities from illegal criminal ones, pointing out that cracking down on these illegal criminal activities is not in the least to attack, but rather to protect normal religious activities. Only then can we successfully win over, unite and educate the broad mass of religious believers, and bring about the normalization of religious activities.

XI

Buddhism, Islamism, Catholicism and Protestantism hold a very important position among our national religions. At the same time they are ranked among some of the more important world religions. All of these have extensive influence in their societies. Catholicism and Protestantism are widespread in Europe, North America, Latin America as well as in other places. Buddhism is strong in Japan and South East Asia, while Islamism is spreading in several countries in Asia and Africa. Some of these religions are looked upon as state religions in a number of countries. At the present time as our country's international contacts increasingly expand, so also do these contacts increase among religious groups. This has an important meaning for extending our country's political influence. But at the same time there are reactionary religious forces from abroad, especially those imperialistic religious forces such as the Vatican and the Protestant foreign mission societies, who strive earnestly to use all possible occasions to carry on their efforts at infiltration 'to return again to the China mainland'. Our policy is one in which we will positively develop friendly international contacts with religions, but we will also firmly resist the infiltration from foreign hostile religious forces.

In accordance with our party's policy, religious persons within our country can and even should engage in mutual visits and friendly contacts with religious persons in other countries as well as develop exchanges in the fields of religious art and culture. But in all of these various contacts, they must firmly adhere to the principle of an independent, self-governing autonomy, and resolutely resist all those reactionary religious forces from abroad who want once again to gain control over religion in our country. They must refuse with determination any meddling and interfering with religious affairs within our country on the part of foreign churches or religious personages, nor must they permit any foreign religious organization (and this includes all the groups and organisms they control) to use any means to come to our country for missionary work, or to send in secretly and distribute on a large scale religious literature.

We must educate all religious organizations and individuals not to make use of any means whatsoever to solicit funds from foreign church organizations, and religious persons and individuals as well as other organizations and individuals in our country must refuse any subsidy or funds offered by foreign church organizations for religious purposes. If in accordance with religious custom foreign believers or overseas Chinese or compatriots from Hong Kong or Macau wish to give some donations or offerings to Buddhist and Daoist temples or churches within our territory, they can accept them. But if there is question of large contributions or offerings, even though it can establish that the donor acts purely out of religious fervor with no strings attached, yet permission must be sought from the provincial, urban or autonomous area governments or from the central government department responsible for these matters before any religious body can accept them on its own.

We must keep a very watchful eye out for and pay close attention to hostile religious forces from abroad who set up underground churches and other illegal organizations. We must firmly crack down on these organizations that, under the guise of religion, carry out destructive espionage. Of course in carrying out this crack down we must make thorough investigations and have irrefutable evidence on hand, as well as choose a favourable occasion, to execute the case in accordance with lawful procedures, and not act rashly and without thought.

The new task now facing us is how to develop friendly relationships with foreign religious groups and yet maintain our policy of independent autonomy. The essential basis for doing this type of work well is to act in accord with the correct general and specific policies of the central government and party. We should handle the national religious question realistically and effectively, strengthen our investigations and studies of the history of religion and its present situation, and make efforts to train talented people able to engage in these international religious activities. Facts prove over and again that if we handle well the national situation, then all hostile religious forces from abroad will have little or no opportunity to exploit the situation to their own advantage. And then the international contacts undertaken by religious groups will make smoother and sounder progress and thus activate the positive function they should have.

XII

The basic guarantee for a successful handling of the religious question is to strengthen our party's leadership. The party's work on religion is an important constituent of the party's United Front and its work among the masses since it touches upon various aspects of social life. This demands of party committees on each level that they must definitely organize all pertinent departments – these include the United Front department, the Bureau of Religious Affairs, the Bureau of the National Minorities, the Department for Politics and Law, the Department for Propaganda, Culture, Education, Science and Technology and Health as well as the Labour Unions, the Youth League, the Women's Federation and all other mass organizations, etc. All these must have a unified ideology, a unified knowledge and understanding, and a unified policy. They must share the labour and take individual responsibility, but act in close coordination, and take a realistic hold on this important task in order to conscientiously and unremittingly carry it through to a successful conclusion.

We must reinforce and strengthen the government organs responsible for religious affairs, to enable all cadres who give themselves to this particular work, to study in a systematic way the Marxist theory of religion, thoroughly understand the party's fundamental standpoint and policy on the religious question, maintain close relationship with the mass of religious believers and consult on equal terms with persons in religious circles in order to cooperate and work together.

An important constituent of the party's theoretical work on religion is to use the Marxist standpoint and method to carry out scientific research on the religious question. Another important task for the party's propaganda line to take up is to use Marxist philosophy in criticizing idealism (this includes theism) and educate the masses, but especially the broad mass of teenagers, in a dialectical and historical materialistic and scientific world view. So we need to strengthen our propaganda in what is related to a scientific and cultural understanding of natural phenomena, of social evolution and of human life, old age, sickness and death as well as good and ill fortune. To establish research teams armed with Marxist ideology to study religious theory and to make efforts to set up research organs and make use of pertinent university disciplines which also study the religious question from the Marxist ideology is an indispensable and very important aspect of the party's theoretical work on this question. Of course when we publish articles in newspapers and magazines which relate to this religious question we should adopt a prudent policy so as not to violate our present policy now in force on the religious question, nor to offend the religious sensibilities of the mass of religious believers. Academic circles should respect the religious ideology of those in religious circles, whereas those in religious circles should in like way respect the research and propaganda activities carried out by these academic circles in their Marxist interpretation of religion.

The central authorities of the party and state once again emphasize and point out that all party members definitely must clearly understand that the party's religious policy is not just a temporary expedient measure, but is based on the scientific theoretical foundation of Marxist–Leninism and Mao thought, whose decisive strategy is to take as its goal the unification of the people nationwide and have them work together to build a powerful, modern socialist state. Given the present condition of socialism, the only correct and fundamental way to solve the religious question lies precisely in safeguarding the freedom of religious belief. It will be only after the gradual development of socialism's economic, cultural, scientific and technological enterprise, as well as by the gradual development of socialism's material and spiritual civilization, that that type of society and level of awareness that gave rise to the existence of religion will gradually disappear. This kind of great enterprise naturally cannot be accomplished within a short period of time, not even within one, two or three generations. This is to say that only after a long historical period and after many generations and the combined efforts of the broad masses of both believers and non-believers, will this come about. Then at that time all Chinese will have within their own country completely rid themselves of what is impoverishing, ignorant and spiritually empty, and will have become a highly developed material and spiritual civilization, able to stand in the front ranks of mankind in a glorious world. At that time the vast majority of citizens in our country will have reached an awareness enabling them to deal with the world and their fellowmen from a scientific viewpoint, and no longer have any need to have recourse to an illusory world of gods to seek spiritual solace. This is precisely what Marx and Engels have said will happen – there will be an age when people will have freed themselves from all alienating forces controlling the world and have come to the stage when they will conscientiously plan and control the whole of social life. This is also what Comrade Mao Zedong meant when he said that the people, relying upon themselves alone, will create a new age both for themselves and for the world. And so only when we enter this new age, will all that mirrors a religious face in our present actual world finally disappear. Each one of us party members, as each succeeding generation goes by, must put forth all our best efforts to bring about this brilliant future.

An Open Letter to the Clergy and Laity[1]

Dear Clergy and Laity in Our Lord,
Under the beneficent light of the Holy Spirit, the Standing Committee of the Chinese Catholic Patriotic Association, the Standing Committee of the Chinese Catholics Religious Affairs Committee and the Bishops' Conference have held a joint meeting in Beijing from July 15–18 [1981].

With elated spirits, everybody reviewed the new dynamic atmosphere which has manifested itself among our Catholics since the third representative meeting of the Chinese Catholic Patriotic Association and the Chinese Catholic Conference. Everyone was unanimous in thanking and praising the Lord.

All the bishops and the members of the Standing Committee present expressed their great indignation and solemnly protested the Roman Curia's disregard for the rights of the Chinese church in its illegally appointing Deng Yiming as Archbishop of Guangdong.

The Roman Curia has consistently been hostile to the Chinese people and has plotted to overthrow the new China. Before the liberation, the Chinese church existed under a colonial status for a long time, manipulated by the Roman Curia and the foreign missionaries. It served the aggressive policies of the imperialists and so harmed our country in many ways.

After the Liberation, the Roman Curia persisted in its stubborn opposition to the policies of the new China, time and again publishing reactionary 'encyclicals' and 'orders', inviting the Chinese clergy and laity to oppose every policy, law and decree of the People's Government.

It called for a 'bloody martyrdom' in support of its political machinations. It fouled up the whole atmosphere. Some people went so far as to commit crimes. If the Chinese church had continued to go on in this way, then it certainly would have met with God's righteous anger and of necessity be spurned by the Chinese people. It would have nowhere to exist, because its actions would be incompatible with the teaching of Jesus to honour God and to love men.

With the silent blessing of God, the Chinese clergy and laity, acting out of

---

[1] This is an English translation of the Chinese text. See *Catholic Church in China* 3 (October 1981): 12–18.

a sense of responsibility and their love for their country and church, launched a patriotic anti-imperialist campaign. They did this in order to uphold the dignity of our country and to serve the interests of the Chinese church.

Their action was modelled upon that of Jesus when he purified the temple. They drew up the policy of an independent, autonomous administration of the church, which would elect and consecrate its own bishops so that the Lord would have good shepherds for his flock in China. In doing this they radically changed the colonial status of the Chinese church. But this just enterprise has all along met with the Roman Curia's unreasonable opposition and sabotage.

During the 10 years of turmoil, the party's and the government's policy of the freedom of religious belief, as well as all its other policies, met with similar serious sabotage. All religious activities were compelled to come to an end.

But after the smashing of the 'Gang of Four', the People's government energetically restored and implemented its policy of the freedom of religious belief. During these past few years, churches all over were opened, one after another. Others are now in the process of a stepped-up renovation in preparation for their opening.

Now the clergy and laity can, in freedom and joy, celebrate feast days, perform the sacraments and celebrate the Holy Sacrifice of the Mass. Some churches have even had an increase in the number of Catholics.

Religious matters have taken on a whole new development. We are now in the actual stage of establishing a seminary for fostering priestly vocations. Under God's care, church affairs throughout the country are thriving, presenting a joyful scene where 'the rivers clap their hands and the hills sing and dance together' (Psalm 98:8).

Now, just when the broad mass of clergy and laity are elated over this revival of the church, the Roman Curia, in accordance with its political aim of showing hostility to our socialist motherland, organised people, under the pretext of visiting relatives or tourists, to come to our country and disseminate secretly reactionary pamphlets, gather intelligence, spread rumours, sow dissension between Catholics and the government, create division within the Catholic church and sabotage the stability and unity prevailing within our country.

What must be especially pointed out is John Paul's disregard for our country's sovereign rights by his presumptuous appointment of Deng Yiming, who still continues to maintain his reactionary stand as Archbishop of Guangdong.

This is in line with the Vatican reactionary policy of continuously and persistently showing hostility to our country. It exposes once again its attempts to sabotage the Chinese church's independence and autonomy. Its aim is to try to make it once again a colonial church. But we firmly believe that this plot of the Roman Curia will never succeed.

Everybody knows that our independence and autonomy is a right which our country's clergy and laity will not permit to be infringed upon and we are perfectly justified in this.

That bishops be elected by the clergy and laity is in accord with the tradition of the apostolic era. Scripture records that, after Jesus ascended into heaven, Mary and the apostles and 120 laity of both sexes, were gathered together united in prayer and elected Matthias to be an apostle.

Afterwards, the apostles, in accord with the Lord's will, dispersed and travelled all over preaching the gospel of salvation. Every time they came to a new place and established the church there, they elected from the Christian community men of proven virtue, character and talent to be bishops and take charge of the church in that locality.

All these bishops were the lawful successors to the apostles. We have several fine examples of this in Paul, who appointed Timothy to be the bishop of the church in Ephesus and Titus to be the bishop of the church in Crete. St. Peter appointed the bishop in Antioch and St. Mark, the evangelist, appointed the bishop in Egypt.[2]

There are other examples as well. The apostles in appointing these bishops did not need the permission of the other apostles. All were lawfully appointed because God was the source of their spiritual power.

After these successors of the apostles passed away, the clergy and laity jointly elected their own bishops. In chapter 5, verse 1 of St. Paul's letter to the Hebrews we have this statement: 'when a man is chosen as high priest, he is appointed on men's behalf as their representative in the things of God'.

We have the example of St. Ambrose, St. Augustine, St. Athanasius, St. John Chrysostom, etc., who, called by God, were chosen and consecrated as bishops by the clergy and laity of their respective locales.

In the Council of Carthage, 254 A.D., presided over by St. Cyprian, we find clearly stated in Article 4: 'The priest, having been judged and approved by the people, proves that he is competent and qualified for this office. Only if he is chosen in the view of all, can we consider him to be chosen by God's authority'.

As history developed, owing to political and economic reasons, kings and emperors controlled the election and appointment of bishops for a time. But the Roman Curia finally came to control these appointments.

The selection and appointment of bishops has very much to do with national interests and the political and religious life of the faithful. No government will allow anyone who rebels against its country's interests to usurp an ecclesiastic office. Hence many countries successively signed agreements with the Roman Curia.

We have for example, Germany, Austria, France, Prussia, Ecuador, Guatemala, Honduras, San Salvador, Haiti, Australia, Italy, Spain and others. These agreements or treaties state either that the country has the right to nominate bishops or that, before they are appointed, the opinion of

---

[2] There is no mention of these appointments in the New Testament.

the government is solicited. Some treaties state that when the bishop takes office, he must swear an oath of loyalty to the state.

Today, the Roman Curia has acted contrary to the Chinese government and the Chinese church by illegally appointing Deng Yiming as Arch-bishop of Guangdong. The Vatican has not only gone against what Jesus did when He founded His church and violated the traditional spirit of the apostolic age but has also disregarded his sovereign rights of the great People's Republic of China.

This criminal action of the Roman Curia is a gross interference in the internal affairs of our country as well as with the rights of the Catholic church. The Chinese people, and this includes our clergy and laity, will in no way tolerate this. Our bishops must be chosen and consecrated by ourselves. We will never permit the Roman Curia to interfere in or control this matter.

Deng Yiming had previously committed serious crimes against his country and its people. After a long period of patient education by the People's government, he was magnanimously released after he had shown signs of repentance.

After his release, he should have sincerely mended his ways by showing his love for his country and observing its laws and continuing to make reparation for his past faults. Instead, he showed little concern for the interests of the Chinese church and willingly offered his services to the Roman Curia's reactionary policies.

He had the effrontery to use a trip to Hong Kong for a medical check-up and a visit to his relatives as a pretext to act against his country and the Chinese church. He made his way to the Vatican to receive his so-called office as Archbishop. He engaged in all sorts of activities behind the back of the Chinese people and the Chinese church.

He has already lost the honour of being a Chinese citizen and a Chinese cleric by violating the principle of the Chinese church's independent and autonomous self-administration, therefore, the clergy and laity of the entire country cast him out.

That Guangdong diocese and the Patriotic Association of Guangzhou have revoked Deng Yiming's position as Bishop of Guangdong diocese and as Vice-chairman of Guangzhou's Patriotic Association is completely correct.[3]

This decision fully expresses both the solemn position taken by the clergy and laity throughout the country and their staunch resolution to persist in maintaining the independent and autonomous administration of the Chi-nese church, while at the same time smashing plots of the Vatican which vainly attempts but without success to gain control once again over the Chinese church.

Dear clergy and laity in Our Lord, Patriotism is a command of the Lord.

---

[3] Bishop Deng Yiming said that he had never been aware of being appointed Vice-chairman of the Guangzhou CPA, still less that he willingly accepted the post.

Our motherland is truly a great country, worthy of our love. Only in socialist new China can the Chinese church cease being in a colonial status.

For more than 30 years, the Chinese Catholic church has followed the teaching of Our Lord and the traditional spirit of the apostolic age, proceeding along the only correct road of an independent, autonomous self-administration. As for the future we shall rely upon the guidance and the help of the Holy Spirit and trust in the compassionate care of Our Lady and never leave this road.

Let us advance in our country and church, and resolutely resist the plots of the Roman Curia as well as all other interference and sabotage coming from foreign reactionary forces, and independently and autonomously carry out the Lord's work within our motherland in an even better way.

Our cause is just. A just cause obtains the blessing of our merciful Father for 'God loves the just man' (Psalm 146:8).

The Standing Committee of the Chinese Catholic Patriotic Association.
The Standing Committee of the Chinese Catholic Religious Affairs Committee
The Chinese Bishops' Conference.
18 July 1981.

The Vatican's Eight-Point Directive on dealings with China

1 Catholic Doctrine affirms with clarity that only those are said to be full members of the church who 'accept all the means of salvation given to the church together with her entire organization, and who – by bonds constituted by the profession of faith, the sacraments, ecclesiastical government, and communion – are joined in the visible structure of the Church of Christ, who rules her through the Supreme Pontiff and the bishops' (L.G., n. 14).

Since 'the lasting and visible source and foundation of the unity both of faith and of communion' (L.G., n. 18) in the Catholic church is the Roman Pontiff, those who do not profess and do not maintain communion with the Pope cannot be considered Catholics. Communion with the Pope is not only a question of discipline, but above all of Catholic faith.

Therefore, the Holy See nourishes profound appreciation and admiration for the bishops, priests, religious and laity who, in every part of the world, in the course of time have always maintained and are maintaining their faith wholly and entirely, including their fidelity to the Roman Pontiff, and encourages them to continue and to grow in their faith.

2 With regard to China, history records the constitution of the Chinese Catholic Patriotic Association in 1957, with the declared intention of renouncing the fundamental ties with the Supreme Pontiff and with the Holy See, and of submitting the community of the Catholic faithful to the direct control of the Civil Authorities.

Notwithstanding the fact that certain more recent positions adopted by some representatives of the Patriotic Association would seem to indicate a certain change of attitude and a tendency on the part of the same Patriotic Association to assume a more political than religious role as a means of communication between the church and the government, constitutive documents and official declarations of representatives of the said Association confirm the initial intentions.

Moreover, it is a fact that the Patriotic Association is still seeking even now to control the choice and ordination of the bishops in each Diocese and the activities of the various diocesan communities.

In view of the doctrinal principles expounded above, no Catholic in conscience can accept the principles of an association which demands the rejection of a fundamental element of his or her faith, such as the indispensable communion with the Roman Pontiff, Visible Head of the church and of the College of the Catholic bishops of the world, which cannot exist without him as Head.

3 From 1958 on, by reason of an initiative of the Patriotic Association, numerous episcopal ordinations took place in mainland China without the necessary consent (apostolic mandate) of the Roman Pontiff.

According to the doctrine of the church and its canonical discipline, such ordinations are to be considered gravely illicit; both the one who receives the ordination and the one who confers it incur a 'latae sententiae' excommunication reserved to the Apostolic See (cf. Decree of the Holy Office dated 9 April 1951 and Canon 1382 of the Code of Canon Law).

To judge from the information at hand, it seems that in such ordinations elements of such a nature to cause them to be considered 'per se' invalid are not present. Naturally, in such situations, a definite judgement is possible only after each case has been attentively and duly examined under every aspect.

4 With regard to the sacraments administered by priests ordained by bishops not recognised by the Roman Pontiff, the presumption remains for the validity of their ordination and therefore also for that of the sacraments administered by them.

With regard to the duty of attendance at Mass and of the reception of the sacraments, Catholics are to look for priests who have remained faithful, that is those in communion with the Pope.

Nevertheless, in order to meet the requirements of their spiritual welfare, Catholics can have recourse to other priests also, on condition that they avoid the occasion of scandal and the danger that such actions might harm the complete content of the Catholic faith which, as has already been noted, requires full communion with the Roman Pontiff.

5 The principles expounded in nos. 1 and 2 require that all 'communicatio in sacris' be avoided with bishops and ecclesiastics belonging to the Patriotic Association. Therefore, on the occasion of visits outside mainland China, such persons may not be invited or allowed to celebrate liturgical acts in churches or Catholic institutions.

The same principles are to be maintained as well for the behaviour of bishops and ecclesiastics who go on a visit to mainland China.

6 The church has the right and duty, in China as well as elsewhere, to have its own seminaries where its clergy are formed.

If, however, that were to be prevented and if it were not possible to adequately form the candidates to the priesthood in another way, even privately, then such candidates could be sent to the seminaries opened under the control of the Patriotic Association, but only on condition that the general orientation and formation imparted there follow the teaching and directives of the church.

Such a possibility should be evaluated according to local circumstances, keeping in mind also the persons who direct such centres of formation.

7 Sacred books, those of the liturgy, catechisms and other teaching texts, are to be used only and in the measure to which they faithfully communicate the doctrine of the church.

8 Any assistance is to be directed to initiatives which serve to maintain the correct doctrine and spirit of faith of the Catholic church.

Regarding assistance to persons or initiatives which do not give such guarantees, each case must be examined in the light of the moral principles concerning cooperation.

The English translation of 'Document 3', 1989

Central Office Document
1989 no. 3

{CONFIDENTIAL}

The Central Office of the Communist Party
and of the State Council
Transmitted to the Central Government's United Front
and the Religious Affairs Bureau of the State Council

Circular on
'Stepping up Control Over the Catholic Church to Meet the New
Situation'

To: The party committees and people's government of each province and
autonomous region, the party committees in the military districts, all
ministries and commissions of the Central Government and State agencies,
party committees in general headquarters, all party committees on all
military levels, all people's organizations:

The Central United Front and the Religious Affairs Bureau of the Council
of State with the approval of the Council of State and the Central
Committee of the Communist Party transmit to you this document on
'*Stepping Up Control Over the Catholic Church to Meet the New Situation*'. In the
light of conditions existing in each local area and department please
proceed to implement this document.

The Central Office of the
Communist Party Central Committee
The Central Office of the
Council of State

February 17, 1989

(This document should also be transmitted to the county party committees,
the county governments and their respective departments.)

Report on stepping up control over the Catholic Church to meet the new
situation.

The Central Committee of the Communist Party, the Council of State:

The religious question is quite complex precisely at the present moment when reform is under way. It is very important to handle this question carefully, emphasizing positive factors while eliminating those elements with potential for creating instability. This question also has consequences for furthering our reform movement and enabling our socialist modernization program to proceed with a hitch. Recently with the approval of the Party's Central Committee and the State Council we have given the concrete situation of the Catholic Church in China full study as it relates to the principle of handling Sino–Vatican relations. We now report our findings and present our opinions as follows:

The Catholic Church has a 400-year history in our nation. It developed more rapidly after the Opium War with the incursions of the imperialist powers. In the early years after Liberation China had altogether 2,700,000 Catholics. Now there are more than 3,300,000. Before Liberation imperialist powers and the Vatican completely controlled the Catholic Church in China. Once the New China was established, the party and the government motivated and encouraged patriotic clergy and the Catholic community to break free from the Vatican's control and set up the Chinese Catholic Patriotic Association. Under the aegis of this Association Catholics were to manage their own church independently and autonomously so that the Catholic Church truly became an enterprise over which Catholics themselves had full say. This indeed had been a major change for the Catholic Church in China. After the Party's Third Plenum of the 11th Central Committee, both the party and government continued to emphasize Catholic Church work, urging it to go on maintaining the aim of independent and autonomous administration of its own affairs. The Catholic Church in China has to stay firmly on this road.

But the Vatican's desire to once again exercise control over the Chinese Catholic Church has never died out. During these past few years the Vatican has vilified and attacked the patriotic Chinese clergy. It has made use of its international status and the faith that the clergy shows towards the Pope to send agents into China. It has also used other clandestine means to appoint bishops secretly and to stir up and support underground forces, in a vain effort to divide the Chinese Catholic Church. According to the facts we have at hand, the Pope has already appointed 25 underground bishops. These bishops in turn have ordained more than 200 priests who are dispersed through 17 provinces and cities. Underground church groups have been organized in Hebei, Fujian, Shaanxi, Wenzhou in Zhejiang, and Tianshui in Gansu provinces respectively. They are a political force defying the government and an element that can seriously affect public security.

In the past we have had some problems in our work dealing with the Catholic Church. The main problems are: we have not fully developed the function of the Patriotic Church organization; the number of patriotic clerics is too small and their aging problem is very serious; we have not been successful in either winning over or breaking up the underground forces; we have been unable to control their activities; we have been negligent in implementing policies dealing with the Catholic Church; a notably large number of church buildings and other real estate have not been returned to their rightful owners. The church's financial situation is, as a result, beset with difficulties and it is short on means of self support. Therefore we must adopt effective measures to augment and improve our work dealing with the Catholic Church.

I

We must firmly implement the policy
of independent and autonomous administration of church affairs
and intensify ideological education of the
clergy and the Catholic Community

In the early years after Liberation, the Central Government decided to permit Catholics, under the premise of freeing themselves from the control of the Vatican, to keep those ties which were purely religious. Self-elected bishops still sought the Pope's approval. The Vatican, however, not only did not approve the selection of these Bishops but it 'excommunicated' them. After 1958 the Chinese Catholic Church could do nothing else but cut all ties with the Vatican. This was the only correct thing to do.

In recent years, because of the Vatican's infiltrating activities, some clergy and Catholics have wavered in regard to the policy of the independent and autonomous administration of church affairs and their thinking has become somewhat muddled. We must, therefore, adopt various ways to explain clearly to the clergy and the Catholic community the present situation. We must teach them that fully upholding the policy of the independent and autonomous administration of its own affairs is the only correct way for the church to go. We must further fully affirm the past contributions made by patriotic clergy and innumerable Catholics in defending China's sovereignty when they implemented this policy of the independent and autonomous administration of church affairs. We must explicitly state that now as in the past and for the future we shall continue to rely upon them to administer church affairs well. We should state once again that the two basic principles that regular Sino–Vatican relationships will never change. These two principles are:

1 The Vatican must break off so-called 'diplomatic ties' with Taiwan and recognize that the People's Republic of China is the only legal government of China.

2 The Vatican must not interfere with China's interior affairs. This includes not interfering with religious affairs as well.

No matter how Sino–Vatican relationships might develop, the Chinese Catholic Church must firmly adhere to and not deviate from the policy of the independent and autonomous administration of church affairs. It must continue to choose and consecrate it own bishops and make its own decisions on all its own internal affairs. This includes church and financial administration and supervision of the clergy. The above-mentioned educational practices will do away with the muddled thinking of the Catholic clergy and masses and strengthen their faith in the autonomous running of their church.

II

Help the Catholic Patriotic Organizations
Reorganize Their Structures
And Build Up A Well Knit Organization

If the Chinese Catholic Church wants to avoid Vatican control over their religious activities and have their own people administer their own church affairs, it will be necessary to take practical measures to strengthen the structure of the Catholic Patriotic Organizations. The party and the government will support and aid the Catholic Patriotic Organizations to support and aid the Catholic Patriotic Organizations to strengthen and increase their effectiveness as well as actively search out patriotic organizations. We must choose suitable candidates as soon as possible and have them consecrated as bishops and assigned to those places lacking bishops. This will insure that the leadership of the Catholic Church will remain in the hands of patriotic forces.

There is also need to reorganize the structures of the present Catholic Patriotic Organizations in an appropriate manner. Before 1980 the Catholic Church had only the one Catholic Patriotic Association. It was very effective in maintaining the principle of independent and autonomous church administration. It upheld China's sovereignty and warded off hostile religious forces from abroad that sought to undermine our autonomy. At the 1980 national meeting of Chinese Catholic representatives the members decided to create the Chinese Catholic Church Administrative Commission and also established the Bishops' Conference which was to consist of legally chosen bishops from each diocese. The Catholic Church now had three national and parallel patriotic organizations. Although each of these three religious patriotic organizations had its own basic function, yet as far as practical work was concerned the Bishops' Conference and the Church Administrative Commission did not develop all their potentialities. The system does not effectively meet the present situation and the needs demanded by work on the domestic and international levels. In line, therefore, with the special characteristics of the Catholic Church we must consolidate the democratic spirit in the church and suitably readjust church structures. To proceed further we must clearly outline each organization's function and regulate their mutual relationships. The important points which must be readjusted are these:

1 The Bishops' Conference must be strengthened enabling it to become a real, effective body in the Chinese Catholic Church. Its basic function will be, in accordance with the Chinese Church's policy of independence and autonomy, to supervise church affairs and administer the church well (this will include explaining theological teaching, formulating church rules, examining and approving bishops to be in charge of dioceses, etc.), as well as being the official representative to other churches abroad.

2 The Chinese Catholic Patriotic Association is a mass national organization made up of clergy and laity. Its basic function is to assist the party and the government in implementing the policy of the freedom of religious belief, help the church enforce the principle of the independent and autonomous administration of church affairs, continue to be the bridge between the Catholic community and the government, actively promote social service, initiate self-supporting enterprises and social projects for the common good and encourage all clerics and lay persons to take part in building up the two civilizations.

3 The Chinese Catholic Church Administrative Commission will no longer be a national organization but will become a specialized committee under the Bishops' Conference in charge of church affairs activities.

4 The supreme authoritative body in the Chinese Catholic Church is the National Congress of Representatives. It has the power to elect the executive committee of the Bishops' Confernece, its chairman, vice-chairman and secretary general, and the leadership structure of the Patriotic Association and to deliberate the work reports of the Patriotic Association and the Bishops' Conference.

The Catholic Patriotic Organizations on the provincial level should also reorganize themselves following the spirit of what is said above. The provincial Patriotic Associations and the Church Administrative Commissions are to be elected by the provincial, congresses of representatives. Their activities will be directed respectively by the National Patriotic Association and the Bishops' Conference.

III

We must continuously make serious efforts to implement
our policy of helping the Catholic Church
solve its problems of self support

Before 1958 the Catholic Church relied upon its rentals from real estate for self support. But owing to the many political campaigns in the past, especially to the 'Cultural Revolution', most if not all of the Church's real estate was confiscated. The resulting decrease in revenues was on such a scale that self-support became almost impossible. Although in recent years the situation has taken a turn for the better, yet the implementation of this policy has proceeded at a snail's pace. For the moment national and provincial patriotic associations need to rely upon government subsidies in order to operate. The grass root churches have for the most part no way to support themselves while patriotic clergy live in desperate circumstances. If this situation is not changed not only will it affect the relationship of the party and the government with Catholic personnel, but the Catholic Patriotic organizations themselves will find it very difficult to organize the great mass of Catholic believers to carry out the policy of independent and autonomous administration of the church.

Each locality, therefore, must seriously see to it that the situation of confiscated churches and church properties is settled. (These properties include churches, seminaries and the lands on which these structures stand.) There will be no need to proceed further in case this matter has already been satisfactorily dealt with in accordance with the State Council and the Party Central Committee's regulations. It is precisely those cases where nothing has been done that require our immediate attention. Those buildings which the church in fact needs must be returned without question. If it is impossible to return them at the moment a contract must be made stating the fact of their eventual return and the reasonable amount of rent to be paid during the period of their use. A reasonable price fixed by national standards must be paid to the church by the unit which presently occupies the property in case the original building has been torn down, changed to another use or sold. If the military is occupying the buildings or property the matter must be resolved in accordance with document no. 46 issued by the Central Government in 1988.

All local areas must actively help the Catholic Church develop its own self-support projects. They can permit Catholic Patriotic Associations, in accord with pertinent government regulations, to take initiatives and freely set up enterprises and social welfare projects that will provide self support. Local government should give these efforts preferential treatment, offering credit, technological assistance and tax rebates. Finance ministries can provide subsidies to pay for the necessary expenses. These subsidies will be given on a temporary basis and will cease once the Patriotic organizations reach the stage of self-support. The subsidies will gradually decrease in proportion as the ability of the Patriotic organizations increase to provide for their own needs.

IV

Catholic Underground Forces must be dealt with
by adopting methods
to win over or isolate their adherents

We designate the underground as consisting of those bishops secretly consecrated by the Vatican and those priests that these bishops have in turn ordained as well as key leaders they control. Most of them believe in the Pope and do not agree with the independent and autonomous administration of the Church. Only very few of them use religion as a pretext to oppose the party and the government, create disturbances and incite others to do so. Therefore, we must make use of all positive means to increase our control over them. We must try to win over the majority and isolate the trouble makers, attacking reactionaries with determination. The present task is to make known government and Party policies and to organize and educate those Catholics who have been deceived. In the case of underground bishops and priests we must treat each case individually winning them over if possible or isolating them if not. Those who wish to accept the government's leadership and show themselves to be patriotic and law abiding, providing they have the necessary qualifications, can be examined by the local Patriotic Association. Once their clerical status has been approved by the Bishops' Conference arrangements can be made for their employment. Those whose political attitude is not so clear or who lack sufficient theological knowledge, can take part in training courses or be sent to seminaries for further training. Once they have changed their positions and they have the requisite religious knowledge arrangements can be made for them. Regarding those underground individuals who continue in their stubborn opposition despite the patient efforts of the government and who carry out confrontational activities, stir up Catholic communities and disturb the social order, we must obtain evidence, expose their crimes publicly and deal severely with them in accordance with the law.

V

Strengthen Our Leadership Over The Catholic Church

The problem of the Catholic Church involves the struggle we are engaged in with the Vatican as it attempts to control the Chinese Catholic Church and our resistance to such attempts. It is a very complicated situation. We should be paying close attention at the present moment to trends taking place in some areas. Underground groups in these areas are running wild; they deceive people and incite them to resist the government. In some places underground forces have publicly proclaimed that they have received the Vatican's special appointment to be "the only legitimate hierarchical bishops". They have attempted to take over control of leadership in the church. The Party and the government must definitely strengthen its leadership work over the Catholic Church. We must fully estimate the problems and difficulties that will arise in the midst of this work so that it will produce solid results. All of our leaders must be of one mind fully realizing the necessity and urgency of this task which this new situation presents us. All levels of leadership must be united in thought and fully recognize the urgency and importance of strengthening Catholic Church work in the new situation. The United Front, the Religious Affair Bureaus, the Public Security Agencies and other pertinent government departments as well as labour unions, the Communist Youth League and

Women's League and all such mass organizations must coordinate their efforts, share responsibility, use all means to unite and educate the Catholic masses, and carry out general administration. Everything will be done under the Party's unified leadership. We need to enhance the role which the Patriotic Association and the patriotic clergy play. We must allow them to carry out those tasks which they can do on their own (such as winning over the underground clergy, restructuring their organization, etc.). We must continue to win over and unify the majority of the clergy and this includes the middle-of-the-roaders as well. We must be careful to differntiate among the various underground forces, i.e., those clergy who, because of their belief in the Pope, are separated from us and those key members of the underground and Catholics whom they influence and control. We must make many patient and meticulous efforts to unite the greatest number of them as possible. Each place must pay close attention to tendencies at work among the underground and use effective measures to prevent them from making any trouble. As soon as any problem arises, each department's forces must be coordinated under the unified leadership of the Party and government, to meet and resolve these problems immediately and in a satisfactory manner.

Unless this report needs further refinement, we propose that it be sent to each department for implmentation.

> The United Front of the Communist Party
> The Religious Affairs Bureau of the State Council
> December 24, 1988

Important terminology: United Front, Religion, Catholic Church

Promulgated on Feb. 23, 1989 by the Central Secretariat of the Central Government.

Selected bibliography

WESTERN BOOKS

Acta Apostolicae Sedis, vol. LXXI, City State of the Vatican.

Abbott, Walter (ed.), *The Documents of Vatican II*, trans. Joseph Gallagher, London: Geoffrey Chapman, 1966.

Amnesty International Report 1986, London: Amnesty International, 1987.

Anglican–Roman Catholic International Commission, *The Final Report: Windsor, September 1981*, London: Catholic Truth Society & SPCK, 1982.

Asia Research Centre, *The Great Cultural Revolution in China*, Tokyo: Charles E. Tuttle, 1965.

Babris, Peter J., *Silent Churches: Persecution of Religion in Soviet Dominated Areas*, Arlington Height, Illinois: Research Publishers, 1978.

Barnett, A. Doak, *The Making of Foreign Policy in China*, London: Tauris, 1985.

Bociurkiw, B. and Strong, John, *Religion and Atheism in the USSR and Eastern Europe*, London: Macmillan, 1975.

Bourdeaux, Michael, *Risen Indeed: Lessons in Faith from the USSR*, London: Darton, Longman & Todd, Keston Book 16, 1983.

Bourdeaux, Michael and Rowe, Michael, *May One Believe in Russia: Violations of Religious Liberty in the Soviet Union*, London: Darton, Longman & Todd, 1980.

Brugger, Bill, *China: Radicalism to Revisionism 1962–1979*, London: Croom Helm, 1981.

Bull, George, *Inside the Vatican*, London: Hutchinson, 1982.

Burkhanov, Sharkkat and Gusarov, Vladilen, *Soviet Power and Islam. – The Soviet Government's Experience in Co-operating With the Muslim Clergy*, Moscow: Novosti Press Agency Publishing House, 1984.

Bush, Richard, Jr, *Religion in Communist China*, New York: Abingdon Press, 1970.

Cameron, Nigel, *Barbarians and Mandarins – Thirteen Centuries of Western Travellers in China*, New York: Walker & Co., Weatherhill Book, 1971.

Canon Law Society of Great Britain and Ireland, in Association with the Canon Law Society of Australia and New Zealand and the Canadian

Canon Law Society, trans. *The Code of Canon Law in English Transla-tions*, London: Collins Liturgical Publications, 1983.

Chao, Jonathan, *Chinese Communist Policy Towards Christianity*, Hong Kong: Chinese Christian Research Centre, 1983.

China: Violations of Human Rights, Prisoners of Conscience and the Death Penalty in the People's Republic of China, London: Amnesty International, 1984.

Ching, Julia, *Probing China's Soul*, San Francisco: Harper and Row, 1990.

Chow Tse-Tsung, *The May Fourth Movement: Intellectual Revolution in Modern China*, Cambridge, Mass.: Harvard University Press, Harvard East Asian Studies 6, 1960.

Chu Hungdah (ed.), *Symposium on Hong Kong: 1997*, University of Mary-land, School of Law, Occasional Papers, Reprints Series in Contem-porary Asian Studies 3 – 1985(86), 1986.

Chu, Theresa and Lind, Christopher (ed.), *A New Beginning: An International Dialogue with the Chinese Church*, Toronto: Canada China Programme of the Canadian Council of Churches, 1983.

Clough, R., *Island China*, Cambridge, Mass.: Harvard University Press, 1978.

Cohen, Jerome A. (ed.), *The Dynamics of China's Foreign Relations*, Cam-bridge Mass.: Harvard University Press, East Asian Research Centre, Harvard East Asian Monographs 39, 1970.

Cohen Jerome and Chu Hungdah, *People's China and International Law: A Documentary Study*, 2 vols, Cambridge, Mass.: Harvard Studies in East Asian Law, Princeton: Princeton University Press, 1974.

Cohen, Paul, *China and Christianity: The Missionary Movement and the Growth of Chinese Antiforeignism 1860–1870*. Cambridge, Mass.: Harvard Univer-sity Press, 1963.

Coleridge, Henry James, *Life and Letters of St. Francis Xavier*, London: Burns and Oates, 1881.

Communism and Christianity in Theory and Practice. Doctrines, Facts, Conclusions, Aids to the Church in Need, UK, 1978.

The Constitution of the People's Republic of China (Promulgated for Implementation on December 4 1984), Beijing: Foreign Languages Press, 1983.

De Smith, S. A., *Constitutional and Administrative Law*, 3 edn, Harmonds-worth: Penguin Books, 1977.

Dunn, Denis, *The Catholic Church and the Soviet Government 1939–1949*, New York: Columbia University Press, 1977.

Detente and Papal-Communist Relations 1962–1978, A Westview Replica edn, Boulder, Colorado: Western Press, 1979.

Dussel, E. D., *Ethis and The Theology of Liberation*, trans. Bernard Mc-Williams, Maryknoll, N.Y.: Orbis Books, 1974.

Dreyer, June, T., *China's Forty Millions*, Cambridge, Mass.: Harvard University Press, 1976.

Dulles, Avery, *Models of the Church*, New York: Image Book, 1970.

Edwards, R. Randle, Henkin, Louis and Nathan, Andrew, J., *Human Rights in Contemporary China*, New York: Columbia University Press, 1986.

Fairbank, John King, *Chinabound*, New York: Harper Row, 1982.
  The United States and China, 4th edn, Cambridge Mass.: Harvard University Press, 1979.
Frankel, Joseph, *International Relations in A Changing World*, new edn, Oxford: Oxford University Press, 1979.
Ginsburg, Norton and Laler, B. A. (ed.), *China: The 80's Era*, London: Westview Press, 1984.
Gittings, John, *The World and China 1922–1972*, New York: Eyre Methuen, 1974.
Gold, Thomas B., *State and Society in the Taiwan Miracle*, New York: M.E. Sharpe, 1986.
Goldman, Merle, *China's Intellectual Advise and Dissents*, Cambridge Mass.: Harvard University Press, 1981.
  Literary Dissent in Communist China, New York: Atheneum, 1971.
Goldman, Merle and Check, Timothy (ed.), *China's Intellectuals and the State*, Cambridge Mass.: Harvard University Press, 1979.
Goodman, David S. G. (ed.), *Groups and Politics in the People's Republic of China*, Cardiff: Cardiff University College Press, 1984.
Goodstadt, Leo F., *Mao Tse-tung: The Search for Plenty*, Hong Kong: Longman, 1972.
Graham, Robert., *Vatican Diplomacy: A Study of Church and State on the International Plane*, Princeton, N.J.: Princeton University Press, 1959.
Gutierrez G., *A Theology of Liberation*. Maryknoll, N.Y.: Orbis Books, 1973.
Hales, E. E. Y., *Revolution And Papacy 1769–1846*, London: Eyre & Spottiswoode, 1960.
Hanson, Eric, *Catholic Politics in China and Korea*, Maryknoll, N.Y.: Orbis Books, 1978.
  The Catholic Church in World Politics, Princeton, N.J.: Princeton University Press, 1987.
Hebblethwaite, Peter, *In the Vatican*, Oxford: Oxford University Press, 1987.
Hinton, Harold, *Communist China in World Politics*, Boston: Houghton Mifflin, 1966.
Hinton, William, *Fanshen: A Documentary of Revolution in A Chinese Village*, Harmondsworth: Pelican Book, 1972.
Hoffmann, Stanley, *Contemporary Theory in International Relations*, Westport, Conn.: Greenwood Press, 1977.
Hong Kong Caritas, *Annual Report on Hong Kong Caritas 1984–1985*.
  Annual Report on Hong Kong Caritas 1985–1986.
Hsu Immanual, Chung-yueh, *China Without Mao: The Search for A New Order*, Oxford: Oxford University Press, 1982.
Karnow, Stanley, *Mao and China – Inside China's Cultural Revolution*, Harmondsworth: Penguin, 1984.
Kim, S. Samuel (ed.), *China and the World*, 2nd edn, San Francisco: Westview, 1989.
Kung, Hans, *The Church – Maintained in Truth*, trans. Edward Quinn, London: SCM Press, 1980.

Kuroyedov, Vladimir, *Church and Religion in the USSR*, Moscow: Novosti Press Agency Publishing House, 1982.

Latourette, K. S., *A History of Christian Mission In China*, New York: Macmillan, 1929.

Liao Kuang-sheng, *Anti-foreignism And Modernization in China 1960–1980*, Hong Kong: Chinese University Press, 1984.

Mabbett, I. W., *Modern China – The Mirage of Modernity*, London: Croom Helm, 1985.

MacFarquhar, Roderick, *The Origins of the Cultural Revolution*. vol. 1 *Contradictions Among the People, 1956–1957*, London: Oxford University Press, 1974.

   The Origins of the Cultural Revolution. vol. 2 *The Great leap Forward, 1958–1960*, London: Oxford University Press, 1983.

MacFarquhar, Roderick, (ed.), *The Hundred Flowers Campaign and the Chinese Intellectual*, New York: Octagon Book, 1974.

MacInnis, Donald, *Religious Policy and Practice in Communist China – A Documentary History*, New York: Macmillan, 1972.

Marx, Karl and F. Engels, *On Religion*, Moscow: Foreign Languages Publishing House, 1957.

Matthews, Robert O., Rubinoff, Arthur G., and Stein, Janice Cross (eds.), *International Conflict and Conflict Management*, Scarborough, Ontario: Prentice-Hall of Canada, 1984.

Maxwell, Robert, *Deng Xiaoping – Speeches and Writings*, New York: Pergamon Press, 1984.

Minamiki, G., *The Chinese Rites Controversy*, Chicago: Loyola University Press, 1982.

Moody, Peter, Jr., *Chinese Politics After Mao: Development And Liberalization 1976–83*, New York: Prager, 1984.

   Opposition And Dissent in Contemporary China, Stanford University, Hoover Institute, 1977.

Munro, Donald J., *The Concept of Man in Contemporary China*, University of Michigan Press, 1977.

Nathan, Andrew, *Peking Politics 1918–23. Factionalism And the Failure of Constitutionalism*, Berkeley: University of California Press, 1976.

Nichols, Peter, *The Politics of The Vatican*, London: Pall Mall Press, 1968.

O'Leary, G., *The Shaping of Chinese Foreign Policy*, London: Croom Helm, 1980.

Pye, Lucian, *Asian Power And Politics: The Cultural Dimension of Authority*, Cambridge Mass.: Belknap Press, 1985.

   The Spirit of Chinese Politics: A Psycho-Cultural Study of Authority Crisis in Political Development, Cambridge Mass.: M.I.T. Press, 1968.

Readings on Faith And Ideology, vol. 1, Manila: Socio-Pastoral Institute, 1986.

Reardon-Anderson, James, *Yenan And the Great Powers: The Origins of Chinese Communist Foreign Policy, 1944–1946*, New York: Columbia University Press, 1980.

Rienstra, M. Howard, *Jesuit Letters From China. 1583–1584*, Minneapolis, Minnesota: University of Minnesota Press, 1986.

Rowbotham, A. H., *Missionary and Mandarins. Jesuits At the Court of China*, Berkeley: University of California Press, 1942.

Schram, Stuart, *Ideology And Policy in China Since the Third Plenum, 1978–84*, University of London, SOAS, Contemporary China Institute, 1984.

The Political Thought of Mao Tse-tung, New York: Praeger, 1969.

Schurmann, Franz, *Ideology and Oganization in Communist China*, 2nd edn, Berkeley: University of California Press, 1968.

The Logic of World Power: An Inquiry Into the Origins, Currents and Contradictions of World Politics, New York: Pantheon Books, 1974.

Schwartz, Benjamin, *Reflections on the May fourth Movement: A Symposium*, Harvard East Asian Monographs 44, Cambridge Mass.: Harvard University East Asian Research Centre, 1972.

In Search of Wealth and Power: Yen Fu and The West, Cambridge Mass.: Harvard University Press, 1964.

Segal, Gerald (ed.), *The China Factor*, London: Croom Helm, 1982.

Segal, Gerald. and Tow, William T., *Chinese Defence Policy*, London: Macmillan, 1984.

Segundo, J. L., *Jesus of Nazareth, Yesterday and Today*, trans. John Druary, Maryknoll, N.Y.: Orbis Books, 1984.

Seldon, Mark, *The Yenan Way in Revolutionary China*, Cambridge Mass.: Harvard University Press, 1971.

Selected Works on Mao Zedong, 5 vols, Beijing: Foreign Languages Press, 1977.

Seymour, James (ed.), *The Fifth Modernization: China's Human Rights Movement, 1978–79*, New York: M. Coleman Enterprise, 1980.

Spence, Jonathan, *The Gate of Heavenly Peace*, New York: Viking Press, 1981.

Stehle, Hansjakob, *Eastern Politics of the Vatican 1917–1979*, trans. Sandra Smith, London: Ohio University Press, 1981.

Swindler L. and Swindler A. (ed. and trans.), *Bishops and People*, Philadelphia: Westminster Press, 1970.

Theology in the Third World, Manila: Socio-Pastoral Institute, 1983.

Tillich, Paul, *Dynamics of Faith*, New York: Harper, 1957.

Torres, C., *Father Camilo Torres' Revolutionary Writings*, New York: Harper, Colophon Books, 1972.

Triska, Jan F. (ed.), *Constitutions of the communist Party States*, Stanford University, Hoover Institute Publications of War, Revolution and Peace, 1968.

Twittchett, D. and Fairbank, J. K., *The Cambridge History of China*, vol. 10, part 1, *Late Ching [Qing], 1800–1911*, in J. K. Fairbank (ed.), Cambridge University Press, 1978.

Van Den Wyngaert P. A., *Sinica Franciscana Vol. 1.*, Florence: Collegium S. Bonaventurae, 1929.

Wang Gunwu, *China and The World Since 1949: The impact of Independence, Modernity and Revolution*, London: Macmillan, 1977.

Weber, Max, *Basic Concepts in Sociology*, trans. H. P. Scher, London: Peter Owen, 1964.

The Religion of China, trans. Hans H. Garth, London: Macmillan Press, 1964.

Welch, Holmes, *Buddhism Under Mao*, Harvard East Asian Series no. 69, Cambridge, Mass.: Harvard University Press, 1972.

Whyte, Bob, *Unfinished Encounter: China and Christianity*, London: Fount Paperbacks, 1988.

Whyte, Martin King, *Small Groups and Political Rituals in China*, Berkeley: University of California Press, 1974.

Williams, G. H., *The Mind of John Paul II: Origins of His Thought and Action*, New York: The Seabury Press, 1981.

Willike, Bernard, *Imperial Government and Catholic Mission in China During the Year 1784–1785*, New York: The Franciscan Institute, 1948.

Wurth, Elmer (ed.), *Papal Documents Related to the New China 1937–1984*, Maryknoll, N.Y.: Orbis Books, Probes Series, 1985.

Yahuda, Michael, *China's Role in World Affairs*, London: Croom Helm, 1978.

Towards the End of isolationism: China's Foreign Policy After Mao, London: Macmillan Press, 1983.

Yang, C. Y., *Religion in Chinese Society*, Berkeley: University of California Press, 1967.

Yip Ka Che, *Religion, Nationalism and Chinese Student. The Anti-Christian Movement of 1922–1972*. Western Washington University, Centre for East Asian Studies, Studies on East Asia vol. 15, Western Washington University Press, 1980.

Young, John D., *Confucianism and Christianity – the First Encounter*, Hong Kong University Press, 1983.

CHINESE BOOKS

Chedi Geduen Jidojiao Yu Meidiguozhuyi De Lianxi [Severing the ties between US Imperialist and Christianity], Xinhua Shishi Congkan no. 91 [Xinhua series on current affairs no. 91], Beijing: Renmin, 1951.

Chen Yuan (ed.), *Kangxi Yu Loma Guanxi wenshu Yingyinben* [Facsimile of the documents relating to Kangxi and the legates from Rome], Zhongguo Shixue Congshu no. 23, Taiwan: Xueshen, 1973.

Dangdai Zhongguo Yanyiusuo (ed.), *Zhonggong Zhongyang Guanyu Zongjiao Wenti Di Luenwen Zhi* [Selected essays on the CCP's religious questions], Xianggang: Dangdai Zhongguo Yanjiusuo, 1972.

Deng Xiaoping Wenxuen (1975–1982) [Selected works of Deng Xiaoping (1975–1982), Beijing: Renmin, 1983.

Diguozhuyi Zenyang Liyong Zongjiao Qinlue Zhongguo [How did Imperialists make use of religion to encroach on China], Xinhua Shishi Congkan no. 92 [Xinhua series on current affairs no. 92]. Beijing: Renmin, 1951.

Fang Hao. *Zhongguo Tianzhujiaoshi Renwu Zhuan* [Biographies of prominent persons in the Chinese Catholic church], 3 vols, Xianggang: Tianzhujiao Zhengli Xuehui, 1967.

Gansusheng Minzu Yanjiusuo, *Yisilan Jiao Zai Zhongguo* [Islam in China], Ningxia: Renmin, 1982.

Gu Zhangsheng, *Chuanjiaoshi Yu Jindai Zhongguo* [Missionaries and contemporary China], Shanghai: Renmin, 1981.

Gu Zulu, *Zhongguo Tienzhujiao Di Guochu He Xianzai* (The past and present of the Chinese Catholic church), Shanghai: Social Science Academy, 1989.

Jiduojiao Renshi Di Aiguo Yundong [The Patriotic Movement of Christians], Xinhua Shishi Congkan no. 74 [Xinhua series on current affairs no. 74], Beijing: Renmin, 1951.

Jin Zhihua (ed.), *Qinglian Rensheng Zhexue* [Philosophy of life for the youth], Beijing: Zhongguo Qinglian, 1986.

Li Jinwei, *Hongweibing Shilu* [Facts about red guards], Xianggang: Shijie Huaqiao, 1967.

Li Weihan, *Tongyi Zhanxian Wenti Yu Minzu Wenti* [Questions on the United Front and nationalities], Beijing: Renmin, 1981.

Li Zhiyue, *Jindai Zhongguo Fan Yanjiao Yundong* [The late 19th century antimissionary movement in China], Beijing: Renmin, 1985.

Lo Guang (ed.), *Tianzhujiao Zaihua Chuanjiao Shiji* [The history of Catholic mission in China], Zhangxiang Historical Series no. 3, Taiwan: Zhangxiang, 1967.

Lu Shiqiang, *Zhongguo Guanshen Fanjiao Di Yuanyin (1860–1874)* [Causes of anti-missionary attitudes of officials and gentry (1860–1874)], Zhongguo xueshu Zhuzuo Jiangzu Weiyuanhui Series no. 16, Taibei: Zhongguo Xueshu Zhuzuo Jiangzu Weiyuanhui, 1966.

Lu Yizhe, *Zhonggong Zenyang Dueidai Zongjiao* [How did the CCP treat religions], Xianggang: Yaoluen, 1953.

Lo Yu and Wu Yan (ed.), *Dalu Zhongguo Tianzhujiao 40 Lian Dashiji* [Major events of 40 years of mainland Chinese Catholic church], Taibei: Furen Daxue, 1986.

Lo Zaufeng, *Zhongguo shehuizhuyi Shichi Di Zongjiao Wenti* [Religious problems in the Socialist Period of China], Shanghai: Shehui Kexue, 1987.

Mao Zedong Xuanzhi 5 vols [Selected works of Mao Zedong], Beijing: Renmin, 1977 (reprint).

Ming Shi [The History of Ming Dynasty], *Lie Zhuan* [Biographies]: *Sheng Oue.* no place, Zhonghua, no date.

Minzu Wenti Yanjiuhui (ed.), *Huihui Minzu Wenti* [Nationality questions on the Hui], Beijing: Minzu, 1980.

'Proceedings of the First International Symposium on Church and State in China: past and present', Tamkang University, Taipei, Taiwan, 1987.

Sun Xinhua, Lei Yun, Wu Hongbin and Jiang Jiandong (eds.), *Zongjiao Wantan* [On religion], Chejiang: Renmin, 1984.

Tianjing Tianzhujiao Gexin Yundong Di Chengjiu [The success of the reform movement of Tianjing Catholics], Xinhua Shishi Congkan no. 88 [Xinhua series on current affairs no. 88], Beijing: Renmin, 1951.

Tianzhujiao Renshi Di Aiguo Yundong [the Patriotic Movement of the Catholics], Xinhua Shishi Congkan no. 84 [Xinhua series on current affairs no. 84], Beijing: Renmin, 1951.

Wang Kecheng and Tang Yunchiao, *Quanyu Dangfeng Wenti* [On the party's discipline], Beijing: Renmin, 1981.

Wang Zhangling, *Mali Zhuyi Yu Zhongjiao Zhi Chongtu* [Conflict between Marxism-Leninism and religion], Taibei: Yaushi, 1982.

Wang Zhixin, *Zhongguo Jiduojiao Shigang* [Brief history of Christianity in China], Xianggang: Jiduojiao Fuqiao, 1959.

   Zhongguo Zongjiao Sisheng Shi Dagang [History of Chinese religious thought], Shanghai: Zhonghua, 1933.

Wu Yan, *Dalu Tianzhujiao Toushi Jianluen Zhonggong Di Zongjiao Zhengce.* [Glimpses of Catholic life style in mainland China and the Chinese Communist policy towards religion], Taiwan: Wendao, 1984.

Xin Zhibo, *Zhongguo Tianzhujiao Ji Chi Jiaolan* [The Chinese Catholics and their plights], Xianggang: Ziyou, 1954.

Zhang Chunshen, *Fandigang Yu Woguo De Waijiao Guanxi* [The diplomatic relations of the Vatican and the Republic of China], Taiwan: Wendao, 1980.

Zheng Yushuo, *Sirenbang Hou De Zhongguo* [China after the Gang of Four], Xianggang: Tiandi, 1979.

Zhonghua Renmin Gongheguo Kaiguo Wenxian [Documents on the establishment of the PRC], 2nd edn, Xianggang: Wenhua Ziliao Gongyingshe, 1978.

Zhonggong Zhongyang Wenxian Yanjiushi (ed.), *Xinshiqi Tongyizhanxian Wenxian Xuanbian* [Selected documents on the new era's United Front], Beijing: Zhongyang Dangxiao, 1985.

Zhonggong Zhongyang Zuzhebu Yanjiushe (ed.), *Zhishi Fengzi Wenti Wenxuen* [Selected essays on the questions of intellectuals], Hunan: Renmin, 1983.

Ziyou Taipingyang Yuekanshe, *Lei Mingyuan Shenfu Zhuan* [The biography of Father F. Lebbe], Saigon: Yuenan Ziyou Taipingyang Xiehui, 1963.

Zhongguo gongchandang Lici Zhongyao Huiyizhi vol. 1 [On important meetings of the CCP vol. 1], Shanghai: Renmin.

WESTERN ARTICLES

'A Tale of Two Churches, The Chinese Catholics' dilemma', *South China Morning Post*, 30 June 1984.

Alexander, Stella, 'Church-state relations in Yugoslavia 1967', *Religion in Communist Lands* 4 (Winter 1977): 238–40.

An Zhiguo, 'About Humanism', *Beijing Review* 51 (December 1983): 4.

'Archbishop of Canterbury on religion in China', *China Reconstructs* (March 1984): 34–5.

Babbio, Alberto, 'Summit Segreto a Roma: Il Papa apre alla Cina?' [The secret summit in Rome: is the Pope open to China?], *Jesus* (Rome) (April 1986): 85.

Barry, Peter, 'Amity: Christian outreach in China', *Tripod* 27 (June 1985): 35–45.

Bociurkiw, Bohdan R. 'The Catacomb Church: Ukrainian Greek Catholics in the USSR', *Religion in Communist Lands* 1 (Spring 1977): 4–12.

Bociurkiw, Bohdan R. 'The shaping of Soviet religious policy', *Problems of Communism* (May–June 1973): 37–51.

'The Uniate church in the Soviet Ukraine: a case study in Soviet church policy', *Canadian Slavonic Paper* 7 (1965): 89–113.

Branett, A. Doak, 'Ten years after Mao', *Foreign Affairs* (Fall 1986): 37–65.

Calle, Jose M., 'Some thoughts to better understanding of the present situation of the Catholic church in China to-day', *Eastern Asian Pastoral Review* 1 (1986): 89–93.

'Casting God in a Communist image', *Universe*, 31 July 1987.

Chan, Gerald, 'Sino-Vatican diplomatic relations: problems and prospects', *The China Quarterly* (1989), 814–36.

Chan, Sylvia, 'Political assessment of intellectuals before the Cultural Revolution', *Asian Survey* 9 (September 1978): 891–911.

De Wcydenthal, J. B., 'The Pope's pilgrimage to Poland', *Religion in Communist Lands* 1 (Spring 1984): 69–76.

De B. Mills, Williams, 'Generational Change in China', *Problems of Communism* (November–December 1983): 16–35.

'Deng Liqun on China's Cultural Policy', *Beijing Review* 51 (December 1983): 5.

Dreyer, June Teufel, 'Limits of the Permissible in China', *Problems of Communism* (November–December) 1980: 48–65.

Griffith, William, 'Sino-Soviet rapprochement', *Problems of Communism* (March–April 1983): 20–9.

Harding, Harry, 'Change and continuity in Chinese foreign policy', *Problems of Communism* (March–April 1983): 1–19.

Henze, Paul B. 'Conspiring to kill the Pope', *Problems of Communism* (May–June 1985): 59–64.

'The Holy Father Will Not Abandon Taiwan', *Asia Focus* (9 May 1986): 8.

Hoffmann, Stanley, 'International Organization and the International System', *International Organization* 3 (Summer 1970): 389–413.

Huan Guocang, 'Taiwan: a view from Beijing', *Foreign Affairs* (Summer 1985): 1064–80.

Hvat, Ivan, 'The Ukrainian Catholic church, the Vatican and the Soviet Union during the Pontificate of Pope John Paul II', *Religion in Communist Lands* 3 (1983): 264–79.

Iserali, Raphael, 'The Muslim minority in the People's Republic of China', *Asian Survey* 8 (August 1981): 901–19.

Keyfitz, Nathan, 'China faces hard choices in its population policies', *The Asian Wall Street Journal*, 28 March 1984.

Macioti, M. I., 'Reflections on the relations between the church and the Christian Democractic party in Italy', *Social Compass* 2–3 (1976): 121–40.

Maddox, Patrick, 'Value change in China', *Problems of Communism* (November–December): 65–8.

Morrison, Peter, 'Islam in China: an update', *Religion in Communist Lands* 2 (Summer 1985): 152–6.

Myers, Ramon, 'The economic transformation of the Republic of China on Taiwan', *China Quarterly* 99 (September 1984): 500–28.

Nethercut, Richard D, 'Leadership in China: rivalry, reform and renewal', *Problems of Communism* (March–April 1983): 30–46.

Nowak, Ian, 'The church in Poland', *Problems of Communism* (January–February 1982): 1–16.

Nye, Joseph S. and Keohane, Robert O, 'Transnational relations and world politics: an introduction', *International Organization* 3 (Summer 1971): 329–49.

Parks, Michael, 'Feud among Chinese Catholics sours hopes for Vatican ties', *Los Angelos Times*, 24 April 1982.

Patterson, George, 'Mao, Marxism and Christianity', *Religion in Communist Lands* 4–5 (July–October) 1974: 20–9.

Pepper, Suzanne, 'Education and revolution: the 847 "Chinese Model" Revisited.'

'The student movement and the Chinese Civil War 1945–1949', *China Quarterly* 48 (October 1971): 698–735.

'Profession of faith of a Chinese priest in Communion with Rome', *China Bulletin* (Rome) 3 (March 1986): 10–11.

Qi Ya and Zhou Jirong, 'Expansionist Soviet global strategy', *Beijing Review* 5 (22 June 1981): 22–5.

'Religious policy', *China News Analysis* 1156 (8 June 1979).

'Resolutely Combat Bourgeois Liberalization', *Beijing Review* 3 (January 1987): 15.

Rudolph, Jorg-Meinhard, 'China's media: fitting news to print', *Problems of Communism* (July–August 1984): 58–67.

Schram, Stuart, '"Economics in command?" Ideology and policy since the Third Plenum 1978–84', *China Quarterly* 99 (September 1984): 417–61.

Shaw Yu-Ming, 'Taiwan: a view from Taipei', *Foreign Affairs* (Summer 1985): 1050–63.

Shen Yifen, 'Some theological reflections on being a local pastor in New China', *China Study Project Bulletin* 29 (January 1986): 11–17.

Skilling, Gordon, 'Independent currents in Czechoslovakia', *Problems of Communism* (January–February 1985): 32–49.

Special Commentator, 'On policy towards intellectuals', *Beijing Review* 5 (2 February 1979): 10–15.

Stehle, Hansjakob, 'The Ostpolitik of the Vatican and the Polish Pope', *Religion in Communist Lands* 1 (Spring 1980): 13–21.

Tang, Edmond, 'The Church in China – after two revolutions', *Pro Mundi Vita: Dossiers* (January 1982), Dossier Asia-Australasia no. 23.

'Youth of the Cultural Revolution – social problems in post-revolutionary China', *Pro Mundi Vita: Dossiers* 2 (1983), Asia-Australasia no. 25.

Vallier, Ivan, 'The Roman Catholic church: a transnational actor', *International Organization* 3 (1971): 479–95.

Wen Ying, 'Religion and Marxism co-exist again in China', *Ta Kung Pao* (English edn), 3 July 1980.

Weng, Byron, 'Taiwan's international status today', *China Quarterly* 99 (September 84): 463–80.

Winchlu, Edwin A. 'Institutionalization and participation on Taiwan: from hard to soft authoritarianism?', *China Quarterly* 99 (September 1984): 481–99.

Wickeri, Philip, 'Church and society in China: theological and historical realities', *China Study Project Bulletin* 29 (January 1986): 27–36.

Whyte, Martin King, 'Corrective labour camps in China', *Asian Survey* 3 (March 1973): 253–69.

Zhao Fusan, 'A reconsideration of religion', *China Study Project journal* 2 (August 1987): 4–22.

Zhao Ziyang, 'Report on the work of the government', *Beijing Review* 27 (4 July 1983): ii–xxiv.

CHINESE ARTICLES

Benbao Pinglun Yuan, 'Jianshe Jingshan Wenmin Fanduei jingshan Wuren' [Build the spiritual civilisation, oppose the spiritual pollution], *Renmin Ribao*, 16 November 1983.

Chen Duxiu, 'Benzhi Zuian Zhi Dabianshu' [In defence of the 'sin' of this journal], *Xinqingnian* 1 (15 January 1919): 15–16.

Fu Tieshan, 'Zhongguo Tianzhujiao Shengzhi Jiaoyou Wei Jiduo Zuo Jiancheng' [The Catholic clergy and laity witnessed Christ], *Zhongguo Tianzhujiao* 4 (March 1982): 30–2.

Gong Zuezeng, 'Guanyu Woguo Shehui Zhuyi Shiqi Zongjiao Fangmian De Jige Wenti' [On a few questions on religious in our state in socialist era], *Shijie Zongjiao Yinjiu* 1 (1986).

Han Yu, 'Jian Ying Fugu Biao' [Treaties dissuading against receiving the Buddha's relics], *Guwen Pinzhu* [Classical proses with commentary and annotations], vol. 3, pp. 18–21.

He Li 'Jiaohui Jieru Zhengzhi Shoudao Jianggao' [The church was warned for being involved in politics], *The Nineties* 3 (March 1987): 44–5.

Hu Shi, 'Wushi Nianlai Shijia Zhexue' [Philosophies of the world during the last 50 years], *Hu Shi Wen Cun* [Completed works of Hu Shi], vol. 2. Shanghai: Yadong, 1924, pp. 217–304.

'Bu Xiu' [Immortality], *Xinqingnian* 2 (February 1919): 19–20.

Hu Yaobang, 'Guanyu Dang De Xinwen Gongzuo' [On the journalistic work of the party], *Hongqi* 8 (1985): 1–4.

'Quanmain Kaichung Shehuizhuyi Xiandaihua Jianshe De Xinjumian' [Open the new phase of the construction of the Socialist modernisation] (A report to the 12th Party congress), *Renmin Ribao*, 8 September 1982.

'Zai Qingzhu Zhongguo Gongchandang Chengli Lushe Zhounian Dahui Shang De Jianghua' [A speech on the Celebration 60th Anniversary of the CCP], *Renmin Ribao*, 2 July 1981.

Ji Wen, 'Lui Binyan Jiangdi Sige Gushi' [The four stories told by Liu Binyan], *The Nineties* (December 1986): 85.

Jiang Wenxuan, 'Tantan Wodang Chuli Zongjiao Wenti De Fan "Zuo" He Fang You', *Shijie Zongjiao Yanjiu* 1 (1987): 104–12.

Lei Zhencheng, 'Dang Duei Zongjiao Wenti De Jiben Zhengce' [The basic policy of the party on religion], *Guangming Ribao*, 27 June 1982.

Li Desheng, 'Jixu Qingdhu 'Zho' De Sixiang Yingxiang Luli Kaichuang Buduei Jianshe De XinJumian' [Continue to eliminate the 'leftist' ideological tendency strive to create a new situation in building up our ranks], *Renmin Ribao*, 13 April 1983.

Li Weihan, 'Mao Zedong Sixiang Zhidao Xia De Zhongguo Tongyi Zhanxian' [The Chinese United Front policy under the guidance of Mao Zedong thought], *Hongqi* 24 (16 Decejmber 1983): 14–23.

Mei Xian, 'Qingbaowang Pianbu De Fandigang' [The Vatican with its intelligence network], *Xinwanbao*, 1 June 1981.

'Women Dang Zai Shehui Zhuyi Shiqi Zongjiao Wenti Shang De Jiben Zhengce' [The basic policy of religious questions of our party in this period of Socialism], *Hongqi* 12 (16 June 1982): 2–8.

Xiao Feng, 'Zonggong Zenyang Duidai Jiaohui He Zongjiao Tu' [How did the CCP treat the church and religious believers], *Zhishi Fengi* 65 (16 November 1970): 13–14 part 1, 66 (16 December 1970): 21–4 part 2, 67 (16 January 1971): 30–2 part 3, 68 (16 February 1971): 29–30 part 4.

Xiao Yinfa, 'Zhengque Lijia He Guangche Dang De Zongjiao Xinyang Ziyou Zhengce' [Correctly comprehend and implement the party's religious freedom policy], *Renmin*, 4 June 1980.

'Xinyang Ziyou Shi Dang Zai Zongjiao Wenti Shang De Yixiang Gang

Ben Zhengce' [Religious freedom is the party's basic policy on religious questions], *Guangming Ribao*, 30 November 1980.

Yang Jingren, 'Xinshichi De Tongyi Zhanxian' [The United Front of the new era], *Hongqi* 7 (April 1983): 2–7.

Ye Zhiying, 'Zhonggong Yu Fandigang Guanxi Zhi Tantao' [An investigation on the Sino-Vatican relations], *Feiqing Yuebao* 10 (April 1984).

'Yijiaobawu (1985) Lian Zhonggong Dueiwai Wenhua Tongzhan Huotang Gaikuang Diaocha', *Zhonggong Yanjiu* 3 (March 1986): 118–28.

Yu Benyuan, 'Zongjiao Xinyang Ziyou Yu Wushenglun Xuanchuan' [Religious freedom and propagation of atheism]. *Shijie Zongjiao Yanjiu* 3 (1986): 131–9.

Yu Chaoqing, 'Zaitan Zongjiao De Benzhi He Zhehui Zuoyong' [Further discuss the nature of religion and its social function], *Shijie Zongjiao Yanjiu* 3 (1987): 121–6.

Zeng Wenjing, 'Xuanchuan Wushenluen He Zongjiao Xinyang Zhiyou Shi Chongtu Ma?' [Is there any conflict between propagating atheism and religious freedom?], *Renmin*, 29 February 1956.

Zhang Youyu, 'Yige Bixu Renzheng Yanjiu Tansuo De Wenti' [A problem having to research seriously], *Zhongguo Faxue* 2 (1987): 1–10.

Zhao Fusan, 'Jiujin Zenyan Renshi Zongjiao De Benzhi' [How to comprehend the nature of religion], *Zhongguo Shihui Kexue* 3 (1986): 3–19.

'Zhonggong Zhongyang Guanyu Woguo Shehui Zhuyi Shiqi Zongjiao Wenti De Jiben Guandian He Jiben Zhengce' (Wenjian no. 19: 1982) [document 19 issued by the CCP Central Committee in 1982 – regarding our nation's basic view points and policies towards religion in the Socialist stage], *Feiqing Yuebao* 10 (April 1983): 82–91.

MISCELLANEOUS

Amnesty International, 'Health concern. People's Republic of China: Fan Xueyan', ASA 17/04/87, 4 July 1987. Newsletter calling for urgent action.

Beijingshi Tianzhujiao Aiguohui, and Beijingshi Tianzhujiao jiaowu Weiyuan Hui (eds.), 'Beijing Jiaoyao Tongxun' [The newsletter of the Beijing Catholic diocese], nos. 1–6. Internally circulated news on the Beijing Catholic diocese.

A collection of clippings from the Chinese and Hong Kong English language press, 1950–1958, on religion and the anti-rightist movement in China, Union Research Centre, Hong Kong (on microfilm).

Delegate's Office for the Chinese Apostolate, 'Correspondence', 1 May 1982–28 December 1987. Semi-internally circulated journal on China of the Society of Jesus' Manila office.

Gong, Pinmei, Bishop, 'Sheng su Shu' [The Letter of Appeal], January 1987. A private letter presented to the Supreme Court of the People's Republic of China.

Heyndrickx, Jerome J. Fr. 'A visit to the Catholic church in China: Beijing – Tianjin – Nanjing – Shanghai – Guangzhou, May 13–June 2, 1985', A confidential report presented to the Vatican and other concerned offices.

Holy Spirit Study Centre, 'Youguan Zhongguo Dalu Zongjiao Jianbao Zhiliao (1980–1983)' [A collection from all English and Chinese press and journals on religion in China (1980–1983)] (Semi-private).

If the Grain of Wheat Dies . . . Fr. Francis Xavier Chu Shu-Tek (no publisher, no date).

Ladany, L., 'A brief assessment of the situation of the church in China', 93, Pokfulam Road, Hong Kong. A printed article for private circulation.

'The Church in China Seen in December 1980', *China News Analysis* Office, Hong Kong G.P.O. 3225, 1981. A printed article for private circulation.

'The Church in China Seen in December 1983', Ricci Hall, 93, Pokfulam Road, Hong Kong. A printed article for private circulation.

Leung, Beatrice K. F., 'Sino-Vatican conflict (1976–1982): political and diplomatic influences on China's policies towards the Catholic church.' M.A. Dissertation, University of Hong Kong, 1983.

Mahon, Gerald, Bishop, 'A visit to the People's Republic of China, Monday 23rd March–Saturday 11th April 1987', A confidential report presented to the Vatican and other concerned offices.

'Report of the European Region to the Chapter', 'Report of the Latin American Region to the Chapter', and 'Report of the Asia-Oceania Region to the Chapter'. Reports presented to the General Chapter of Missionary of the Oblates of Mary Immaculate, Rome, September 1986.

Triviere, Leon, Father. *The Catholic Church in China* (no publisher, no date). This book contains good documentary on the conflict between the Chinese Catholic church and the PRC in the early 1950s.

The Silent Church (no publisher, no date).

Wu Chengchun, John, Bishop, 'Statement on the Catholic church and the future of Hong Kong', Catholic Information Service, 23 August 1984. (A declaration made by the Catholic bishop of Hong Kong).

INTERVIEWS

Father Franco Belfiori, S. J., the Italian adviser of Bishop Dominic Deng in the controversy over the appointment of the archbishop. He works closely with bishop Deng. The writer had the chance to talk with him many times on Sino-Vatican relations. The most recent talk was held on 4 August 1987.

Cardinal Casaroli, The Secretary of State, City State of the Vatican (8 February 1987).

Cardinal Caprio, the former secretary of Msgr. A. Riberi. He was expelled from China together with Riberi in 1951 (14 September 1986).

Msgr. C. Celli, Director, China Desk, Secretariat of State, City State of the Vatican (28 March 1985, 15 September 1986).

Bishop Dominic Deng Yiming. Being a friend of Bishop Deng, the writer was able to discuss Sino-Vatican relations with him more than once, most recently on 14 July 1987.

Msgr. Gidoni, Director of the China Section, the Sacred Congregation for the Evangelization of Peoples (Propaganda Fide), the City State of the Vatican (18 March 1985).

Father Gelinas, S.J., was expelled by the Chinese government from Shanghai in the 1950s, then he went to work in Vietnam. He was expelled again when Saigon was taken over by the Vietnamese Communists in 1975. He kept a very detailed record on church-state relations in Vietnam under the Communist regime, and was able to compare the treatment of the Catholic church by these two Asian Communist countries (13 February 1986).

Father Francis George, the Assistant Superior General, the Missionary of the Oblates of Mary Immaculate (22 March 1985).

Father Paul Pang, the Director of the Overseas Chinese Apostolate, Sacred Congregation for the Evangelisation of Peoples (17 March 1985, 14 September 1986).

Bishop Wu Cheng Chun, the Catholic Bishop of Hong Kong. The interview was held immediately after his second trip to China, February 1986 (13 February 1986).

Sister Bernadette Yuen, the Assistant Superior General of the Sisters of the Precious Blood. She was one of the delgates to accompany Bishops Wu on his trip to Guangdong (12 February 1986).

Sisters Yang Guilan and Chen Guinien, sisters of the Precious Blood. They were sent to conduct mission work in Weizhou, Guangdong before 1949, and have never left their mission place since then. Even now they are still conducting mission work in Weizhou. Two long interviews had been conducted on how they braved the purges, especially in the Cultural Revolution and how they have conducted mission work in rural areas (29 and 30 December 1981).

MEETINGS OF CHINESE RELIGIOUS LEADERS

1 On 23–31 December 1980, the writer joined a group of Catholics from Hong Kong which attended the Christmas celebration in the Cathedral of Guangzhou. The whole programme was organised by *YI* [Messenger] (a pro-CPA group in Hong Kong). Because of the warm relationship of *YI* with the CPA, the writer, together with a Hong Kong priest, was able to meet the assistant director of the Religious

Affairs Bureau of Guangdong Province to discuss religious matters with him.

2 In September 1981 the writer participated in a religious conference on 'China: A New Beginning', held at Montreal, Canada organised by the China Program of the Canadian Churches Council. China sent a Christian delegation to this, the first time they had been allowed to attend a religious conference abroad. During the eight days of the conference the writer had the opportunity of making personal contacts with the Chinese delegates such as Bishop K. H. Ting, the Protestant leader of the group, and Catholic delegates such as Bishop Michael Fu, Bishop Tu Shihua, Father Wang Zicheng and other Protestant delegates.

3 In September 1984, 1989, and 1990 the writer made a couple of weeks trip to Beijing, Nanjing, Guiyang Hanzhou and Guangzhou, not only to meet religious personnel there but to meet ordinary Chinese in the hope of feeling the pulse of social life in China.

4 The writer was able more than once to meet members of Chinese Protestant delegations when they visited Hong Kong at various times between 1982, 1985, 1988, 1989 and 1990.

Index

LSE MONOGRAPHS IN INTERNATIONAL STUDIES

Titles out of print

KIN WAH CHIN
The defence of Malaysia and Singapore
The transformation of a security system 1957–1971
RICHARD TAYLOR
The politics of the Soviet cinema 1917–1929
ANN TROTTER
Britain and East Asia 1933–1937
J. H. KALICKI
The pattern of Sino-American crisis
Political military interactions in the 1950s
ARYEH L. UNGER
The totalitarian party
Party and people in Nazi Germany
ALABA OGUNSANWO
China's policy in Africa 1958–1971
MARTIN L. VAN CREVELD
Hitler's strategy 1940–1941
The Balkan clue
EUGEN STEINER
The Slovak dilemma
LUCJAN BLIT
The origins of Polish socialism
The history and ideas of the first Polish socialist party 1878–1886